THIS IS OUR FAITH

Series Authors: Janaan Manternach
Carl J. Pfeifer

Authors: Yvette Nelson
Mary Lou Ihrig

Contributing Authors: Kate Sweeney Ristow
Sister Cecilia Maureen Cromwell, I.H.M.
Patricia Frevert

SILVER BURDETT GINN
PARSIPPANY, NJ

THIS IS OUR FAITH
SCHOOL PROGRAM

Contributing Authors: James Bitney, Sister Cecilia Maureen Cromwell, I.H.M., Patricia Frevert, Robert M. Hamma, Mary Lou Ihrig, Paula A. Lenz, Judene Leon, Yvette Nelson, Sister Arlene Pomije, C.S.J., Sister Carolyn Puccio, C.S.J., Anna Ready, Kate Sweeney Ristow, Sister Mary Agnes Ryan, I.H.M., Sister Maureen Shaughnessy, S.C., Brother Michael Sheerin, F.M.S., Barbara Carol Vasiloff

Opening Doors: A Take-Home Magazine: Peter H.M. Demkovitz, Janie Gustafson, Margaret Savitskas

Day to Day: Skills for Christian Living: Susan G. Keys

National Catechetical Consultant:
Kathleen Hendricks

Advisory Board:
Rev. Louis J. Cameli
Philip J. Cunningham
Sister Clare E. Fitzgerald
William J. Freburger
Greer G. Gordon
Sister Veronica R. Grover, S.H.C.J.
Rev. Thomas Guarino
Rev. Robert E. Harahan
Rev. Eugene LaVerdiere, S.S.S.
Rev. Frank J. McNulty
James O'Toole
Rev. Msgr. John J. Strynkowski

Consultants: Linda Blanchette, Anita Bridge, Fred Brown, Rod Brownfield, Sister Mary Michael Burns, S.C., Pat Burns, Bernadine Carroll, Mary Ellen Cocks, Sister Peggy Conlon, R.S.M., Mary Ann Crowley, Pamela Danni, Sister Jamesetta DeFelice, O.S.U., Sister Mary Elizabeth Duke, S.N.D., Mary M. Gibbons, Yolanda Gremillion, Sister Angela Hallahan, C.H.F., Alice T. Heard, Sister Michele O'Connoll, P.B.V.M., Sister Angela O'Mahoney, P.B.V.M., Sister Ruthann O'Mara, S.S.J., Sandra Okulicz-Hulme, Judy Papandria, Rachel Pasano, Sallie Ann Phelan, Sister Geraldine M. Rogers, S.S.J., Mary Lou Schlosser, Patricia Ann Sibilia, Margaret E. Skelly, Lisa Ann Sorlie, Sister Victorine Stoltz, O.S.B., Sister Nancy Jean Turner, S.H.C.J., Christine Ward, Judith Reidel Weber, Kay White, Elizabeth M. Williams, Catherine R. Wolf, Florence Bambrick Yarney, Kathryn K. Zapcic

Nihil Obstat
Kathleen Flanagan, S.C., Ph.D.
Censor Librorum
Ellen Joyce, S.C., Ph.D.
Censor Librorum

Imprimatur
✠ Most Reverend Frank J. Rodimer
Bishop of Paterson
November 22, 1996

The *nihil obstat* and *imprimatur* are official declarations that a book or pamphlet is free of doctrinal and moral error. No implication is contained therein that those who have granted the *nihil obstat* and *imprimatur* agree with the contents, opinions, or statements expressed.

ACKNOWLEDGMENTS

"An African Creed," by Father Vincent Donovan, reprinted from *Epistle to the Masai,* published by Fides Claretian Publications, 221 W. Madison Street, Chicago, IL 60606

Excerpt from *The Catholic Heritage* by Lawrence S. Cunningham. Copyright © 1983 by the author. Reprinted by permission of the Crossroad Publishing Company.

Quotation from *Patrology,* Volume II. used by permission of Paulist Press, Mahwah, NJ

Excerpt from *Ten Christians* by Boniface Hanley, O.F.M. Courtesy of Ave Maria Press.

Quotation from *Mater et Magistra (On Christianity and Social Progress)* by Pope John XXIII, translated by William J. Gibbons, S.J., © 1961. Courtesy of Paulist Press.

"Spirit of God" Words and music by Miriam Therese Winter. Copyright © Medical Mission Sisters, 1965. Reproduced with permission of copyright owner.

Excerpts from *Vatican Council II: The Conciliar and Post Conciliar Documents, New Revised Edition* edited by Austin Flannery, O.P., copyright © 1992, Costello Publishing Company, Inc., Northport, NY are used by permission of the publisher, all rights reserved. No part of these excerpts may be reproduced, stored in a retrieval system, or transmitted in any form or by any means—electronic, mechanical, photocopying, recording or otherwise, without express permission of Costello Publishing Company.

Excerpts from *The New American Bible* © 1991, 1986, 1970 by the Confraternity of Christian Doctrine, Washington, D.C. 20017 Used with permission. All rights reserved.

Excerpts from the English translation of *Rite of Baptism for Children* © 1969, International Committee on English in the Liturgy, Inc. (ICEL); excerpts from the English translation of *The Roman Missal* © 1973, ICEL; excerpts from the English translation of *Rite of Penance* © 1974, ICEL; excerpts from the English translation of *Rite of Confirmation,* Second Edition © 1975, ICEL; excerpts from *Pastoral Care of the Sick: Rites of Anointing and Viaticum* © 1982, ICEL; excerpts from the *Order of Christian Funerals* © 1985, ICEL. All rights reserved.

Contents 〜〜〜〜〜

Let us Pray

Let Us Pray

Sign of the Cross

In the name of the Father,
    and of the Son,
    and of the Holy Spirit.
Amen.

Señal de la Cruz

En el nombre del Padre,
    y del Hijo
    y del Espíritu Santo.
Amén.

Lord's Prayer

Our Father, who art in heaven, hallowed be thy name;
thy kingdom come; thy will be done on earth
    as it is in heaven.
Give us this day our daily bread;
and forgive us our trespasses as we forgive those
    who trespass against us;
and lead us not into temptation, but deliver us from evil.
Amen.

Padre Nuestro

Padre nuestro, que estás en el cielo, santificado sea tu nombre;
venga a nosotros tu reino; hágase tu voluntad en la tierra
    como en el cielo.
Danos hoy nuestro pan de cada día;
perdona nuestras ofensas, como también nosotros perdonamos
    a los que nos ofenden;
no nos dejes caer en la tentación, y líbranos del mal.
Amén.

Hail Mary

Hail Mary, full of grace,
    the Lord is with you.
Blessed are you among women,
    and blessed is the fruit
    of your womb, Jesus.
Holy Mary, Mother of God,
    pray for us sinners, now,
    and at the hour of our death.
Amen.

Ave María

Dios te salve, María, llena eres de gracia,
    el Señor es contigo.
Bendita tú eres entre todas las mujeres,
    y bendito es el fruto
    de tu vientre, Jesús.
Santa María, Madre de Dios,
    ruega por nosotros, pecadores, ahora
    y en la hora de nuestra muerte.
Amén.

Glory Be to the Father

Glory be to the Father,
    and to the Son,
    and to the Holy Spirit.
As it was in the beginning,
    is now, and ever shall be,
    world without end.
Amen.

Gloria al Padre

Gloria al Padre,
    y al Hijo,
    y al Espíritu Santo.
Como era en el principio,
    ahora y siempre,
    por los siglos de los siglos.
Amén.

Let Us Pray

A Morning Prayer

Loving God, bless the work that we do. Watch over us and guide us in school and at
home. Help us to realize that everything we do gives praise to you. We make this
prayer in Jesus' name.
Amen.

Evening Prayer

O Lord, support us all the day long, until the shadows lengthen and the evening
comes, and the busy world is hushed, and the fever of life is over, and our work is
done. Then, Lord, in your mercy grant us a safe lodging, and a holy rest, and
peace at last, through Jesus Christ our Lord.
Amen.

Grace Before Meals

Bless us, O Lord,
and these your gifts,
which we are about to
receive from your
goodness,
through Christ our Lord.
Amen.

Grace After Meals

We give you thanks
for all your gifts,
almighty God,
living and reigning
now and forever.
Amen.

Prayer of Sorrow

My God,
I am sorry for my sins with all my heart.
In choosing to do wrong
and failing to do good,
I have sinned against you
whom I should love above all things.
I firmly intend, with your help,
to do penance,
to sin no more,
and to avoid whatever leads me to sin.
Our Savior Jesus Christ
suffered and died for us.
In his name, my God, have mercy.

Revised Rite of Penance

Prayer for the Holy Spirit

Come, Holy Spirit, fill the hearts of your faithful
and kindle in them the fire of your love.
Send forth your Spirit, and they shall be recreated;
and you will renew the face of the earth.

Let Us Pray

Nicene Creed

We believe in one God,
    the Father, the Almighty,
    maker of heaven and earth,
    of all that is seen and unseen.

We believe in one Lord, Jesus Christ,
    the only Son of God,
    eternally begotten of the Father,
    God from God, Light from Light,
    true God from true God,
    begotten, not made, one in Being with the Father.
    Through him all things were made.
    For us men and for our salvation
        he came down from heaven:

by the power of the Holy Spirit
    he was born of the Virgin Mary, and became man.

For our sake he was crucified under Pontius Pilate;
    he suffered, died, and was buried.
    On the third day he rose again
        in fulfillment of the Scriptures;
    he ascended into heaven
        and is seated at the right hand of the Father.
He will come again in glory to judge the living and the dead,
    and his kingdom will have no end.

We believe in the Holy Spirit, the Lord, the giver of life,
    who proceeds from the Father and the Son.
    With the Father and the Son he is worshiped and glorified.
    He has spoken through the Prophets.
    We believe in one holy catholic and apostolic Church.
    We acknowledge one baptism for the forgiveness of sins.
    We look for the resurrection of the dead,
        and the life of the world to come. Amen.

Beginning the Journey

Together this year we will explore the nearly two thousand year journey of the Catholic Church. We will examine the life of the Church as Jesus' community and learn about the challenges experienced by the Church in the past and the present. We will also consider our role in today's Catholic Church and how we are called to continue Christ's work, looking forward to the final fulfillment of God's kingdom of peace, love, and justice at the end of time. We will learn how the heritage of the Catholic Church is renewed in each of us as we follow Jesus' way of love. We begin our journey by reflecting about the Church in the world.

What are some of the things you have wondered about the Catholic Church?

_____

_____

_____

How do you think an eighth grade class can be an example of the Church community?

_____

_____

_____

What talents, gifts, and abilities are you willing to share with others to carry on Christ's mission and the Church's work in the world?

_____

_____

_____

Prayer for the Journey

Gathering

Leader: We come together to commit ourselves to the journey of faith. We pray for openness and trust as we discover the history of the Catholic Church and identify the work to which each one of us is called by God. We ask for God's presence and the Holy Spirit's guidance as we journey together. We ask these things through Christ, our Lord.

All: Amen.

The Word of God

Reader: [Reads Ephesians 4:1-6]

All: Thanks be to God.

Response

Group 1: Help us to discover your call in each of our lives, O Lord.

Group 2: Unite us in love with the believers of every time and age.

Group 1: Help us to see in the Church your plan for the establishment of perfect peace, love, and justice in the world.

Group 2: Help us to develop the gifts and talents we will need to be your people—the Church of the future.

All: Be with us on our journey of faith, O Lord. Let us walk always in your light.

Presentation of Symbols

Conclusion

Leader: May the Lord guide us on our journey.
May Jesus be our companion.
May the Holy Spirit give us direction and help.
May the Lord bless and keep us always.

All: Amen.

THIS IS OUR FAITH

A Preview of Grade 8
For Your Family

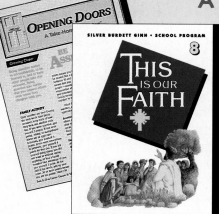

You are invited!

Accept our invitation to accompany your child on his or her faith journey this year. As illustrated by the commitment page and the gatefold on the Grade 8 pupil edition cover, the learning process is like a journey of discovery. We hope that you also will choose to commit yourself to this journey with your son or daughter and be supportive as he or she studies the truths taught by the Catholic Church.

This Year in Grade 8

The theme of Grade 8 is the Church. Students survey the major historical periods of the Church in order to come to a deeper understanding and appreciation of their heritage. Students will be encouraged to see how their own lives reflect the beliefs and commitment of the Church community by participating in the worshiping life of the Church through personal prayer, Mass and the sacraments, and living a Christian way of life. Students will learn that Jesus calls his followers to live lives of compassion, care, and concern for their fellow human beings, particularly those in need.

OPENING DOORS
A Take-Home Magazine™

At the end of each unit, students will find an issue of *Opening Doors: A Take-Home Magazine.* This magazine includes features on Catholic family values and communication skills ("Growing Closer"), personal growth and spirituality ("Self"), material on the Mass ("A Closer Look"), and Catholic identity and heritage ("Being Catholic"). Watch for it!

Your Adolescent

Eighth graders are continuing to mature in a number of areas. Friends are very important, but sometimes the eighth grader is able to stand against the group in certain situations. Interest in sexuality continues to develop, although eighth graders usually have friends of both sexes.

Eighth graders need to belong to a group of trusting and caring people who allow them the freedom to be responsible. They need supportive reinforcement from parents and other adults and guidance in making wise decisions. Eighth graders are sensitive to criticism but know that such correction is often necessary and helpful. They have a genuine interest in sharing what they have and in helping others. They also can become angry and aggressive when frustrated.

Be Affirming

Show your appreciation and belief in your child by taking a few minutes this week to treat him or her like an adult. Encourage an adult conversation with your child about his or her interests or hobbies.

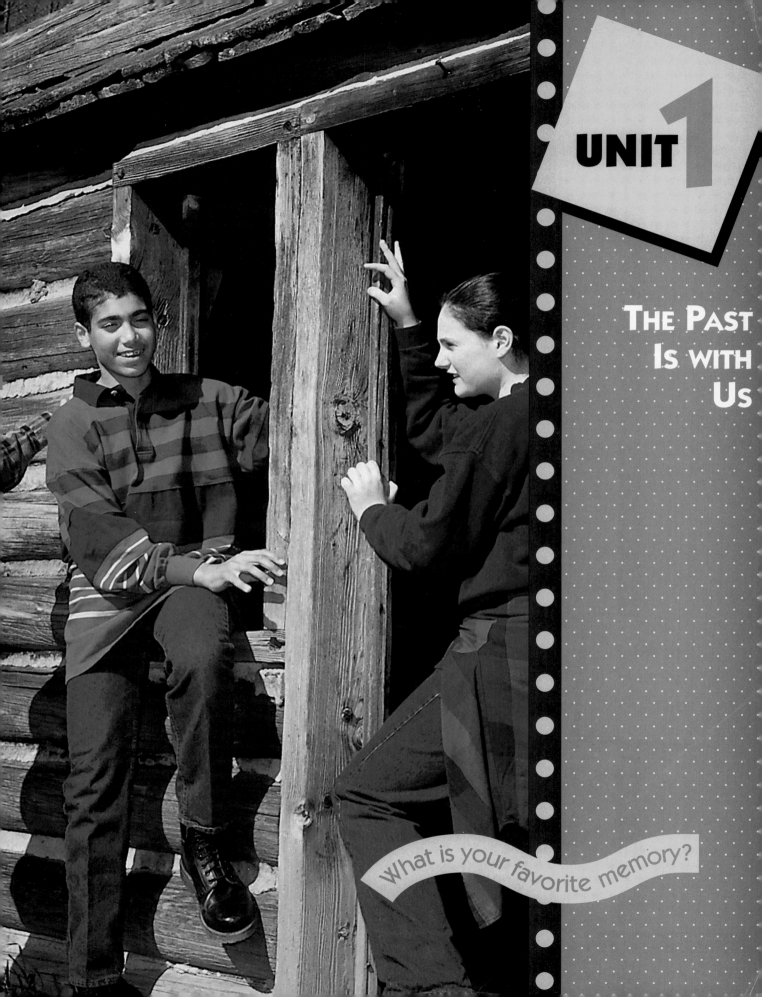

THE PAST IS WITH US

What is your favorite memory?

A WELCOMING PEOPLE

BELONGING

Most Catholics belong to parishes—communities organized so that Catholics can worship and share their faith together. You and your family probably belong to a parish. Every parish has its own personality. What is your experience of parish life?

TO WHAT GROUP DO YOU BELONG?

Activity

Mark all the statements that apply to you and add your own statement, if you wish.

_____ My parish is large.

_____ I like the music at Mass in my parish.

_____ I don't like my parish.

_____ My parish is small.

_____ I don't know anything about my parish.

_____ My parish has lots of activities for everyone.

_____ I like that my parish reminds other people about Jesus and his mission.

_____ I don't belong to a parish.

Other: _____

_____

What do you think might be the best thing about a parish community?

_____

_____

A Welcoming Community

After Jesus' resurrection and ascension, a group of his close friends were staying together. They were Jewish, and the Holy Spirit came upon them as they celebrated together the Jewish feast of Pentecost. Filled with courage, these disciples went out to tell people about Jesus Christ. These events mark the beginning of the Church established by our Lord.

Those who first accepted the good news about the risen Christ were Jewish and formed small communities in the neighborhoods of Jerusalem. The members of the communities became very close. They shared everything they owned so that no one was in need. They ate and prayed together. They shared the Eucharist. They listened to the teachings of the apostles. They followed Jesus' way of love (Acts 2:42–47; 4:32–35).

Onlookers frequently admired how they cared about one another and how full of joy they were. The number of the followers of Jesus continued to grow as the communities welcomed those who accepted Jesus.

Paul, who had been a forceful persecutor of the followers of Jesus, was converted to Christ and welcomed by those he had persecuted. He and another follower of Jesus, Barnabas, preached about Jesus among Jewish communities in other parts of the Roman Empire. Paul became, with Peter and James, one of the important leaders of the early Church.

When **Gentiles**, or people who were not Jewish, began responding to the good news of Jesus Christ, the communities of Jesus' followers had to decide whether or not to accept them. The apostles called a **council**, or meeting, in Jerusalem. They decided that a Gentile could become a follower of Jesus without becoming Jewish first.

New communities, or churches, developed. One of the earliest of these communities in the Roman Empire gathered regularly in the home of Lydia, a businesswoman in Philippi. Also, Priscilla and her husband Aquila, who were tentmakers, were leaders of the community in

Ephesus. Their hospitality was well-known. And it was in Antioch that the communities were first called **Christians**, or followers of Jesus. The apostles were succeeded by men who were specially chosen as bishops. Ignatius, the bishop of the Christians in Antioch, was the first to call the Church **catholic**, meaning "welcoming the whole world."

Activity

List four things that impress you about the early church.

1. _____

2. _____

3. _____

4. _____

Vocabulary

Gentiles: people who are not Jewish

council: meeting of Church leaders

Christian: follower of Jesus Christ

catholic: welcoming or open to the whole world

PERSECUTED COMMUNITIES

While Christians had become open to the whole world, the world was not open to them at first. Beginning about thirty years after Pentecost, the Romans periodically persecuted Christians because they refused to offer incense to the emperor, who was considered divine, and to the other Roman gods. This refusal made many Romans believe that the Christians were not loyal to the emperor and the government. Christian men, women, and children became **martyrs** when they were killed for their faith in Christ.

Seneca, a famous Roman philosopher who was also the tutor of the emperor Nero, wrote about the way that some Romans regarded the martyrdom of Christians as entertainment: "By chance I attended a midday exhibition, expecting some fun, wit and relaxation… But it was quite the contrary… These noon fighters are sent out with no armor of any kind; they are exposed to blows at all points, and no one ever strikes in vain. . . . Man, a sacred thing to man, is killed for sport and merriment." Seneca also told how this affected him: "I have come home

more greedy, more cruel and inhuman, because I have been among human beings."

In Rome, the martyrs were sometimes buried in underground cemeteries called **catacombs**. The Christian communities honored the martyrs and looked up to them. Despite persecutions, the Christian communities continued to grow.

People wondered what it meant to be a Christian and why Christians did not give up their faith when they were persecuted. In a letter written to Diognetus, who was a non-Christian, an unknown Christian explains, "Christians are in the world as the soul is in the body… The soul dwells in the body but is not part of the body. So Christians live in the world but are not of the world." This means that Christians recognized that faith in Jesus was worth more than anything in the world.

The writer of this letter to Diognetus also explains some Christian beliefs: "We marry and have children, but we do not kill babies that we do not want. We welcome all to share our food, but we do not share our wives. We live on earth but have our home in heaven. We obey the laws but, in our own lives, go beyond the laws."

BEYOND THE JEWISH COMMUNITIES

Persecution from Roman authorities was not the only challenge that the Christian communities faced. Christians found themselves in an increasingly awkward and strained relationship with the Jewish communities to which they belonged.

The first Christians were Jewish and lived and worshipped in Jewish communities. Their Scriptures were Jewish and many of their prayers, hymns, and worship practices were Jewish at first. But as the number of followers of Jesus grew, and the leaders of the followers of Jesus accepted Gentiles among them, the Jewish leaders felt that the teachings of Moses and the prophets were being undermined.

The New Testament records increasing controversy between Jewish and Christian groups and shows Christians being expelled from synagogues. It also tells stories of how apostles such as Paul turned their attention to preaching among the Gentiles. Gradually, Christian and Jewish groups would lead more and more separate lives until, after decades, these two religions became completely separate.

Activity

Imagine that you are a newly baptized Christian in the early Church. You and many Christians you know try to avoid trouble, but you already know of people who have been martyred.

1. For what reasons did you become a Christian?

   _____

   _____

   _____

   _____

   _____

   _____

2. What difficulties and dangers will you face when practicing Christianity?

   _____

   _____

   _____

   _____

   _____

   _____

   _____

   _____

Vocabulary

martyrs: people killed for being witnesses for Christ

catacombs: underground Christian cemeteries

Activity

THE GROWING CHURCH

As time passed, the Church became more organized, with the bishop of a local area as the center of unity. The Churches of Alexandria, Jerusalem, Antioch, Constantinople, and Rome became the most important. These cities were centers of learning for groups of Christians throughout the Roman Empire.

Church leaders, such as Ignatius of Antioch, Clement, Irenaeus, and Origen, wrote important works of theology. These writings helped Christians grasp better the meaning of the life and teachings of Jesus. These writings also helped explain to non-Christians what Christians believed.

Sunday, the Lord's day, became the Christian Sabbath. A liturgy, or service, of the Word was joined to the liturgy of the Eucharist. Some Christians began to lead lives of fasting and prayer, sometimes withdrawing to deserted areas to seek holiness away from the distractions of the world. Most Christians, however, gathered in homes to pray and break bread together.

Deacons were chosen to assist Church leaders (Acts 6:1–7). In some areas of the Roman Empire, deaconesses were also chosen.

Because individuals who became Christians were from many different peoples in the Roman Empire, they did not share the same language, the same customs, or the same ideas about how women and men should interact. In some places, women and men lived very separate lives and did not often meet together in public. Church leaders respected the different customs that people had.

The role of deacon and deaconess are described in an ancient Church manual, called the *Didascalia Apostolorum*. This Church manual describes how Christians are to live and worship. It tells bishops to choose deacons: "a man for the execution of the many things that are necessary, and a woman to serve among women. For there are houses where you cannot send a deacon to women. . . . but you can send a deaconess." The manual describes, for example, how a deaconess was the one who should help a woman out of the water after she was baptized and was the one who should anoint her. It would not have been proper for a man to do it, although he was the one who would say the prayers.

By the end of the last major persecution in 312, the Church looked different from the first Jewish Christian communities in Jerusalem. However, the Church was still made up of people who committed their lives to Jesus Christ and to one another and who were alive with the warmth and life of the Spirit.

LET OTHERS LEARN FROM YOUR LIVES

Ignatius was one of the most loved and admired bishops in the early Church, and one of the most influential. No one knows much about his childhood or youth. He was probably born about the time Jesus died. According to legend, he was a disciple of Jesus' apostle John and was consecrated bishop of Antioch by Peter.

As bishop, Ignatius guided the growing Church in Antioch for forty years. During the persecution by Emperor Trajan about 107, Ignatius was arrested for being a Christian. The Roman judge condemned him to death and sent him by ship to Rome.

During the journey to Rome, Ignatius wrote seven letters to various Christian communities. These letters not only describe the trip to Rome, but show Ignatius to have been a man of great faith and strength.

Ignatius was guarded by ten soldiers who treated him badly during the trip. But at every port at which the ship stopped, hundreds of Christians came out to meet him and to cheer him on his way to martyrdom. Ignatius prayed with them and encouraged them to be faithful to Jesus Christ.

To the Christians in Rome, where he was soon to die, Ignatius wrote: "Pray for me that God gives me grace. . . . not only to be called but to be Christian . . . I am God's wheat and am to be ground by the teeth of wild beasts that I may become the pure bread of Christ."

In another letter, Ignatius described to the Ephesians how Christians are to live: "Let others learn from your lives. In the face of people's hatred, be patient; faced with their boasts, be humble; answer their insults with prayers; in the face of their errors, be strong in your faith; against their anger, be gentle. Do not seek revenge. Let our love show them we are their brothers and sisters."

In a letter to the Christians in Smyrna, he was the first to use the title *Catholic Church.* Ignatius wrote that the bishop, as leader of the

Christian community, represented Christ: "Wherever the bishop is, there let the people be, for there is the Catholic Church." He also insisted on the unity of the Christian community in the Eucharist.

Ignatius arrived at Rome on the last day of the public games. The guards led him to the stadium where thousands gathered to watch the games and the deaths of condemned Christians. Ignatius was fed to hungry lions as the crowd cheered.

The Church celebrates the feast of Saint Ignatius of Antioch each October 17.

Activity

If one of the Christian leaders of the early Church traveled through time to your school, what would you want to tell him or her about being a Christian today?

_____

_____

_____

_____

Activity

When have you disagreed with someone about a matter which you both considered to be very important? Answer the following questions to recall how you handled the situation.

1. What was the argument about?

_____

_____

2. Who was involved in the disagreement?

_____

_____

3. How was the argument resolved?

_____

_____

4. Name at least one other way the argument could have been resolved (even if this would not have been your choice).

_____

_____

CHRISTIAN BELIEFS

Admitting Gentiles to the Christian communities not only helped the Catholic Church to grow, it also challenged Christians to preach and explain their beliefs to people who were not Jewish and who were not familiar with the Old Testament. As more and more non-Jewish people became Christian and the Church became separate from Jewish communities, non-Jewish ideas and ways of thinking began to influence Christian thought. In particular, Christian ideas began to be influenced by Greek philosophy.

Using Greek philosophy to explain their ideas, some Christian thinkers denied the goodness of creation, saying that the material world kept souls trapped. They said that God would save only a small, elite group of individuals who had received secret knowledge and that the God of the Old Testament was not really God, but a lesser divine being. They also denied the humanity of Jesus, teaching that as the Son of God, he just appeared to be human. These ideas threatened to destroy the Church.

Christians have always discussed among themselves how to understand Jesus and his mission, but with the spread of new ideas from Greek philosophy these discussions became especially important in the first centuries of the Church. Bishops soon found themselves with the responsibility of deciding which ideas were helpful in understanding Jesus and which were not. Beginning in the fourth century, Christians focused their thinking on how to understand who Jesus was and what his relationship was to God the Father and the Holy Spirit.

These arguments and discussions went on for most of the first eight centuries of the Church's existence. Some of the suggested ideas distorted and threatened to destroy the Christian faith. The bishops declared such ideas to be **heresy**, that is, the denial of Church doctrine. The Church was called upon time after time to clarify its faith in Christ Jesus. The early **ecumenical**, or worldwide, councils—at Nicea (325), Constantinople (381), Ephesus (431), and Chalcedon (451)—condemned the beliefs of people such as Arius and Nestorius, for their teachings about the nature and person of Jesus Christ. From the first two councils came the Nicene Creed, which we still recite at Mass today.

At the Council of Nicea, for example, the bishops of the Church were called on to state Jesus' relationship with God the Father. Was Jesus made by the Father at some point in history (implying that there was a time when the Word of God did not exist)? This is what an Egyptian priest named Arius taught. Or, as Church leaders such as St. Athanasius believed, was Jesus begotten of the Father—the same substance of the Father (and thus, in existence

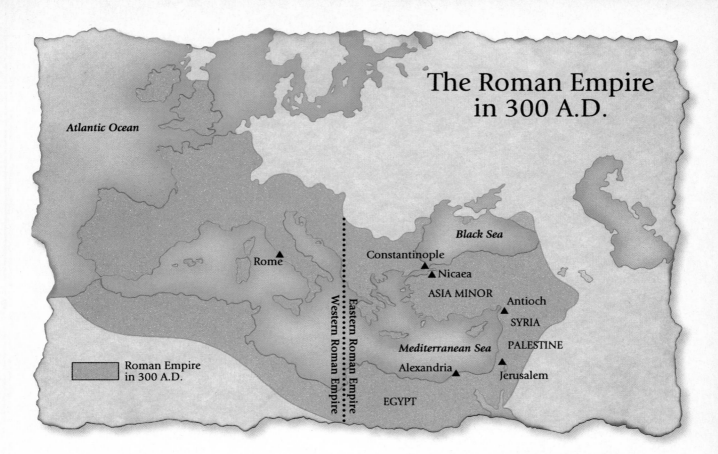

The Roman Empire in 300 A.D.

Atlantic Ocean

Black Sea

Constantinople

Nicaea

ASIA MINOR

Antioch

SYRIA

Mediterranean Sea

PALESTINE

Alexandria

Jerusalem

EGYPT

Rome

Eastern Roman Empire

Western Roman Empire

Roman Empire in 300 A.D.

eternally, as God is)? The bishops fought bitterly over this theological issue at the council. The bishops decided that Jesus, the Word of God, was truly divine and of the same substance as God the Father.

Theological issues and questions continued to arise during the first centuries of the Church. Was Jesus both God and man? Was he one person or two? How could he be one person with two natures? Who was Mary? Was she the mother of Jesus the human being? Was she the mother of God? What is the Trinity? Who are the persons of the Trinity? How are they distinct and at the same time one? These and other important questions about Christian beliefs pushed Church leaders and teachers to express the message of Scripture in philosophical language.

Those most responsible for clarifying the Church's faith in Jesus Christ included Pope Leo I, and Bishops Athanasius, Ambrose, and Augustine, among others. Many of these are honored today as saints and **Church Fathers**—great teachers of the first eight centuries.

Vocabulary

heresy: the denial of a Church doctrine

ecumenical: worldwide

Church Fathers: great Christian teachers of the first eight centuries

WE BELIEVE

The Church began on Pentecost through the coming of the Holy Spirit to the disciples of Jesus. Through the guidance of the Holy Spirit, the Christian communities, despite persecutions and other challenges, grew to become a Church open to the whole world.

Constantine saw a cross in the sky and heard a voice say, "In this sign you shall conquer!"

According to legend, Constantine immediately ordered his soldiers to paint the cross on their helmets, shields, and swords. Constantine's army won the battle.

The next year, Constantine officially recognized Christianity as a legal religion in the empire. Now Christians could worship in public, build churches, and hold public office. Pagan temples were turned into churches. Bishops became high-ranking government officials and the Church took on the organization of the empire. For example, the word *diocese* originally referred to a division of territory within the empire.

It is possible that Constantine himself became a Christian on his deathbed. Constantine probably saw Christianity as a way to unite the once-strong Roman Empire, crumbling from within and threatened from without by enemies during his lifetime.

In the year 380, Emperor Theodosius made the Catholic Church the official religion of the Roman Empire. Now the Church could truly be open to the whole world. In succeeding centuries, the Church became powerful and acquired more of the governing practices and structures of the Roman Empire. In fact, the Church itself became the single most identifiable characteristic of the empire that had once persecuted and tried to destroy it.

The identification of the Church with the empire had its dangers, however. The Church faced all the temptations that come with worldly power and status. Worldly goals could lead to greed, arrogance, and the oppressive use of power. These characteristics are opposite the goals of Christian faith: to serve and to love. The Church also faced the danger of forgetting that God is the focus of all life.

With the Church's new position in the empire, Christians had a new, important responsibility in how they chose to live and act for others. In this regard, Christians sometimes chose wisely and sometimes chose foolishly in the following centuries.

Activity

What is it like to be an outsider?

_____

_____

What is it like to be someone's favorite?

_____

_____

CHURCH AND EMPIRE UNITE

Until about 300, Christians were an illegal, politically powerless, and frequently persecuted minority. This began to change when Constantine became emperor of Rome. In 312, just before an important military battle,

UNDERSTANDING HISTORY

In this chapter, some of the main ideas and events of the first three centuries of the Church's history have been presented. History is commonly thought of as a series of known facts put in their proper order. But history is actually a process of discovery and interpretation. Historians look at evidence from the events they are researching, and then they interpret this evidence in order to explain it to people living today. To write about events, historians must make decisions about which facts are the most important and which tell something that will help people to understand the events better.

A primary source is a firsthand account of something that happened in the past. Primary sources include diaries, autobiographies, and eyewitness reports. Primary sources provide the evidence that historians look at. A secondary source is a summary of primary sources or other secondary sources. Biographies, encyclopedias, and textbooks are secondary sources. Historians create secondary sources, but they also use them to help make sense of the evidence they have collected from primary sources.

Activity

Choose something that happened last week in your school or parish. Write about the event in the form of a primary source. Then write about the event in the form of a secondary source.

Primary Source:

_____

_____

_____

_____

Secondary Source:

_____

_____

_____

_____

Activity

Each statement below describes either a primary source or a secondary source. Write **P** in the blank before each statement that describes a primary source. Write **S** in the blank before each statement that describes a secondary source.

_____ Seneca wrote about his experiences at the games.

_____ A college professor writes a two-volume history of the Church.

_____ Someone wrote a church manual called the *Didascalia Apostolorum*.

_____ A Christian wrote a letter to his friend Diognetus.

_____ An encyclopedia article describes the life of Constantine.

Praying with the Early Church

Just as we do, the Christians of the early Church gathered to pray and sing together. Their prayers and hymns expressed what they believed about Jesus. Many of these prayers and hymns have survived over the centuries and are still found in the Church's worship today.

Some of these prayers and hymns were included in the books of the New Testament as the books were written. Scholars believe, for example, that parts of the first chapter of the Gospel of John are from an early Christian hymn. The hymn explains in poetic language that Jesus is the Word of God and we can recognize the divine wisdom of God in Jesus. The hymn also expresses clearly that the Word of God has always existed, since the very beginning. Made man, Jesus guides and helps us to understand who God is.

The hymn probably reminded the early Christians about who Jesus was for them. The poetic style of the hymn tries to express Jesus' divine nature as the Son of God by capturing the feeling of mystery, wisdom, and grandeur.

This hymn is shown here. We do not know what it sounded like when it was sung, but it was most likely sung during worship.

In the beginning was the Word,
   and the Word was with God,
   and the Word was God.
He was in the beginning with
   God.
All things came to be through him,
   and without him nothing came to
   be.
What came to be through him was
   life,
   and this life was the light of the
   human race;
the light shines in the darkness,
   and the darkness has not
   overcome it.
The true light, which enlightens
   everyone,
   was coming into the world.
He was in the world,
   and the world came to be through
   him.
And the Word became flesh
   and made his dwelling among us,
   and we saw his glory,
   the glory as of the Father's only
   Son,
   full of grace and truth.

John 1:1–5, 9–10, 14

CHAPTER REVIEW

Match the names of these early Christians with the statements that best describe them.

1. I was an apostle, and I wrote many letters to Church communities.

2. I was a bishop and a martyr. I wrote letters, too.

3. I was a businesswoman, and a Christian community met in my home.

4. We were non-Jewish people who were welcomed into the Church.

5. Our theological writings helped the early Christians understand the meaning of Jesus' life.

6. I traveled with Paul.

7. I was a Roman philosopher who did not like the Roman games in which Christians were martyred.

8. We were tentmakers, just like Paul, and we lived in Ephesus.

_____ Ignatius of Antioch

_____ Seneca

_____ Clement, Irenaeus, Origen

_____ Lydia

_____ Barnabas

_____ Paul

_____ Gentiles

_____ Priscilla and Aquila

Write a paragraph telling what the important decision of the Council of Jerusalem was and why it was important.

_____

_____

_____

Respond to the following questions based on what you have learned in this chapter.

1. What is a *martyr?*

_____

_____

2. Why did the Romans persecute Christians?

_____

_____

Your every act should be done with love.
1 Corinthians 16:14

3. Members of the early Church gave their lives for their beliefs in Christ. Though you do not face the threat of death, discuss how you can take courageous stands for your Christian beliefs.

2 A THRIVING PEOPLE

BEING OURSELVES

The events that happen in our lives help make us who we are. Every now and then we need to pause and reflect on our life experiences and recognize how they change us and help us grow.

WHAT HELPS YOU TO GROW AS A PERSON?

Activity

On the lines below, name four important things that have happened in your life. Then tell how each helped you to grow as a person.

1. Because _____ happened,

   I grew _____

2. Because _____ happened,

   I grew _____

3. Because _____ happened,

   I grew _____

4. Because _____ happened,

   I grew _____

Name one thing you hope will happen to you in the future and explain why.

_____

_____

_____

_____

_____

_____

_____

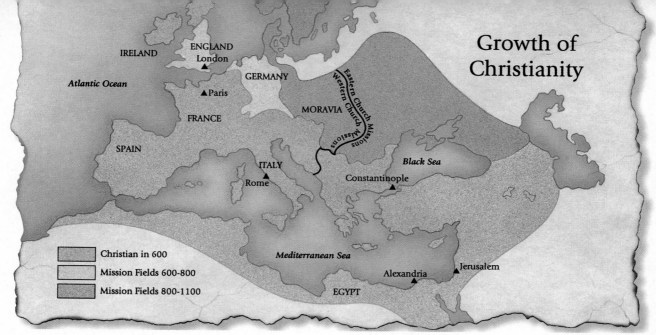

Growth of Christianity

IRELAND
ENGLAND
London
Atlantic Ocean
GERMANY
Paris
MORAVIA
FRANCE
Eastern Church Missions
Western Church Missions
SPAIN
Black Sea
ITALY
Constantinople
Rome
Mediterranean Sea
Jerusalem
Alexandria
EGYPT

Christian in 600
Mission Fields 600–800
Mission Fields 800–1100

THE CHURCH EXPANDS

One of the things that the emperor Constantine did was to move the captial of the Roman Empire from Rome, in the West, to Constantinople, in the East. In an age without electronic technology, communication between the two parts of the empire was slow—sometimes taking as long as a year. Also, the western part of the empire suffered a series of attacks from Europe by Germanic invaders. These Germanic peoples succeeded in conquering Rome in 410 and were ruling parts of the Western Roman Empire by 476.

Guided by the Holy Spirit, the Catholic Church continued to grow and was led by the bishops, the successors of the Twelve chosen by Christ. Missionaries such as St. Patrick worked among the people of Europe, and helped to Christianize them. Sts. Cyril and Methodius worked among Slavic people and Christianized what became Eastern Europe and Russia.

Disputes about Christian beliefs also continued. In the East these were so important that one Church leader, St. Gregory of Nyssa, said, "Every part of the city is filled with such talk: the alleys, the crossroads, the squares, the avenues… If you inquire about the quality and price of bread, the baker will reply: 'The Father is greatest and the Son is subject to him.' "

Church leaders such as St. Augustine (354–430) worked to clarify the Church's beliefs. A brilliant thinker, Augustine admitted in his autobiography the *Confessions* that, as a student, "I did not love learning, and I hated being driven towards it." His writings on sin, grace, and the sacraments remain an important influence on Christian thinking even today.

Another teacher, St. Jerome (345–420), translated the books of the Bible from languages such as Greek to Latin so that Western Catholics could read them. His translation is called the Vulgate. He helped to decide the **canon**, or list, of the books of the Bible. Jerome is also known for the guidance he gave others about faith. On the education of women, he wrote, "Let her treasures be not silks or gems but manuscripts of the holy scriptures…"

Justinian and his wife Theodora became emperor and empress in 527 and strengthened the empire to keep it from splitting. They made a collection of laws that eventually became the basis of **canon law**, the collection of laws of the Catholic Church.

Vocabulary

canon: a list of the books of the Bible

canon law: the collection of laws of the Catholic Church

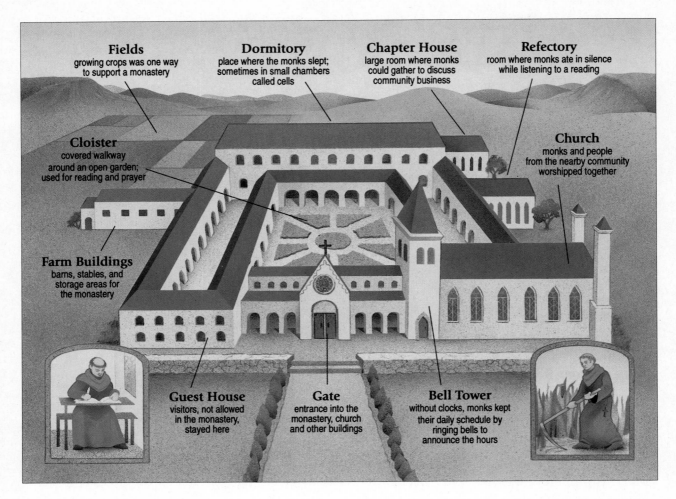

Fields
growing crops was one way to support a monastery

Dormitory
place where the monks slept; sometimes in small chambers called cells

Chapter House
large room where monks could gather to discuss community business

Refectory
room where monks ate in silence while listening to a reading

Cloister
covered walkway around an open garden; used for reading and prayer

Church
monks and people from the nearby community worshipped together

Farm Buildings
barns, stables, and storage areas for the monastery

Guest House
visitors, not allowed in the monastery, stayed here

Gate
entrance into the monastery, church and other buildings

Bell Tower
without clocks, monks kept their daily schedule by ringing bells to announce the hours

THE RISE OF MONASTERIES

Some Christians began to feel that Christ was calling them to follow him in a way that more closely resembled the zeal and devotion of the martyrs. They tried to live as **hermits** — completely alone, fasting and praying continuously. St. Anthony of the Desert (250–356) was one of these Christians. Trying to live a holy life alone was very difficult, however. Many failed, and a few even lost their minds from loneliness. Some hermits began living near one another, meeting for Mass and meals. Pachomius, an Egyptian hermit, formed a **monastery**, a community of monks, or men who live in religious life together. He also founded a convent for women.

St. Basil (329–379), the bishop of Caesarea, is considered the father of monasticism in the eastern part of the Roman Empire. He wrote a rule, or description of daily life, for monks and nuns in the eastern part of the empire. It is still used today by Eastern Christian monks and nuns throughout the world. St. Benedict of Nursia (480–547) is considered the father of monasticism in the western part of the Roman Empire. He also wrote a rule that is still followed by many religious today. It is called the Benedictine Rule. Along with his sister, St. Scholastica, who began a monastery of nuns, Benedict guided a religious movement that has influenced Western Christianity down to the present day.

Monasteries became particularly important in those areas of Europe and the Middle East that were threatened by invasion by non-Christians. In a time that was difficult and dangerous, monks and nuns kept learning alive by copying by hand books which otherwise would have been lost. Monasteries were centers of faith and learning after the collapse of the Roman Empire.

AN IRISH ABBESS

Born around 450, Brigid lived in Ireland. Little is known of her life, but there are many legends about her generosity and miracleworking. One story says that she angered her father because she gave his expensive sword to a poor leper.

Another story says that when she was sent to collect the butter made from the family cows' milk, she gave it all to the poor. When she got home, God provided her with more butter than she had originally. Yet another story says that she was so holy and pure that when she touched a wooden pillar near the altar in a church, the pillar grew roots and branches and healed those who touched it.

Brigid became a nun, and she persuaded a holy man named Conleth to found a double monastery with her at Kildare, which means "church of the oak." A double monastery is one in which there is a house for monks and a separate house for nuns, but both communities share the same church.

Brigid was full of fun and energy. She loved books, music, and art. She saw to it that beautiful copies of the Bible were made at Kildare. Most of all, though, she loved people — especially the poor. She traveled all over Ireland in a horse-drawn chariot to start other monasteries and to help the needy in remote areas.

Another legend about her life tells how she and Sister Dara, a blind and holy nun, once sat up all night talking about their faith in Jesus. As the dawn came, Brigid saw that the sky was so lovely she prayed that Sister Dara could also see it. When Brigid touched the blind nun's eyes, Sister Dara was healed. She looked for a while at the beautiful sky and then said, "Close my eyes again, for when the world is so visible to the eyes, God is seen less clearly to the soul." So Brigid prayed once more and Sister Dara was blind again.

Brigid died at Kildare around 525. Considered a saint, she was buried beside Sts.

Patrick and Columba. Together, the three are considered the patron saints of Ireland. We celebrate Brigid's feast on February 1.

Activity

Name one thing about Christianity that has influenced your life. Explain how it has played a role in making you who you are.

_____

_____

_____

_____

_____

Vocabulary

hermits: people who remove themselves from others and live alone

monastery: a religious community of monks or nuns; also, the building in which they live

How many religious traditions are represented among the people you know? Circle the religious faiths that are listed. Add others if they are not listed here.

Christianity   Hinduism   Judaism   Islam   Sikhism   Bahaism   Buddhism

_____

Are people of all religious beliefs and backgrounds made to feel welcome in your neighborhood and school? Give a reason for your answer.

_____

Do disagreements over religious beliefs ever occur between people you know? Why or why not?

_____

EAST AND WEST GROW APART

By the seventh century, government in the western part of the Roman Empire had collapsed. Life became dangerous as the West became isolated, impoverished, and subject to violence and bloodshed. Travel and trade declined. In these times, Western Christians looked to the bishop of Rome for authority and leadership in both political and religious matters.

In the eastern part of the Roman Empire, where the emperor lived, people saw the emperor as the ruler of the kingdom of God on earth and not only looked to him for political leadership, but for religious leadership as well. Soon there was tension between the authority of the emperor and that of the bishop of Rome, now referred to as the pope.

Christians in the eastern part of the Roman Empire were also faced with the influence of a new religion: Islam. The word *Islam* means "submission to God." This religion was founded in the early seventh century by Mohammed, an Arab who is considered by Muslims to be the last and greatest of the prophets. Muslims believe in one God—Allah—and have five main religious duties: to pray five times a day, facing in the direction of the holy city of Mecca; to give to the poor; to profess their faith by reciting a creed daily; to fast every day from dawn to dusk during the month of Ramadan; and to journey once in their lives to Mecca, if possible. Friday is kept as a weekly day of worship, and the Koran is the name of the Muslim book of Scriptures.

Islam became the religion of armies from Arabia that began to conquer the surrounding territories. By the end of the seventh century, Muslim armies not only succeeded in conquering much of the Eastern, or Byzantine, Empire, but parts of the West as well. Muslim armies conquered Palestine, Syria, North Africa, and parts of Spain. Much of the Byzantine Empire had been lost to them, but Constantinople itself had been successfully defended.

Islam also influenced Eastern Christianity— for example, by making it distasteful to use images of God, Jesus, Mary, and the saints in prayer. The veneration of images and statues was considered idolatry, or the setting up of false gods. In 726 the emperor forbade the use of images in Christian churches. In the West, images were felt to have a place in prayer and this law was overlooked. The eastern and western parts of the empire grew further apart.

THE CHRISTIAN COMMUNITY SPLITS

There had always been cultural and religious differences between the two halves of the Roman Empire. For example, Greek was the language of the East, and Latin was the language of the West. Church organization and worship practices varied as well.

Now, increasingly, there were theological differences, too. In 589 a Western council had decided to add the Latin word *filioque*, meaning "and the Son," to the Creed, after the words saying that the Holy Spirit proceeds from the Father. Christians in the East protested, saying that this denied that God the Father was the source of everything.

Several centuries later, in 876, a council in Constantinople condemned the pope for the *filioque* clause and because he acted without the permission of the emperor in political matters. In 1054, when a papal assistant excommunicated the bishop of Constantinople without, as it turned out, papal permission, the bishop of Constantinople excommunicated the pope in retaliation. Since then, Eastern and Western Christians have gone their separate ways.

This division resulted in the development of the Orthodox churches primarily in Russia, Eastern Europe, Asia Minor, and the Middle East. The Catholic Church turned its attention to Europe.

Over the centuries, there have been failed attempts to reconcile the two halves of Christianity. Since Vatican II, new efforts have begun.

Activity

Just as Christians of the eastern and western parts of the Roman Empire grew apart, we sometimes experience the loss of a relationship. Give a real-life example showing how each Scripture passage below can help us strengthen our relationships.

"Everyone should be quick to hear, slow to speak, slow to wrath."

1James 1:19

_____

"As I have loved you, so you also should love one another."

John 13:34

_____

"The community of believers was of one heart and mind, and no one claimed that any of his possessions was his own, but they had everything in common."

Acts 4:32

_____

Activity

As we grow, we become more responsible and have the ability and freedom to do more in our lives. It can be easy, however, to think that our freedom to act means we can do anything we want, regardless of the consequences. With freedom comes responsibility. Explore this idea by answering the questions below.

At school, what is one thing you expect of a good teacher?

_____

_____

What is an example of something a good teacher would never do?

_____

_____

If you were a teacher, how would you treat your class?

_____

_____

THE CHURCH IN THE WEST

Through missionary activities among the Germanic peoples, Gregory the Great (pope, 590–604) united western Europe. He believed that the Church and the State formed one society, called **Christendom**. The pope should rule in spiritual matters and the emperor in material affairs. But the pope was supreme.

In practice, this idea only worked once. Pope Leo III needed the help of a Frankish king named Charlemagne to keep Rome from being attacked by the Lombards, a Germanic people. Charlemagne helped and then gained control of almost all of western Europe. On Christmas Day in 800, Charlemagne went to Rome and was crowned Holy Roman Emperor by the pope—even though there was still an emperor in the eastern part of the empire.

In *The Song of Roland*, a heroic poem that commemorates Charlemagne's bravery, Charlemagne kneels in prayer before battle against a Muslim army. Then, "His prayer is done; rising, he stands erect; the sign of power he makes on brow and breast." This is an example of the sign of the cross as a sign of political power and military might.

Years later, when Charlemagne died, his empire was divided among weaker kings. These kings warred against each other and the popes. When kings were strong enough, they ignored the popes altogether.

Henry IV of Germany, for example, argued with the pope over the right to appoint bishops. At the time, bishops, continuing in roles they had had in the later years of the Roman Empire, were still political rulers as well as spiritual leaders. Pope Gregory VII, a pope who reformed the Church and improved its laws and the quality of the clergy, excommunicated Henry.

In 1077, Henry knelt in the snow outside a castle in Canossa, Italy—to beg the pope's forgiveness. The pope forgave him, and Henry then proceeded to do whatever he wanted, ignoring the pope. The clash of political wills between kings and popes would continue for centuries.

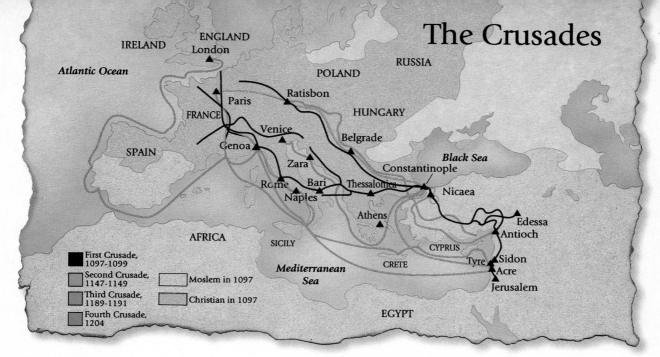

The Crusades

Map legend:
- First Crusade, 1097–1099
- Second Crusade, 1147–1149
- Third Crusade, 1189–1191
- Fourth Crusade, 1204
- Moslem in 1097
- Christian in 1097

THE CRUSADES

"God wills it!" cried the soldiers who rushed Jerusalem and fought viciously to conquer it. "God wills it!" they cried, and in the words of one eyewitness, "The streets ran with blood." The siege, or military blockade, of Jerusalem, was part of the **Crusades**, the name given to nine military attempts between 1095 and 1217 by Western Christians to liberate the holy places of Palestine from the Muslims. The crusaders wanted to control the places where Jesus and the apostles lived and taught.

The word *crusade* is taken from the word *cross* because the cross was used as a symbol and battle standard for the Christian armies. The First Crusade was called after the Byzantine emperor, under attack from Muslim invaders, asked the pope for help.

In many ways the Crusades became an excuse for brutality, greed, and ruthless ambition, but they had important lasting effects. For example, on their way to Jerusalem, the soldiers of the First Crusade slaughtered thousands of the Jews who lived in Europe. Then the Fourth Crusade helped to put an end to the Byzantine Empire when in 1204 the crusaders sacked and pillaged Constantinople, the city revered by Eastern Christians. Other Crusades helped to strengthen the power of European kings against the pope. Some Italian cities with harbors, such as Venice, became important trading and shipping centers. Although the Crusades helped awaken Europe from the collapse of the Roman Empire, they never accomplished their goal. The last crusader stronghold of Acre, in Palestine, fell in 1291 to a Muslim army.

Vocabulary

Christendom: the one society that Church and State formed together

Crusades: nine military attempts to liberate Palestine from Muslim control

WE BELIEVE

Christ calls his Church and each of its members to follow him as closely as possible. He calls most Christians to follow him through everyday family life and work. He calls others to follow him in religious communities and leadership in the Church.

A Special Place

Early in the eleventh century, Catholics from Normandy, France, invaded southern Italy, which had been divided between Eastern Christian and Islamic rulers for two centuries. The Normans captured Sicily and carved out small kingdoms for themselves. Although many Muslims fled, many also remained, and for a while, Sicily was a center of Muslim learning—ruled by Christians. Gradually, however, Sicily became more and more Christian.

In Sicily, about five miles from the city of Palermo, is the Cathedral of Monreale. This cathedral, built around 1174, is important because it tells us much about the Church during this period.

Monreale was built as a monastery for Benedictine monks by William II, a crusader from Normandy, France. The design and artwork of the cathedral combine Roman, Byzantine, and Arab styles.

The floor plan is that of a basilica, which was a plan frequently used by Roman administrators for their public buildings and which is still used by Western Christians for churches. This plan is a rectangle with two rows of columns down the length of the building and a smaller square or rounded area at one end. The main hall of the building is called the nave, and the smaller area is called the apse.

The marble pavement of the cathedral is Arabic, and the walls are decorated with Byzantine mosaics, or pictures made with tiny pieces of colored stone.

Activity

Monreale shows influences that gave the Church its character during this time. For each term below, describe this evidence.

The Christianization of Europe:

_____

Eastern Christianity:

_____

Islam:

_____

The Crusades:

_____

The Roman Empire:

_____

THE CHURCH THEN

Between the fourth and twelfth centuries, the Catholic Church changed a great deal. Once despised and persecuted, Christians found themselves with authority and responsibility, and they struggled to use their power wisely. In times that were often hard and violent, Christians themselves were sometimes guilty of brutality and cruelty — as during the Crusades, for example. Yet there was also much good.

Christians spread the good news of Jesus Christ throughout Europe and Russia. They struggled to bring order and justice to society as the Roman Empire weakened, and they expressed their faith in different ways through theology, art, worship, and prayer.

. . . AND NOW

Today, Catholics still face the challenge of living their faith in difficult times. Each generation must deal with the question of how it will express its faith and how it will respond to the problems of the age.

As in the past, Catholics in this century must decide how to handle war, poverty, hunger, and injustice. Yet we must also decide how to use technology wisely, employing it to better the lives of others. We must also decide how to use medical advances, for example, so that the rights of the weak, the elderly, the poor, the sick, and the unborn will not be disregarded. We have many opportunities challenging us to better the world.

Activity

In the first column of the chart below, identify five things you think were positive achievements for the Church between the fourth and twelfth centuries. In the second column, identify five things you would like to see the Church accomplish during your lifetime. On the lines below the chart, tell why you have one of these hopes.

The Church Then	The Church Now

_____

_____

_____

Praying an Eastern Christian Hymn

Eastern Christians call the Mass the Divine Liturgy. While Roman Catholics consider the Mass, in part, to be a Eucharistic meal in memory of Jesus' Last Supper, Eastern Christians emphasize that the Divine Liturgy is part of heavenly worship — that each time the Divine Liturgy is celebrated, heaven and earth meet, and human beings and angels give glory to God at the same time.

One of the more important hymns of the Divine Liturgy is called the "Trisagion" (treye-say-yahn), or "Hymn of Angels." It is sung to accompany the procession of the Gospel book to the lectern for the readings. (In the Mass, an "Alleluia" is sung before the readings, except during Lent. The "Trisagion" occurs at a similar point in the Divine Liturgy.) The "Trisagion" is an ancient hymn and has been sung at the Divine Liturgy since the fifth century.

The hymn glorifies the three Persons of the Trinity. "Holy God" refers to God the Father, "Holy and Mighty" refers to Jesus, and "Holy and Immortal" refers to the Holy Spirit.

It is customary to bow from the waist and make the Sign of the Cross each time the first part of the "Trisagion" is sung and once when the "Glory Be to the Father" is sung. The melody of the "Trisagion" varies according to the liturgical season and holy day. This is true for all chants and hymns of the Divine Liturgy in Eastern Christianity.

Holy God, Holy and Mighty, Holy and Immortal, have mercy on us. (*Sung three times.*) Glory be to the Father and to the Son and to the Holy Spirit, now and for ever, world without end. Amen.
Holy and Immortal, have mercy on us.

CHAPTER REVIEW

Answer each of the following questions in a sentence.

1. Why do men and women become monks and nuns?

   _____

2. How did monasteries help the people of Europe in a difficult and violent age?

   _____

3. Why did Christianity split in half in 1054?

   _____

   _____

4. What did Charlemagne accomplish?

   _____

   _____

5. Why did Pope Gregory VII and King Henry IV of Germany argue?

   _____

Respond to the following questions from what you learned in this chapter.

1. What was meant by *Christendom*?

   _____

   _____

2. Why did the popes and bishops sometimes find it necessary to govern like heads of state?

   _____

   _____

   _____

Repay to Caesar what belongs to Caesar and to God what belongs to God.
Mark 12:17

3. Discuss what you would tell someone who insists that the Church should not be involved in politics.

A CREATIVE PEOPLE

FREEING GIFTS WITHIN

WHO DO
YOU THINK
IS A CREATIVE
PERSON? WHY?

Once a young boy saw his neighbor carrying a block of stone down the street. The boy helped carry the stone to the woman's workshed.

The next day the curious boy visited the woman to see what she was doing with the stone. He saw the woman hitting the stone with hammers and chisels. The woman told him that she was a sculptor.

Each day the boy came back and sat watching the sculptor strike the stone. Each day the stone became smaller and smoother. It seemed to become more alive.

Then one morning the boy walked into the sculptor's shed. The sculptor stood there smiling at a beautiful stone lion.

The boy was amazed. "How did you know there was a lion in the stone?" he asked the skillful sculptor.

Activity

How do you think the sculptor answered the boy? Write the answer here.

_____

_____

_____

_____

_____

From Countryside to Town

The Middle Ages (900–1400) was an amazingly creative time for Europe. The Crusades helped to change society by bringing spices, silks, and other luxuries back to Europe. Towns sprang up along the major travel routes of the crusaders to the Holy Land. Trade and commerce grew in Christendom and between Christendom and the Arab world. A new class of people emerged — merchants, businesspeople, bankers, artisans, and craftspeople.

Jewish citizens of medieval kingdoms also contributed much to the creativity of this time. Their skilled labor and learning in many occupations helped to build the strength of medieval society. Their knowledge of trade, medicine, and navigation made them valuable, if frequently despised. From time to time throughout the Middle Ages, Christians persecuted the Jewish people and failed to recognize that persecution was wrong.

The performing arts flourished during this time. Entertainers traveled the roads putting on plays, telling stories, singing songs, and sharing tales of romantic love. From these grew great works of literature, drama, and music.

From Monasteries to Cathedrals

The new towns replaced the monasteries as the centers of life and culture. Townspeople built great cathedrals, such as those at Chartres, Rouen, and Gloucester — to raise people's hearts to God. Skilled architects, craftspeople, artists, and thousands of laborers worked long years to create these magnificent houses of worship.

From Cathedrals to Universities

Bishops began schools connected with the new cathedrals. The best of these cathedral schools became universities, the earliest of which was in Bologna. Other important universities

were soon to appear in Paris, Oxford, Cambridge, Naples, Cologne, Heidelberg, and Salamanca, where they still exist today.

Famous teachers, such as Abelard in Paris, attracted students from all over Europe. About the year 1100, Abelard took the first steps toward a scientific method of asking new questions and doing careful research to find new answers. Gratian, an Italian monk, developed canon and civil law using Abelard's new method.

Scholasticism, an important way of doing philosophy and theology, was based on Abelard's method and enabled scholars to suggest answers to difficult questions. By looking first at one side of an issue and then at the other, scholars were able then to combine the strongest and most persuasive parts of each. The work *Summa Theologiae* by St. Thomas Aquinas is a brilliant example of scholastic theology. Western thinkers are still heavily influenced by this two-part approach.

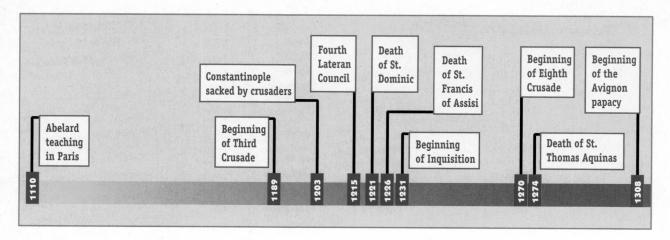

1110	1189	1203	1215	1221	1226	1231	1270	1274	1308

Abelard teaching in Paris (1110)

Constantinople sacked by crusaders (1203)

Beginning of Third Crusade (1189)

Fourth Lateran Council (1215)

Death of St. Dominic (1221)

Death of St. Francis of Assisi (1226)

Beginning of Inquisition (1231)

Beginning of Eighth Crusade (1270)

Beginning of the Avignon papacy (1308)

Death of St. Thomas Aquinas (1274)

FROM MONKS TO MENDICANTS

New religious communities of men and women became even more influential than the early monks and nuns. The new community members were called friars (or brothers) and sisters. St. Francis of Assisi, a merchant's son, founded the Franciscan Order around 1209. The Franciscans were men committed to poverty and to renewing the faith of Christians in the towns. Francis' friend St. Clare began the Franciscan sisters, known as Poor Clares.

St. Dominic began another new religious order, the Dominicans, who focused on preaching. Dominic also started communities of Dominican sisters. The friars were called **mendicants** because they supported themselves by begging. Lay people united with Franciscans and Dominicans by forming **third orders** to work with the mendicants.

FROM SERVICE TO POWER

The medieval papacy grew even stronger than it had been before. Rome became the most powerful center of the Christian faith. In the East, Constantinople was conquered by the Muslim Turks in 1453. After this event, Eastern Christianity barely survived under Islamic rule, although Eastern Christianity flourished in Russia. In Rome Western Christianity expressed its power and prestige in Europe. The bishops of Rome were considered by Western Christians to be the successors of St. Peter and the vicars of Christ on earth.

Popes were now elected by **cardinals**, advisors who were selected by the pope and who were assisted by a **curia** of officials. From time to time popes called councils to root out any abuses that had risen and to put down heresy. One such council, called the Fourth Lateran Council, was held in 1215.

Another effort to suppress heresy was the Inquisition, which began in 1231. It was the responsibility of the clergy who were appointed as inquisitors to identify heretics and encourage these people to repent their mistaken beliefs. Any denial of a Catholic teaching or even suspicion of unusual opinions could result in being denounced to the Inquisition. Punishment included heavy penances, fines, and the confiscation of property. If someone were judged to be stubborn in believing a heresy, he or she would be turned over to the civil authorities for execution—usually burning at the stake.

Although begun to maintain Catholic unity, abuses quickly crept into the Inquisition's activities. Torture became an important part of questioning. Also, not just heretics, but anyone who seemed to be a threat to peace and order could be denounced to the Inquisition and his or her property awarded to the accuser. In the fifteenth and sixteenth centuries, the Spanish Inquisition accused, tortured, and ultimately was responsible for the executions of thousands of Spanish Jews and Muslims. The hope for a united Christendom had turned into an oppressive abuse of power.

Activity

All sorts of situations call for creative thinking. Look at the following list and rate your own creativity in each situation.

	Grim	Great
Drawing	☐	☐
Doing a puzzle	☐	☐
Singing or playing an instrument	☐	☐
Taking photographs	☐	☐
Playing sports	☐	☐
Dancing	☐	☐
Making things	☐	☐
Writing poems and stories	☐	☐
Helping and caring for others	☐	☐
Bringing people together	☐	☐
Being persuasive	☐	☐
Entertaining others	☐	☐

Imagine that at the end of this school year, you will be given an award for your creativity. Write about some of the gifts you have used to earn this award.

_____

_____

_____

_____

_____

_____

_____

Vocabulary

mendicants: religious persons who supported themselves by begging

third orders: lay communities closely united with religious orders of men or women

cardinals: advisors selected by the pope

curia: officials who assist the pope or a bishop

Manor

Pasture

Workshop

Water Mill

Church

Serfs' Houses

First Field

Third Field

Barn

Second Field

THE FEUDAL AGE

Throughout the Middle Ages, most people lived under a system called **feudalism**. This was a social system that was based on loyalties and protections, rather than laws. To find protection from Germanic invaders, people depended upon powerful lords who would fight for them. In return, people owed the lords allegiance and a portion of the goods from their farms. The lords maintained order in society.

Over the centuries, the lords gained more and more power until most ordinary people were **serfs**, or poor farmers. Serfs were tied to the farms on which they were born. They could not leave and seek out a better arrangement with another lord. Feudalism was at its peak in Europe between 900 and 1200, but loyalties and protections continued to be important as late as the 1600s.

The feudal system—the lords, manor houses, and serfs—was a very important part of the Church's life, too. Most bishops of the Church

were feudal lords, and they controlled their own serfs and properties. They made everyday decisions about the lives of the townspeople in their jurisdiction. The serfs on their farms were required to work a certain number of days each year on the Church's land. Serfs were also required to give a portion of their harvest to the Church. This form of taxation, called **tithing**, included the grain the serfs grew, a portion of their livestock, their garden produce, and anything else they might have earned.

LIVES OF FAITH

As poor as they were, serfs often had great faith. Their understanding of Christian faith was very different from ours, however. A serf of the Middle Ages was usually not educated at all and could not read or write. Since the printing press had not yet been invented, there were very few Bibles, and these were very expensive and kept in the great churches and monasteries.

Serfs sang songs about their faith and told one another stories about the miracles of Jesus, Mary, and the saints—and some of these stories were more entertaining than they were pious. The serfs also fasted and prayed on holy days. But their Christianity was mixed up with local superstitions about the weather and how to cure illnesses. They still visited local witches and wizards who might know something about an herbal cure that no one else knew. And even though they were Christian, they did not always behave with the respect and submission that the great lords and bishops of the feudal age had come to expect.

Activity

Imagine that one morning you wake up and find the world very different from what it is today. In this new world, there is no separation of Church and State. In many ways, the world is back in the Middle Ages. Every year on April 15 your family pays its taxes to the parish priest. And the governor of the state has decided that a person cannot get a driver's license if he or she does not celebrate the sacrament of Reconciliation regularly. Work with others in your class to explore this new world.

Name three other ways in which your life might be different.

_____

_____

_____

What do you think should happen in this new world to people who are not Catholic?

_____

_____

If this happened, do you think the world would be better or worse than it is now? Give reasons for your answer.

_____

_____

_____

_____

Vocabulary

feudalism: a social system based on loyalties and protections

serfs: poor farmers who could not leave the farms where they were born

tithing: a form of taxation; a portion of the harvest given to the Church

Activity

On a separate sheet of paper, brainstorm as many creative responses as possible for each of the situations listed below.

• Your younger brother or sister is crying.
• A neighborhood ballfield may be turned into a parking lot.
• You need to throw a party in a half hour.
• An elderly person in your parish is lonely.
• You just won a million dollars.

THE CHURCH IN NEED

By the fourteenth century the Church seemed to be going through a storm. Many popes and bishops lived like worldly princes. Catholics knew little about their beliefs. But the major crisis of the time was caused by the fact that the popes no longer lived in the city of Rome.

They had moved to Avignon, which is in southern France. The reason for this situation was a bitter argument between King Philip of France and Pope Boniface about political authority. The French king had ended the argument by taking control of the papacy. The popes lived in Avignon from 1305 to 1377 and continued to be controlled by the French kings.

A woman named Catherine, who was noted for her holiness, was anxious to heal the Church. She visited Pope Gregory XI in Avignon and pointed out the necessity of returning the papacy to Rome, saying, "No longer resist the will of God, for the starving sheep wait for you to return to the see of St. Peter." Pope Gregory listened to her and returned to Rome in 1377.

After Gregory's death, Urban VI was elected pope. He was incompetent and, possibly, insane. The cardinals asked him to step down, and when he refused, a group of them elected someone else pope. This created scandal and disorder because there was more than one pope. The **Great Schism** continued from 1378 to 1417, when the cardinals and kings of Europe worked to stop the claims of rival popes.

The Great Schism was ended by the Council of Constance (1414) at which the bishops of the Church worked together to determine who the pope should be. They persuaded one pope to step down and deposed another. They then elected Martin V to be the new pope. Although one of the rival popes, Benedict XIII lived until 1423, claiming all the while to be the true pope, the bishops of the Church accepted Martin V as the pope.

After this, the bishops of the Church insisted upon more power and authority in religious matters so that never again could a king or an incapable pope control the Church. The term **conciliarism** describes the idea that the bishops meeting in a council have the highest authority in the Church. Yet over the centuries the question of who has the highest authority in the Church—the pope or the bishops—continued to be an issue for awhile.

A YOUNG WOMAN WHO BROUGHT REFORM

Born in 1347, Catherine Benincasa grew up in a large family in Siena, Italy. Her father owned a successful cloth-dying business. Though she had no formal education, Catherine was an intelligent and cheerful girl who learned to read but not to write.

As a teenager she surprised and angered her parents by announcing that she would not marry. Nor did she want to become a nun. The family was unhappy but finally let Catherine do what she felt God wanted her to do.

She became a member of the Dominican Third Order, a group of laypersons who lived in their own homes, but affiliated themselves with the Dominicans. For three years Catherine faithfully performed her household duties and prayed a great deal. She took food and clothing to the poor and cared for the sick. When a terrible epidemic, called the Black Death, struck the people of Siena, Catherine tirelessly cared for its victims. Many men and women joined in her efforts.

Catherine was very upset by the serious problems she saw in the Church. She dictated hundreds of letters to kings, bishops, princes, cardinals, generals—even to the pope—trying to spark the needed reforms. She acted as a diplomat and peacemaker. Catherine went to Avignon and convinced Pope Gregory XI to move the papacy back to Rome as a needed step toward Church reform.

Catherine also dictated a spiritual book, the *Dialogue,* about her relationship with Christ. Written in four essays, Catherine emphasized living as a Christian and God's love. She guided many men and women to holiness.

Working so hard for peace in Italy and for reform in the Catholic Church, Catherine was only thirty-three when she suffered a stroke and died in 1380. She was canonized in 1461, and in 1970, Pope Paul VI named her a Doctor (teacher) of the Church. April 29 is the feast day of St. Catherine of Siena.

Vocabulary

Great Schism: the period of time during which there was more than one pope

conciliarism: the idea that the council of bishops has supreme authority in the Church

WE BELIEVE

In the midst of challenges, the Holy Spirit helps the Catholic Church to adapt creatively to the needs of the times. The Spirit gives individual Christians creative abilities to build up and renew the Church.

THE RENAISSANCE

The Crusades opened the rest of the world to Europeans. Western Christians became aware of the achievements of Arab scholars. Arab mathematicians, for example, had mastered algebra and were skilled cartographers, or mapmakers. In Cairo, Egypt, there was an observatory where astronomy was studied.

When Muslim Turks conquered Constantinople in 1453, Eastern Christian scholars there fled to Italy—taking with them the writings of the Greeks. This introduction of Arab learning and the rediscovery of classical Greek and Roman learning was the beginning of the Renaissance, which means "rebirth."

ACHIEVEMENTS AND LEARNING

During the Renaissance a new emphasis was placed on the beauty of nature and the dignity and uniqueness of each individual. This was called humanism, because it celebrated the ability of human beings to reason and to learn about themselves and their world. It also celebrated human feelings and the human ability to appreciate music, literature, and art.

Fabulous paintings and sculptures were produced during the Renaissance by artists such as Michelangelo and Titian. Many of these artists were hired by wealthy merchants and princes to create works of art for them. But the greatest employers of artists were the popes and bishops who had works such as the Sistine Chapel in Rome created for them.

Increasingly, education was no longer restricted to religious topics, as it had been during the Middle Ages. Now there was interest in economics and politics. The roots of modern medicine and science can also be found in the Renaissance.

One of the most brilliant men of the age was Leonardo da Vinci. An accomplished artist who painted the *Mona Lisa* and *The Last Supper*, Da Vinci was also a scientist and an inventor. He performed autopsies on corpses to learn more about the human body from both the scientific and artistic points of view. His inventions included plans for a flying machine and an armored car. He wrote, "Just as iron rusts without use, and water becomes putrid and with the cold freezes, so talent without exercise deteriorates."

THE GROWTH OF FAITH AND DEVOTION

During the Renaissance there was a renewed interest in religion. With the rediscovery of Greek writings, new and more accurate translations of the Bible were made, based on the original Greek texts. New insights into the Scriptures resulted.

People began to think that holiness could be achieved by ordinary people. For example, Thomas á Kempis (1380–1471), a monk, wrote *The Imitation of Christ*. This book describes how ordinary people can live their lives and become friends with Jesus by taking up their crosses in life. This book is still read by Catholics.

The Renaissance was a creative rebirth that invigorated Western European society. Knowledge increased, and people had a new appreciation for the dignity and abilities of human beings.

Activity

Design an invention that could help, teach, or comfort a very young child. Sketch your ideas on the graph paper. Then write a description of your invention and give it a name.

PRAYING WITH DANCE

Many religions include dance as a form of prayer and worship. In some religions, dance is used as part of a ritual for doing magic. In others, dance is a way to honor and praise God.

The Old Testament shows us that the ancient Hebrews used dance as a spontaneous way to give glory to God. For example, when the ark of the covenant was brought to Jerusalem, King David "came dancing before the LORD with abandon, as he and all the Israelites were bringing up the ark of the LORD with shouts of joy and to the sound of the horn" (2 Samuel 6:14–16). The Bible also describes David as "leaping" before the Lord.

Dancing to give honor and glory to God was also known during the Renaissance. In sixteenth-century Spain, dance was used on special holy days to praise God. Unlike David's wild dancing, however, this dance was more like a procession—somber and regal in style.

Today, dance is occasionally used at Mass. Called liturgical dance, it generally includes the movements of ballet and modern dance as part of a procession or meditation. True liturgical dance is neither a performance nor an entertainment but a natural and heartfelt way to praise God through movement.

As physical beings, we use movement all the time to praise God. We kneel, genuflect, and make the Sign of the Cross to give glory and honor to God. And some of us are talented enough to dance before the Lord, as David did.

Activity

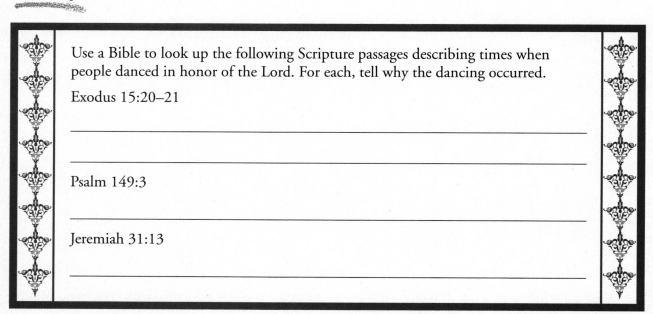

Use a Bible to look up the following Scripture passages describing times when people danced in honor of the Lord. For each, tell why the dancing occurred.

Exodus 15:20–21

_____

_____

Psalm 149:3

_____

Jeremiah 31:13

_____

CHAPTER REVIEW

Match the words in Column 1 with their definitions in Column 2.

Column 1

_____ third orders

_____ St. Catherine of Siena

_____ Scholasticism

_____ serfs

_____ Great Schism

_____ curia

_____ cathedrals

_____ Avignon

_____ friars

_____ feudalism

_____ Leonardo da Vinci

_____ Renaissance

Column 2

1. rebirth; a time of new learning and knowledge
2. lay communities united with religious orders
3. a way of answering philosophical and theological questions
4. a social system based on loyalties and protections
5. officials who assist the pope or a bishop
6. city in France where the popes lived for awhile
7. period in the Church's history when there was more than one pope
8. brilliant inventor, artist, and scientist
9. holy woman who worked to have the popes return to Rome
10. poor farmers who depended on lords for protections
11. mendicants
12. magnificent buildings built for prayer and worship

Write a paragraph describing some of the creative achievements of the Church during the Middle Ages and Renaissance.

_____

_____

_____

_____

Respond to the following questions based on what you have learned in this chapter.

1. What is *conciliarism*?

_____

_____

2. Why do you think people such as Francis and Dominic chose to go to the people in the cities and towns?

_____

_____

3. Discuss what events today call for creative solutions by Christians.

Do not quench the Spirit.
1 Thessalonians 5:19

4 A REFORMING PEOPLE

ROUGH TIMES

Think of a group to which you belong. Does it seem as alive and interesting as it was when you first joined? Does the group seem to have lost something of its old spirit? Why do you think it has? If the group has kept its spirit, why do you think this is so?

Most groups start out with enthusiasm, high ideals, and exciting activities. After a while many of them experience a loss of energy. This loss of spirit can be the result of many things. The group may have achieved its basic purpose and may not know where to turn next. Or, group members may be quarreling with one another. Other groups go through periods during which members experience some loss of spirit and then later their enthusiasm sparks back to life.

WHAT MAKES YOU FEEL BETTER WHEN TIMES ARE ROUGH?

Activity

Why do you think some groups experience a loss of energy after a while?

_____

_____

_____

Why is it often harder to renew a group that has lost its spirit than it is to start a new group?

_____

_____

_____

_____

_____

_____

In Need of Reform

The Renaissance changed European society in many ways. It helped Europeans to feel optimistic about improving their lives in many areas.

One of the many inventions created during the Renaissance was the printing press. In 1456, Johannes Gutenberg invented the type mold and movable type—metal blocks that spelled out words and could be used over and over again. This was part of the invention of the printing press, a technological leap forward that revolutionized the way knowledge was communicated. The first book that Gutenberg printed was the Bible.

In the Middle Ages only the Church, the aristocracy, and the wealthy could afford to own books, because books were made one at a time, by hand. Once the printing press was invented, books could be mass-produced cheaply and quickly and many people could afford them.

Books helped to spread learning and knowledge throughout Europe. More and more people learned to read. There was an explosion of ideas and information.

At the same time that European society was being improved by the inventions, art, literature, and political and economic developments of the Renaissance, there was also a renewed interest in religion and faith. Now that European Christians could read about the early churches in the Bible for themselves, they began to improve the sorry state that the Church had fallen into. Although the popes and leading bishops had become important patrons of the arts, improving filthy, crowded medieval towns by adding open squares and beautiful buildings, such projects cost a great deal of money. The princes of the Church became very much like the princes of the world—more interested in money and political intrigue than in living holy lives.

For example, Church property was an important source of Church income that was sometimes exploited for personal profit. A bishop might buy or sell for a fee the rights to the income of Church land to another bishop or

priest. This corrupt and dishonest practice was known as **simony**, or the buying and selling of spiritual things.

Another corrupt practice for moneymaking was the buying and selling of indulgences. An **indulgence** is the removal of all or some of the punishments for sins that have already been confessed and forgiven. This practice had been a way for the Church to show forgiveness and lessen harsh penances for sin. Now, however, an indulgence could be bought for a fee. It could even be bought for someone who had already died and was presumably suffering for the sins of his or her earthly life.

Vocabulary

simony: the practice of buying and selling of spiritual things

indulgence: the removal of all or some of the punishments for sins that have already been forgiven

Activity

THE PROTESTANT REFORMATION

It was Martin Luther, an Augustinian monk who lived in Germany, who unleashed a powerful but divisive reformation of the Church in 1517. Luther challenged the practice of selling indulgences and other forms of Church corruption. He called Christians to return to the Bible and to faith.

Luther went too far in his teachings, however. He said that God saves people because of their faith alone and the good that they do does not count in God's eyes. He also taught that there are only two sacraments—Baptism and the Eucharist.

The biggest problem for Luther, however, was the authority of the popes and the Church councils. He and the leaders of the Church quarreled about the meaning of an important Scripture passage about Church authority: "I will give you the keys to the kingdom of heaven. Whatever you bind on earth shall be bound in heaven; and whatever you loose on earth shall be loosed in heaven" (Matthew 16:19). In the end, Luther rejected the Church's claim to the keys of the kingdom of heaven as described in this passage. He only accepted the authority of the Bible. He said that the Church leaders had become tyrants who tried to keep Christianity from people.

After the Church excommunicated him in 1520, Luther continued his work. He translated the Bible into German so that the German people could read it. He wrote catechisms to teach people his ideas, and he is considered the founder of the Lutheran Church.

Because his works were quickly printed and read by thousands all over Europe, Luther became very popular. Ideas about reform quickly spread to other countries.

Other reformers worked to spread their own ideas about what Christianity should be like. They were called Protestants, because they protested against the Church. John Calvin (1509–1564), a French scholar who lived in Geneva, Switzerland, taught that God alone decided who was to be saved and that no one could do anything to change God's decision.

Another reformer, Ulrich Zwingli (1484–1531) lived in Zurich, Switzerland. He wanted to get rid of anything about religion that was superstitious and not based clearly on the Bible. He persuaded the city government of Zurich to draw up a religious code that set up Protestant Christianity in the city. The Bible was accepted as the sole authority in religion. The Mass was done away with, and all paintings and statues were taken out of the churches.

In England in 1534, King Henry VIII, angry because the pope refused to let him divorce his wife, made himself head of the Church of England—the Anglican Church. Protestants in England were especially influenced by the ideas of John Calvin.

Activity

Below is a statement that Luther made in answer to the bishops and the emperor Charles V. Next to it is a statement that Charles V made about Luther. After reading both, answer the questions.

LUTHER'S ANSWER

Since Your Imperial Majesty and Your Highnesses insist upon a simple reply, I shall give you one—brief and simple but deprived neither of teeth nor horns. Unless I am convicted of error by the testimony of the Bible (for I place no faith in the mere authority of the pope, or of councils, which have often been wrong, recognizing, as I do, no other guide but the Bible), I cannot and will not retract my statements, for we must never act against our conscience.

STATEMENT OF CHARLES V

A single monk, led astray by private judgment, has set himself against the faith upheld by all Christians for more than a thousand years. He believes that all Christians up to now have been wrong. I am now sorry that I have so long delayed moving against him and his false doctrines. I have made up my mind never again to listen to him. He is forbidden to preach and to win over men with his evil beliefs and incite them to rebellion.

What is the main point of what Luther is saying?

_____

_____

Why has Charles V decided not to listen to Luther any more?

_____

_____

Activity

Mark some of the ways you think work best to end an argument.

_____ Change the topic.   _____ Shout.   _____ Discuss the problem calmly.

_____ Ignore the person.   _____ Compromise.   _____ Agree with the person.

_____ End the relationship.   _____ Apologize.   _____ Negotiate with the person.

_____ Get even.   _____ Force the issue.   _____ Overlook the problem.

Remembering Jesus' command to love one another, suggest several Christian ways to end an argument.

_____

_____

MAJOR RELIGIOUS DIVISIONS

NORWAY
SCOTLAND
Stockholm ▲
SWEDEN
DENMARK
Moscow ▲
IRELAND
ENGLAND
RUSSIA
London ▲
Atlantic Ocean
GERMANY
Warsaw ▲
Paris ▲
POLAND
FRANCE
HOLY ROMAN EMPIRE
HUNGARY
CRIMEA
MOLDAVIA
SWITZERLAND
PORTUGAL
SPAIN
ITALY
BULGARIA
Black Sea
Madrid ▲
Rome ▲
OTTOMAN EMPIRE
Constantinople ▲
Mediterranean Sea
Jerusalem
Alexandria ▲
EGYPT

Roman Catholic
Anglican
Lutheran
Orthodox
Calvinist
Moslem

THE CATHOLIC REFORMATION

There were many people who wanted to reform the Catholic Church from within instead of leaving it. These people did not go as far as Luther, Calvin, and Zwingli. They accepted the teachings and practices of the Church and the authority of the popes and Church councils. The movement to reform the Church from within is called the Counter-Reformation or the Catholic Reformation. It sought to preserve and improve the Catholic faith.

New religious orders were founded to meet the needs of the Church. The Society of Jesus, or Jesuits, founded in 1534 by St. Ignatius Loyola, established colleges in Europe to educate Catholic youth.

In 1535, St. Angela Merici began an important community of religious women, the Ursulines, to educate Catholic girls and young women. St. Teresa of Avila reformed the Discalced (barefooted) Carmelites, a group of contemplative nuns. St. Philip Neri began the Oratorians, a community of priests dedicated to spiritual reform.

There were other changes in Catholic life as well. More frequent confession and Communion were encouraged. The education of priests was improved. Catholics sought to renew their faith by having a new interest in the humanity of Jesus and by desiring to get closer to God. People were encouraged to pray regularly and to recognize that they could cooperate with grace when they felt God acting in their lives.

The first Catholic hymnal was printed in 1537, and people were encouraged to sing at Mass. (Before this, choirs had done the singing.) Music was important because it was a way to elevate the soul to focus on the Spirit. The use of art in churches reflected the idea that God uses beauty and grandeur to attract the soul.

BEARING ARMS FOR THE CHURCH

As a young man, St. Ignatius Loyola (1491–1556) was a soldier in the Spanish army. During a battle his legs were injured when he was hit by a cannonball. He was taken to a nearby castle where he slowly recuperated. To pass the time, he began to read books on the life of Christ and the saints. He underwent a conversion. He decided that, rather than being a soldier for an earthly king, he would become a knight for Christ.

After he recovered he went on a pilgrimage and then went to France, where he spent some time caring for the sick and leading a life of prayer. It was here he began to write a book called *Spiritual Exercises*, which is still used.

He wrote: "Going for long and short walks and running are physical exercises; so we give the name of spiritual exercises to any process which makes the soul ready and able to rid itself of all irregular attachments; so that, once rid of them, it may look for and discover how God wills it to regulate its life."

Ignatius went to Paris and studied at the university there from 1528 to 1535. There he felt called by God to start a new religious order. He and several friends joined together to form the Society of Jesus. At first they thought they would work in Jerusalem and try to convert the Muslims who held the city.

But soon they decided that the way they would "bear arms for God" was to protect the Church from enemies — especially the Protestants, who seemed to be dividing the Church in some places in Europe. The Society of Jesus — also called Jesuits — grew rapidly and established schools all over Europe. They also became missionaries throughout the world. Their spirit today is that of their founder, Ignatius Loyola, who taught them to seek God's will and to obey it, no matter what the cost may be.

Today, the Church considers Ignatius to be a saint. We celebrate his feast day on July 31.

Activity

Reform requires significant change. What are some ways that people today might reform their lives?

_____

_____

_____

_____

_____

_____

What is one change that you would like to make in your life to become a better person?

_____

_____

_____

_____

_____

_____

THE COUNCIL OF TRENT

A new pope, Paul III, wanting to reform the Church, called an ecumenical council in 1545. This council, which became known as the Council of Trent, reaffirmed these Catholic teachings: (1) the Church's tradition, along with the Bible, is important; (2) good works as well as faith are important for salvation; (3) there are seven sacraments; and (4) the pope has authority over the entire Church.

The bishops at the Council of Trent faced questions of faith and the moral reform of the Church. They discussed both of these problems. Issues of doctrine received more of their attention, however. Among the topics they discussed were justification, or what is necessary to have a right relationship with God, and how Christians discover God's revelation both in Scripture and in tradition—the teachings and the practices the Church has always held.

The bishops also discussed how the sacraments work and taught that the sacraments do not depend on the strength of the faith of the Christian receiving them, but celebrate God's grace in and of themselves. The bishops emphasized the real presence of Jesus Christ in the Eucharist. They also required Catholics to celebrate the sacrament of Reconciliation each year and receive communion at least once a year as well.

The Council of Trent called for the spiritual renewal of the Church and had a catechism of Catholic doctrine written. It also recommended establishing seminaries to train priests. Sts.

Charles Borromeo and Francis de Sales were two bishops who worked hard to carry out the Church's reforms.

In the end, however, although the Council of Trent did much to renew the Catholic Church, it failed to unite Protestants and Catholics. This is because, from the beginning of the Reformation, political and economic matters played a big role in the religious disputes.

For example, although Luther first called for reform in 1517 when he nailed to the cathedral door in Wittenburg his ninety-five theses, or points for discussion, it was not until 1545 that the bishops and princes of Europe could agree on holding the council in Trent. And even then there were problems about who would attend the council and what their roles would be. The emperor wanted the council to resolve practical matters, such as trying to agree with Protestant positions whenever possible. But Lutheran representatives did not arrive at the council until 1551, six years after it had begun; and when they finally arrived, they wanted the discussions to begin over again. The bishops refused and focused their attention on stating what the Church stood for and what beliefs one had to have to be Catholic.

While the Catholics worked for renewal within the Church, religious disputes among Protestants led to the rise of more and more religious groups who held very rigid opinions about their particular view of Christianity. Such disagreements soon led to war, and over the next century, the wars of religion in Europe and England brought great suffering to many.

Activity

Complete the following chart to identify the causes and effects of the Reformation. For each fact write in the missing cause or effect. (Hint: Chart is read across.)

FACT	CAUSE	EFFECT
1. The Bible was the first book to be printed.	Gutenberg invented the printing press in 1456.	_____ _____ _____
2. There were corrupt practices for raising money in the Church.	Church leaders lived and acted like the princes of the world.	_____ _____
3. Luther refused to accept the authority of the pope and Church councils.	He only accepted the Bible as the authority for Christians.	_____ _____
4. In the sixteenth century there were calls for reform and much discussion about religion.	_____ _____ _____	Catholics and Protestants did not reunite.

Activity

Complete the following survey to reflect on ways you can renew your faith and grow closer to God. Mark as many choices as you wish.

_____ Write a confidential letter to God.

_____ Visit a beautiful church.

_____ Work for others in a service project.

_____ Learn a way to meditate.

_____ Learn a way to pray, using Scripture.

_____ Sing a favorite hymn.

_____ Create a prayer corner in your classroom.

_____ Start and keep a spiritual journal.

_____ Create a class collection of prayers.

_____ Create a work of religious art.

_____ Other: _____

_____

_____

_____

_____

WE BELIEVE

The Catholic Church is continually guided and renewed by the Holy Spirit. We are called to respond to new challenges and opportunities in the light of the Church's two thousand years of experience and wisdom.

The illustration shows a tree with "Christianity" on the trunk. The main branches and sub-branches are labeled: Catholic Church; Orthodox Church (1054); Anglican; Episcopal (1789); Methodist (1733); Lutheran (16th century); Reformed (16th century); Presbyterian (17th century); Congregational (17th century); Baptist (17th century).

CHRISTIANITY TODAY

Since the time of Martin Luther and the Reformation, Christians have continued to discuss and disagree with one another about their beliefs and practices. Today, there are at least several hundred Christian groups, or denominations, in the United States alone. Most of these are Protestants.

The largest Christian denomination in the United States is the Catholic Church, with about 22% of the U.S. population. The next largest are the Baptist Churches, followed by the Methodist Church, the Lutheran Churches, the Presbyterian Churches, and the Episcopal Church.

Other rapidly growing Christian groups in the United States include evangelical and fundamentalist Christians. These Christian groups interpret the Bible literally and use it as their rule for prayer, worship, and everyday life. These groups look for a life-changing, personal conversion (born-again) experience of Jesus as Lord and Savior as a sign of a person's faith.

Eastern Christians are found in the United States as well, and they make up about 2% of the Christian population. Eastern Christians are not considered Protestants, because the break between Eastern, or Orthodox, Christians and Catholics came in 1054—several centuries before the Reformation.

Although the Reformation was a time of great and, unfortunately, divisive change, Christianity is always in a state of growth and renewal because the Holy Spirit is always prompting and guiding people of faith. Today, the Catholic Church is still continually renewing itself and trying to live out the good news of Jesus Christ. Because we are imperfect people, we do not always do it well, but with the support of the Spirit and one another, we can struggle to live better lives of faith in Jesus Christ.

Activity

Explore your ideas about how strong the Catholic Church is today. For each 'Good Job' response, write 10 points. For each 'OK Job' response, write 5 points. For each 'Bad Job' response, write 0 points. The total number of points is the grade you give the Catholic Church. How well do you think the Church does in each of the following areas?

	Bad Job	OK Job	Good Job
1. The Church is found throughout the world.	_____	_____	_____
2. The Church does a lot for the poor, the sick, and the elderly.	_____	_____	_____
3. The Church educates people about the faith.	_____	_____	_____
4. The Church encourages people to be generous.	_____	_____	_____
5. The Church works for peace and justice in the world.	_____	_____	_____
6. The Church is a community of Jesus' followers.	_____	_____	_____
7. The Church provides comfort and guidance for people.	_____	_____	_____
8. The Church brings the Word of God to people.	_____	_____	_____
9. The Church shows care and concern for people.	_____	_____	_____
10. The Church provides leadership in a sinful world.	_____	_____	_____

Activity

Consider the life of the Church today in terms of your own parish. Name three things you like about your parish. Then name three things you wish were different about your parish.

Likes

1. _____

2. _____

3. _____

Wishes

1. _____

2. _____

3. _____

Give your reasons for one of the things you wish was different.

_____

_____

The idea behind Taizé is one of simplicity. The community emphasizes the Christian call to follow Christ and to do so by leaving behind all the demands and distractions of life. By simplifying one's life, by giving away possessions, and by opening one's heart to others, one will discover the joy of being alive. This joy will shine through, touching the lives of others. And it is in this joy that one will find the true meaning of community, of oneness with Jesus and with others. This is the core of the Christian message.

Activity

Why do you think Christians remain divided today?

_____

_____

_____

If you had the opportunity to talk to Christian leaders from around the world, what would you say to them about Christian unity?

_____

_____

_____

Create an ecumenical prayer to pray with your class for Christians in your family and community. Pray for specific leaders and churches.

_____

_____

_____

_____

_____

_____

PRAYING FOR CHRISTIAN UNITY

In this century, some Christians have recognized that it is sad that there are so many divisions separating Christians from one another. They started a movement called ecumenism which works for Christian unity. Through prayer and discussion, perhaps many of the divisions that have broken up the Christian community can be healed.

One example of the kind of healing that can take place among Christians is found in the monastic community of Taizé. This group of monks is not Catholic, but Protestant. Founded in 1940 by Roger Schutz, Taizé is located in France. It is an ecumenical monastic center at which Christians from many denominations can meet and pray together. Retreats and study centers for all Christians are held at Taizé in order to further Christian unity. This is the main work of this monastic center: the reconciliation of Christians. Catholics, Eastern Orthodox Christians, and Protestant Christians have prayed together and met here.

CHAPTER REVIEW

Circle the correct answer or answers. Be ready to support your choices during a class discussion.

1. Martin Luther disagreed with:
   a. the granting of indulgences.
   b. the Church's belief that Jesus is human and divine.
   c. the Church's insistence on the value of good works.

2. This caused the split between Catholics and Protestants:
   a. the printing press.
   b. disagreement with some of the teachings of the Church.
   c. the Crusades and Holy Wars.

3. The council that was called in 1545 and that reformed and renewed the Church was:
   a. the Council of Jerusalem.
   b. the Second Vatican Council.
   c. the Council of Trent.

4. This council reaffirmed these Church teachings:
   a. Scripture and tradition are sources of faith.
   b. there are seven sacraments.
   c. the Bible is not important.
   d. the Pope has limited authority over the Church.

Write a paragraph describing some of the reasons that the Reformation occurred.

_____

_____

_____

_____

_____

Respond to the following questions based on what you have learned in this chapter.

1. What is an *indulgence*?

_____

_____

2. What new religious orders were founded to solidify the Catholic Counter-Reformation?

_____

_____

_____

Repent, therefore, and be converted.
Acts 3:19

3. Discuss several reforms suggested by Luther or others that have taken place within Catholic life since the Reformation.

UNIT 1 ORGANIZER

Use the following chart to summarize the information, events, and ideas that you have learned about in this unit. Fill in the squares with the correct answers. Be sure to allow enough space for your answers.

	The Early Church	Eastern Christianity	The Middle Ages	The Reformation
Who were some of the important people?				
What was one major event that happened during this period?				
When did it occur?				
Why did it happen?				
What was the outcome?				

UNIT **1** REVIEW

Fill in the blanks to complete the sentences.

1. _____ is the saint and Church Father who translated the Bible into Latin.

2. _____ is a word used to describe the denial of a Church doctrine.

3. _____ are the followers of Jesus Christ.

4. A collection of laws of the Catholic Church is called _____ _____ .

5. _____ objected that the popes lived in Avignon, France.

6. The _____ _____ was when there was more than one pope.

7. _____ is the king who begged the pope's forgiveness by kneeling outside his castle in the snow.

8. _____ and _____ were two reformers who, along with Luther, left the Catholic Church during the Reformation.

9. _____ was the apostle who preached to and converted the Gentiles.

10. _____ is a saint who started a double monastery in Kildare, Ireland.

Match the first part of the sentence with the correct second part.

_____	1. Council of Trent	**a.**	a community of monks or nuns
_____	2. Deaconness	**b.**	the city in the Holy Land that the crusaders tried to capture
_____	3. Ignatius of Loyola	**c.**	the city where the pope lives
_____	4. Teresa of Avila	**d.**	the capital of the eastern part of the Roman Empire
_____	5. Monastery	**e.**	the founder of the Discalced Carmelites
_____	6. Jerusalem	**f.**	a woman chosen to minister to other women
_____	7. Constantinople	**g.**	the soldier who wanted to bear arms for Christ
_____	8. Rome	**h.**	the council that met to end the Reformation
_____	9. Renaissance	**i.**	the removal of punishment for sins that are forgiven
_____	10. indulgence	**j.**	the time when Europe experienced a rebirth in knowledge

UNIT 1 REVIEW

Mark the following statements by writing **T** for each true statement and **F** for each false one.

_____ 1. The Crusades were wars to gain control of the Holy Land.

_____ 2. Eastern and Western Christians never grew apart.

_____ 3. Great cathedrals were built to raise people's hearts to God.

_____ 4. Monks and nuns preserved the faith and learning of Europe when it was under attack by invaders.

_____ 5. Gentiles are those who belong to the Jewish community.

_____ 6. Augustine was the first one to call followers of Jesus Christians.

_____ 7. Anthony, a young Egyptian, responded to God's call to holiness by living by himself in the desert.

_____ 8. St. Basil the Great, St. Benedict of Nursia, and St. Scholastica were responsible for the growth of monasticism.

_____ 9. The Franciscans, begun by Francis of Assisi, were committed to poverty and to renewing the faith of Christians in the towns and cities of Europe.

_____ 10. Martin Luther was a monk who worked to reform the Catholic Church from within.

_____ 11. Charlemagne was crowned emperor of both the eastern and western parts of the Roman Empire.

_____ 12. Eastern Christians looked to Rome for leadership, while Western Christians depended on the emperor in Constantinople.

_____ 13. Feudalism was a system based on loyalties and protections, and many bishops were feudal lords.

_____ 14. The crusaders succeeded peacefully in restoring the Holy Land to Christian control.

_____ 15. Pope Gregory the Great refused to allow the Germanic invaders to become Christian.

Write a paragraph about the following statement. Be sure to include examples.

The Church is continually prompted towards renewal by the Holy Spirit. This renewal was particularly evident in the sixteenth century.

_____

_____

_____

_____

Inner Conflict and External Pressure

At one time or another, almost everyone experiences stress. The feeling itself can be expressed in a number of ways, including muscular tension, inability to sleep or sleeping too much, being easily frustrated, feeling irritable or moody, losing one's temper, and in some cases, quiet retreat or withdrawal from everyday activities.

Sometimes the feeling of being stressed can be a positive experience, especially when it motivates us to make important changes in our lives. However, these feelings can also have negative consequences for personal health and relationships with others. Part of growing and maturing is learning how to manage effectively the stress that we experience.

Activity

Mark the things in the list below that are sources of stress for you. Is there one thing that stands out as the most stressful in your life right now?

___ getting in a fight with a friend

___ worrying about an upcoming test

___ feeling overwhelmed by too much to do

___ not having enough friends

___ not getting along with your parents or guardians

___ being pressured by friends to do things you do not want to do

___ not feeling smart enough

___ feeling disliked by a teacher

___ worrying about what others think of you

___ having someone close to you die

___ getting a bad grade

___ going to a new school

___ worrying about making mistakes

___ not having enough money

___ significant changes in your family

___ the expectations of parents or guardians about your performance in school

___ worrying about how you look

___ having someone close to you fall ill

___ worrying about being safe at school or in your neighborhood

___ Other: _____

Listening to Self-Talk

When you think about the things that cause stress in your life, you can probably identify some that are related to other people's expectations, behavior and attitudes, or events outside your immediate control. What you tell yourself about these experiences and events, however, is a critical factor in whether or not one of these cause you to feel stressed.

For example, two students may be asked to give oral reports in social studies class. One student looks forward to the event and sees it as an opportunity to demonstrate what he or she knows. The other student feels self-conscious and nervous and wishes he or she could hand in a written report instead. The event—giving an oral report—is the same for both, but one student feels energized and the other feels stressed.

HINTS FOR MANAGING STRESS

- Get adequate rest and exercise. The physical tension that builds from stress needs to be released in a positive way.

- Eat a healthy diet. A healthy diet helps maintain physical and mental well being. Too much caffeine and sugar can aggravate the physical tension you feel when stressed.

- Manage your time. This prevents feelings of overload that can lead to feelings of stress. Plan ahead for future events that you know require your time. Waiting until the last minute increases your anxiety and stress, which can inhibit your best effort.

- When feeling overwhelmed by too much to do, make a list. Just creating the list can lessen the feeling of being stressed. Cross off items as you complete them. This will help you to feel satisfied and in control.

- Make time to relax. Your body as well as your mind need time to do nothing.

- Take note of the things you tell yourself about the stressors in your life. Are you telling yourself that you must be perfect?

Activity

On a separate sheet of paper, write a paragraph about something in your life that is causing you to feel stressed. Then create a plan to manage your stress by identifying one or two things you could do.

Prayer

Jesus, I know you are with me always. Keep me near as I cope with the stress in my life. Help me to find safe and helpful ways to manage stress and to cope with events that contribute to my feelings of being stressed.

OPENING DOORS
A Take-Home Magazine™

BE ASSERTIVE!

Being assertive means to act confidently, to be listened to, and to have other people take you seriously. Being assertive also means that you respect others even when they disagree with you.

How assertive are you? During the next week keep track of how assertive you were with your family each day. If you were assertive, give yourself 3 points. If you were pushy, whiny, or manipulative (these are all aggressive behaviors), give yourself 5 points. If you were somewhere in between, give yourself 4 points for that day. If you felt yourself doing things you did not want to without saying anything, or had a family member take advantage of you, give yourself 1 point. At the end of the week, add up your score. 30 or more points means you are too pushy. Under 10 points means you let yourself be treated like a doormat. Between 10 and 30

points means that you are like most people—assertive at times, nonassertive at other times, and sometimes too aggressive.

FAMILY ACTIVITY

Have family members try the activity described above to help identify one another's behavior. Encourage one another to be more assertive, rather than aggressive or nonassertive.

What does it mean to be assertive, nonassertive, or aggressive?

Assertive people care about others and realize that it is okay to have needs. They speak up for themselves and their opinions, listen to others, and cooperate with others.

Nonassertive people always do what they do not want to

do and they get pushed around. They never admit that they have needs and they are afraid to express their opinions.

Aggressive people ignore the needs of others. They do not listen and they push others around. They put their own needs first, complain frequently, and manipulate others.

HOW TO BE ASSERTIVE

The best way to be assertive is to be open with others about how you feel. Always be clear and specific.

Jesus was assertive. People knew where he stood, but he was not aggressive. He did not force his disciples to listen to him. He did not make the Pharisees do what he wanted. He was direct about what he thought.

THE INNER VOICE

We have an inner voice, a conscience, that signals us to do good. A conscience tells us when we are acting as we should, helps us to make decisions, and warns us when we should not do something.

Complete the following to explore how you listen to your conscience.

1. When your conscience bothers you, you are likely to . . .
get a stomachache
feel tired
explode at nothing
make jokes
feel guilty or uneasy

2. When you feel shame or regret, you will confide in . . .
a family member
a friend
a priest
a teacher
nobody

3. The word that describes you best is . . .
responsible
indecisive
impulsive
obedient
rebellious

4. Which word describes a mistake you are most likely to make?
selfish
passive
bossy
dishonest

5. For the kind of mistake you identified above, what response are you most likely to make?
apologize
resolve not to do it again
confess or discuss the mistake with someone
not recognize the mistake until much later

6. Regarding sensitive subjects, such as abusing drugs

2

and experimenting with sex, you are likely to . . .

> choose friends whose values are the same as yours

> openly disagree when your friends' attitudes are different from yours

> not discuss these issues with friends or with anyone else

> be swayed by the opinions of your friends and relatives

7. A personal strength that helps you face your weaknesses is . . .

> humor
> understanding
> humility
> perseverance
> honesty

8. Regarding the influence of others, you are . . .

> easily influenced by the opinions of friends

> always wondering what other people think of you

> not interested in what others think

Look over your answers. Are there other ways that your conscience—your inner urge toward good—affects you? Are there times when you confuse your conscience urging you with what you want to do?

Our conscience is formed by what we learn as we grow up. The teachings of the Church, the examples of our teachers and parents, and the good influences of our friends and relatives all affect our ability to know right from wrong, and help to form our conscience. Our conscience acts as an inner guide for our life—if we take the time to listen and think before we act.

Given the chance, your conscience will do more than alert you to coming trouble. Your conscience can guide you in many other ways, helping you to discover your own unique gifts and ways you can help others.

Is Your Conscience Always Right?

Keep your conscience healthy by . . .
- learning and following the teachings of the Church
- reading and studying Scripture
- choosing good friends and good role models
- taking the advice of those inner feelings that encourage you to do what is right, especially when it is difficult to do so

Our conscience helps us in our own life with the personal events and issues with which we must deal. However, our conscience also expands beyond our immediate concerns to include all those who are affected by the groups to which we belong. Some issues are collective—that is, they are the acts of a group for which all the members of the group are responsible—for example, when a strong nation robs a weaker nation of its resources. How can you get involved in righting the injustices done to others?

FROM THE PAST

Did you know that Saint Paul wrote to the people of the city of Corinth to tell them to stop partying and getting drunk at their eucharistic celebrations?

Perhaps there's more to the story of the Mass than you thought. You have already learned that in the early Church the Mass was a meal, a community gathering at which people remembered what Jesus did at the Last Supper. They brought bread and wine with them and met together in one another's homes. They prayed and read Scripture. Sometimes, as with the Corinthians, though, they needed to be reminded of the real purpose of the Eucharist.

Did you know, however, that there was not just one way to have this eucharistic celebration? Christian communities in different places did things differently. In one place the celebration was in Greek because that was the language the people spoke. In another place the celebration was in Latin because that was what those people spoke. Some people used regular loaves of bread. Others used unleavened bread. Different prayers were prayed. Different Scripture verses were read. While the expressions differed, the meaning of the celebration was the same.

Today we call these different ways to celebrate the Eucharist *rites.* There are six major rites in the Catholic Church. All of the people who belong to these rites are truly Catholics. The rite that most people think is the *only* way to be Catholic is the Roman, or Latin, Rite. Although the Roman Rite is the largest rite, it is only one of the rites of the Catholic Church.

THE ROMAN RITE MASS

Over the centuries the Church changed. The Mass with which you are familiar—the Mass of the Roman Rite—also changed. It became more elaborate and formal. Although at first, Latin was the language people spoke where the Roman Rite was practiced, after several centuries the people spoke other languages and very few people understood Latin. However, the Mass was still in Latin. Even the Scripture readings were in Latin. Many people did not understand the Mass. They kept themselves busy by reading their prayer books, saying the rosary, lighting candles, or walking around the church to pray the Stations of the Cross. Women had to cover their heads and, in a hurry, might pin a piece of tissue to their hair just to meet this requirement.

The Mass no longer appeared to be a true community celebration. There were no lectors or eucharistic ministers. The priest did everything and the people watched. Until the middle of the twentieth century, only choirs sang. There was no Sign of Peace.

The altar was against the wall and the priest stood before it with his back toward the people. No one brought bread with them to church anymore as they had done in the early Church, and no one except the priest could receive from the cup. Communion was no longer either a leavened or unleavened loaf of bread but a thin, unleavened wafer made from wheat. The Mass appeared not to be a meal to be shared by the followers of Jesus as much as the event at which special words were spoken that turned the bread and wine into Jesus' Body and Blood. Communion could only be received on the tongue because it was considered a terrible thing to touch Jesus—the host. People had to swallow it whole or wait until it melted in the mouth.

All of this changed with the Second Vatican Council (1962–1965), which reformed the Mass. Vatican II reminded people of the purpose of the celebration of the Eucharist and made it more of a community-centered celebration. Still, some people say the old way was better because it was mysterious and gave a real feeling of the sacred. What do you think?

Talk to your grandparents, religion teacher, or other adult about the changes the Church has experienced in the past 25 years since Vatican II.

CHANGES

Using the following clues, identify some of the changes in the Mass since Vatican II.

1. The Mass is now described as a _____.
2. For centuries, people did not sing at Mass. Now there is more _____.
3. Before, people could receive the host but not the _____.
4. Women had to cover their _____.
5. The _____ was turned around to face the people.
6. Lay people who read Scripture during Mass are called _____.
7. The language of the Roman Rite Mass used to be _____.
8. Lay people who help to distribute Communion are called _____ _____.
9. Today you can receive Communion in the hand or on the _____.

Answers on page 6.

1. _ E _ _
2. _ u _ _ _
3. c _ _
4. h _ _ _ _
5. a _ _ _ _
6. _ _ _ _ _ r _
7. _ _ _ i _
8. _ _ _ _ _ _ _ _ _ _ _ _ _   _ _ _ _ s _ _ _ _
9. t _ _ _ _ _

OUR FATHER

Imagine that you lived during the 1300s. The English you would speak would be very different from the English of today. Here is the Our Father the way it looked six hundred years ago. Can you read it?

Fadir, halewid be thi name. Thi kyngdom come to. Gyue to vs to day oure eche dayes breed. And forgyue to vs oure synnes, as and we forgyuen to ech owynge to vs. And leed not vs in to temptacioun.

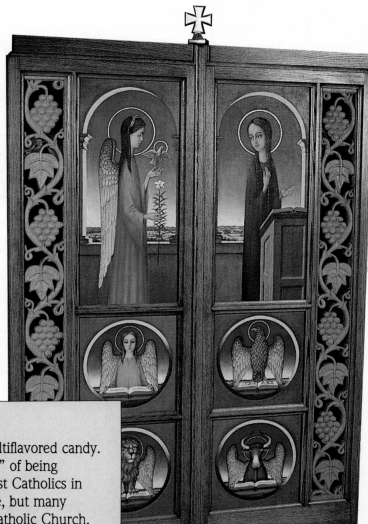

Icons of the Annunciation and the four evangelists.

RITES

In a way, the Catholic Church is like a multiflavored candy. There are many different ways, or "flavors," of being Catholic. These flavors are called *rites*. Most Catholics in the United States belong to the Roman Rite, but many belong to one of the Eastern Rites of the Catholic Church. The major Eastern Rites are the Alexandrian Rite, the Antiochene Rite, the Armenian Rite, the Byzantine Rite, and the Chaldean Rite. The Byzantine Rite is the most widely used rite after the Roman Rite. In the United States, Catholics of the Byzantine Rite celebrate the Eucharist in English, Old Slavonic, or Ukrainian. They make the Sign of the Cross from right to left, they use icons (pictures) rather than statues, and their churches have domes rather than steeples.

Answers 1. meal 2. music 3. cup 4. heads 5. altar 6. lectors 7. latin 8. eucharistic ministers 9. tongue

Looking Ahead

In Unit 2, you will learn about the changes and reforms the Catholic Church went through in order to work more meaningfully to transform the world in the light of Christ's gospel. We, the Church, have something to contribute to the world today and are called to stand, like Jesus, for and with the poor.

UNIT **2**

PEOPLE OF THE FUTURE

Who can you rely on in tough times?

A Growing People

Valued and Valuable

Kathy and George were curious. They had never been in the attic of Grandpa's house. With a flashlight, they began to explore it. There was so much dust, they sneezed and coughed. They opened up boxes of old books and magazines. They laughed at dusty old hats.

Kathy pulled a gray sheet covering something large. "George, look at this!" she shouted as the sheet fell to the floor. George ran over to see what she had found.

"I really like it," Kathy said. "It's just an old rocking chair," George answered without enthusiasm.

Ignoring her brother's tone, Kathy demanded, "Help me take it downstairs."

Reluctantly, George helped dust off the rocking chair and carefully carried it downstairs.

Grandpa recognized the chair immediately. "It's a fine chair," he said wistfully. "Your grandmother used to spend many an hour in it." Then he was quiet. He seemed to be remembering.

Later that afternoon Kathy and George cleaned and polished the chair until it looked almost new. Then they found a place for it in the living room, right near the big front window.

That evening Grandpa rocked back and forth in the chair, telling them stories about their grandmother.

"Thank you, Kathy. Thank you, George," he said. "You've given me something valuable."

Discuss

1. Why was the old rocking chair valuable to Grandpa?

2. How did Kathy and George respond when they discovered how much the old chair meant to their grandfather?

3. How was the old rocking chair valuable to Kathy and George?

HOW DO YOU SHARE WHAT IS IMPORTANT TO YOU?

GOING FORTH

Jesus entrusted his disciples with something of great value—his mission. Yet he did not want his disciples to keep quiet about it. He wanted them to go out and share it with the world: "Go, therefore, and make disciples of all nations, baptizing them in the name of the Father, and of the Son, and of the holy Spirit, teaching them to observe all that I have commanded you" (Matthew 28:19–20).

Our Lord knew that sharing something so great was going to be difficult, and so he instructed the disciples how to go about it. He told them to travel as simple laborers: "Do not take gold or silver or copper for your belts; no sack for the journey, or a second tunic, or sandals, or walking stick" (Matthew 10:9–10).

And, knowing that there would be those who would not recognize the value of the word being preached, Jesus told the disciples, "Whoever will not receive you or listen to your words—go outside that house or town and shake the dust from your feet" (Matthew 10:14).

The disciples went to **evangelize**, or preach the good news of Jesus' kingdom. They traveled far from Judea and Galilee and began Christian communities in many places.

Activity

People have different reactions about the things that are most important to them. Some people want to hide them; others want to share them. What do you value most in the world? Why?

_____

_____

_____

Would you ever share this with someone? Why or why not?

_____

_____

_____

How valuable is the Christian faith to you?

_____

_____

Do you want to share it with others? Why or why not?

_____

_____

_____

What challenges would you be willing to face to share your faith with others?

_____

_____

_____

Vocabulary

evangelize: to preach the good news of God's kingdom

TO ALL THE WORLD

Beginning with the Renaissance, European merchants and explorers traveled throughout the world. They traded with other peoples and began colonies in places that were new to them. The Europeans were largely intent on making their fortunes—whether by trade, mining, or farming. They were ambitious and sometimes greedy and brutal in establishing themselves and protecting their economic interests.

Wherever the Europeans went, they took their religion. Clergy often went in the very first ships to visit a place. They went as chaplains to the European traders and as missionaries to the new country.

Sometimes when the Europeans arrived, they found that Christianity was already known to some extent. For example, there had been Christians in India from the time of the early Church. Legend has it that the apostle Thomas preached in Malabar in southern India and was martyred in Mylapore, where his tomb is still venerated today. There had also been small groups of Christians in China from the time of the early Church, but these few communities were not well-known.

Mostly, however, European clergy came into contact with peoples who were completely unfamiliar with the Church and with the person and teachings of Jesus Christ.

TO CHINA AND JAPAN

The first missionaries to the East were Franciscans, Dominicans, and Jesuits. One of the more famous missionaries was St. Francis Xavier (1506–1552). He was a Jesuit and a friend of St. Ignatius Loyola. Francis set off for India in 1541. He visited Indonesia and spent two years in Japan, ministering to the growing Church there. Francis had ambitious missionary plans and baptized thousands at a time after preaching to a large crowd.

Other Jesuits, however, used a different technique. They appealed to the intellectual class of the peoples they visited and spent their efforts teaching about Christianity as well as languages, such as Italian, Spanish, and Latin.

Protestant missionaries who traveled with English and Dutch merchants watched Catholic progress with interest and even copied the Jesuit missionary technique. In many places, such as Japan and India, Protestant and Catholic missionaries competed with one another for converts. Orthodox Christianity, however, did not arrive in Asia from Russia until the eighteenth century.

The early successes of the sixteenth and seventeenth-century missionaries did not last. In China and Japan fierce persecution almost destroyed the Church. Today Catholicism is still not widespread in Asia.

A RESPECTFUL EUROPEAN IN CHINA

In 1583, when Matteo Ricci arrived in China, Europeans were generally not welcomed there. The Chinese people felt that Europeans held little respect for them or their ancient culture. They were wary of the Spanish and Portuguese merchants, who often took advantage of them.

Ricci was different. He was an Italian who spoke fluent Chinese. He was a European professor but wore the dress of a Buddhist monk, which he later changed to the robes of a Chinese scholar. He was a Jesuit priest, but he knew and respected the wisdom of Confucius.

The Chinese called him Li Madou and his small house was always open to guests. He spent hours talking with visitors. He showed them his books and art works from Europe and his guests were fascinated by his collection of scientific instruments—sundials, clocks, glass prisms, navigational instruments—and a remarkable world map he had made. He also wrote a total of twenty books in Chinese.

Most of all, the Chinese were impressed by the learned and kindly man himself. Together they spent hours in conversation about Confucius. Father Ricci also told them about Jesus Christ. He was impressed with the goodness and sensitivity of the Chinese and believed that Christ had already influenced them in this way. He formed close friendships with some of the Chinese scholars. Some of them became Catholics. Father Ricci allowed the converts to use some of their Chinese customs in the celebration of the liturgy.

This respectful approach eventually allowed Father Ricci access to the emperor of China in 1601. The emperor was so impressed with this respectful foreigner and his knowledge that he offered him a house on the imperial property.

Some of China's most powerful leaders and scholars became Christians because of Father Ricci. He died in 1610, after more than twenty-five years of intense missionary work.

Activity

1. Name two ways used by missionaries to preach the word of God.

   _____

   _____

   _____

2. Why was Father Ricci successful in China?

   _____

   _____

   _____

3. How did the missionaries arrive in other countries?

   _____

   _____

   _____

   _____

CHRISTIANITY IN AFRICA

During the first two centuries of the early Church, Christianity had grown rapidly in North Africa. In the seventh century, when Muslim armies conquered much of North Africa, the Church there largely disappeared— except for some Christian communities that survived in Egypt and Ethiopia.

Christianity arrived in Africa again between the late fifteenth and seventeenth centuries with Franciscans, Dominicans, Jesuits, and other religious orders who accompanied European traders, especially the Portuguese. In the Congo, King Nzinga and some members of his family were baptized in 1491. The king's oldest son, Alfonso, who was also a Catholic, eventually took control of the kingdom.

Success in the Congo and other places of Africa was shortlived. With the beginnings of European involvement in the African slave trade in the seventeenth century, however, Africans had less and less interest in Christianity. Although slavery had been part of human societies for centuries, the kind of slave trade that the European traders practiced included attacking and destroying villages and marching off entire sections of the population which were then sold into slavery in the West Indies. Alfonso and other African kings naturally objected to this injustice and brutality and there was increasing violence and hostility between Europeans and Africans.

When Alfonso died, the Church in the Congo did not thrive. Because the Church had been a foreign influence in Africa and had not become the faith of the people with an African clergy, it did not grow.

It was not until the nineteenth century that missionaries returned and preached the gospel with more success. These missionaries attempted to spread their message by educating children and establishing hospitals and other health care facilities. Racism and political problems continued to limit the growth of the Church even through much of the twentieth century.

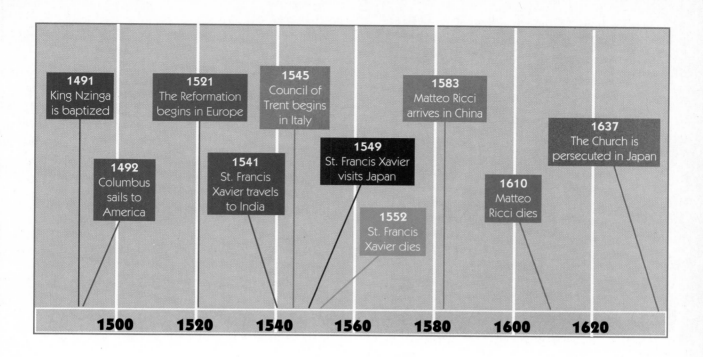

1491
King Nzinga is baptized

1492
Columbus sails to America

1521
The Reformation begins in Europe

1541
St. Francis Xavier travels to India

1545
Council of Trent begins in Italy

1549
St. Francis Xavier visits Japan

1552
St. Francis Xavier dies

1583
Matteo Ricci arrives in China

1610
Matteo Ricci dies

1637
The Church is persecuted in Japan

1500   1520   1540   1560   1580   1600   1620

Activity

Use the time line to answer the questions below.

1. What was happening in Europe between 1490 and 1545?

   _____

   _____

   _____

2. When did St. Francis Xavier begin his travels in the East? Where did he travel?

   _____

   _____

   _____

3. Which of the events marked on the time line do you think is the most important? Give a reason for your answer.

   _____

   _____

   _____

   _____

Activity

What are some of the qualities you think a good missionary needs?

_____

_____

_____

What are some of the reasons you think someone would want to share his or her faith with someone else?

_____

_____

_____

What are some ways Christians whom you know share their faith with others every day?

_____

_____

_____

Activity

1. Name three cities or places in the United States that have Catholic names.

   _____

   _____

   _____

   _____

2. Based on what you have learned so far about the expansion of the Catholic Church, how do you think the Catholic faith came to the Americas?

   _____

   _____

   _____

   _____

CHRISTIANITY IN THE AMERICAS

Just as in other parts of the world, missionaries arrived in the Americas with explorers and traders. The Spanish and Portuguese arrived in Central and South America and then pushed south and north—eventually as far as areas known today as Florida, New Mexico, Arizona, and California.

The Christian missionaries had more success in the Americas than in other parts of the world. The missionaries worked with the peoples they encountered. They taught the native peoples farming methods and crafts, and sometimes, reading and writing. Gradually, the population of Latin America became overwhelmingly Catholic.

The missionaries frequently saw how traders exploited and oppressed the native peoples. The Europeans saw the potential in the land and the raw materials that were available, but these were useless without sufficient labor. So the Europeans enslaved many of the peoples they encountered. The missionaries often found it necessary to speak out against their own countrymen and the wrongs they did.

Bartolomé de Las Casas, a Dominican missionary, was the first European to expose the oppression of the native peoples of Latin America: "In three or four months, there died more than 6,000 children, by reason that they [the Spaniards] had plucked away from them their fathers and mothers, which they sent into the mines." The Spanish were forcing the people to mine gold and silver, which were then sent to Spain.

Other missionaries also spoke out about what their fellow Europeans were doing. The Jesuits in particular helped the people by establishing special settlements for their protection. Junipero Serra, a Franciscan, started many of these mission settlements in California.

Yet despite the good the missionaries tried to do in this way, sometimes the native peoples were encouraged to become too dependent on the missionaries for leadership and knowledge. Tribal customs and traditions were frequently lost.

Although the native peoples were sometimes treated cruelly, the message and promise of Christianity took root in Central and South America. St. Martin de Porres, for example, was born in Lima, Peru, and spent his whole life as a Dominican lay brother, working for the poor and outcast in a colonial society that rigidly defined people by color and class.

Gradually, over the centuries, these Latin American colonies gained their independence from European countries. Because the Church in these countries had grown and had also developed its own clergy and religious orders, it stood on its own and Christianity flowered through the faith of the people.

IN NORTH AMERICA

The first attempts to spread the Catholic faith in North America were made by Spanish missionaries beginning in the 1500s. In the early 1600s, French Jesuits brought Catholicism to the north central and northeastern sections of the North American continent. Priests such as Jacques Marquette and Isaac Jogues worked with the native peoples. Many of the missionaries established "praying villages" where Christian converts could live their faith in peace. One of the most famous of these converts is Kateri Tekakwitha (1656–1680), called the "Lily of the Mohawks", who risked her life to become Christian.

Despite these early missionary efforts, however, the story of the Catholic Church in North America was very different from that of the Church in Central and South America. In North America, colonists from Europe displaced the native peoples. Among these European immigrants to America were large numbers of Catholics.

Activity

Pretend you are a non-Christian living in a non-European country in the sixteenth or seventeenth century. You have the opportunity to speak with a European Christian missionary. What would you like to say or ask?

_____

_____

_____

_____

_____

_____

THROUGHOUT THE WORLD

Today, the Catholic Church is found throughout the world. For example, there are approximately 430,000 Catholics in Japan, where once the efforts of the missionaries were destroyed. The nations of Africa are the fastest-growing parts of the Catholic Church with nearly 100 million Catholics and about 400 dioceses and archdioceses. In Latin America, still mainly Catholic, there are approximately 400 million Catholics.

The total worldwide Catholic population is nearly 1 billion people—making the Catholic Church the largest Christian denomination in the world. (There are nearly 2 billion Christians in the world and 1 billion Muslims.)

The Catholic Church grew because people, like the missionaries, bravely set out to share with others what was of great value to them—their faith. It also grew because some people who heard the word of God found something of value in it and discovered faith within themselves.

Today, we Catholics are found in so many places and yet we are one. We share the same faith in Jesus and celebrate the same Eucharist at Mass. And we have the same call as did the first disciples of Jesus all those centuries ago: to share our faith with others.

Activity

Complete the following open-ended statements to express your opinions about understanding and sharing your Catholic faith.

1. If Jesus visited my home today and asked me to share my faith with others, I would

   _____

   _____.

2. I think the best way for me to share my faith is

   _____

   _____.

3. One way I would not be willing to share my faith is

   _____

   _____.

4. One thing I think all Catholics can do to live their faith is

   _____

   _____.

Activity

Mark the ways in which you are willing to share your faith with others. Then identify three more things that Catholics can do to share their faith.

_____ Read Bible stories to younger children.

_____ Answer questions about my faith.

_____ Learn more about my faith.

_____ Pray for missionaries.

_____ Live my faith every day.

_____ Read the diocesan newspaper with my family.

_____ Collect money for the missions and for religious education.

1. _____

   _____

   _____

2. _____

   _____

   _____

3. _____

   _____

   _____

WE BELIEVE

The Catholic Church is universal and includes people from various countries and cultures throughout the world. Together we are all part of the body of Christ.

PRAYING WITH OTHER CATHOLICS

Catholics are found throughout the world, and no matter where they live, they share the same faith. They do not always pray in exactly the same way, though. Because prayer is always an expression of who we are and what our unique relationship with God is like, Catholics have many different prayer forms.

You may know someone who has a great devotion to the rosary, or a family who always prays together before and after meals. You may know someone who prays in a different language or who has different holiday customs from you even though he or she is Catholic. The prayers that Catholics pray are rich in variety and style. This is one of the great treasures of the Church. Catholics share so much that is the same and they have an interesting and rich prayer life through which to express themselves.

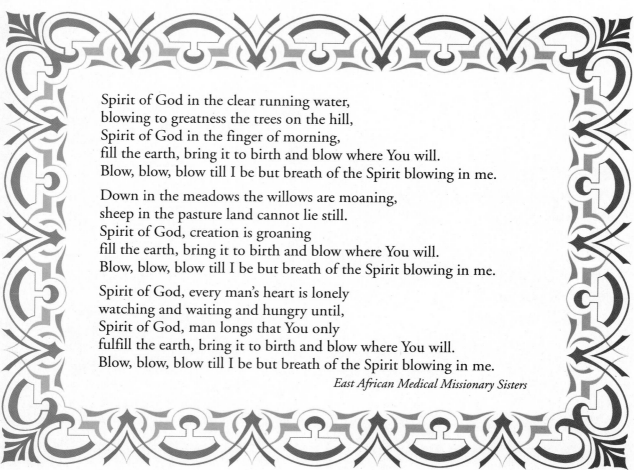

Spirit of God in the clear running water,
blowing to greatness the trees on the hill,
Spirit of God in the finger of morning,
fill the earth, bring it to birth and blow where You will.
Blow, blow, blow till I be but breath of the Spirit blowing in me.

Down in the meadows the willows are moaning,
sheep in the pasture land cannot lie still.
Spirit of God, creation is groaning
fill the earth, bring it to birth and blow where You will.
Blow, blow, blow till I be but breath of the Spirit blowing in me.

Spirit of God, every man's heart is lonely
watching and waiting and hungry until,
Spirit of God, man longs that You only
fulfill the earth, bring it to birth and blow where You will.
Blow, blow, blow till I be but breath of the Spirit blowing in me.

East African Medical Missionary Sisters

CHAPTER REVIEW

Use the words below to complete the sentences.

Malabar	St. Francis Xavier	Jesuits	Matteo Ricci	Ethiopia	Nzinga
Franciscan	Arizona	Bartolomé de Las Casas		Kateri Tekakwitha	

1. _____ was an African king baptized by Portuguese missionaries.

2. The Apostle Thomas may have preached in _____ India.

3. _____ is called the "Lily of the Mohawks."

4. The _____ were a religious order which evangelized in Asia.

5. After Muslim armies conquered much of Northern Africa, Christians could only be found in _____ .

6. The Spanish even pushed into what is called _____ today.

7. _____ was a missionary who went to India and Japan.

8. _____ was a missionary who worked in China.

9. Junipero Serra was a _____ who evangelized California.

10. _____ objected to the way the Spanish treated the native peoples.

For each place, name one person or event that is part of the Church's story of growth and expansion there.

Asia	Africa	The Americas

Respond to the following questions based on what you have learned in this chapter.

1. What does it mean to *evangelize*?

_____

_____

2. How did the Church grow over the centuries?

_____

_____

3. Discuss some of the things all Catholics have in common.

"Go, therefore, and make disciples of all nations."
Matthew 28:19

6 An American People

New Beginnings

Throughout our lives we are called upon to make new beginnings. Sometimes we choose these, but many times we do not. We move to new places, attend new schools, and join new parishes.

One of the most difficult of new beginnings is arriving in a new place and struggling to make a new life for oneself. This demands courage and great inner strength. Throughout the Bible, there are many accounts of brave adventurers called by God to leave friends, relatives, and possessions to follow new ways.

> WHAT IS IT LIKE TO START SOMETHING NEW?

Activity

Choose one of the Bible passages to read. Then write whom God called and what risks were involved in making the journey of faith.

Genesis 12:1–9

_____

_____

Exodus 13:17–14:22

_____

_____

_____

Luke 5:1–11

_____

_____

_____

Acts 9:1–9

_____

_____

_____

AMERICAN CATHOLIC SETTLERS

The seeds of the Catholic Church in North America were planted by the Spanish and French Catholic missionaries who bravely preached the good news to the native peoples.

Then, between 1607 and 1733, British immigrants founded thirteen colonies on the eastern seaboard of North America. Mostly Protestants, the settlers strongly opposed the Catholic Church. In fact, except for Maryland and Pennsylvania, the colonies forbade the practice of the Catholic faith.

Nevertheless, when the colonies rebelled against England and drew up their Declaration of Independence in 1776, one of its signers, Charles Carroll, was a Catholic. A little more than a decade later, the First Amendment to the new United States Constitution guaranteed religious freedom to all citizens of the new nation, and the Catholic Church was free to flourish.

Baltimore, Maryland, became the seat of the first American Catholic diocese. Its first bishop was John Carroll, a cousin of Charles Carroll.

John Carroll (1735–1815) faced many challenges to lead the Catholic Church in the United States. Among these he had to defend the Church against anti-Catholic prejudice. He believed in the United States and what the country stood for. He wrote that in America "general and equal toleration, by giving a free circulation to fair argument, is the most effectual method to bring all denominations of Christians to a unity of faith."

In 1809, St. Elizabeth Ann Seton, or Mother Seton as she is more commonly known, founded the Sisters of Charity, the first American religious community. Mother Seton was raised a Protestant and was a widow with five children when she converted to Catholicism and decided to begin her order. She and her sisters soon started the first parochial school in Emmitsburg, Maryland. About this school she wrote that she had a "plan for establishing an institution for the advancement of Catholic female children in habits of religion." Her order also began the first Catholic hospital in Philadelphia. In 1975 she was canonized as the first American-born saint.

Activity

Answer the following questions to express your opinions about lives of faith.

1. How was Mother Seton a person of faith?

_____

_____

2. What could you admire about her?

_____

_____

3. How can learning about other Catholics help you to strengthen your own faith?

_____

_____

THE CHURCH IN THE UNITED STATES

At first, the Catholic Church in the United States was small, but it soon began to grow. Catholics went west with other settlers. Many had been living in Maryland, and some of these moved on to Kentucky. Since there were few priests, when a priest did visit an area, he not only said Mass (perhaps the first Mass the people had attended in a year or more) but also heard confessions, performed marriages, and baptized children. After staying for several days, he went on to the next frontier community.

Other priests and religious sisters ministered to the native peoples by starting missions and schools. Catholic lay people and missionaries, such as Jesuit Father Pierre de Smet and Sacred Heart Sister Rose Philippine Duchesne were among the American Catholics who lived their faith on the western frontier.

Immigrants from Ireland and Germany began to arrive in great numbers about the year 1850. These new arrivals were mostly Catholic, poor, and uneducated. They faced hostility and prejudice from Protestant Christians and were not only kept out of jobs but also were the victims of rioting and violence. Yet many new parishes, schools, and religious orders were started.

Mother Frances Xavier Cabrini, an Italian immigrant, arrived in New York in 1889. She worked among the Italian newcomers, building schools and hospitals. In 1946 she was the first American citizen to be canonized.

A second, even larger wave of immigrants began shortly after 1900. These immigrants were also Catholic, poor, and uneducated, but they came mainly from Poland, Eastern Europe, and Italy. They brought with them different customs and traditions and faced hostility not only from Protestant Christians but from other Catholics as well. Most of these immigrants settled in the big cities and industrial areas of the Northeast and Midwest and began their own parishes and schools.

In places with large Catholic populations, it was not unusual to have several different parishes, each with parishioners of a different ethnic background.

The bishops of the Catholic Church tried to help the constant stream of immigrants. Three councils of the American bishops met in

Baltimore in 1852, 1866, and 1884 to consider important issues facing the American Catholic Church. From these meetings came the ideal of a parochial school for every parish, and the introduction of the *Baltimore Catechism*, a book that was used to teach Catholic doctrine for several generations.

Another important result of these councils was the effort to send priests to work among African Americans. Before the Civil War, Catholics had not done much to speak out against slavery. Some Catholics even owned slaves. After the Civil War, however, Rome asked the American bishops to minister to African Americans.

Yet African American Catholics continued to experience racism and prejudice from other Catholics. They were not allowed to join religious orders, and few African American men were ordained to the priesthood. Augustus Tolton (1854–1897) was one of the first African American priests in the United States. Today there are nearly one million African American Catholics in the United States.

By 1914, nearly one out of five Americans was Catholic. The great influx of Catholic immigrants renewed the anti-Catholic feelings among American Protestants. In 1928, Alfred E. Smith was badly defeated in the presidential elections, in large part because he was Catholic.

The Catholic Church continued to grow in the United States. New Catholic schools, colleges, and universities opened. Many young people became priests, sisters, and brothers, and not only worked among Catholics in America, but went as missionaries to all parts of the world. In 1960, John F. Kennedy became the thirty-fifth President of the United States—and the first Catholic president.

Today, the Catholic Church is by far the largest church in the United States. It has greatly benefited from the **religious pluralism** and democratic ideals of the United States. Catholics are influential in all areas of American life and are active in the struggle for human rights, social and economic justice, and world peace.

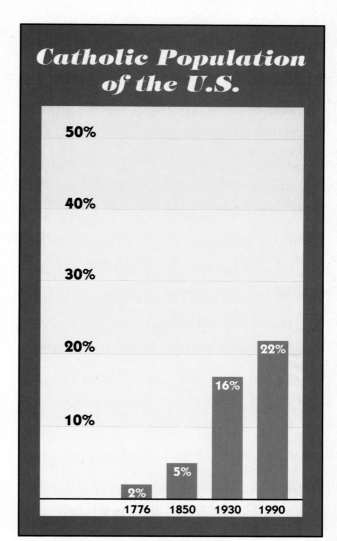

Catholic Population of the U.S.

Vocabulary

religious pluralism: the free existence of religion in a country or a society

WE BELIEVE

In the United States, the Catholic Church has benefited from religious pluralism, and its members have contributed to efforts aimed at social justice and peace.

A GREAT CATHOLIC WOMAN

Elizabeth Lange was born in Cuba some time around 1800. Her parents had fled there to avoid Haiti's racial violence against Black people.

In 1817 her parents arranged for Elizabeth to sail to the United States. She made her way to Baltimore, where she suffered from racial discrimination at a time when slavery was still a reality in many parts of America. However, she found a home with the French-speaking Black refugees who gathered for Mass each week in the basement of Saint Mary's Seminary.

Elizabeth was dismayed to discover that there was no public education at that time for Black people in the United States. She knew that without education, Black children would never achieve real freedom and equality.

So Elizabeth started a small free school for Black people in her own home. She taught them to read and write. She read the Bible with them every day. Soon another refugee from the Caribbean, Marie Balas, joined Elizabeth.

A friend, Father Joubert, was so impressed with the women's efforts that he suggested they form a religious community dedicated to the education of Black children. Lange and Balas were enthusiastic about the idea because at that time Black women were not allowed to join religious orders in the United States.

Their new community, the Oblate Sisters of Providence, was approved in 1829. They met with strong prejudice from many white Catholics. The sisters had to support themselves and their students by taking in laundry.

Finally in 1847, Father John Neumann, (since honored as a saint), supported and encouraged them. With his help, the Oblates grew, expanding their work to other cities.

Mother Elizabeth Lange, a pioneer in the American Catholic Church, joined in the struggle for equal rights and social justice for all people. She died in 1882.

Activity

How do people today still take a stand against prejudice and discrimination?

_____

_____

_____

_____

Write about ways in which you can make a stand against prejudice and discrimination.

_____

_____

_____

_____

Activity

Create a time line, using some of the facts that you have learned about the history of the Catholic Church in the United States.

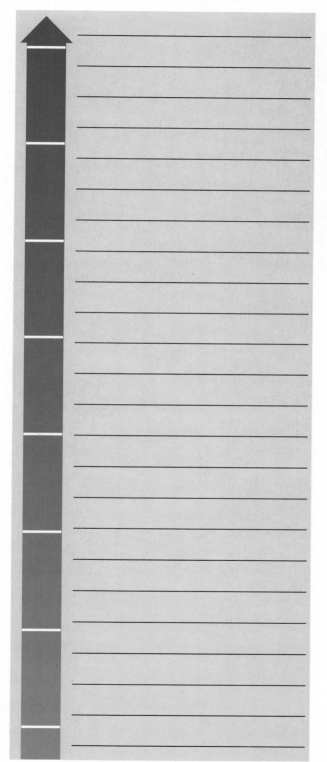

Activity

What is your own Catholic history like? Write a paragraph that describes your life as a person of faith. Be sure to include sacraments that you have received, other Catholics who have played an important role in your life, the parishes you have belonged to, and the name of the Catholic school you attend.

Activity

Name an important event in your life.

_____

_____

Explain why you consider this event to be important.

_____

_____

_____

WRITING HISTORICAL ACCOUNTS

Writing a historical account is not just a matter of getting the facts and dates in the right order. It is providing explanations of how and why things happened. When historians write their explanation of the events, they are interpreting the events. They are writing factual *stories*. Historians interpret the facts to explain the events.

Read the sentences below. These sentences use the same basic facts, but they emphasize different aspects of the facts by focusing on different details.

1. In 1920, the bishop gave permission to the people for a church to be built in Mayerville.

2. Working together, the people of Mayerville built their own parish in 1920. Their parish was a symbol of their faith. They brought bricks from their backyards and built the church with their own hands.

3. The church in Mayerville was built in 1920 of brick.

The first example emphasizes the role of the bishop and reminds us that the parish in Mayerville is part of the universal Church. The second example emphasizes the people of the parish community and how much the church meant to them. The third example emphasizes the physical building.

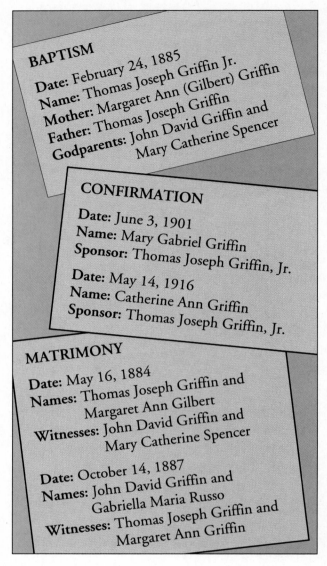

BAPTISM
Date: February 24, 1885
Name: Thomas Joseph Griffin Jr.
Mother: Margaret Ann (Gilbert) Griffin
Father: Thomas Joseph Griffin
Godparents: John David Griffin and
Mary Catherine Spencer

CONFIRMATION
Date: June 3, 1901
Name: Mary Gabriel Griffin
Sponsor: Thomas Joseph Griffin, Jr.

Date: May 14, 1916
Name: Catherine Ann Griffin
Sponsor: Thomas Joseph Griffin, Jr.

MATRIMONY
Date: May 16, 1884
Names: Thomas Joseph Griffin and
Margaret Ann Gilbert
Witnesses: John David Griffin and
Mary Catherine Spencer

Date: October 14, 1887
Names: John David Griffin and
Gabriella Maria Russo
Witnesses: Thomas Joseph Griffin and
Margaret Ann Griffin

Activity

Look at the notes above taken from parish records. Then write a paragraph explaining what you have learned from this information. What details will you include?

_____

_____

_____

_____

_____

_____

WRITING ABOUT YOUR PARISH

Learn more about the story of our Catholic community and its faith by writing about the history of your parish. Consider collecting information from some of the following sources.

> Parish records
> Parish notices and letters
> Parish bulletins
> Photographs
> Interviews with older parishioners
> Old maps and blueprints
> Parish religious order records
> Town histories
> Newspaper articles
> Diocesan records
> Home movies and videos

Organize your information to tell the story of your parish. What facts and details will you choose? What kind of story do you want to tell?

Activity

Use the following questionnaire to help you look for specific kinds of information. Be sure and jot down other questions too.

1. When was your parish established? _____
2. Who was the bishop of the diocese at the time your parish began?

   _____

   Who was the first pastor?

   _____

   How long did he serve? _____
3. When was your parish dedicated?

   _____

   How was its name chosen?

   _____

   _____

   How many families were registered at the

   beginning? _____ How many are

   registered now? _____
4. If your parish has a school, when was it

   begun? _____
   What religious order first staffed the school?

   _____

   How many students are enrolled now? _____
5. Where are people of your parish buried?

   _____

   _____
6. Other things that make your parish unique:

   _____

   _____

   _____

Activity

Some European Christians came to America in search of religious freedom. Do you experience the United States today as a Christian nation? Why or why not? Mention some specific practices, values, ideas, and symbols to support your answer.

_____

_____

_____

_____

_____

_____

_____

CHRISTIANS IN AMERICA

The people of our nation belong to many races and are members of many religious faiths. The Constitution of the United States provides for the freedom of all faiths. The Constitution forbids the establishment of one official religion and so our country will never become another Christendom. Yet our Christian values can help us make good choices that benefit all people in our nation.

The Christian ideals and values we hold have much to contribute to American society and culture. The Catholic Church's teachings continue the ideals and values of Christ. The Catholic Church's teachings have much to offer Americans trying to build a just and peaceful society.

Jesus clearly spoke of our role as Christians in our world. In the Sermon on the Mount (Matthew 5:1–12), we learn that we will be at peace when we seek God's justice, when we hunger and thirst for holiness, when we are merciful, and when we are willing to face persecution to overcome evil. Jesus reminds us that we are truly happy when we live simply.

Activity

What are some ideals and values of Jesus Christ that might help make our country a better place to live? Name two and describe how a Catholic citizen might work to influence law or policy.

1. _____

_____

_____

_____

2. _____

_____

_____

_____

FREEDOM AND RESPONSIBILITY

Church and state are not easily separated. Sometimes people feel compelled to protest laws and practices they do not agree with. Over such issues some citizens choose to break the law in good conscience. Sometimes the courts have upheld their right to disobey; sometimes not.

Use this questionnaire to assess your own opinions on matters of religious freedom, responsibility, and the state's right to govern. Read each statement carefully, and then circle the number that reflects your response.

1. I strongly agree	**2.** I agree		
3. I disagree	**4.** I strongly disagree		

1 2 3 4   A citizen has the right to refuse to fight in a war.

1 2 3 4   A citizen has the obligation to defend our nation.

1 2 3 4   Catholics should vote for candidates who agree with Church teachings.

1 2 3 4   Catholics should vote for the candidate they feel will best carry out the duties of his or her office.

1 2 3 4   Catholics should rely on their priest's opinion about whom to vote for.

1 2 3 4   United States taxes should support Catholic and other private schools.

1 2 3 4   Bible reading and prayer should be allowed in public schools and at public events.

1 2 3 4   Priests should speak about politics.

1 2 3 4   The Church should speak out about social and economic problems.

1 2 3 4   Only a Christian should ever be President of the United States.

1 2 3 4   The state should close shopping malls on Sunday, the Lord's day.

1 2 3 4   United States taxes should not be spent on abortion or birth control.

1 2 3 4   When Catholics disagree with a law of the United States, they are free to break that law because they follow the Church, not the state.

Look over your responses. Do you think separation of church and state in our country is good for both the Church and the state? Why or why not?

_____

_____

_____

Activity

As Catholics in the United States, not only do we have the right to practice our religion freely, but we also have the opportunity to work for justice and peace in our society.

Underline and be ready to defend the two most effective ways you think a Catholic can be a force for justice and peace.

- Promoting good TV and movies
- Helping to feed the poor and shelter the homeless
- Watching the news and reading the newspaper
- Demonstrating in the streets
- Writing people in Congress
- Praying
- Setting good examples
- Standing up for the poor and powerless

PRAYING IN HOSPITALITY

The Statue of Liberty is a symbol of the American people's hospitality—the warm and generous treatment of all others, whoever they may be. This symbol challenges the citizens of the United States to warmly welcome people from other places who may have customs, practices, and religious beliefs far different from our own. The Statue of Liberty is a symbol that challenges us to share this country's resources with those who wish to live here.

Hospitality requires generosity, but sometimes—especially when resources are expensive or in short supply—it is particularly hard to be hospitable. We may resent or fear those whom we do not understand or know. We may think that others do not deserve our hospitality or that we are not the ones who should be generous.

When fear and resentment make hospitality impossible, as Christians we must rise above the differences that separate us. We must promote healing through patience, dialogue, courtesy, good intentions, and willingness to build trust—including seeking forgiveness for any hurt we may have caused. We must do all we can to work with the Spirit who is love and generosity.

A PRAYER FOR HOSPITALITY

Open us, O Lord,
to your gift of hospitality.
Bless us with insight
into hearts seeking welcome,
with graciousness to receive their gifts,
and with love to share our gifts.

Grant, O Lord,
that we may become
a hosting people, an inviting people,
until we share eternal hospitality
with you in heaven.
Amen.

Activity

Work with your class to plan a prayer celebration for a spirit of hospitality. Jot down your ideas below.

1. Words of hospitality:

   _____

   _____

2. A sign or gesture of hospitality:

   _____

   _____

3. Ideas for praying for hospitality:

   _____

   _____

Explain how each person or group contributed to the Church in America.

1. Father Augustus Tolton

   _____

   _____

2. John Carroll

   _____

   _____

3. Elizabeth Ann Seton

   _____

   _____

4. John F. Kennedy

   _____

   _____

5. Elizabeth Lange

   _____

   _____

Respond to the following questions based on what you have learned in this chapter.

1. What is *religious pluralism*?

   _____

   _____

2. What most contributed to the growth of the Catholic Church in the United States?

   _____

   _____

   _____

Where the Spirit of the Lord is, there is freedom.

2 Corinthians 3:17

3. Discuss what you think the Catholic Church in the United States has to offer.

A CHANGING PEOPLE

7

CHANGES

Throughout our lives, we experience many changes. Some of these are major and affect us deeply. Others are minor and hardly affect us at all.

Think about your life and how things have changed since you were young. Express your opinions below about some of the changes you have experienced.

HOW HAS YOUR LIFE CHANGED SINCE YOU WERE YOUNG?

Activity

Think about how things were when you were eight or nine years old. Then think about how things are today.

1. My favorite TV Show

   Then: _____

   _____

   Now: _____

   _____

2. A news headline

   Then: _____

   _____

   Now: _____

   _____

3. A popular movie

   Then: _____

   _____

   Now: _____

   _____

CHANGES IN THE WORLD

Many things happened in the nineteenth century that affected and changed the Church and how people thought about being Catholic. New ideas about society, science, philosophy, and government forced Catholics to ask questions about what they believed and who they were as persons of faith.

For much of the nineteenth century, the Catholic Church was largely found in Europe although there were growing numbers of Catholics throughout the world. During this time, however, Europe was wracked with political unrest. There were revolutions in France, Germany, Spain, and Italy. The French revolution was the first of these and had the most influence on the life of the Church. The revolutions challenged the Church's political power and worldly influence. They stripped the Church of land, artworks, and universities. Especially in the French revolution, clergy and religious were oppressed, and some were killed. Others fled to America for religious freedom.

In addition to the changes brought by revolution, there were also new ideas introduced by science and philosophy. Scientific advances had been made in the late eighteenth century, during a time called the Age of Enlightenment. These scientific advances caused people to question other accepted ideas, including religious ones. In the mid-nineteenth century, for example, Charles Darwin published his book *The Origin of Species* (1859), which suggested that all forms of life evolved over millions of years on Earth, rather than being created all at once. This made people question how and when God created the universe.

Other people began to ask questions about the role of religion in society, especially when there was so much poverty and oppression. Karl Marx, a philosopher, suggested that religion only kept people enslaved and ignorant of the real causes of their misery and poverty. Other people also said that by standing for faith, the Catholic Church was actually standing for ignorance and backwardness instead of progress.

THE CHURCH RESPONDS

In some places the Catholic Church found it was unwelcome or actually made illegal. Church leaders and the politicians of these nations signed **concordats**, treaties or agreements, permitting the Church to exist within these countries. This happened in France, for example, in 1801.

People who took their faith seriously defended the Church. These people responded to the anti-Catholic ideas of the nineteenth century by pointing out that the most important thing was not the Church as a political power but the Church as the Body of Christ, a community of grace in heaven and on earth. In England, a theologian named John Henry Newman converted to Catholicism from the Church of England. He emphasized the importance of faith, the Church, and the role of all the baptized in the Church.

Vocabulary

concordat: a treaty or agreement permitting the Church to exist and work within a country

Activity

Things do not always go as planned. Name and explain a time when something did not happen the way you wanted it to.

_____

_____

We all face such obstacles in our lives. Name two other examples of common obstacles that people may face in their lives.

_____

_____

A STRONGER CHURCH

During the revolutions of the nineteenth century, the Church was still a political power. The pope ruled the Papal States, a territory in Italy. A strong movement began to unite all of Italy, including the Papal States. In 1870, war broke out, and the pope lost the Papal States.

Pius IX, who was then pope, protested this. He refused offers from the government of Italy for a financial settlement. He declared himself a "prisoner of the Vatican." It was not until 1929 that a concordat called the Lateran Treaty was signed between Pope Pius XI and the government of Italy. By that agreement the pope was recognized as the independent ruler of Vatican City in Rome.

The papacy had lost all its political power. Yet Catholics and non-Catholics alike began to look to the pope more as a spiritual leader. The pope spoke to the whole world with spiritual and moral authority. Losing the Papal States had been a blessing in disguise. Although less of an earthly ruler, the pope had become a stronger spiritual leader.

THE FIRST VATICAN COUNCIL

In 1869, Pope Pius IX opened Vatican I, the first council to be held in the Church since the Council of Trent in the sixteenth century. This council defined the doctrine, or teaching, of **papal infallibility**. This doctrine means that when the pope speaks in Christ's name, he is kept from all error in matters of faith. The Council stated that the pope has infallibility "with which the Divine Redeemer has willed that His Church. . . should be equipped."

This does not mean that a pope is perfect. Nor does it mean that everything the pope says on any subject is right. The pope is infallible when he speaks with the full authority of his office on matters of faith. This doctrine assures us that the pope teaches with the guidance of the Holy Spirit and that his teaching is free from error.

The teaching of papal infallibility reminds us that the pope, as head of the Church, has an authority and power greater than any earthly power. It reminds us that the pope is Christ's representative on earth. And, most importantly, it tells us that God will always be faithful to the Church.

A MORE DEVOUT CHURCH

In the rapidly changing and challenging times of the nineteenth century, Catholics discovered how deep their faith actually was. They discovered a deeper devotion to Mary, for example. The doctrine of the Immaculate Conception was declared in 1854, and the Church approved of the visions of Mary experienced by St. Bernadette at Lourdes in 1858. The Church would also later approve the appearances of Mary at Fatima in Portugal in 1917.

Catholics also discovered a deeper devotion to the person of Jesus. St. Thérèse of Lisieux, for example, who lived in France, saw herself as a little child, dependent upon God and called to love Jesus in little, hidden ways every day. In her autobiography, she said, "I want so much to love him! To love him more than he has ever been loved!"

This devotionalism expressed itself in frequent reception of the Eucharist and the sacrament of Reconciliation, praying the Rosary, going to Mass frequently, and saying prayers to the saints for their intercession in problems and in times of illness.

Activity

Problems and obstacles can also be seen as opportunities. Answer the following questions to explain how this can be so.

1. What good came out of the Church losing the Papal States?

   _____

   _____

   _____

2. What is papal infallibility a sign of?

   _____

   _____

   _____

3. When you are faced with problems and obstacles in your own life, how do you think your faith can help you?

   _____

   _____

   _____

WE BELIEVE

The Holy Spirit continually guides the Church. Even during times of great change, the Church always has the opportunity and authority to transform the world in the light of Christ's gospel. Every member of the Church has something to contribute to this transformation.

Activity

Describe your idea of a perfect day.

_____

_____

_____

_____

Name one thing that would make your life
perfect.

_____

_____

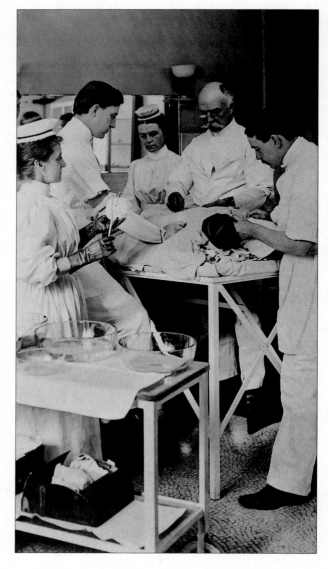

THE TWENTIETH CENTURY

The first part of the twentieth century saw a
rapid growth in ideas and inventions. There was
also the development of cities and new
industries. People believed that the world was
becoming a better place, because they could see
progress all around them. In fact, the first two
decades of this century are sometimes referred to
as the Progressive Era. It was a time of optimism,
and people worked for better labor conditions,
improved health care, and more education.

The Catholic Church led the way in many of
these areas. For example, Pope Leo XIII had
alerted Catholics to the needs and rights of
laborers, who were overworked and underpaid,
and who had to work in unsafe factories. He
published an encyclical, or papal letter, called
Rerum Novarum, or _On the Condition of the
Working Classes_ (1891).

In this letter the pope condemned the misery
that most of the world's population found itself
in. He said, "Every principle and every religious
feeling has disappeared from the public
institutions and so, little by little, isolated and
defenseless workers have found themselves in
time at the mercy of inhuman masters and
victims of the cupidity of unbridled
competition." The pope condemned the human
greed that oppressed people.

Other popes also called on Catholic lay
people to become involved in working to
bring about a world of justice and peace.
Catholics started hospitals and schools to
help better the conditions in which many
poor people lived.

The early twentieth century was also a time
of great missionary outreach. For example, Pope
Benedict XV asked missionaries to train men to
become priests and men and women to join
religious orders in the mission countries. Pope
Benedict did not think it was right that in
some places only Europeans were the priests
and religious. All Christians are called by
God to serve the Church and humanity in
different ways.

A TIME OF SUFFERING

The optimism of the first part of the twentieth century ended with the crushing tragedy of not one but two world wars (1914–1918 and 1939–1945). As a result of the violence and destruction of both world wars, people in many countries and continents died or faced poverty and starvation. In some places they faced political and religious oppression as well.

The suffering caused by these wars was horrifying. During World War II, for example, Adolf Hitler and the Nazis attacked the Jewish citizens of Germany and other European countries. The Jewish people had their freedoms taken away and they were rounded up and placed by the millions in concentration camps. Before Hitler was stopped, his government killed more than six million Jews from all over Europe. This became known as the Holocaust.

Yet Jewish people were not the only ones deliberately exterminated by the Nazis. Those who were mentally challenged, incurably ill, and those who opposed the Nazis were also put to death. Many Catholic priests and Protestant ministers were murdered by Hitler and the Nazis.

Among those who were killed by the Nazis was Edith Stein, a young Jewish woman who converted to Catholicism after reading the autobiography of St. Teresa of Avila. She became a Carmelite nun known as Sister Teresa Benedicta of the Cross. In 1943 she was arrested by the Nazis and sent to the camp at Auschwitz where she died in the gas chamber. In 1987 she was beatified. She may be canonized in the future.

Some Catholics did what they could to stop the Nazis. They worked in the underground resistance movement. They helped Jewish families to escape. In Rome, Pope Pius XII helped to provide shelter and protection for the many refugees of the war. The Vatican itself also shielded several thousand Jewish refugees.

After World War II ended, many of the countries of Eastern Europe came under the control of the former Soviet Union. At this time the Soviet Union was run by the Communists, members of a political system that had taken its teachings from Karl Marx. The Communists hated all religions and did all they could to destroy them. They closed churches and imprisoned or killed church leaders who refused to accept communism. A number of Catholics in Eastern Europe were killed.

In 1937, Pope Pius XI had written an encyclical called *Divini Redemptoris* and spoke out against the evils of communism. In it he said, "Communism is intrinsically perverse, and one cannot accept collaboration with it in any area on the part of anyone who wants to save Christian civilization." For most of the second half of the twentieth century, the Church had to struggle to survive in communist countries.

A Time of Change

Even while there was much suffering in the world, the Church gave the world spiritual strength and leadership. During this time there was a renewed interest in the Bible, the liturgy, and ecumenism (uniting with other groups of Christians).

The liturgical movement tried to help people better understand the Mass. Until the 1960s, the official prayers of the Roman Rite were almost all said in Latin. The Mass was in Latin and the sacraments were celebrated in Latin. But most Catholics were not able to understand Latin. People sometimes used other, private prayers at Mass, such as the Rosary.

Among other things, the liturgical movement encouraged people to use missals to understand the Mass. In a missal the words of the Mass were printed side by side in Latin and in English, for example. In this way, people could follow what was going on.

The biblical movement was connected to the liturgical movement. Catholics began to read and study the Bible more. Biblical scholars used new, critical techniques to deepen knowledge and understanding of the intentions of the writers of the biblical books.

The term *ecumenical movement* is used to describe the efforts among Christians from different Churches to work for unity. The leaders of the ecumenical movement were mainly Protestant. In 1948 a number of Protestant churches organized the World Council of Churches in Amsterdam, the Netherlands. Although the Catholic Church is not a member of the World Council of Churches, from time to time Catholic representatives discuss theological issues with Protestants in an effort to build understanding.

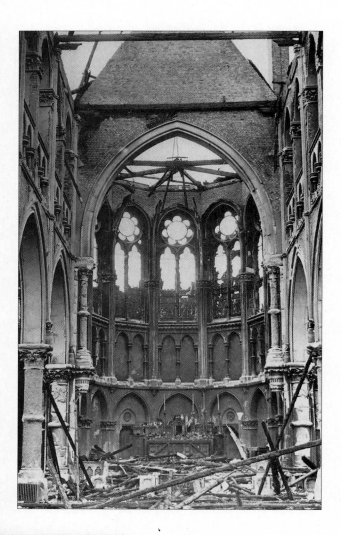

Activity

Read the following Scripture passages and then tell what you think they are saying the Church should be like.

1. Corinthians 12:12–13

   _____

   _____

   _____

2. Acts 2:42

   _____

   _____

3. Acts 6:1–4

   _____

   _____

4. John 13:34–35

   _____

   _____

   _____

5. Romans 12:6–8

   _____

   _____

   _____

6. What does being Catholic mean to you?

   _____

   _____

   _____

   _____

   _____

   _____

The events of the first half of the twentieth century caused people to become more aware of problems of injustice. As a result of the world wars, there were new ideas, changing values, and challenges to authority. The Catholic Church, as a community and as an international institution, turned its attention to the crises of the modern age. The Church became especially concerned with people who were struggling as a result of the changing nature of the world. In the second half of the twentieth century, the Catholic Church has had the opportunity to become the servant to those who were oppressed.

After World War II

When the war ended in 1945, the world was a very different place from what it had been before. There was much less optimism about what human beings could accomplish and much more awareness of the horrible brutality that human beings were capable of. There was also a deep suspicion about authority and the ways in which people in power could act, for better or worse. But at the same time, there was a new interest in religion and spirituality.

Catholic scholars, in particular, looked closely at the Bible and the writings of the early Church Fathers to reflect deeply on what Christian faith should be. Theologians such as Yves Congar, Jean Daniélou, Karl Rahner, and Henri de Lubac wrote about the importance of going back to the sources of Christianity in order to renew the Christian faith.

Not all Catholics agreed with these theologians, however. Some Catholics, including Pope Pius XII, were concerned about where some of these new theological ideas might lead. These Catholics saw the evils of communism and the changes the world had gone through in the twentieth century, and they recognized that many people were in danger of losing their faith. They felt that in order to keep the Catholic faith alive and well it was important to have a strong pope and clear statements about doctrine. They relied on the authority of the papacy to lead the Church in the world.

Other Catholics, including the next pope, John XXIII, thought differently. They, too, saw the changes and dangers in the world and felt that the Church could do more. They agreed with what some of the new theologians were saying and looked forward to renewing the Church by going back to the sources of the faith. It was only by reading the Bible and the writings of the Church fathers, they felt, that the Church could find a way to renew itself and speak more effectively in the modern world.

OPENING CHURCH WINDOWS

When Pope John XXIII died on June 3, 1963, the whole world wept. A gentle and humble man, Pope John was loved by Catholics and non-Catholics alike.

Television, newspapers, and magazines told the story of Pope John's remarkable life. They carried pictures of the pope visiting prisoners in a Roman prison on Christmas Day. There were pictures of him enjoying a glass of wine with family and friends. There were pictures of the pope receiving the daughter of the Russian leader, Nikita Khrushchev, and her family at the Vatican and blessing them, even though they claimed they did not believe in God.

The media reported stories about how approachable the pope was. It was said that his brothers were very nervous when they visited the new pope in the Vatican for the first time. "Don't be afraid," the pope had said to them with a smile. "It's only me." He, like them, was a peasant from a remote Italian village. John never forgot his roots.

He seemed to be smiling most of the time. Reporters passed along some of the jokes. "How many people work in the Vatican?" someone asked the pope one morning. "About half!" the pope answered with a twinkle in his eye.

"Good Pope John," as people of all faiths called him, seemed to be everyone's grandfather. He was seventy-six years old when the cardinals elected him pope in 1958. John brought with him years of experience as an administrator of a diocese and as a Vatican diplomat to Bulgaria, Turkey, and Paris. When he became pope, few expected anything new from someone of John's age.

To everyone's amazement, Pope John XXIII unleashed a youthful spirit of renewal in the Church. Pope John knew the Church's history and loved the Church's ancient traditions. But he lived fully in the present and loved the modern world. John had a great dream for the future—a dream in which the Church appreciated the best of the world while sharing with the world the light of Christ. Several

years before he died, he called the Second Vatican Council.

Most of all, Pope John XXIII respected and loved people of all faiths, races, and nations—people of influence and people of poverty. In return, people everywhere loved him. Our Church and our world are better today because of good Pope John.

Activity

"Opening Church windows" is a metaphor for Pope John XXIII's actions toward renewal. Think of other metaphors for promoting renewal within the Church. Write them on the lines below.

_____

_____

_____

_____

_____

PRAYING ABOUT OUR GIFTEDNESS

John Henry Newman, the English convert who became a cardinal, believed that personal holiness could be found in the commitment a person made to fulfilling the responsibilities he or she had been given. Newman said that every person has a sacred obligation to develop the gifts and talents bestowed on them by God.

Newman wrote, "God has created me to do some definite service. God has committed some work to me which has not been given to another. I have a part in a great work. I am a link in the chain, a bond of connection between persons. God has not created me for naught. I shall do good. I shall do God's work."

Talking about our gifts and talents sometimes makes us feel as if we are bragging or calling too much attention to ourselves. On the other hand, talking about our gifts might make us feel inadequate, as if we are nothing special or just like everybody else. But Cardinal Newman was right. God has given each of us special gifts which the Holy Spirit helps us to develop.

Activity

Read the Scripture passages listed below and then write what each one says about using our gifts and talents.

1. Peter 4:10–11

_____

_____

2. Romans 12:6

_____

_____

3. James 1:16–17

_____

_____

4. Timothy 4:14

_____

_____

Interview a partner about his or her interests and hobbies. Find out what your partner likes to do and would like others to know about himself or herself. Write on the lines below the good things you discovered.

_____

_____

Based on the good things you discovered about your partner, write a petition thanking God for him or her. In your petition, mention what makes your partner special.

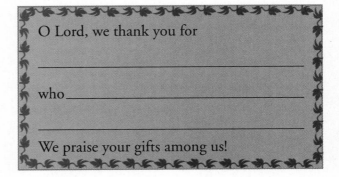

O Lord, we thank you for

_____

who_____

_____

We praise your gifts among us!

CHAPTER REVIEW

Use your own words to explain the meaning of each word or term below.

1. Concordat

_____

_____

2. The Papal States

_____

_____

3. Ecumenism

_____

_____

4. Communism

_____

_____

5. Vatican I

_____

_____

Respond to the following questions based on what you have learned in this chapter.

1. What is *papal infallibility*?

_____

_____

_____

2. Why was the liturgical movement of the twentieth century important?

_____

_____

Behold, I make all things new!
Revelation 21:5

3. Discuss why it is important to know the past in order to renew the present for the sake of the future.

8 A GLOBAL PEOPLE

WHAT'S POSSIBLE?

Optimism is a quality that can help us see obstacles as challenges and opportunities rather than as stumbling blocks. It helps us to think positively and creatively about everyday life. Along with a feeling of well-being, an optimistic attitude can get us through difficult and confusing times.

Activity

How optimistic a person are you? Rate yourself on the following categories. The more "yes" answers you have, the more positively you probably look at life.

1. I believe that people are good.

    No   Yes

2. Things work well most of the time.

    No   Yes

3. When I meet someone for the first time, I assume I am going to like him or her.

    No   Yes

4. When asked to try something new that is not harmful or dangerous, I am interested.

    No   Yes

5. When faced with problems, I assume I can handle them.

    No   Yes

6. When faced with problems, I don't give up.

    No   Yes

7. I am interested in learning new things.

    No   Yes

8. When things are going wrong, I think, "It's just one bad day."

    No   Yes

AN OPTIMISTIC COUNCIL

When the bishops of the world gathered in 1962 to open the Second Vatican Council, or Vatican II, Pope John XXIII criticized the "prophets of doom" who feared change. Describing his task as one of "opening the windows of the Church to the modern world," John looked with optimism on the Church's role in the modern world.

John's successor, Pope Paul VI, led Vatican II to its completion in 1965. During the Council, the world's bishops, aided by the Church's best theologians, dramatically renewed the Church.

The council taught that God speaks to us through **signs of the times**, the major experiences and issues of our age. Although we have a teaching mission in the world, we must learn from it as well.

Vatican II emphasized community living in Christ's Spirit. Priests are ordained to serve the community but all Christians share in the priesthood of Christ to some degree. **Collegiality**, a shared responsibility and cooperation, is to characterize the Church.

The Catholic Church must be open to the work of all religious faiths for Christian unity. Vatican II reemphasized the importance of the Church's worship, or liturgy, and Christ's priesthood and ministry. The Church's worship is the sign and source of our life as Catholics.

Activity

What are two ideas that resulted from the Second Vatican Council?

_____

_____

How do you think the Church can be optimistic in our world today?

_____

_____

_____

_____

_____

How do you think Christian faith can make you an optimistic person?

_____

_____

_____

_____

_____

Vocabulary

signs of the times: major experiences, issues, and values of our age through which God speaks to us

collegiality: shared responsibility and cooperation

CHANGING CHURCH PATTERNS

The population of the Church is shifting its numbers from Europe and North America to the south, to the newly industrializing countries of Latin America and especially to Africa. Soon seven out of ten Catholics will be living in one of these two regions.

The Church in these newly industrializing nations is already revealing a creative power that is influencing the entire Church. In many of these places, centuries-old patterns of injustice and oppression are being changed.

For example, particularly in Latin America, poor Catholics are united in small, organized groups of Christian families called base Christian communities. These vary in size but typically number about fifty men, women, and children. All are poor. Most cannot read or write. Lay people elected by the community are responsible for the direction of the community. Since there is a shortage of priests, a priest visits whenever possible to celebrate the Eucharist with them. The rest of the time, lay persons lead the community in prayer.

The typical base Christian community gathers every week. Members come together to
- reflect on and talk about their lives
- reflect on and talk about a biblical story that relates to their lives
- pray together
- plan practical actions that will help one another and will change the conditions that cause their poverty
- share food, drink, and fellowship

These base communities are linked in a network of communities within a city or country. In some places in Central and South America, rulers suspect any group of people who organize to better their lives. These rulers fear that the base communities will oppose the existing, oppressive government. In an effort to break up these communities, priests, nuns, and lay people who work in base communities have been killed. However, in the face of death, members of base communities continue to meet, pray, and support one another. And they continue to seek to change the unjust situations that rule their lives.

Throughout the world today many people participate in the Church's life more actively than in the past. There is more shared responsibility and support among Catholics. As a result of what is happening in the Church in the newly industrialized nations, parish communities throughout the world resemble more the first Christian communities founded by Jesus' apostles in Jerusalem during the first century.

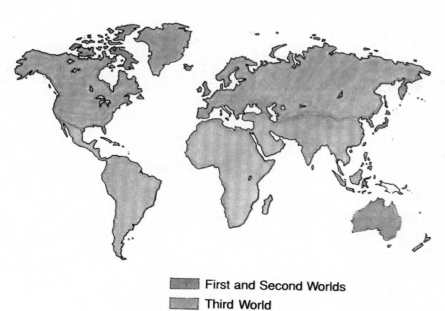

 Newly industrialized nations have 75% of the world's population.

 Only 11% of educational spending is allotted to newly industrialized nations.

 In newly industrialized nations, ten out of every 100 babies die during infancy.

 Newly industrialized nations have only 30% of the world's food.

 Only about 15% of the world's energy is spent in newly industrialized nations.

 Only about 8% of world industry is found in newly industrialized nations.

First and Second Worlds

Third World

ABOUT OUR NEIGHBORS

One of our Christian obligations is to care for our neighbors. Learning about where our neighbors live, and under what conditions, is an important first step in the caring process. Look at the map below to learn about the areas and the statistics of the newly industrializing nations.

People in these nations frequently live in great poverty. Their nations lack what is necessary for human survival.

Activity

The following percentages represent the five major divisions of the world's population.

64% Asia
14% Africa and the Middle East
9% Europe
7% South and Central America
6% North America

What would you expect to find out about how the world's resources are divided?

_____

_____

_____

How do you feel about how the world's resources are actually divided?

_____

_____

_____

How do you think Jesus would respond to this injustice? How will you respond?

_____

_____

_____

Activity

In school, students are frequently asked to work together in small groups. What is one positive thing about working in small groups?

_____

What is one problem that can arise?

_____

DESCRIBING THE CHURCH

In a landmark book, *Models of the Church*, Jesuit theologian Father Avery Dulles uses five images to describe the Catholic Church. In this way, Dulles summarizes ideas about the nature and function of the Church. Dulles' images characterize the Church as Institution, Community, Sacrament, Herald, and Servant. The first two images describe what the Church *is*; the last three identify what the Church *does*.

THE CHURCH AS INSTITUTION

In this model, the Church is described as a society that teaches, sanctifies, and governs. The authority to perform these three functions has been handed down in the Church from the time of the apostles. Today, the pope and the bishops perform these roles, acting as the **magisterium**, or the teaching office of the Church.

The institution of the Catholic Church gives organization as well as a strong sense of mission and identity. The Church exists to bring about the salvation of all people through Jesus and to further the kingdom of God by working to break down the unjust social structures that enslave people and keep them from sharing in the goodness of life.

An example of the Church as an institution working for justice is found in many of the United States bishops' pastoral letters, including *Economic Justice for All*. In this letter, the bishops examine whether or not the economy of our nation protects or undermines the dignity of every human person. The document cries out for just wages, employee rights, an end to human starvation caused by greed, and the commitment of both Church and society to work together for economic justice for each member of the human family.

THE CHURCH AS COMMUNITY

This model describes the Catholic Church as a family joined together in love because of their faith and unity in Jesus. We are called by Jesus himself to be a community founded on love. "This is my commandment: love one another as I love you" (John 15:12). We are called to be a visible sign of the invisible Lord continuing his work through us. Our concern for others imitates the first Christian community, who shared all things and divided their possessions among themselves according to need.

An illustration of the Church's care for all of its members is found in recent events regarding women. In the early Church, women performed the role of deaconess. In the following centuries, however, women were denied leadership roles, and their contributions to the Church were not recognized. This has been a source of pain for many.

Pope John Paul II publicly acknowledged this pain in 1995, when he issued a letter to the women of the world. In the document, he expressed sorrow and regret that women had "often been relegated to the margins of society and even reduced to servitude." The pope praised "the genius of women" throughout the Church's history, and he called for women to have just social, economic, and political rights. The document presents new hope that the Church will be more sensitive to women.

THE CHURCH AS SACRAMENT

This model recognizes that the Church draws believers together to witness and worship so that we can grow to be better signs of Jesus Christ. The Church as sacrament calls us to be a light to the world (Matthew 5:16) and a sign of the Lord's grace and presence in the world. Through the grace we receive in the sacraments, we are called to become grace—God's life—for others. We must never forget the true miracle of the sacraments—that the risen Christ is with us, inviting us to reflect the light of his love to the world.

Today, the Rite of Christian Initiation of Adults (RCIA) is a powerful example of the model of the Church as sacrament. This ancient rite, in which adults are fully initiated into the community at the Easter Vigil through Baptism, Confirmation, and Eucharist, was restored to the Church in the 1970s.

Persons wishing to join the Church become **catechumens** and enter into a period of study, prayer, and preparation to be welcomed into the Church community. As the catechumens grow in faith, the members of the parish community are challenged to renew their own faith and to be examples to the catechumens through their witness to the power of Jesus in their own lives. By helping others to become members of the Catholic Church, we can deepen our own faith.

Vocabulary

magisterium: the official teaching office of the Church. The responsibility for teaching the authentic message of Jesus is carried out by the pope and bishops.

catechumens: persons wishing to join the Catholic Church who enter into a period of study, prayer, and preparation

THE CHURCH AS HERALD

This model describes the Church as a response to Jesus' command to "make disciples of all nations" (Matthew 28:19). A herald is a messenger—and we are called to be the messengers of God's word in our lives. By recognizing how Jesus is good news for us, we can make the gospel come alive through our own words and actions.

Pope John Paul II is the most visible herald of our times. He has traveled more than any other pope. He has listened to the cares and concerns of people from every part of the world and responded with a compassionate call to love, peace, and justice.

In 1981, the pope was shot in St. Peter's Square in Rome. While still in the hospital, he broadcast a radio message in which he said that he was praying for his would-be assassin. Later, he went to the jail to visit the man who shot him. The pope spoke with him, prayed with him, forgave him, and blessed him. John Paul II heralds Jesus' message of love and forgiveness.

THE CHURCH AS SERVANT

In this model, the Church is described as reaching out to the people with whom Jesus identified himself—those who are poor, outcast, sick, suffering, and victims of oppression and prejudice. In the Gospel of Matthew, we read that Jesus said, "Whoever wishes to be great among you shall be your servant" (Matthew 20:26).

We see the Church as servant in countless worldwide organizations, such as Maryknoll (the Catholic Foreign Mission Society of Maryknoll), whose priests, sisters, brothers, and lay volunteers spread the good news to people in over twenty-nine countries around the world. The workers of Catholic Relief Services respond to the needs of the poor, suffering, and forgotten people in more than seventy-five countries. We see the Church as servant in people such as Mother Teresa and countless volunteers who staff soup kitchens, operate shelters for the homeless, and offer friendship and support to those who suffer from AIDS and other terminal illnesses.

We also see the Church as servant in our local parish communities. Our fellow parishioners take the Eucharist to shut-ins. Members of the social concerns committee provide clothing and food to people who need help. Youth ministry groups pack food baskets at holidays so that poor families will have special holiday meals. Young children across the country save dimes and quarters to help children they have never met. The Church as servant is a ministry in which we all share.

Activity

Imagine that you must help the parishes described below. Mark each of your choices for action. Then write other suggestions for change on the lines provided.

St. Maurice Parish has 100 families and is an old, inner-city parish. Members of the parish are struggling to meet the needs of the area. The parish has a self-help program for senior citizens, a food pantry for the unemployed, and a Catholic school for children in the neighborhood. The parish feels strongly about all of these ministries, and it needs to continue offering help. But the parish is going into debt. What do you recommend?

_____ Have fundraisers to make money.

_____ Recruit volunteers.

_____ Appeal for help from the richer parishes in the diocese.

_____ Close the school.

_____ Close the parish.

_____ Discontinue the ministries to the elderly, the poor, and the children.

_____ Other _____

_____

You belong to St. Isidore Parish, an 80-family rural parish. Ten miles to the south is Sacred Heart, a parish of 50 families; and eight miles north is St. Andrew's parish, a parish of 100 families. The three parishes share one priest. Father Behen comes to your parish to celebrate Mass on Saturday evenings. The bishop of your diocese says he has no more priests and Father Behen will not come to your church anymore. What should your parish do?

_____ Use videos and call experts to train lay teachers and leaders.

_____ Train lay people to lead prayer and communion services.

_____ Close the parish.

_____ Close all three parishes and build one that is centrally located.

_____ Try to find a priest who can be hired from somewhere else.

_____ Other _____

_____

What is one problem facing the Church that you are concerned about?

_____

_____

How would you like to see this problem resolved?

_____

_____

WE BELIEVE

We the Church share in the mission of Jesus Christ and are called to spread the good news throughout the world. As Institution, Community, Sacrament, Herald, and Servant, the Church continues Jesus' mission in the world.

In Our Lives

We learn what it means to be faith-filled people and to live lives of goodness by the examples of those around us. Throughout our lives we look to the people whom we admire, imitating their qualities and learning from them.

Activity

Complete the following activity about the people you admire and the qualities you would like to have. You can name any person more than once.

Person:
Quality I admire:
Example:

Person:
Quality I admire:
Example:

Person:
Quality I admire:
Example:

Person:
Quality I admire:
Example:

Person:
Quality I admire:
Example:

Person:
Quality I admire:
Example:

A Woman for the Times

Pinamen McKenzie (1873–1962) was a Montagnais woman who lived in the traditional ways of her people in northern Canada. She married and had four daughters, but was widowed when she was thirty-eight. She devoted the rest of her life to the poor, to children, and to prayer.

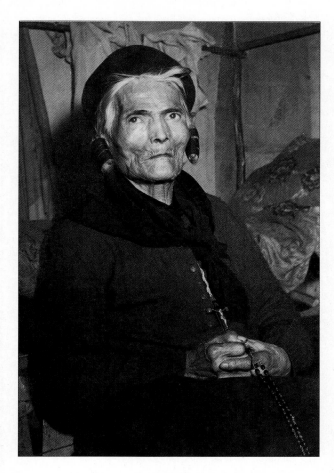

For the Montagnais, life was hard. The native people of the village where Pinamen lived in Labrador were poor, illiterate, and suffered frequently from illness and hunger. There were no priests or religious brothers and sisters to strengthen the people in their faith. Pinamen visited the sick, praying by their bedsides, and sometimes she gathered children to sing to them. She begged for the poor, gathering contributions by canoe in the summer or by dogsled in the winter.

Pinamen prayed unceasingly—even during her daily chores—and she went to church every morning. She taught her people how to pray and everything else she knew about being a Christian.

She herself lived simply, preparing skins for tanning and guarding the campsite. Even in winter months she lived in a tent.

Pinamen's life is remarkable because she almost singlehandedly kept the Catholic faith alive in this remote region of Canada. For twenty-five years there was no priest among her people. It was she who led and guided the community. It was she who planted the seeds of faith in the hearts of her people and nurtured this faith by prayer, word, and example.

When Pinamen died on June 21, 1962, her people gave her the title *Mishta*, which means "Great and Dauntless." Mishta Pinamen is a woman for our times because she shows us that faith is not dependent on power and position, but on sacrifice, endurance, goodness, and love.

Activity

What is one thing Mishta Pinamen's story teaches you about faith?

_____

_____

_____

_____

What are some examples of sacrifice and goodness that you have seen people make?

_____

_____

_____

_____

_____

PRAYING FOR OUR GLOBAL FAMILY

As the Catholic Church tries to meet the needs of our modern world, one of its greatest challenges is to incorporate the rich diversity of the worship customs and traditions of all of its members around the globe. Native American Catholics, such as Mishta Pinamen, bring to the Church the gift of profound respect and gratitude for all of God's blessings in creation. Native Americans often pray using images of creation, such as the wind, as a way of remembering God's presence all around us.

Activity

To complete the Prayer of the Four Winds below, first read the prayers about the wind of the East and the wind of the West. Then write prayers for the wind of the South and the wind of the North.

Think about the wind of the South as God's breath nourishing us through family, friends, and the harvest of food. Think about the wind of the North as God's breath protecting us from hard times and calling us to show care for others.

We bless you, O Lord, for the wind of the East, the breath of God. Lord, you wake all of creation with your rising sun. May we always walk in your light and live to serve you by our words and actions.

We thank you, O Lord, for the wind of the West, the breath of God. With the setting of the sun, we are reminded of the shortness of life. Creator God, you give us rest at the end of the day, rest which renews in us a desire to live according to your call. We know that one day we will live forever in your never ending light.

We praise you, O Lord, for the wind of the South, the breath of God. Lord, you

_____

_____

_____

_____

We honor you, O Lord, for the wind of the North, the breath of God. Lord, you

_____

_____

_____

_____

For each term below, write a sentence that explains how the term describes the Church.

Institution

_____

Community

_____

Sacrament

_____

Herald

_____

Servant

_____

Respond to the following questions based on what you have learned in this chapter.

1. What is the meaning of *collegiality*?

_____

_____

2. What are some of the characteristics of the Church in newly industrialized nations?

_____

_____

_____

_____

_____

_____

_____

Blessed are you who are poor, for the kingdom of God is yours.
Luke 6:20

3. Discuss the characteristics of the Church in the modern world that you see in your own parish.

UNIT 2 ORGANIZER

Create a time line by identifying some of the more important events in the life of the Church since the seventeenth century. Give a reason for each choice by telling why each event is so important. Start your work at the bottom of the time line.

_____

Event: _____

Reason: _____

_____

_____

Event: _____

Reason: _____

_____

_____

Event: _____

Reason: _____

_____

_____

Event: _____

Reason: _____

_____

_____

Event: _____

Reason: _____

_____

_____

Event: _____

Reason: _____

_____

UNIT 2 REVIEW

Mark an **X** in the space next to the best answer to each sentence.

1. When Jesus' disciples went out to evangelize, they

   _____ went into the desert to pray.

   _____ preached to other Christians.

   _____ preached the good news of Jesus' kingdom.

2. The Church flourished in Latin American countries because

   _____ European countries ruled their colonies strictly.

   _____ these countries had their own clergy and religious.

   _____ the people were forced to remain Catholic.

3. Religious pluralism means

   _____ many religions freely exist in a society.

   _____ there is only one religion in a society.

   _____ one religion is the official religion but others can exist.

4. The term *papal infallibility* means that

   _____ the pope is as perfect as God.

   _____ when the pope speaks authoritatively in Christ's name he is kept from error in matters of faith.

   _____ the pope knows everything.

Place a **T** before each true sentence and an **F** before each false sentence.

1. _____ When Christian missionaries from Europe arrived in India, they found small groups of Christians already there.

2. _____ St. Francis Xavier was a famous missionary in South America.

3. _____ Matteo Ricci was a missionary who respected Chinese culture and learning.

4. _____ Slavery and racism were problems that limited the growth of the Church in Africa.

5. _____ In the United States, the Church has suffered from religious pluralism.

6. _____ Settlers of the thirteen American colonies always accepted the Catholic Church.

7. _____ The arrival of Catholic immigrants in the mid-nineteenth century and the early twentieth century helped the Church in the United States grow.

8. _____ African Americans were enthusiastically welcomed into the Catholic Church.

9. _____ Revolutions in Europe challenged the Church's political power and worldly influence.

10. _____ As a result of the wars and suffering of the twentieth century, people became more aware of problems of injustice.

UNIT **2** REVIEW

Write a brief answer to each question.

1. What did Vatican II reemphasize?

   _____

   _____

2. Who are some important people in the history of the Catholic Church in North America?

   _____

   _____

   _____

List five images of Church and then give an example of each.

1. _____

   _____

   _____

2. _____

   _____

   _____

3. _____

   _____

   _____

4. _____

   _____

   _____

5. _____

   _____

   _____

Special Skills for Managing Stress

A helpful way of lessening the physical sensations of stress is to relax physically. Controlling one's breathing is one important way to help the body become relaxed.

DEEP BREATHING

1. Begin by sitting quietly and comfortably. Close your eyes.

2. Breathe in and out three times through your nose. Listen to your breathing. Inhale and exhale. Try to block out any distracting sounds. Concentrate on your breathing. Listen to its rhythm.

3. Take a deep breath and feel the sense of fullness in your chest. Hold your breath as you slowly count to three. Then slowly exhale. Do this again and this time as you exhale, gently blow your stress away.

4. Repeat by inhaling, holding your breath, counting to three, and exhaling, blowing the stress away again. Continue until you begin to feel relaxed. Gradually return to your normal breathing rhythm.

This deep breathing exercise is easy to do any time or any place you feel stressed. You can use this exercise quietly without anyone being aware of what you are doing. Its calming effect can be helpful when confronting events that are particularly stressful such as tests, oral reports, and conflicts with friends or family members. You might also find this to be helpful when trying to fall asleep at night. Deep breathing is also a useful way to quiet yourself in preparation for prayer and meditation.

MEDITATION

Another way we can manage stress in our lives is to recognize our complete dependence on God. When we acknowledge that God should be our first priority and sole focus, stress becomes much more manageable in our everyday lives. When God is first in our lives, everything else is less important and we are able to keep our perspective on what really counts and what does not.

We can remind ourselves that God is the most important thing in our lives by praying and meditating regularly. Meditation is a form of prayer in which we quiet ourselves and listen to God. We use our thoughts, imagination, and emotions in meditation. For us Christians, meditation always focuses on trying to understand the will of God for us. When we meditate we quietly reflect upon and listen to the inner voice of the Holy Spirit in our minds and hearts. We think about our relationship with God and respond to God's call to us. A common way to meditate is to use Scripture stories. When we meditate using a Scripture story we prayerfully participate in the images and events of the Biblical story.

1. Begin by sitting quietly and comfortably. Close your eyes and try to block out any distracting sounds and thoughts.

2. Imagine you are among a small group of people who have gathered to see Jesus. The sun is hot, and the ground is dry and dusty. You find a seat in the shade of a palm tree and wait for him to pass by.

3. Hold this image in your mind while your eyes are closed. See the people waiting for Jesus. Imagine how they are dressed, what they look like, and what they are saying.

4. Jesus and his disciples are approaching. He comes near you, seeking refuge from the heat in the shade of the tree, and sits down beside you. Jesus looks at his disciples and asks them, "Who do people say I am?" They reply, "Some, John the Baptist; others, Elijah; and still others, one of the prophets." Jesus thinks for a moment, and looking into your eyes, asks, "Who do you say that I am?"

5. What do you feel and think when Jesus asks you who you think he is? Allow your body to continue to feel relaxed. Listen to the rhythm of your breathing. Concentrate on what Jesus has just asked you. Gradually return to your normal breathing rhythm and then open your eyes.

Prayer

Continue the meditation by writing a dialogue between Jesus and you in the space below.

Jesus: And you, who do you say I am?

I: _____

Jesus: What do you think it was like for me when I was your age?

I: _____

Jesus: What is hard about your life right now?

I: _____

Jesus: Will you remember that I am with you always?

I: _____

OPENING DOORS
A Take-Home Magazine™

COMPROMISE and COOPERATION

Compromise is the art of giving up something in order to get something. Suppose that you and your brother are fighting over riding a bike. Fight long enough and neither of you will even get time to ride it. In order to get some time to ride the bike, you have to give up some riding time.

THE ART OF COMPROMISE

How do you compromise?

1. Decide on what you actually want. Your goal is probably to get some *thing*, not to win by getting some *one*.

2. Look for areas of agreement. You and your brother may both hate to wash the dishes. Already you have more in common than you think. How can *both* of you achieve your goals?

3. Be willing to give something up. Perhaps you would like to get out of doing dishes on Saturday, but Sunday dishes don't bother you as much. Your brother may be more than willing to do dishes on Saturday to avoid doing more dishes on Sunday. Make a deal!

4. Be flexible. Once you say, "I'm not giving up my bike on Saturdays," it becomes too difficult to change your position.

5. Be gracious. Regardless of the outcome, always be kind. If you didn't get your way, be nice about it. You do not know when you will next need to compromise.

6. Don't gloat over "having won" an argument or a conflict. Make your sister feel bad for letting you have the TV this time and you might not get it from her again.

FAMILY ACTIVITY

Find out how members of your family are likely to compromise by asking their solutions to the problem below.

You have to give your friend an important homework assignment. Your sister has to arrange a ride to work tomorrow. Who should use the phone first?

Possible Compromises
1. The older one goes first.
2. The younger one goes first.
3. It doesn't matter who goes first, each gets fifteen minutes.
4. Flip a coin to decide.
5. Other:

In what areas do family members need to work on the fine art of compromise?

RELATIONSHIPS

What are the qualities you find most attractive in someone? Decide how important each of the following qualities is to you (or add other qualities) and finish the pie to illustrate how big a slice each quality should get in terms of its importance.

Qualities

cuteness	sense of humor
popularity	kindness
talents (athlete, musician, actor or actress, etc.)	generosity
	wealth
	friendliness
toughness	courtesy
intelligence	

Your relationships with others affect you profoundly. A good relationship can help you to grow and develop your talents and abilities, opening you to others and helping you to be a better person. A bad relationship can drain you, close you off from your other relationships with family and friends, and keep you from being your best self. How do you know if a relationship is good or not?

You've heard the old saying, "Love is blind." Well, that's an exaggeration, but it is true that when you really like someone you tend to forgive and overlook faults that you should notice. There are clues to the quality of a relationship.

1. Qualities: The qualities you admire in someone tell a lot about the qualities you would like to have yourself. Sometimes, however, we admire a quality but find it difficult to be close to the person. If you like someone because he or she is popular, do not expect to become his or her only friend. If you like someone for his or her toughness, do not expect him or her to be tough with everyone else and sensitive with you.

2. The Other Person's Friends: The friends someone has tell you about that person's values and interests. If his friends drink and smoke and he spends much of his time with them, he probably does, too. If her friends do drugs and she says they are her best friends, be careful. She might be doing drugs, too.

3. Personal Behavior: If the person you like is destructive or violent, lies to everyone, or has other bad habits, sooner or later you will feel the effects of this bad behavior. You will not be the exception. He or she will lie to you, damage property, or become violent toward you.

Jesus taught us to love and care for others. This means that we should treat others with respect and courtesy and be concerned about them. However, this does not mean that we are responsible for another person's happiness or can solve another's problems. We should not stay in an unhealthy relationship.

No two people are alike. There will always be differences. Most differences can be worked on, discussed, and a solution found if both people are willing. However, some people cannot do this. Do not stay in a relationship in which the other person gets physically violent, uses alcohol or drugs, is nasty and hurts your feelings constantly (even if he or she apologizes each time), lies continually, or steals or destroys property. You are worth more than this kind of person can appreciate.

A TIME OF CHANGE

The 1960s. Hippies. Woodstock. The Beatles. Miniskirts. Bellbottoms. Tie-dyeing. Psychedelic. Vietnam. Flower Power. War protests. Draftcard burning. JFK. The Age of Aquarius. Civil Rights. The Doors. Robert Kennedy. The Black Panthers. Feminism. The Church.

THE CHURCH??

That's right. Many important things happened to the Church in the sixties, and the Church led the way in working for justice in many of the important events and movements of the sixties. Catholics worked for civil rights, for an end to the war in Vietnam, and in the women's movement. Catholic priests and nuns became a visible presence and spoke out on political issues. Some Catholics were pleased by this involvement and others were shocked. This kind of social involvement would have been unthinkable just a few years before.

The Second Vatican Council, or Vatican II, began in 1962 and made the Church's involvement in the issues of the 1960's possible.

When the Council ended in 1965, the changes it proposed were far-reaching. You have learned in Chapter 7 how Vatican II helped to renew the Church.

Some people welcomed the changes of the Council. Others were more cautious. Others felt that the Council had not gone far enough. For many Catholics, the sixties became a period of experimentation while the Church began to put into practice the changes of the Council.

Experimentation is testing, trial and error—when both good and bad suggestions are attempted. Some of the changes Catholics tried in the sixties were good and worked well, but others, though well-intentioned, did not work. Many of these experiments had to do with the Mass.

The Second Vatican Council made changes in the Mass to help Catholics celebrate better as a community. Some people felt that the Council had not made enough changes and they experimented with other ways to change the Mass. People tried home Masses, outdoor Masses, and Masses in other places less formal than a church in order to create a warm, friendly atmosphere. People sat on the floor and used coffee tables or other tables as altars. People tried using readings other than Scripture. Members of the community were invited to give homilies. "Dialogue homilies" led by the celebrant gave the members of the community an opportunity to share their opinions and ideas. Some thought that perhaps bread and wine were no longer meaningful symbols for the Eucharist and suggested using crackers and cola. Others designed new vestments and used symbols taken from popular culture, such as cartoon characters, in place of Christian symbols. Chalices and patens were redesigned to be less ornate, simpler.

Liturgical dance, using modern dance techniques, was used for Entrance Processions and at the Preparation of the Altar. Slide shows were presented after Communion. Different types of music, such as folk, rock, and jazz, were used. Trying to make the celebration of the Eucharist more like a party, some decorated for Mass using balloons and streamers and distributed candy after Communion. Clowns tried to point to the joyousness of the occasions.

Although done with good intentions, many of these attempts did not help people to celebrate the presence of Jesus. People found out that Scripture is important, a nice reading from somewhere else just is not as good or as appropriate. Bread and wine are the best symbols for the Eucharist, and cartoon characters do not carry the same meaning as Christian symbols.

The changes that worked were those that helped people to recognize Jesus' presence in God's word, in Communion, and in the community of his disciples. The celebration of the Eucharist is warmer and more community-centered than it appeared to be before Vatican II. Our music is more varied and our prayers express our praise and thanks to God.

Renewal of any kind is frequently difficult and controversial. The sixties were such a time for the Church. Renewal affected all areas of Catholic life, including the Mass. Today, our Eucharistic celebration is still our greatest act of worship because through the celebration of the Eucharist, we are united with Jesus and the Church community as we share a special meal.

SANDRO BOTTICELLI (FILIPEPI)
FIORENTINO N.1444/45-M.1510

A FAMILY AFFAIR

Did you know that sainthood seemed to run in some families? Saints who were mother and child: Saints Monica (mother) and Augustine (son); Saints Bridget of Sweden (mother) and Catherine of Sweden (daughter); Saints Margaret (mother) and Matilda (daughter).

Saints who were brother and sister: Saints Scholastica and Benedict.

Saints who were brothers: Saints Cyril and Methodius.

Saints who were husband and wife: Saints Isidore the Farmer and Mary de la Cabeza; Saints Henry II and Cunegunda. (Can you name another famous husband/wife pair?)

DID YOU KNOW?

The United States Catholic Conference has its own system for rating movies. The ratings given to movies can be found in diocesan newspapers and other Catholic publications.

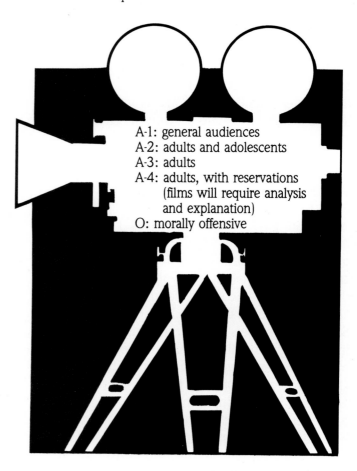

A-1: general audiences
A-2: adults and adolescents
A-3: adults
A-4: adults, with reservations (films will require analysis and explanation)
O: morally offensive

WOULD YOU BELIEVE?

Our farewell "goodbye" is a contraction of the words *God be with you.*

Looking Ahead

In Unit 3 you will learn about Catholic worship and prayer. Catholic worship is rich and includes personal and communal prayer and official liturgy. Catholic prayer has traditionally been expressed not just in words but through many forms of art and beauty. Catholic prayer is sacramental, with seven major sacraments and many sacramentals. Instituted by Christ, the Eucharist is the central celebration of the Church, celebrating the presence of the risen Christ with his followers and their union with him and one another.

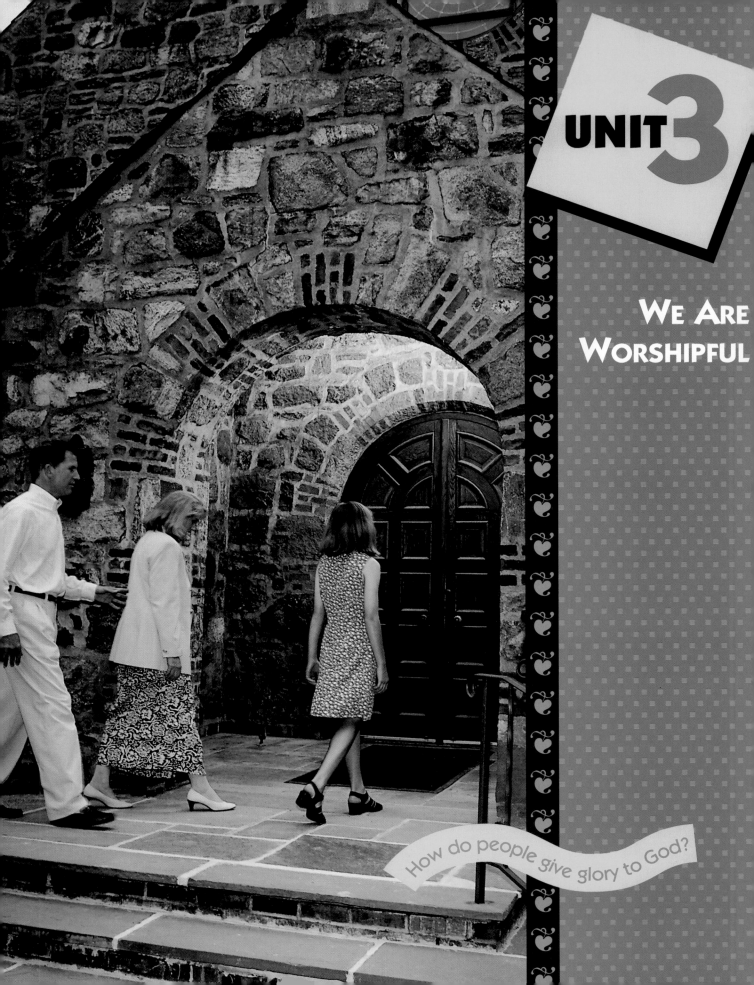

UNIT 3

WE ARE WORSHIPFUL

How do people give glory to God?

9 A PRAYERFUL PEOPLE

RELATIONSHIPS

Throughout our lives we will share many different kinds of relationships. Although we will probably be acquainted with many people, we will only be close to a few of these. And even then, we may not remain close to the same people throughout our lives. Our relationships will grow and change, just as we do.

WHO IS IMPORTANT IN YOUR LIFE?

Activity

Who are some of the people you feel closest to?

_____

_____

How do you know when you are close to someone?

_____

_____

_____

What do you think are three signs of closeness?

_____

_____

_____

_____

How do people become closer?

_____

_____

_____

_____

How do people become farther apart?

_____

_____

_____

_____

THE PRAYER OF JESUS

Jesus' life is an example of how we can live in God's presence and how we can respond to the Lord in prayer. As did many Jewish people of his time, Jesus probably prayed daily with his family and celebrated the annual Jewish feasts with his people. As an adult, he prayed at the Temple in Jerusalem, and he gathered in the synagogue with his fellow Jews on the Sabbath.

Jesus prayed often to God, his Father. He prayed when he was happy: "At that very moment he rejoiced [in] the holy Spirit and said: 'I give you praise, Father, Lord of heaven and earth, for although you have hidden these things from the wise and the learned you have revealed them to the childlike' " (Luke 10:21). He also prayed when he was afraid. In the garden on the night before Jesus died, he prayed: "Father, if you are willing, take this cup away from me; still not my will but yours be done" (Luke 22:42).

Jesus tells us that we can pray as he prays. Find and read Luke 11:11–13. In this parable, Jesus asks us to think of the person whom we most trust and on whom we depend. Jesus reminds us that this person tries to help us. We can think of God as being like this trusted person. God is our Father and will never fail us. Jesus shows us that God is on our side and wishes for us more than we can know.

Jesus can be our model for prayer. Prayer is our response to God in all of our experiences, in all of our moods, in our successes and in our failures.

Discuss

Another parable about prayer can be found in Luke 11:5–10. Look up this reference in the Bible and read the parable. Then discuss together what Jesus is teaching us about how we should pray.

Activity

Here are five common definitions of prayer. Circle the number of the definition that is closest to your own understanding of prayer. If you know another definition of prayer that you like better, write and explain it.

1. Prayer is the saying of prayers.

2. Prayer is conversation with Christ.

3. Prayer is lifting our minds and hearts to God.

4. Prayer is a radical response to life.

5. Prayer is simply resting in God's presence.

_____

_____

_____

THE LORD'S PRAYER

Jesus not only gave us a good example of how we can pray in our daily lives, he also taught his followers to pray. In the Gospels of Matthew and Luke, we read about the prayer that Jesus himself gave us to pray. This prayer is called the Our Father, or Lord's Prayer. It is a key prayer of the Church.

In the Lord's Prayer, we address God as Father, recognizing that we are God's children and acknowledging his majesty and glory. In this prayer we ask for God's continual care and turn toward him with humble, trusting hearts. Through praying the Lord's Prayer frequently, we can enter more deeply into our covenant, or relationship with God.

Activity

You have probably been praying the Lord's Prayer for years without giving much thought to what you were praying. Explain what each of the phrases of the Lord's Prayer means.

Our Father

_____

_____

Who art in heaven

_____

_____

Hallowed be thy name

_____

_____

Thy kingdom come

_____

_____

Thy will be done on earth as it is in heaven

_____

_____

Give us this day our daily bread

_____

_____

And forgive us our trespasses

_____

_____

As we forgive those who trespass against us

_____

_____

And lead us not into temptation

_____

_____

But deliver us from evil.

_____

_____

THE PRAYER OF MARY

We can learn much from the way in which Mary, the mother of God and our mother, prayed throughout her life. She showed her trust and humble faith in God when she generously offered her whole being to do his will in becoming the mother of God. When the messenger of the Lord appeared to Mary, she responded in faith and acceptance.

This is the most important lesson we can learn in prayer. God continually seeks out each one of us in our everyday lives.

In the Gospel of Luke, we can read the Magnificat (Luke 1:46–55). The Latin word *magnificat* means "proclaims" or "praises." In this prayer, Mary proclaims and praises God. This prayer expresses Mary's faith in all the good things that God did for the people of Israel and recognizes the good that God continues to do.

Through Mary's example of trust in God and her willingness to accept anything he asked of her, we see an example of what our faith and trust in God can strive to be.

What other prayers do you know?

_____

_____

_____

Activity

Circle the prayers that you know. Plan to learn the others that are listed below.

Hail Mary
Lord's Prayer
Glory Be to the Father
Prayer to the Holy Spirit
Prayer of Sorrow
Angelus
Prayer of St. Francis
Grace Before Meals
Grace After Meals
Act of Faith
Act of Hope
Act of Love
A Morning Offering
An Evening Prayer

Describe an experience of prayer in your own life. What was the situation? Why did you pray? What did you learn about prayer from this experience?

_____

_____

_____

_____

_____

_____

HUMAN RESTLESSNESS

Have you ever had the experience of wanting to do something, but having no idea what? This is a common human experience of restlessness. We are frequently restless. For generations, people have interpreted this experience as a need for power, wealth, land, prestige, fame, and so on. Yet even achieving these goals usually does not stop the restlessness. We continue to long for something that we cannot quite express.

Activity

When have you had an experience of restlessness?

_____

_____

_____

How do you think this human longing might be managed?

_____

_____

_____

THE INNER LIFE OF PRAYER

Throughout history there have always been some people who understood that the longing and restlessness that human beings experience cannot be soothed by worldly achievements. They recognized that the longing that human beings experience is really a longing for God.

Prayer is a way of expressing this longing for God. Young children are taught that prayer is talking to God. As we grow older, we realize that prayer is not so much in the words that we speak but in the relationship we yearn to have with God. We pray from our hearts, by expressing our longing and need to be close to God.

Prayer is the expression of this relationship between us and God, our Father. For Christians, prayer is an inseparable part of faith. To live a life of prayer is to pray continually and strive to place ourselves in the presence of God always.

Even the best Christians, however, have times when it is difficult to pray. This is because in our prayer lives we are drawn closer to, and learn to trust and depend more and more on God. There may be times when we are easily distracted or do not feel like praying. There may be times when we doubt that prayer is doing any good at all and wonder whether God is there.

At these times, it is important to remember that even Jesus had to face temptation (Matthew 4:1–11). He also found strength in prayer when he struggled in the garden of Gethsemane (Matthew 26:36–44). Perseverance and trust in God can help us through these times.

SHE TOOK THE WORLD INTO HER PRAYER

Thérèse Martin was born in 1873 in the town of Alençon, France. She was the youngest of nine children. Her mother died when she was just four years old. Thérèse's loving and attentive father taught her about a loving and attentive God.

When Thérèse was a child, she knew that great saints were filled with the glory of God. She wondered how a person as small and unworthy as she could be filled with the glory of God. Her sister, Pauline, finally found a way to address Thérèse's concern.

One day, Pauline placed before her two containers—one was their father's large drinking mug and the other was a thimble from the sewing box. Then Pauline filled both containers with water and asked, "Which is the fuller, Thérèse?"

Then Thérèse knew that she and everyone, child or adult, could indeed be full of the glory of God. Everyone was God's delight, if only they knew it.

Thérèse was determined to follow her vocation to know God. Two of Thérèse's older sisters became Carmelite nuns. Thérèse wanted to follow them, but she was only fifteen years old. The bishop said she would have to wait until she was older. But Thérèse persisted. During a visit to Rome with her family, Thérèse stepped forward to ask Pope Leo XIII to let her become a Carmelite. The pope did not object, so when they returned to France, Thérèse joined the Carmelite convent at Lisieux.

Thérèse spent her life devoted to a routine of prayer and work. She lived a quiet and simple life at the convent, but in time her superiors took notice of her prayerful life and her care for the other sisters. Thérèse's superiors asked her to write her autobiography. Thérèse did so.

In her writings, she described the simplicity of her prayer and the value of her life as a well-loved child of God. She firmly believed that her "little way" of prayer, trust, and love could lead

all people to God. She prayed for people everywhere as well as for those with whom she lived. She prayed especially for those who served God as missionaries.

Pope Pius XI canonized Thérèse in 1925, and two years later, named her copatron of the world missions. The Church celebrates the feast of St. Thérèse of Lisieux each October 1.

Discuss

1. What do you think St. Thérèse of Lisieux meant by saying that everyone is God's delight?

_____

_____

_____

2. What do you think of the "little way"?

_____

_____

THE PRAYER OF THE CHURCH

After Pentecost, the early Christians lived by following Jesus' word and example. Prayer marked the life of the original Christians in the neighborhood communities of Jerusalem. The Church in Jerusalem consisted of Jewish followers.

The first Christians in Jerusalem probably went to the Temple daily, and in their homes they celebrated the Eucharist together. They prayed the psalms. They created new prayers to the Father in the name of Jesus, and in the Holy Spirit. They also prayed to Jesus Christ. They continued to pray at the regular Jewish prayer times—morning, midday, evening. They prayed kneeling or standing, often with arms outstretched and raised. They prayed silently and aloud, and they often prayed by singing.

The ideal of the early Christians was summed up by St. Paul: "Pray without ceasing. In all circumstances give thanks, for this is the will of God for you in Christ Jesus" (1 Thessalonians 5:17–18).

GROWING IN PRAYER

From these prayerful beginnings, the early Christians kept alive Paul's ideal of continual prayer. As hermits prayed in solitary stillness, other Christians were building churches. They gathered together to pray and to celebrate the Eucharist, and their morning and evening prayer was centered on the psalms.

This was the beginning of what came to be called the **Liturgy of the Hours** or Divine Office, the Church's official prayer at certain hours of the day and night.

In later centuries, monks and nuns made the Liturgy of the Hours central to monastic life, expanding it to include other hours of the day and night. They adapted the Roman way of telling time to divide each day into eight sections. Prayers were said at each time of the day. The eight times of day were Matins (traditionally beginning with midnight), Lauds (sunrise), Prime (about 6 A.M.), Terce (about 9 A.M.), Sext (about noon), None (about 3 P.M.), Vespers or evensong (sunset), and Compline (9 P.M.). Over the centuries Matins and Lauds were sometimes combined together for morning prayer, as were Prime, Terce and Sext for daytime prayer. Compline and Vespers were also combined.

Over time lay people in parishes developed forms of prayer more adapted to their lifestyle, which centered on family life and work. Besides praying some of the psalms, they prayed the Lord's Prayer, Hail Mary, and other vocal prayers. At the sound of the church bells three times a day, people stopped work at home and in the fields to pray the Angelus. The Rosary, a popular form of prayer, developed with 150 Hail Mary's in place of the 150 psalms, or psalter, prayed each day in the monasteries.

One of the oldest forms of prayer is the Jesus Prayer, in which one repeats the word *Jesus*, or the sentence *Jesus Christ, Son of God, Savior, have mercy on me*, in rhythm with one's breathing. Similar brief aspirations that could be prayed easily and often even as one worked became popular. They include *My Lord and my God* and *Jesus, Mary, and Joseph*.

Today there are many forms of prayer for Catholics to participate in. There are forms of morning and evening prayer that include hymns, psalms, a reading of Scripture, and intercessions, or prayers of petition. The Catholic tradition of prayer is rich and varied. It follows the exhortation, "Let the word of Christ dwell in you richly, as in all wisdom you teach and admonish one another, singing psalms, hymns, and spiritual songs with gratitude in your hearts to God." (Colossians 3:16).

Activity

Think about what happened to you yesterday. Then complete the log below. Then write a short, simple prayer that you might have prayed—or did pray—at that time.

Morning

Event: _____

Prayer: _____

Afternoon

Event: _____

Prayer: _____

Evening

Event: _____

Prayer: _____

What are some ways that you can include prayer in your life every day?

_____

_____

Vocabulary

Liturgy of the Hours: the Church's official prayer at certain hours of the day and night; also called the Divine Office. It consists of psalms, readings, hymns, and prayers.

WE BELIEVE

The Church came to be in an experience of prayer. Prayer continues to be the Church's vital breath. Various forms of prayer grew up over the centuries as Catholics faced new challenges and cultures. We need to draw on the Church's rich and varied heritage of prayer as we seek to be united with Christ.

Activity

Think about your friends and then complete the following statements.

The best way to keep a friend is _____

_____

_____

The best way to lose a friend is _____

_____

_____

The key to a close friendship is _____

_____

_____

A Rich Tradition

The Catholic tradition of prayer helps us to pray in many different ways. As Catholics we are called to praise God, to thank God for all our gifts, to offer prayers of petition, and to express sorrow for wrongdoings. We are called to gather in public worship and to retreat in private prayer. Public worship and shared prayer help us to continue working and resting in God's presence.

When we spend time alone in prayer, we deepen our friendship with God. We begin to see God in all the events and people of our daily lives. As Catholics, we can look to the lives of the saints as examples. For many centuries great men and women have taught others to pray and be attentive to God's presence. Saints such as Bernard, Francis of Assisi, Teresa of Avila, and Ignatius Loyola taught others how to pray always. These saints have taught us to be with and talk to God as one would be with and talk to a very close friend. They taught us about meditation and contemplation.

Meditation is a prayerful reflection. When we meditate, we are thinking, wondering, or imagining about something. We use our minds and our emotions to enter more deeply into God's presence. Meditation is somewhat like mulling over something or wondering about the mystery of it all. You can meditate on almost anything: a personal experience, a world event, a truth of faith, a person or a thing, a biblical text or story, a prayer, a symbol or picture—or anything else.

Contemplation is different from meditation, although some people confuse the two. Contemplation is a prayerful "seeing" of God in nature or people. It is a quiet resting in God's presence. Contemplation is a gift from God and can be sought after through frequent prayer and meditation. It is a gift in which a person enters into the presence of God and is in a continual state of prayer, even while he or she is working and taking care of others. The contemplative has an inner life that is continually directed toward and focused on God.

How to Meditate

There are many different kinds of meditation techniques to help you turn your attention to God. Here is one way to meditate.

1. Prepare: Find a quiet place. Take a relaxed position. Play some quieting music. Breathe slowly and deeply.

2. Picture: Read a biblical story slowly. Try to imagine the scene, picturing details about the place and the people. Hear the words. Imagine how each person feels.

3. Ponder: Mull over the story. Try to get behind the situation, words, and actions that you have just pictured in your imagination. Ask yourself questions. Who are the people involved? Why those particular people? What are they saying and doing? Why that word? Why that gesture or action? What difference does it make? How does it make me feel? Why?

4. Pray: Begin to talk with God or Jesus Christ. Let the words just come as if you were talking with a friend. The words may be words of praise, thanks, petition, or sorrow.

Since meditation and prayer should be translated into how you live, decide on something you will do as a result of this meditation.

Activity

From the time of the early Christians, the Church has always prayed. To search for your own reasons to pray, answer these questions.

1. Praise: What is there about God that makes you want to praise God?

   _____

   _____

   _____

2. Thanksgiving: What is in your life today for which you would most like to thank God?

   _____

   _____

   _____

3. Petition: What do you feel most moved to pray for?

   _____

   _____

   _____

4. Sorrow: For what would you like to ask God's forgiveness?

   _____

   _____

   _____

Vocabulary

meditation: prayerful reflection on an event, object, truth, or text

contemplation: a prayerful "seeing" of God in nature or people; a quiet resting in God's presence

Praying with Our Imagination

In this chapter, you have learned that you can meditate about almost anything. Here is a another way to meditate. A guided meditation is a journey of the imagination. It is a special way of being with Jesus through a story that, through our imaginations, takes us to another place or even another time.

As we listen to a story read aloud by someone else, we place ourselves at the center of it. During our journey in the story, we encounter Jesus and begin a dialogue in which we share our thoughts, feelings, joys, and disappointments. We speak these words silently, in the quiet of our hearts.

Then we invite our Lord to respond to us, once again in the silence of our hearts. We may feel Jesus' love, comfort, and encouragement. At the end of our meditation, we can express our belief in Jesus, thank him for being with us, or promise to meet again in prayer soon. Then we leave our journey behind and return to this place and time, knowing that we can visit with Jesus again, anytime and anywhere.

Activity

Answer the questions below to plan how you might create a guided meditation to share with your class.

1. Where will you take your classmates during the meditation? A deserted beach? A rowboat on a lake? A quiet trail? Their own rooms?

   _____

   _____

2. How will they meet Jesus? How will they recognize him?

   _____

   _____

3. How will you invite your classmates to speak to Jesus? What will you suggest they say?

   _____

   _____

4. What will Jesus say in return?

   _____

   _____

5. How will the meditation end? How will you get your classmates back to here and now?

   _____

   _____

Circle **T** if the sentence is true. Circle **F** if the sentence is false.

1. We should only pray when we are happy and feel good about ourselves.　　T　F

2. Jesus is our best model for prayer.　　T　F

3. Contemplation is a quiet resting in God.　　T　F

4. The Liturgy of the Hours is based on the eight-part day of monastic life.　　T　F

5. When we pray, we can bring before God all of our thoughts and concerns.　　T　F

6. The Liturgy of the Hours is the same as the Divine Office.　　T　F

7. Thérèse of Lisieux thought that God was like a stern and unapproachable judge.　　T　F

8. Jesus prayed only in the Temple.　　T　F

9. Jesus taught us to pray by addressing God as Father.　　T　F

10. We do not learn how to pray from Mary's example.　　T　F

Respond to the following questions based on what you have learned in this chapter.

1. What is *meditation*?

_____

_____

_____

2. How is the Liturgy of the Hours the prayer of the Church?

_____

_____

_____

_____

Pray at every opportunity in the Spirit.
Ephesians 6:18

3. Discuss some of the reasons why people find it difficult to pray.

10 A PEOPLE OF SIGNS

INSIGHT THROUGH MUSIC

Sometimes words are inadequate to express what we are feeling and thinking. At those times we can use different artistic expressions to capture the essence of what we are experiencing. In this way, we use art and music to communicate with others about who we are, our relationships, and our needs and hopes.

HOW DO PEOPLE EXPRESS THEIR DEEPEST FEELINGS?

Activity

Consider how different artistic expressions help you to better understand and express personal experiences that are not easily put into words.

1. How does music help you understand what words alone cannot express?

_____

_____

2. Why is music so important to people?

_____

_____

3. Give an example of how music conveys feelings and ideas through sound.

_____

_____

_____

JESUS, THE IMAGE OF GOD

The life and work of Jesus Christ reveal to us who God is and what God is like. Jesus reflects the light of God's love. At the beginning of the Gospel of John, we read about Jesus, the Image of God: "And the Word became flesh and made his dwelling among us, and we saw his glory, the glory as of the Father's only Son, full of grace and truth" (John 1:14).

Jesus' revelation about his Father's love helps others realize that all people are made in the image and likeness of God. We share in God's life and love. This is explained further in one of the letters in the New Testament.

"For the life was made visible; we have seen it and testify to it and proclaim to you the eternal life that was with the Father and was made visible to us—what we have seen and heard we proclaim now to you, so that you too may have fellowship with us; for our fellowship is with the Father and with his Son, Jesus Christ" (1 John 1:2–3).

The Gospel of John gives us some signs or images that show us who Jesus is. Here is a list of images that John used to describe who Jesus is for us.

> Way, Truth, Life
> Living Water
> Bread of Life
> True Light
> Good Shepherd

John 10:11

_____

John 8:12

_____

John 14:1–7

_____

Activity

Look up the following verses from the Gospel of John. Then write the image next to each citation.

John 4:10

_____

John 6:35

_____

Activity

Think about what you know about Jesus and how he is an image of God for you. Give examples of what you know and believe about God because of what you have learned about who Jesus is.

_____

_____

_____

Activity

Many people express themselves through their clothing, hair, and jewelry. These outward things can tell you what a person thinks of himself or herself.

What are some things that clothing can tell you about someone?

_____

_____

_____

What does your fashion style tell about you?

_____

_____

_____

_____

IMAGES OF TRUTH

Frequently, we choose to express our faith through words of prayer. Even in prayer, however, there are times when words are inadequate for what we need to express. At these times we can use art, music, and other artistic expressions to communicate to God, our loving Father, what human words fail to say. Just as Jesus is the image and reflection of all that God is and promises to us, art and music can be images of who we are and what we hope for—images rising in prayer to God.

EXPRESSIONS OF PRAYER

From the earliest days of the Church, Christians have prayed in creative ways. The earliest Christians stood to pray, their arms raised upward, or their hands placed in blessing on the head of the one for whom they prayed. These Christians prayed with music and song, too. In fact, the earliest parts of the New Testament are selections from early Christian hymns. The early Christians prayed by using symbols, the most important being the breaking of the bread—in which the risen Christ himself is present.

During the Roman persecutions, the Christians painted pictures of Jesus on the walls of the catacombs where they hid. Their faith in Jesus, the Good Shepherd, was frequently illustrated in paintings and statues.

CENTURIES OF ART

Once Christianity was made legal by Constantine, Christians built great churches in which to pray. Inside these places of worship were beautiful images that expressed the Christian faith. Christians of this time painted **icons**, or sacred images of Jesus Christ, his mother Mary, and the saints. The Church taught that these icons were a way of expressing the divine reality that could not be expressed in words. The icons were regarded as channels of prayer.

Christians began making crosses covered with jewels or featuring the figure of the risen, victorious Christ. In later centuries, as the Catholics of Europe shared in the sufferings brought on by the breakdown of the Holy Roman Empire, they pictured Jesus differently—as suffering on the cross. Such images were expressions of prayer and helps to prayer.

Medieval Christians also developed dance and drama to express their faith. They considered the graceful movements of the dancer an inspiration to pray.

Perhaps the most dramatic expression of prayer in symbol and image was the creation of the great cathedrals. The light that filled them symbolized God's presence. Stained-glass windows, statues, and sculptured symbols were created to raise the spirits of those who prayed within the cathedrals. The lofty spires of the cathedrals had a similar effect on all who looked upon them. These grand cathedrals and smaller churches that dotted Europe were expressions of praise and worship by the townspeople who built them.

BEAUTY AND PRAYER

Catholic tradition has always appreciated beauty in the expression of prayer. Unlike believers of various times and places who have maintained that images and physical beauty distract from union with God, Catholics have recognized that what we can see, hear, smell, touch and feel—places, actions, and things that are genuinely beautiful—are great helps to prayer. In fact, these things can themselves become the finest expressions of praise, thanksgiving, petition, and sorrow.

The Catholic Church continues to cherish prayer inspired by images, sounds, and symbols. We can pray not just with words but also through our use of glass and stone, candles and incense, time and space, music and song, color and shape, gesture and action. In short, we can pray with all that is beautiful. Such prayer reflects our Catholic belief in Jesus Christ.

Vocabulary

icons: sacred images of Jesus Christ, his mother Mary, and the saints

WE BELIEVE

Catholic prayer is expressed not just in words but through many forms of art and beauty. Since God creates all things and became a man in Jesus Christ, all things are graced by God's presence. Anything that is good, true, or beautiful can become an expression of prayer for a Catholic.

A PRAYERFUL ARTIST

Michelangelo Buonarroti, one of the greatest artists of all time, was a sculptor, a painter, an architect, and a poet.

This artistic genius was born in Italy in 1475. He was inspired to be an artist while he was a youngster. His father did not like the idea, preferring that his son become a merchant or businessman. But when Michelangelo was thirteen, his father allowed him to study under a famous painter.

A year or so later, the teenaged Michelangelo heard the powerful preaching of a famous Dominican priest named Girolano Savonarola. The priest's words left a profound impression on the sensitive artist. From that time on, Michelangelo saw his artistic work as an expression of his religious faith. He believed that artists who work within the Church should lead good lives. He also believed that their art, which flowed from their own faith, should evoke feelings of prayer and piety in those who viewed it.

For Michelangelo, to make something beautiful was a sacred task. He tried to create works of art so beautiful that they might lead people to open their hearts to God, the source of all beauty. Michelangelo's art seems to express and to evoke the deepest human longings for the divine. Inspired, the artist prayed with paintbrush, hammer, chisel, and poetic word, creating for the glory of God.

For sixty years, Michelangelo worked on art projects for the popes. As an architect, he helped to design St. Peter's Basilica in Rome. As a sculptor, he created world-famous statues of Moses and David and the Pietà—which depicts Mary holding the dead body of Jesus. As a painter, Michelangelo decorated the walls and ceilings of the Vatican's Sistine Chapel with overpowering images of the creation and last judgment.

Millions of people each year continue to wonder at the size and beauty of St. Peter's Basilica in Rome. Michelangelo's Sistine Chapel

paintings draw tourists from around the world. Few artists have ever created more moving, prayerful images than did Michelangelo.

Activity

If you were a painter, what event in the life of Jesus would you choose to illustrate? Why?

_____

_____

_____

_____

_____

_____

_____

Activity

List some of the images, paintings, or sculptures that are found in your parish church.

_____

_____

_____

_____

_____

Select one of these images and describe it below.

_____

_____

_____

_____

What do you think the artist was trying to express about the subject of this piece of art?

_____

_____

_____

Do you think the artist did a good job? Why or why not? What would you have done in his or her place?

_____

_____

_____

_____

Activity

In the spaces below, list several common ideas and feelings that people have about God.

_____

_____

_____

_____

_____

What is the strongest feeling you have about God?

_____

_____

_____

ARTISTIC PRAISE

Michelangelo praised God with hammer and chisel, paintbrush and palette, and poetic word. Throughout history, other people have praised God through melody, harmony, and poetic word. From the beginning of the Church, music has been a way to express the soul's heartfelt longing for and praise of God. From Gregorian chant to Schubert's "Ave Maria" to Liszt's "Dante Symphony," music has inspired and stirred the hearts and faith of Christians.

Perhaps the psalms of the Old Testament are one of the most important examples of the kinds of music that human beings have used to pray. Many of the psalms indicate that they were meant to be sung. Some psalms include instructions that they were to be sung by the leader of worship or by the chorus. Sometimes the instruments that were to accompany the singing were also specified. Lyres, harps, flutes, and even several instruments that are still unknown to us were called for.

Although we do not know what the psalms would have sounded like when they were sung centuries ago, they still appeal to the senses and include many wonderful images. With your class, read the following section of Psalm 150 aloud.

Praise him with the blast of the
         trumpet,
      praise him with lyre and harp.
Praise him with timbrel and dance,
      praise him with strings and pipe.
Praise him with sounding cymbals,
      praise him with clanging cymbals.
Let everything that has breath
      praise the LORD! Alleluia.

Psalm 150:3–6

MUSIC AND SONG

Music is still an important part of our worship. It has been a tradition for only the past several centuries that churches are equipped with organs. This was not always the case. For much of the history of Christianity, chant and song without the use of instruments was the way in which Christians praised God through music. Today we have a wide array of instruments that are commonly used in worship and prayer celebrations. Guitars, pianos, electric keyboards, tambourines, maracas, and woodwind instruments such as flutes are just some of the instruments frequently used. Recorded music is not supposed to be used. Our prayer should always be live—and from the heart.

The songs we use to praise God are drawn from a variety of sources. Some are ancient and have been sung in worship since the earliest times. The "Holy, Holy, Holy" for example, has been sung in one form or another since at least the fourth century. Others are more recent and are the creations of professional liturgical composers and musicians. No matter the origin, the music with which we praise God should inspire us and remind us of all that we are called to be.

Activity

Read the psalm on page 150 again and think about how it might sound if the instruments mentioned in the psalm were to be used. Describe your impressions below.

_____

_____

_____

_____

How do you think music intended to pray to God should sound?

_____

_____

_____

_____

What instruments do you think you would use most? Why would you use these?

_____

_____

_____

_____

_____

What do you think the words in music for prayer and worship should be about?

_____

_____

_____

_____

_____

THE WONDER OF NATURE

The first story of creation in the biblical Book of Genesis tells us that after each step of creation, God looked at what had been done and saw that it was good. In our lives we recognize the goodness of creation and see the hand of God reflected in all of nature. Our heartfelt response to the beauty, majesty, and power of nature is our prayer to God.

Nature inspires us to prayer in many ways—in thanksgiving for its grandeur and simplicity; in petition against its power and destructiveness; in praise of its maker; and in sorrow for our neglect and willful disrespect of its resources and destruction of life. It does all this because ultimately, nature reminds us of the reality of God.

But now ask the beasts to teach you,
> and the birds of the air to tell you;
Or the reptiles on earth to instruct you,
> and the fish of the sea to inform you.
Which of all these does not know
> that the hand of God has done this?
In his hand is the soul of every living thing,
> and the life breath of all mankind.

Job 12:7–10

We can meditate on nature and so come to a deeper awareness of our own role in God's plan. By allowing the wonder of nature to touch us, we will also deepen our faith. Not only are there relationships among all forms of life, God is in relationship with everyone and everything. We need to acknowledge the responsibility we have toward nature to care for and encourage life in all its forms.

Recognizing the connection between God, nature, and ourselves, we are moved to work with nature, rather than against it. We are challenged to participate in the renewal of life. However we choose to participate—whether by recycling, planting, or caring for animals—our work becomes our prayer. It becomes our response to the goodness of God that we see reflected in nature.

Activity

What is one experience of nature that you will never forget? Why?

_____

_____

_____

_____

_____

Activity

Read each of the Scripture verses below. Then tell what image of nature each verse uses and what that image tells us about God.

Psalm 89:10

Image: _____

Shows that God is: _____

Psalm 28:1

Image: _____

Shows that God is: _____

Psalm 97:1–6

Image: _____

Shows that God is: _____

_____

Think of three images of nature that tell you something about God. Explain each.

1. Image: _____

    This shows that God is: _____

    _____

2. Image: _____

    This shows that God is: _____

    _____

3. Image: _____

    This shows that God is: _____

    _____

    _____

PRAYING THROUGH ART

Artists sometimes attempt to communicate different religious themes and ideas through their art. One artist might focus on the glory and majesty of God; another, on the goodness of creation. Artists might try to communicate the sinfulness and depravity of human nature or the rapture of divine grace.

Some artists work in a realistic style. That is, they try to express their religious ideas by illustrating a Bible story or event just as it might have happened. Other artists work in styles that are more abstract. These abstract styles do not try to make something look realistic. Instead, abstract art challenges the viewer to experience an emotion or a viewpoint about the world, God, or humanity.

Much of contemporary art tries to express the pain and suffering of human existence. To many, these works do not inspire as much as cause discomfort. Their bleakness is meant to remind us about the agonies, tragedies, and horror of life.

One artistic style that has always been considered a sacred form of art is iconography, or the making of icons. Creating an icon is considered a prayer, and icons are said to be "written," not drawn. Like modern abstract art, an icon does not attempt to show us what a saint actually looked like, for example, but what his or her saintly qualities were. Because a strict life of prayer and fasting was valued, many icons show saints who look thin and stern. These figures do not look as if they ever gave into selfishness.

Iconography also has a fixed way of showing certain religious themes. The artist does not have the freedom to do whatever he or she wants, but shows the symbols and images that indicate specific Christian beliefs. For example, stars indicate the heavens. Creating an icon which gives expression to the qualities of holiness is a way of sharing faith with others—and this is one of the goals of Christian prayer.

BRANCUSI, Constantin *Bird in Space*. (c. 1941) Bronze, 6′ (182.9 cm) high, two-part stone pedestal 17 3/8″ (44.1 cm) high. The Museum of Modern Art, New York. Gift of Mr. and Mrs. William A. M. Burden. Photograph © 1996 The Museum of Modern Art, New York.

Discuss

1. What should religious art show?

2. How should religious art make you feel?

3. What kinds of art do you think could be considered prayers? What kinds could not?

Activity

On a separate sheet of paper, create your own religious image. Here are some ideas to help get you started.

• The feeling of being loved by God

• The feeling of being abandoned by God

• The confusion felt when it's hard to distinguish between right and wrong

• The feeling of being generous and serving others

• The feeling of being willing to take on a challenge for the sake of faith in God

CHAPTER REVIEW

Match the words in the first column with their descriptions in the second column.

Column 1

1. Jesus
2. Michelangelo
3. Psalms
4. Nature
5. Cross
6. Cathedrals
7. Sistine Chapel

Column 2

_____ where the figure of the risen, victorious Christ was placed

_____ songs found in the Old Testament

_____ expressions of praise and worship of medieval townspeople

_____ a frequent subject for Christian artists

_____ draws us to recognize the connectedness of all life

_____ the artist who was also a sculptor and poet

_____ the building that contains images of the creation and the last judgment

Write a paragraph describing five ways that the Church prays through image and symbols.

_____

_____

_____

_____

_____

_____

Respond to the following questions based on what you have learned in this chapter.

1. What is an *icon*?

_____

_____

2. What kinds of art can be an expression of prayer and worship?

_____

_____

_____

_____

3. Discuss why you think Catholics continue to create artistic ways of praying in addition to praying with words.

Praise him with lyre and harp, Praise him with timbrel and dance.
Psalm 150:3-4

11 A SACRAMENTAL PEOPLE

WHAT ARE COMMON SIGNS AND SYMBOLS FOUND IN EVERYDAY LIFE?

POWERFUL SYMBOLS

We use signs and symbols to express our deepest thoughts, emotions, and beliefs. Persons, places, things, actions, gestures, sounds, or smells can be signs that reveal invisible realities.

Symbols bring meaning and purpose to our lives. Symbols express or reveal the powerful forces that shape the way we live. Discuss the meanings of the symbols pictured in the photographs above.

Activity

Name a sign or symbol that expresses each of the following ideas.

1. Victory _____

_____

2. Friendship _____

_____

3. Peace _____

_____

NEW MEANING IN JESUS

As Jews, Jesus and his disciples lived in a world filled with Jewish **ritual**. These included the weekly Sabbath, circumcision, the yearly celebration of Passover, and prayer and sacrifice in the Temple. There were also ritual washings and anointings.

These and other rituals drew their meaning both from natural human experiences and from the Jewish people's unique experiences of God (the faith stories of past events). For example, water was used in ritual washings because it symbolized cleansing, dying, and being reborn. To this the Jewish people brought their memories of how God had dealt with them and what was revealed to them through the symbol of water: the destruction of the great flood, the great rescue from Egypt through the Sea of Reeds, and the crossing of the Jordan River into the promised land.

Jesus cherished all the Jewish rituals because these reminded the people of God's saving presence and activity. He used them to celebrate his Jewish faith all his life.

The Church took the rituals and symbols of Jewish religious life and, in the light of Jesus' resurrection, recognized new meanings in them. For example, in the Gospel of John, Jesus tells the Samaritan woman at the well, "Whoever drinks the water I shall give will never thirst; the water I shall give will become in him a spring of water welling up to eternal life" (John 4:14). The water Jesus gives will not only cleanse or quench thirst, but will bring life with God.

Activity

Look up the following passages from Scripture and identify the Jewish symbols and the new meaning Jesus gave them.

1. Matthew 28:18–20

   _____

   _____

2. Luke 22:19–20

   _____

   _____

3. John 20:22–23

   _____

   _____

Discuss

What are some Christian rituals and symbols that are important to you and your family? Why are they important?

Vocabulary

ritual: a formal religious ceremony that proceeds according to set rules

ABOUT THE SACRAMENTS

After Jesus' resurrection, he not only commissioned his disciples to undertake the ministry he had begun, but he also promised to be with his disciples as they exercised that ministry.

Fired by the gift of the Holy Spirit at Pentecost, the disciples took up the mission and ministry that Jesus had left to them. They began teaching, forgiving, healing, uniting, encouraging, calling people to greater openness to God and service to their neighbors, working for a better world, and looking forward to the fulfillment of the kingdom of God at the end of time.

The disciples baptized new followers with water. They gathered regularly to celebrate the eucharistic meal. They also prayed over the sick and anointed them with oil; forgave sinners; and laid hands on the heads of new leaders of the growing Church communities.

They understood these actions to be special signs of Christ's presence. They also recognized that in these signs they received God's **grace.** Grace is God's gift of God's own life and presence to people. St. Augustine called this kind of action a sacrament and defined a **sacrament** as a "visible sign of invisible grace" or "sign of sacred reality." In other words, a sacrament is a special sign within the life of the

Church through which Christ truly becomes present with us and acts in our lives.

Seven sacraments became central to Catholic life. By the twelfth century, the theologian Peter Lombard used the word *sacrament* to refer to the following: Baptism, Confirmation, Eucharist, Reconciliation (or Penance), Anointing of the Sick, Matrimony, and Holy Orders. Lombard saw these as signs and causes of God's grace.

In the sixteenth century, at the Council of Trent, the Church formally defined the seven sacraments of the Catholic Church. In these sacred actions, the faithful share in the life, presence, and mission of Christ. Celebrating the sacraments not only brings us closer to the Lord but to one another in the Lord.

The promise of the risen Christ to be with us always is especially fulfilled in the ministry of the Church and in the sacred actions of the sacraments. The sacraments reveal Christ's presence and bestow God's grace. They also help us recall and celebrate who we are called to be as Christians.

Activity

1. Which sacraments help us better understand that we are called to commit ourselves to the service of others?

   _____

   _____

   _____

   _____

2. Which sacraments help us better understand what it means to be a people who reach out to welcome and include others?

   _____

   _____

   _____

   _____

3. Which sacraments help us better understand what it means to be a people who are peacemakers, people who strengthen and heal one another?

   _____

   _____

   _____

   _____

4. What is a sacrament?

   _____

   _____

   _____

   _____

Vocabulary

grace: God's gift of God's own life and presence to people

sacrament: a special sign within the life of the Church through which Christ truly becomes present with us and acts in our lives

WE BELIEVE

The Catholic Church defines seven sacred actions as sacraments, special signs of Christ's grace and our faith. They are Baptism, Confirmation, Eucharist, Reconciliation, Anointing of the Sick, Matrimony, and Holy Orders. They are actions of the risen Christ, acting through his Church to love, heal, and call us to transform our lives and our world. The sacraments celebrate the meaning of Christ in our most important life experiences.

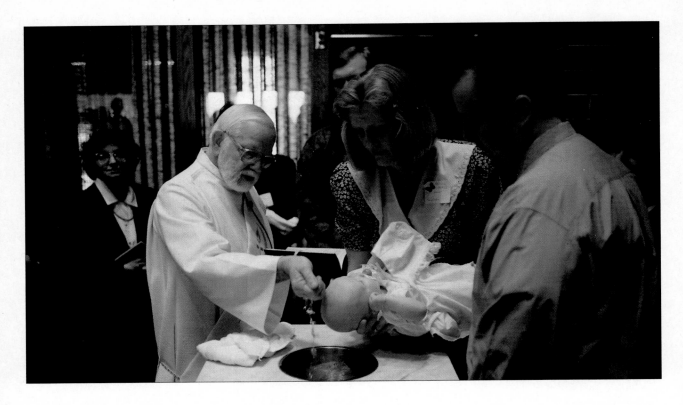

Activity

What sacraments have you received?

_____

_____

_____

_____

What sacramental celebrations have you participated in, although you may not have received the sacrament being celebrated?

_____

_____

_____

_____

_____

_____

THE SACRAMENTS OF INITIATION

There are three sacraments through which we become full members of the Church. These are called the sacraments of initiation: Baptism, Confirmation, and Eucharist.

Baptism: This sacrament unites us with Jesus and welcomes us into the Christian community. We receive the Holy Spirit and are freed from original sin and personal sin. Since the beginning of the Church, children as well as adults have been baptized into the Church. This sacrament is received only once.

Confirmation: This sacrament of initiation strengthens the new life we received at Baptism. The Holy Spirit strengthens us in our faith, helps us to live our faith more responsibly, and helps us to share our faith with others. This sacrament is received only once.

Eucharist: This sacrament is also the central celebration of the Church and our greatest act of worship. The Eucharist celebrates the death and resurrection of Jesus and the real presence of Jesus' body and blood under the appearances of bread and wine. This sacrament should be received frequently.

THE SACRAMENTS OF HEALING

There are two sacraments of healing: Reconciliation and Anointing of the Sick. These sacraments celebrate Jesus' forgiveness and healing.

Reconciliation: This sacrament is also called the sacrament of Penance. Some people refer to it as the sacrament of forgiveness, the sacrament of repentance, and the sacrament of conversion. In this sacrament, we are forgiven by God and the Church after we have acknowledged our sinfulness. We must regret the wrong we have done (or the good we have failed to do), and experience a conversion of our hearts—that is, a sincere willingness to change.

This sacrament is always celebrated with a priest. We may celebrate it individually or with a group. However, confessing our sins is usually done individually with the priest and is a necessary part of the sacrament.

When we go to confession, we tell our sins to the priest and receive our penance—a prayer or act of kindness the priest gives us to show that we are sorry and wish to change. We say aloud an act of contrition, or prayer of sorrow. The priest then forgives us. This is called absolution.

We should celebrate the sacrament of Reconciliation any time we feel the need for God's mercy and forgiveness or if we have committed a mortal sin.

Anointing of the Sick: This sacrament of healing brings Jesus' healing, forgiveness, comfort, and strength to those who are seriously ill, elderly, or in danger of death. During the celebration of this sacrament, the priest prays for three things: (1) easing of the person's suffering, with strength to cope with it; (2) physical healing of mind and body; and (3) forgiveness of the person's sins.

Anointing of the Sick can be celebrated more than once—whenever a person is ill, seriously injured, or having serious surgery. People who are elderly, even if they are not sick, may also celebrate this sacrament. Anointing of the Sick can be celebrated at home, in church, in a hospital, or in a nursing home.

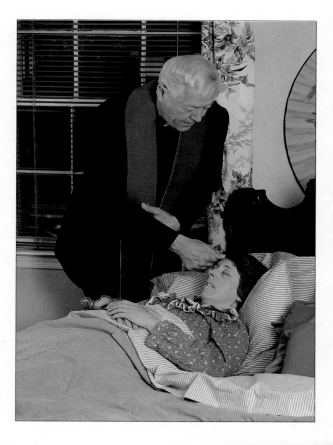

THE SACRAMENTS OF COMMITMENT

Matrimony and Holy Orders are the two sacraments of commitment and service. In these sacraments the Church celebrates two ways that people serve others by sharing their gifts.

Matrimony: The sacrament of marriage, called Matrimony, celebrates the promise that a man and woman make publicly to love each other as husband and wife for the rest of their lives.

The sacrament of Matrimony begins a permanent and sacred bond that cannot be broken through a divorce by a court of law. The Church recognizes that sometimes it is possible to determine that the sacred bond established in this sacrament did not occur. Then the Church can declare that the marriage is annulled. It is important to understand that a decree of annulment does not end a marriage. Instead it is the official judgment of the Church that the sacramental bond of Matrimony was never established in the first place, despite appearances to the contrary.

Through this sacrament, the Holy Spirit strengthens and guides married couples to help them remain faithful to their promises to each other. By their love, the husband and wife are to be a sign of God's love and faithfulness for all people and of Christ's love for the Church.

Holy Orders: This is the sacrament in which men are ordained bishops, priests, and deacons to serve the Church in a special way. Bishops carry on the work of the apostles and serve the Church by leading a diocese. Priests, like bishops, celebrate the sacraments, proclaim God's word, and guide the Church community. Deacons baptize, proclaim the gospel, witness marriages, preside at funerals, and serve the community.

Celibacy, or the state of not being married, characterizes the clergy of the Catholic Church in the United States. A permanent deacon can be married, but if his wife should die, he is not permitted to remarry. In this way, ordained men can give their lives wholly to the service of others and not be torn between their obligations to loved ones and the Church community.

In the Roman Catholic Church, women cannot be ordained. There has been much controversy about this. The pope's position is that since Christ established the sacraments and women have never been ordained, this is something that cannot be done.

BRINGING SACRAMENTS TO PEOPLE

Born in 1786, a time between the American and French Revolutions, Jean Vianney grew up on his family's farm in a small French village. By the time he was four years old, all churches in France were closed by government order. Outlawed priests came to the Vianney farmhouse during the night to celebrate the Eucharist secretly with the family and with their neighbors.

Young Jean understood that the priests and people were risking their lives to have Mass. He himself made his first Communion and first confession in secret.

As a youngster, Jean considered becoming a priest himself. But he had to work with his parents on the farm to help support the family. He was not even able to go to school. When he was sixteen, the French government allowed the churches to reopen. Jean told his parents then about his desire to become a priest. At first his father refused permission, but Abbé Balley, a priest in a nearby village, convinced Jean's father to let his son study with him. Later Jean went to the seminary at Lyons, but he failed his courses and was asked to leave. So Abbé Balley continued to teach him. Jean was not confirmed until he was twenty-one. Eight years later, on Abbé Balley's recommendation, Jean was finally ordained a priest.

Father Jean Vianney was a pastor in the small village of Ars, about twenty miles from his home. The townspeople were not religious and they sometimes made life difficult for their new pastor. However, he prayed and fasted, visited their homes, taught catechism, gave most of his possessions to the poor, and preached strong sermons. Within a few years, Father Vianney had dramatically changed the lives of his parishioners. Popularly known as the Curé of Ars, Father Vianney became famous all over France for his remarkable ability to help people through the sacrament of Reconciliation.

Catholics traveled great distances to be absolved by this holy priest.

Before long, Father Vianney was spending most of his day and much of the night celebrating this sacrament. He sat in the small confessional for hours in summer and in the freezing winter cold, bringing the mercy of Christ to people each day. He did this for twenty-five years. By the time he died in 1859 at age seventy-three, people considered him a saint. Pope Pius XI canonized him in 1925 and named him patron of parish priests four years later. We celebrate the feast of Saint John Vianney each August 4.

Activity

Briefly describe what someone might mean by saying that Jean Vianney was a sacrament of God's love in Christ for others.

_____

_____

_____

_____

OTHER SIGNS OF CHRIST'S PRESENCE

The sacraments were instituted by Christ, but there are other signs and actions that remind us of Christ's presence as well. We call such a blessing, action, or object a **sacramental**.

A sacramental is not the same as a sacrament. Sacramentals do not give us the grace of the Holy Spirit in and of themselves the way sacraments do. Sacramentals give grace by the Church's prayer and remind us of the presence of Christ.

A sacramental always includes a prayer, often with a sign, such as the laying on of hands, the sign of the cross, or the sprinkling of holy water. Other sacramentals include the veneration of relics, the rosary, the wearing of medals, pilgrimages, and visits to shrines. These expressions of our faith can remind us of Christ's presence in our lives and this, in

turn, can help us to become holier, more faith-filled people.

Another important type of sacramental is a blessing. When we bless someone or something, we are praising and thanking God for giving us him, her, or it. By praying a blessing, we praise God for the gifts he gives us—the people in our lives, meals, objects, and even places.

Some blessings have a deeper purpose. These may consecrate, or dedicate, persons to God—such as when a man or woman joins a religious order. Other blessings consecrate things to God—such as when an altar or vestments are blessed.

Sacramentals remind us of the presence of Christ in our lives. They are not the source of magical powers and do not contain holiness. They are signs and actions that, when accompanied by prayer, can help us to become more open and aware of Christ's action in our lives.

Activity

For each sacramental listed below, explain how you think it might remind someone of Christ's presence and action in his or her life.

Praying the rosary _____

_____

_____

Hanging a crucifix in a bedroom _____

_____

_____

Visiting a shrine _____

_____

_____

Saying grace before and after meals _____

_____

_____

Making the sign of the cross with holy

water _____

_____

_____

_____

_____

_____

Activity

How does a sacramental differ from a sacrament?

_____

_____

_____

_____

_____

_____

_____

Vocabulary

sacramental: a blessing, an action, or an object that reminds us of Christ's presence with us

PRAYING WITH HOLY WATER

Holy water is one of the most common sacramentals. Because water is necessary for the survival of all forms of life, it is a symbol of life. No one knows when water began to be blessed before it was used in Baptism and other Christian rituals. The simplest way to bless water is to pray over it and then make the sign of the cross over the water. Usually this is done by a priest.

In addition to Baptism, holy water can be used to bless people at Mass on Sundays, for example. Sometimes a green leafy branch is dipped into a bowl of holy water and then the water is sprinkled on the assembled people. More frequently, however, the water is sprinkled by using a handheld cylinder called an aspergillum.

We may bless ourselves upon entering a church by dipping our fingertips into a holy water font. And we may use holy water in our homes to bless those objects and places we use every day.

All these uses of holy water remind us of our Baptism and call us to live as Jesus taught us. While water is a sign of the sacrament of Baptism, when we use holy water to bless ourselves and other people and objects, we are using it as a sacramental.

Most of us were probably baptized when we were infants and do not remember the promises that our parents and godparents made for us at that time. It can be meaningful to renew our baptismal promises from time to time to remind ourselves of this important sacrament that we have already received. After renewing the baptismal promises, use holy water to make the sign of the cross.

Leader: Let us renew the promises we made in Baptism, when we rejected Satan and his works and promised to serve God faithfully in the holy Catholic Church. Do you reject sin, so as to live in the freedom of God's children?

All: I do.

Leader: Do you believe in God, the Father Almighty, creator of heaven and earth?

All: I do.

Leader: Do you believe in Jesus Christ, his only Son, our Lord, who was born of the Virgin Mary, was crucified, died, and was buried, rose from the dead, and is now seated at the right hand of the Father?

All: I do.

Leader: Do you believe in the Holy Spirit, the holy Catholic Church, the communion of saints, the forgiveness of sins, the resurrection of the body, and life everlasting?

All: I do.

Activity

How can you use the sacramental of holy water in your daily life?

_____

_____

_____

Circle **T** if the sentence is true. Circle **F** if the sentence is false.

1. Sacraments do not really make Christ present to us, they are just symbolic.
   T   F

2. Jesus disregarded the symbols of the Jewish faith.   T   F

3. A sacramental shares God's grace with us through its own holiness and power.   T   F

4. The early Christians called signs and actions of Jesus' presence and activity, "sacraments."   T   F

5. The seven sacraments were formally defined by the Church at the Second Vatican Council.
   T   F

Group the seven sacraments into their three categories.

1. Sacraments of initiation

   _____

   _____

2. Sacraments of forgiveness and healing

   _____

3. Sacraments of service and commitment

   _____

Respond to the following questions based on what you have learned in this chapter.

1. What is a *sacrament*?

   _____

   _____

2. To what actions do the sacraments call us?

   _____

   _____

   _____

   _____

And behold, I am with you always, until the end of the age.
Matthew 28:20

3. Discuss why we need the Church and sacraments to celebrate Christ's presence in our lives.

12 A Eucharistic People

SPECIAL CELEBRATIONS

Very often, when we want to celebrate something special, our celebration centers around a meal of some kind: birthday parties, award banquets, wedding receptions, and family reunions.

When we share meals together, we share more than food. We share conversation, memories, one another's company, one another's troubles and triumphs, and one another's presence, pride, and joy. We renew and strengthen existing relationships as well as establish new ones.

WHAT BRINGS PEOPLE TOGETHER?

Activity

Describe a celebration meal you were part of and particularly enjoyed. Mention the group you were with and the celebration's purpose, the presence of any people special to you, any special food or drink, conversation or memories shared.

_____

_____

_____

_____

_____

SPECIAL MEALS WITH JESUS

The Gospels tell us that Jesus shared many meals with many different people. Throughout his years of ministry, he ate with his disciples, his friends, tax collectors, and those who were considered sinners.

Around the feast of Passover, Jesus gathered his friends to partake of a very special meal, which we have come to call the Last Supper.

At this meal, Jesus did something uniquely different. "Then he took the bread, said the blessing, broke it, and gave it to them, saying, 'This is my body, which will be given for you, do this in memory of me.' And likewise the cup after they had eaten, saying, 'This cup is the new covenant in my blood, which will be shed for you' " (Luke 22:19–20).

Jesus transformed this ordinary Jewish meal with his apostles into the memorial of his sacrifice to his Father for our salvation. He is the Lamb of God, the bread broken for all people. He is the cup of wine, the blood poured out to save us from death.

Furthermore, Jesus invited his followers to continue sharing the meal, promising them that whenever they did so, he would be with them. And so, we know that Jesus himself is present with us when we share the Eucharist together.

Activity

How does Jesus keep his promise to us?

_____

_____

Look up and read each of these passages from Scripture. Use the questions below as points of discussion with your class.

> John 13:1–17
> 1 Corinthians 11:23–26
> Luke 24:13–35
> John 21:1–14

1. In John's account of the Last Supper, what did Jesus do to demonstrate that remembering him meant serving one another?

2. In Luke's resurrection story, how did the disciples recognize the presence of Jesus?

3. In John's resurrection account, how did the disciples know that the man on the shore was Jesus?

4. What do you think verse 26 of the passage from 1 Corinthians 11 means?

5. Which verse in the Corinthians passage shows Jesus' ministry being carried out?

CELEBRATION OF THE EUCHARIST

After Jesus returned to God, the Christian community gathered regularly on Sunday, the "Lord's Day," for the "breaking of the bread." This meal was often joined to a regular sharing of food. As time went on, however, the ritual meal soon became separate. Other elements were added to the meal: an opening greeting, one or more Scripture readings, a homily, prayers of petition, the sharing of the meal, and a formal dismissal.

Eventually the celebration of the Eucharist everywhere came to include a scriptural prayer service combined with the ritual meal. All Christian communities followed the same pattern, but each developed its own style. For example, even though there were prayers, Scripture readings, and hymns, these varied from place to place.

By the time Christianity had become the established religion in the Roman Empire and large churches had been built, the celebration of the Eucharist had evolved into different forms. In the eastern part of the empire, where the emperor lived in Constantinople, the Mass, called the Divine Liturgy, was celebrated in Greek, the language of the people there. And it was celebrated with elegance and great formality.

In the western parts of the empire, the Mass was celebrated in Latin, the common language. Here, too, the Mass became more formal. Throughout Christianity, bishops and priests presided at and led the Mass.

The word **Mass** comes from the Latin word *missa*, meaning "sent." This word was used at the end of the celebration of the Eucharist.

Over the centuries, attitudes about the Mass shifted from seeing it as a meal between friends to seeing it as a formal and elaborate ritual of sacred mystery and holiness. As fewer and fewer people knew Latin, the Mass seemed to become even more mysterious and more sacred. And since the clergy conducted the ritual and people participated by attending the Mass, it was no longer experienced simply as a meal of fellowship.

The Mass had become a ritual of such holiness and awe that Christ seemed far away and people seemed too sinful to be worthy of his presence. Many people stopped receiving Communion. Instead, they looked at and adored the host held high by the priest.

As time went on, there were attempts to help people better understand and participate in the celebration of the Eucharist. Some of these attempts were made in the late nineteenth and first part of the twentieth centuries. They reached their peak in the 1960s at the Second Vatican Council.

One of the major goals of the Council was to restore full participation for all who celebrated the Eucharist. The language of the Mass was changed from Latin to the vernacular, the language of the people. Altars, which had long been placed against the back walls of churches, were turned to face the people. The many roles that lay people had once exercised in celebrating the Eucharist were also restored: lectors, eucharistic ministers, hospitality ministers. The role of the assembly (the people) at the celebration of the Eucharist was once again of major importance.

Today we recognize that the celebration of the Eucharist is the celebration of all those who are present. Attention is placed on the presence of Christ not only in his body and blood under the appearances of bread and wine, but also in the Scriptures read and in the words and actions of the whole community. So the Eucharist has two main parts: the Liturgy of the Word and the Liturgy of the Eucharist. Those present at the Eucharist participate in and celebrate the presence of the risen Christ in all of life, his sacrificial death and resurrection, and their unity with him and with one another.

Activity

Imagine you have a non-Catholic friend who asks you to explain what the Mass is. Be sure to include your own experience.

_____

_____

_____

_____

_____

Vocabulary

Mass: another name for the Eucharist, taken from the Latin word *missa*, which was used at the end of the celebration.

WE BELIEVE

The Eucharist is the central celebration of the Church. Instituted by Christ, the Eucharist is a fellowship meal celebrating the presence of the risen Christ with his followers and their union with him and with one another. The Eucharist is a remembrance and a reenactment of the Last Supper, a celebration of the sacrificial death and resurrection of Jesus Christ, and a call to serve others.

Activity

Complete the following to express your experience of Mass.

List three feelings you think people probably experience most often at Mass.

_____

_____

_____

Name three words that describe what happens at Mass.

_____

_____

_____

Give words or phrases that describe how the celebration of the Eucharist looks, sounds, smells, and tastes.

_____

_____

_____

_____

_____

_____

A Thankful People

The Mass is the most important act of worship for Catholics. It is also referred to as the Lord's Supper, the breaking of the bread, and the memorial of the Lord's passion and resurrection. The Mass may also be called the Holy Sacrifice because it makes present Christ's sacrifice on the cross as well as the Church's offering to God of all that the Father has given us. It can also be referred to as the celebration of the Eucharist.

The word *Eucharist* comes from the Greek word *eucharistein*, which means "to give thanks." Eucharistein, in turn, comes from two other Greek words, *eu*, meaning "good" and *charis*, meaning "gift." Literally, and in the original sense, Eucharist means "to show good favor or thanks." When we call ourselves a Eucharistic People, we are saying that we are people filled with thanks for the gift of the presence of the risen Lord among us.

When we celebrate the Eucharist, we are giving thanks to God in Christ. When we share the body and blood of Christ at the Eucharist, we are committing ourselves to be thankful people, people who look for and celebrate the presence of the risen Christ in our lives.

The Eucharist is sometimes called the Most Blessed Sacrament because it can be considered the sacrament of all sacraments. It is also called Holy Communion because in this sacrament we unite ourselves with Christ as a single body of his believers.

THE PRESENCE OF CHRIST

In the celebration of the Eucharist we offer in thanksgiving what God has given us: bread and wine. We remember how Jesus gave us his body and blood at the Last Supper and how he sacrificed himself for us by dying on the cross. We also recognize his presence with us at Mass through the power of the Word and the Spirit.

There are two parts of the Mass: the Liturgy of the Word and the Liturgy of the Eucharist. During the Liturgy of the Word several Scripture passages are proclaimed. Jesus is especially present with us in the reading of the Gospel.

During the Liturgy of the Eucharist, we bring our gifts of bread and wine to the altar. The priest prays over the gifts and calls upon the Holy Spirit to change the bread and wine into the body and blood of Christ. Using the words and actions of Jesus at the Last Supper, the priest consecrates the bread and the wine.

Jesus is truly present under the appearances of the bread and wine we share at Mass. The Eucharist still has the appearance of ordinary bread and wine, but through the power of the Holy Spirit, has become Jesus' body and blood.

This sacred mystery, in which bread and wine are changed into the body and blood of Christ, is called **transubstantiation**.

The Eucharist unites us with Jesus and the Church community. Jesus is also present in the people gathered to celebrate the Eucharist, in the Word that is proclaimed, and in the priest who presides.

The Eucharist is the central worship of Catholics. Because it is such an important part of who we are as followers of Jesus Christ, it can be very difficult to explain everything that Catholics believe about the Mass. As we grow in faith, we continue to learn more and deepen our understanding about the celebration of the Eucharist.

Vocabulary

transubstantiation: the mystery in which bread and wine are changed into the body and blood of Christ

WORSHIPING TOGETHER

When we celebrate the Eucharist, we celebrate with more than the words we pray and sing. We are aware of the presence of Christ with us in every detail of our celebration—the music we hear, the gestures and movements we make, the way the priest and others dress, and the sacred vessels we use.

The altar is the table around which we gather. It should be centrally located or raised up a step so everyone can see it. On or near the altar are candles and a crucifix. The sacramentary, the book containing the prayers of the Mass, is also on the altar. The lectionary is the book which contains the collection of readings from the Bible. These readings are arranged according to the liturgical year rather than in the order in which they are found in the Bible. The lectionary is placed on a nearby lectern, or pulpit, the stand from which Scripture is read by a lector and the priest or deacon. Another term for the lectern is the ambo.

The two principal vessels used during the Mass are the chalice, or cup, and the paten, or plate. During the Preparation of the Gifts, wine and water are brought to the altar in small bottles called cruets. The bread is also brought to the altar. The wine will be poured into the chalice, and the bread, usually in the shape of flat round wafers called hosts, will be placed on the paten.

In the church, there is probably a tabernacle, a safelike container in which consecrated hosts are kept. Tabernacles are frequently located to the side of the main altar and are carefully made and designed. A tabernacle might be lined with cedar or white or gold silk. The ciborium is the covered cup-like container or dish which contains the consecrated hosts. A sanctuary lamp is usually kept lit near the tabernacle to show that the Blessed Sacrament is reserved there.

LITURGICAL VESTMENTS

At the celebration of the Eucharist, the priest and deacon wear vestments. The alb is a long, loose-fitting, white tunic worn under the other vestments. The cincture is the cord used as a belt for the alb. Over this the priest wears a chasuble. The chasuble is decorated in the appropriate color for the time of the liturgical year. During Lent, for example, a chasuble would be purple while during Ordinary Time it will be green. A stole, a narrow strip of cloth worn over the shoulders, is worn either under or over the chasuble. The stole is a sign of priestly office. The stole is also in the appropriate color for the liturgical season.

There are other ministerial vestments as well. A cassock is a full-length black robe. A surplice is a white linen half-robe with wide sleeves that is worn over a cassock.

Activity

Write how each of the following helps you experience the presence of Christ.

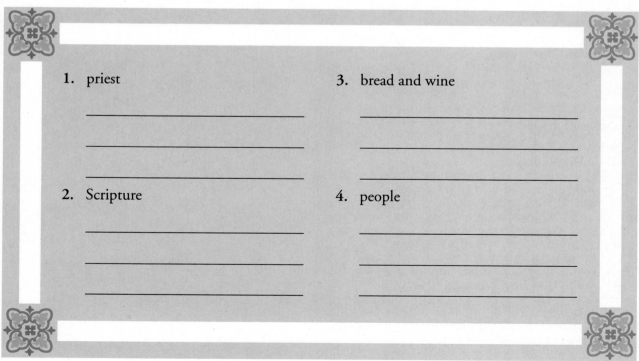

1. priest

    _____

    _____

    _____

2. Scripture

    _____

    _____

    _____

3. bread and wine

    _____

    _____

    _____

4. people

    _____

    _____

    _____

A BRILLIANT THEOLOGIAN

John Damascene (645–750) came from a well-to-do family. His father held important administrative positions in the government in Damascus, Syria. John was well-educated and began his career in government service, following in his father's footsteps. Yet after awhile he felt something was missing in his life and he entered a monastery near Jerusalem and was ordained a priest.

In the monastery, John led the life of an intellectual. He taught other monks, preached in Jerusalem, and wrote over 150 theological works. From time to time, bishops asked his advice on questions of faith.

John was devoted to Mary, and the sermons he preached about the Mother of God are among his most famous works. He preached at least three sermons at places in Palestine where important events in the life of Mary were believed to have occurred.

Although brilliant, John was very humble. He did not want to become famous for his own opinions. Instead, he wanted to strengthen people's understanding of the Church's teachings. He was careful not to create new ideas about Christian beliefs. He was proud to stay within the traditional thinking of the Church.

Today John's theological writings are still read. The *Catechism of the Catholic Church* contains references to his works. From John Damascene we learn more about the human and divine natures of Jesus Christ as well as how Christ is present with us today at Mass and in the sacraments. John explained that it was through the Holy Spirit that the bread and wine offered at Mass become the body and blood of Christ.

John died at his monastery near Jerusalem in 750. Around the twelfth century his body was removed from the monastery and taken to Constantinople where it was venerated. St. John Damascene is considered a great theologian and his feast is December 4.

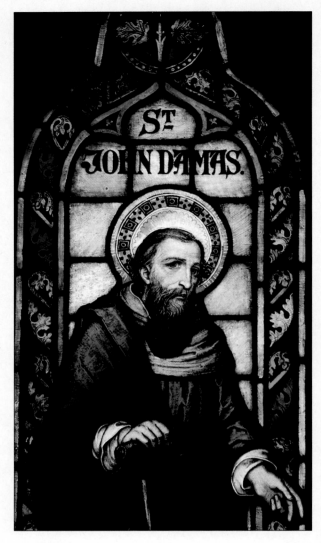

Activity

What are some of the contributions that St. John Damascene made to the Church?

_____

_____

_____

_____

What was St. John Damascene's attitude toward fame?

_____

_____

HOW TO GET MORE OUT OF MASS

The only way to get more out of going to Mass is to put more into participating in the celebration of the Eucharist. It is helpful to realize that Mass is not a performance for entertainment purposes. It is a ritual, and ritual actions do not become meaningful when they are varied and exciting but when people enter into their meaning through quiet, reflective attention and repetition. When we come to celebrate the Eucharist, we lift our minds and hearts to God in prayer.

A church is a sacred place, and celebrating the Eucharist is a sacred action. Human beings have long known that certain places and actions are especially powerful in making God's presence known to us. Feelings associated with the sacred include awe, peace, and joy.

It can help to find a good place to sit—not too hot, not too cold, and no glare from the sun shining through the windows. Use the hymnal, a book of the readings, or a missal of the Mass to follow along if the prayers are not completely familiar. Pay attention to the words and try to join in. Listen to the homily. Stand, kneel, and sit when everyone else does.

The Mass is not a performance that is going to inspire anyone who just happens to walk into the church. Participating as fully as possible is the best way to get more out of Mass.

Activity

What are some common problems that people have concentrating at Mass?

_____

_____

What are some things you think people can do to overcome these difficulties?

_____

_____

While it's true that prayer can occur outside of Mass and people might feel close to God at times other than Mass, what do you think makes Mass a special opportunity to deepen one's relationship with God?

_____

_____

PRAYING AT A FELLOWSHIP MEAL

For centuries, Christians not only celebrated the Eucharist together, but shared other meals as well. They did this to become closer to one another in fellowship and mutual support. Such a meal is called an agape, or love feast. Agape is a Greek word for love, or charity. Agape does not refer to romantic love but to the selfless giving for which the earliest Christian communities were known.

Love feasts were held to help Christians encourage one another in imitating Christ's love for everyone. The food was simple and plain. Prayers might be said and hymns sung, but this was not a formal ritual. Sometimes the poor and the suffering were invited to share in the meals as a form of charity and poor relief. Other times an agape might be held to honor the dead and the martyrs.

There were apparently many forms of agape, but the main intention of all of them was for Christians to encourage one another in imitating Christ.

Today there are many occasions in our parishes and communities for which an agape might be held. Small groups of Christians could meet to share food, pray together, discuss their faith, and study Scripture. An agape could become an opportunity to share a meal with those who are lonely, weak, poor, or in need of support. An agape could also be a fundraising event to relieve some crisis or social problem.

Activity

Plan an agape for your class. Tell why you would hold the agape.

_____

_____

What prayers or Scripture readings would you include?

_____

_____

What simple food would you serve?

_____

_____

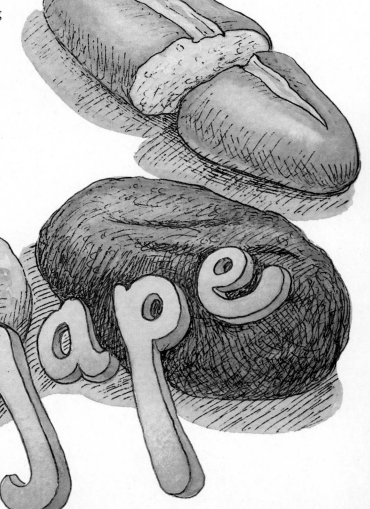

CHAPTER REVIEW

Complete the following sentences by filling in the blanks.

1. Before he died, Jesus shared a meal with his disciples. We call this meal the

   _____ .

2. At first, the Mass was celebrated in the two main languages of the Roman Empire:

   _____ and _____ .

3. People's participation in the Eucharist was renewed because of the work done at

   _____ .

4. The word *Eucharist* means _____ .

5. The term _____ refers to the real presence of Christ under
   the appearances of bread and wine consecrated at Mass.

Write a paragraph to describe the elements of the Mass in which we recognize the presence
of Christ.

_____

_____

_____

_____

Respond to the following questions based on what you have learned in
this chapter.

1. What does the word *Mass* mean?

   _____

   _____

2. What is so special about the food and drink of the Eucharist?

   _____

   _____

3. Discuss why you think many young people feel that Mass is boring.

**Do this in
memory of me.**
Luke 22:19

Complete the web below by summarizing key ideas about each topic that you have studied in this unit. Draw lines from each oval and write the important words and phrases on these lines.

Mass

Prayer

We Are Worshipful

Sacraments

Creative Signs and Expressions

UNIT **3** REVIEW

Match the words in Column 1 with the definitions in Column 2.

Column 1

1. Liturgy of the Hours
2. meditation
3. contemplation
4. icons
5. ritual
6. sacrament
7. *missa*

Column 2

_____ sacred images of Jesus, his mother Mary, and the saints

_____ the Church's official prayer at certain hours of the day and night

_____ a Latin word once used to dismiss the people at the end of the Eucharist

_____ a prayerful "seeing" of God in nature or people

_____ a visible sign of invisible grace

_____ prayerful reflection on an event, object, truth, or text

_____ a set of symbolic actions

Complete each sentence by supplying the correct word(s).

serve	resurrection	Mass	Liturgy of the Eucharist	sacramentals
Last Supper	Incarnation	faith	signs	Liturgy of the Word	grace	creation

1. Prayer with images, sounds, and symbols reflects our Catholic belief in God's

   _____ and in Christ's _____ .

2. The seven sacraments are special _____ of Christ's

   _____ and our _____ .

3. Blessings, actions, or objects that remind us of Christ's presence and care are called

   _____ .

4. The Eucharist has two main parts: the _____

   and the _____ .

5. The Eucharist, or _____ , is a remembrance, or reenactment,

   of the _____ , a celebration of the sacrificial death and

   _____ of Jesus Christ, and a call to _____ others.

UNIT  3 REVIEW

Identify the sacraments according to category and then write a sentence about each one.

Sacraments of Initiation

1. _____

2. _____

3. _____

Sacraments of Healing

1. _____

2. _____

Sacraments of Commitment

1. _____

2. _____

Think about and answer the following question. How is the Mass our greatest act of worship?

_____

_____

_____

_____

_____

_____

_____

_____

Getting Along with Adults

Adolescence is an exciting and often chaotic time of change in a young person's life. It is a time of letting go of childish ways and becoming more adult. It is also a time for striving to be more of your own person with an identity separate from your family.

Freedom and independence are special priorities during adolescence. It may seem that your parents or guardians and other adults are too strict about granting these to you. This is because with independence comes additional responsibility and sometimes adults worry that a young person cannot or will not handle this responsibility. Tension and conflicts can occur as you and the adults around you try to discover a proper balance between your need for freedom and what is reasonable, appropriate, and safe.

Activity

In what areas of your life do you want more freedom?

1. _____

2. _____

3. _____

How can you convince the adults in your life that you can handle more freedom and independence? Here are some ideas.

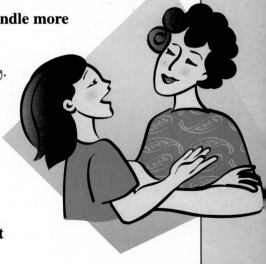

- Be able to say "yes" to what is right and "no" to what is wrong.
- Be able to set and keep limits on what you will and will not do.
- Communicate honestly with the adults in your life.
- Share with the adults in your life the mistakes you have made as well as the successes you achieve.
- Tell the adults in your life what you have learned about the mistakes you have made.

What are some of the most common issues that cause conflict between young people and adults?

A Parent's Letter

When Kate was graduating from the eighth grade, her mother wrote her a letter. This letter let Kate know more about how her mother felt and how her mother recognized that she was growing up.

Dear Kate,

You have now successfully completed the first eight years of your education and soon you will be moving on to high school. You bring me great joy and I want you to know that I love you very much. My hope for you is that you will always love yourself as much as I love you. If you do, I know the decisions you make will be good ones.

I know you think that I'm overprotective and that I worry about you too much. I guess I think that's part of my job as a parent. I am trying, however, to recognize that you are growing and maturing and need more freedom to make your own choices.

It's hard for me to let you go because I know our world is not always a very friendly place. I expect that you will make mistakes, yet I want our relationship to be one in which you can share those mistakes with me.

I will always be here for you. We can solve every problem together. May God bless you and keep you safe on your journey toward adulthood.

Love,
Mom

Activity

Write a letter to one of your parents, guardians, or other significant adults telling about the difficulties and joys of growing up. Describe the kind of relationship you want to have with him or her. Include any advice you would give to him or her about raising you.

_____

_____

_____

_____

_____

Prayer

Jesus, help me to find my way during this time of change and growth. Help me to live honestly in my relationships with others and to act responsibly. Help my parents and guardians to recognize my steps toward maturity and to be understanding when I make mistakes.

OPENING DOORS
A Take-Home Magazine™

LISTENING

How many commandments did God give to Noah on Mount Sinai? If you said ten, you weren't really "listening" to the question. Noah had the ark. Moses had the commandments. (See if you can stump your family with this one.)

Who's the best listener in your family? the worst? Poll family members to decide who deserves these titles in your family.

What makes someone a good listener? Listening requires you to attend closely to what people say and to understand what they are saying. Since it is a skill, like any other skill, it requires practice. If your grandfather is difficult to follow sometimes, then you should listen to him more often, not less, in order to become a better listener.

Listening requires you to have *empathy* for others. Empathy is the ability to understand how others are feeling. When your dad yells at you for not keeping your room neat, the empathetic listener might realize that part of what your dad might be feeling is the stress of being a single parent and not just anger over a sloppy room.

Listening requires you to think more about others. Sometimes we think so much about what we are going to say next that we forget to listen to the other person. If you answered that God gave Noah ten commandments, you were thinking more about what you thought you read than what was really there. Listening can be like that. If you're mentally rehearsing what you're going to say to your sister in an argument, you may miss that she actually agrees with some of what you've said already. What kind of listener do you think Jesus was? What qualities did he have that helped him to be a good listener?

FAMILY ACTIVITY

Tonight talk to your family's best listener. Ask what makes him or her a good listener. What qualities does he or she have that make a good listener? Ask why he or she thinks that listening is so important.

PRESSURE

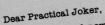

Dear Practical Joker,

You probably know that you should apologize to your classmate. From your letter you also seem to have learned not always to go with the crowd but to follow what you know is right. This takes courage, but you have already taken the first step — realizing beforehand that although the joke was funny, it might not have been worth the consequences.

Anita

Dear Anita,

I'm sick of my best friend. She never wants to have any fun. I want to go to a great party with the most popular kids in school, but of course she doesn't want to go. She says there's going to be drinking at the party. Just because we're at the party doesn't mean we have to drink. I don't want to go to this party by myself. How can I get my best friend to go with me?

Party Person

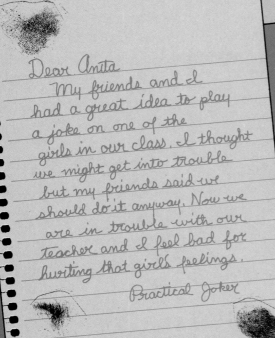

Dear Anita
My friends and I had a great idea to play a joke on one of the girls in our class. I thought we might get into trouble but my friends said we should do it anyway. Now we are in trouble with our teacher and I feel bad for hurting that girl's feelings.

Practical Joker

Dear Family Baby,

No one gets to do what he or she wants to do all the time. Responsibilities and caring for others come first many times in life. Check with other family members. You might be surprised to find out that your dad would really rather stay home and watch TV but his love and responsibility toward your aunt makes him put aside what he wants to do for her sake.

Anita

ANITA

Dear Party Person,
If your best friend really does not want to go, you should respect her decision. It sounds like she does not want to go because she is not comfortable with the people who will be there and their likely behavior. You should consider her reasoning yourself. Are you sure you are not confusing your desire to escape boredom with a willingness to do anything? You probably will feel pressured to drink at this party. Instead of causing problems with your best friend, it might be better to think of something that both of you can enjoy and avoid a potentially bad situation.

Anita

Dear Anita,
My family is driving me crazy. They treat me like a little kid. My best friend's family lets him have more freedom than I do. I never have any fun. My friend wants to go to the mall on Saturday, but I have to go visit some old aunt. It's not fair.

Family Baby

When do you feel pressured?

_____ to be part of a group
_____ to rebel against authority (teachers, parents)
_____ to prove yourself
_____ to joke around/act silly
_____ to say and do things you don't mean
_____ to drink or take drugs
_____ to stay out late
_____ other: _____

Inside yourself you know what you *should* do. That's why you feel pressured. You feel the tug between what you should do and what others are encouraging you to do. How can you handle the pressure?

It takes guts to walk away from a potentially bad situation. It takes courage to say, "No, I can't," or "No, I don't want to." Sometimes it takes more courage than you have. It's easier if you avoid getting yourself into a bad position in the first place.

Here are some guidelines.
1. Avoid trouble *before* it happens.
2. Think things through. Don't assume that because you're with your friends everything will be fine. Play with fire and you're going to get burned. Use common sense. Don't say, "Oh, I'll only try it once." Once is all it takes.
3. Do not put yourself in places where trouble is likely to occur. If you are with friends and some guys turn up who get into trouble, you can bet that there's going to be trouble with them around.
4. Be true to yourself and to the Christian values and beliefs that you have been taught.

When all else fails, say no and walk away. It's better to have one moment of embarrassment than a major problem.

No one can avoid pressure all the time, but you can minimize it by avoiding situations and the people with whom trouble is likely to occur.

Sing, Sing a Song

The music we use at the celebration of the Eucharist not only is music we should enjoy hearing and singing; it is music that should help us to feel the presence of Jesus with his community.

List here some of your favorite songs (or music artists) which would NOT help your parish community feel the presence of Jesus at the celebration of the Eucharist.

_____

_____

_____

The music we use at Mass is liturgical music. That is, it should be music suitable to praise and worship God. Much of the music we listen to and enjoy is secular, that is, music that does not help us to focus on God. Secular music may be very good music. It may move us emotionally and even help us to understand ourselves and others better, but its purpose is not sacred. It is not meant to be used in worship. In sacred music, the words we sing are drawn from Scripture, the prayers of the Mass, or other prayers.

The music at Mass might be led by a song leader or the parish music minister. There might be a choir or a small group who sing as well. It is important that we sing at least some of the music used at Mass because we are there to participate in the eucharistic celebration. We are not there to watch a performance by music artists.

Many different instruments can be used. Most frequently, organs and guitars are played. Pianos, brass ensembles, and electronic keyboards also are used. Some singing might be done without instrument accompaniment. We call this type of singing a capella, singing in "chapel style" as monks and nuns did for centuries.

The music we sing at our eucharistic celebrations comes from many different sources. You might have heard Gregorian chant, traditional hymns like "Amazing Grace," classical music from composers like Beethoven and Bach, gospel music, folk music, and modern religious hymns. Parishes use many different hymnals and missalettes. Instrumental music may be played on organ and guitar, and this music also comes from many different sources.

What kind of music do you enjoy hearing and singing at worship with your parish community?

Sunday liturgies. Here are the parts of the Mass at which music is most commonly used.

Gathering Song

Gloria

Kyrie

Responsorial Psalm

Gospel Acclamation

Preparation of the Gifts

Holy, Holy, Holy

Memorial Acclamation

The Great Amen

Lamb of God

Communion Hymn

Closing Hymn

Circle the instruments below that you would use to create liturgical music.

It is possible to sing the entire Mass. Famous composers like Bach, Bernstein, and Duke Ellington have composed such Masses, although their compositions are not commonly sung at

piano	clarinet	ukulele
synthesizer	bassoon	harp
harpsichord	bagpipe	harmonica
organ	violin	steel drum
accordion	cello	electric drum
marimba	bass	bongos
trumpet	electric bass	snare drum
trombone	electric guitar	bass drum
tuba	acoustic guitar	tom-toms
saxophone	banjo	cowbell
flute	mandolin	handbells
piccolo	cymbals	maracas

CATHOLIC LEGEND and LORE

The story of the Holy Grail has been told by a number of different authors and there are many different versions. The best known comes from the tales told about King Arthur's court. According to the tales, the Holy Grail is the cup from which Jesus drank at the Last Supper. After Jesus' death and resurrection, Joseph of Arimathea had it and brought it to England where it disappeared. Others say that angels guard it or that knights guard it on a mountaintop. When it is approached by anyone who is not pure, the Grail disappears. This popular story has lived in the imaginations of people for nearly eight hundred years.

RELIGIOUS LIFE

Members of religious orders take vows of poverty, chastity, and obedience. Some religious orders also have a vow of stability, which is a vow to stay in the monastery or convent where the members made their profession. This vow is meant to help the religious community to be more like a family. Diocesan priests are bound to celibacy and obedience to their bishops, but do not take a vow of poverty.

DID YOU KNOW?

Saint Francis of Assisi was first to create a crèche, or manger scene, for Christmas. He preached at this scene on each of the twelve days of Christmas.

Looking Ahead

In Unit 4 you will learn the basic beliefs of the Church. The Church's creeds, developed over centuries, sum up Catholic beliefs about God, other human beings, creation, and the meaning and purpose of life. We know and worship God as Trinity—Father, Son, and Spirit. Filled with trust in God's justice and mercy, we look forward to the final coming of God's kingdom at the end of time.

WE ARE
FAITHFUL

What brings people together?

13 A BELIEVING PEOPLE

EVERYDAY BELIEFS

> NAME A BELIEF ABOUT LIFE THAT YOU HOLD STRONGLY.

What do you think it means to be a teenager? Ideas about teens and their lives can be seen on television, in the movies, and in music.

What are some commonly held beliefs about teenagers?

_____

_____

_____

What do you believe about teenagers?

_____

_____

_____

Why do you think some of these beliefs may be true?

_____

_____

_____

Why do you think some of these beliefs may be false?

_____

_____

_____

WHAT WE HOLD DEAR

Although the followers of Jesus believed in him, they did not have a lengthy, formal set of **beliefs**. The Church began with men and women whose lives were touched by Jesus Christ. The disciples of Jesus lived with him during his ministry. They watched him die, and then they experienced him alive again. On Pentecost they experienced the power of his Spirit. Their **faith**, their firm belief in Jesus, changed their lives.

Jesus calls us to have strong faith. He asks us to believe in the promise of the kingdom of God—the fulfillment of God's rule of peace and justice at the end of time—and to hold this belief close to our hearts. He told us the following parable to help us understand and treasure the presence of God in our lives.

> The kingdom of heaven is like a treasure buried in the field, which a person finds and hides again, and out of joy goes and sells all that he has and buys that field.
>
> *Matthew 13:44*

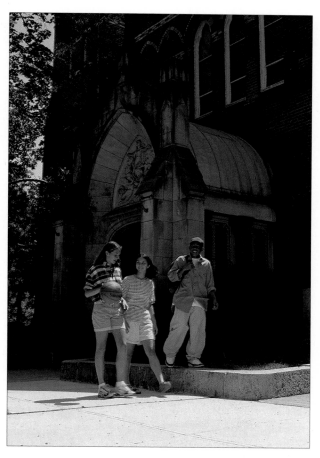

Give an example of a Christian belief that is important to you.

_____

_____

Why is this belief important to you?

_____

_____

Activity

What are several of the most important Christian beliefs?

_____

_____

_____

_____

Where do you think these beliefs came from?

_____

_____

_____

_____

Faith and Doctrine

The experiences of the first Christians raised questions for them. "Who is Jesus Christ—really?" "What difference does he make?" "How does accepting him and his teachings affect our lives and our Jewish beliefs?"

Their questions forced the early Christians to rethink their beliefs, all that they held to be true, and to consider how they wanted to express their faith. They showed what they believed by how they lived and prayed and by the images and symbols they created.

The early Christians believed that Jesus was divine as well as human. So they gave him the name *Lord*, a title that previously had only referred to God in the Old Testament. For example, "Jesus Christ is Lord" (Philippians 2:11).

This raised another basic question for the Jewish Christians: "How could Jesus be God, since there is only one God?" Even before the last book of the New Testament was completed, the new Christians expressed their faith in one God who is Father, Son, and Spirit. This belief is stated in the instruction of Jesus about baptizing new disciples. "All power in heaven and on earth has been given to me. Go, therefore, and make disciples of all nations, baptizing them in the name of the Father, and of the Son, and of the holy Spirit" (Matthew 28:18–19).

As Christians were asked about their faith, they gradually developed statements that expressed their beliefs. These are called **doctrines**, or official Church statements of belief. These doctrines state the great mysteries that the Church holds dear.

Heresy and Truth

Questions about Christian beliefs sometimes led to intense debate within the Church. In the early centuries of Christianity, several disagreements about doctrine shaped how Christians would express their beliefs down through the centuries.

In the fourth century, a priest named Arius, from Alexandria in Egypt, taught that, in the Trinity, God the Son was inferior to God the Father. He also taught that the Son of God was created by God. Arius said that even though Jesus Christ was God's highest creation and more than a mere man, he was not divine in the same way as God. The Council of Nicea in 325

condemned Arius' position and decreed that God the Father and God the Son are of the same substance.

A bishop of Constantinople named Nestorius believed that human nature was too sinful to be combined with divinity in Jesus Christ. In fact, Nestorius considered the human Jesus and the divine Son of God to be two persons. The Council of Ephesus in 431 taught that Jesus has two natures, human and divine, but that Jesus is one Person. Twenty years later the Council of Chalcedon restated the Church's teachings about Jesus.

Perhaps the most threatening of all the theological disputes was the lengthy and sophisticated dispute with Gnosticism. This heretical philosophical approach was heavily influenced by non-Christian Greek ideas. It taught that God was remote and separated from the world. In fact, all matter was evil and Jesus Christ, as the Son of God, would never have taken on our sinful human nature. The influence of Gnosticism lasted for centuries and heavily influenced Christianity. Bishops and theologians such as Irenaeus refuted the teachings of the Gnostics in detail.

In later times, theologians such as John Henry Newman (1801–1890) recognized that the Church, in interpreting the teachings of Jesus Christ, had developed its doctrines over the centuries and expressed them with more and more detail. Today, the Holy Spirit still empowers the Church to distinguish between false teachings and authentic insights into doctrine.

Activity

What are some of the questions that you or people you know have about the Church's teachings?

_____

_____

_____

_____

_____

_____

How do you think you might find the answers to these questions?

_____

_____

_____

_____

_____

_____

_____

Vocabulary

doctrines: official Church statements of belief

✦ ✦ ✦ ✦ ✦ ✦ ✦ ✦ ✦ ✦ ✦ ✦ ✦ ✦ ✦

PROFESSING A CREED

The faith of Christians is professed in summary statements called **creeds**. One of the earliest creedal statements is found in Paul's first letter to the people of Corinth:

> For I handed on to you as of first importance what I also received: that Christ died for our sins in accordance with the scriptures; that he was buried; that he was raised on the third day in accordance with the scriptures; that he appeared to Kephas, then to the Twelve.
>
> *1 Corinthians 15:3–5*

As more people wanted to become Christians, the Christian communities developed a creed in the form of questions that were asked as part of the baptismal ritual. The new Christian answered each question with "I believe." Here is the wording of an early creed.

> Do you believe in God the Father Almighty? Do you believe in Jesus Christ, the Son of God, born of the Holy Spirit of the Virgin Mary, who was crucified under Pontius Pilate and died [and was buried], and rose on the third day, alive from the dead, and ascended into heaven and sat down on the right hand of the Father, who will come to judge the living and the dead?

> Do you believe in the Holy Spirit, and the holy Church, and the resurrection of the flesh?

These questions, with several additions, are still asked of people today when they are about to be baptized. The additions reflect further developments in Christian belief.

The early Christians developed a more extensive creed, which is called the Apostles' Creed. The Apostles' Creed states the beliefs that are central to our faith: the Trinity, the life of the Church, and eternal life. It reminds us about the content of our beliefs.

Another important statement of Christian beliefs is the creed that is part of each Sunday celebration of the Eucharist, the Nicene Creed. This developed as Christians in the fourth century expressed their belief in how Jesus could be both a man and God, both God's Son and the son of Mary. The creed was formulated at the Council of Nicea in 325, developed a bit more, and reached its present form at the First Council of Constantinople in 381.

The Church continues to hold dear to its heart its faith in God and in his will for all humankind. In each century, believing Catholics take on the challenge to profess the ancient statements of faith.

DOCTRINE TODAY

In every generation new problems give rise to new questions. These continue to challenge us to rediscover the meaning of our faith in Jesus Christ. New insights give us new ways to remain faithful to the beliefs for which early Christians lived and died.

The Church continues to develop its understanding of what it means to be a follower of Jesus. This is called the **development of doctrine**. It is an attempt to understand and express the faith clearly. Just as all the Christians before us, we are given the opportunity to restate the traditional faith in words that respond to the issues and concerns that people have in our world today.

Activity

Express in your own words one of the statements of the Nicene Creed. Restate the belief in words that relate to your experience of everyday living.

_____

_____

_____

_____

_____

_____

_____

_____

_____

Vocabulary

creed: a formal summary of basic beliefs

development of doctrine: the growth of the Church's understanding of what it means to be a follower of Jesus Christ

◆ ◆ ◆ ◆ ◆ ◆ ◆ ◆ ◆ ◆ ◆ ◆ ◆ ◆ ◆ ◆

WE BELIEVE

The Church expresses its faith in various ways. These include the way Catholics live and worship and the kind of images and symbols used in worship. Faith is also expressed in formal statements, or creeds. These creeds developed in response to new questions and new ways of understanding. They express the core of what Catholic Christians believe. The Church continues to develop its understanding and expression of these basic beliefs or doctrines.

Activity

Imagine that you have come from another country or culture and are learning about what it means to be an American from watching television. Complete the following flowchart about what you have learned.

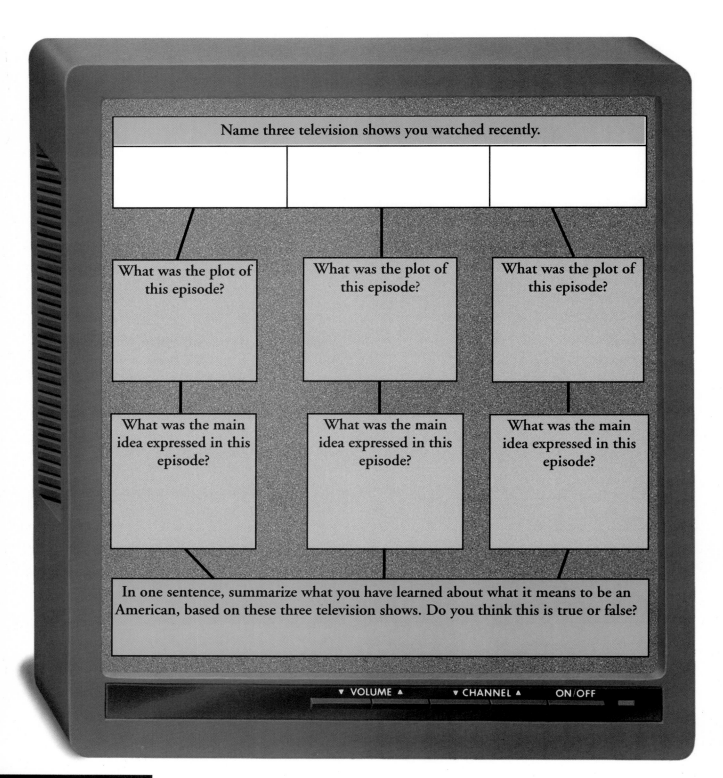

Name three television shows you watched recently.

What was the plot of this episode?

What was the plot of this episode?

What was the plot of this episode?

What was the main idea expressed in this episode?

What was the main idea expressed in this episode?

What was the main idea expressed in this episode?

In one sentence, summarize what you have learned about what it means to be an American, based on these three television shows. Do you think this is true or false?

▾ VOLUME ▴   ▾ CHANNEL ▴   ON/OFF

A Man of Strong Beliefs

John Henry Newman was born in London in 1801, the oldest of six children. The Newman family belonged to the Anglican Church.

During a five-month illness when he was a teenager, John read many books about Jesus. He became convinced that Jesus Christ is both human and divine. John became interested in the teachings of the early Church. He also became very aware of God's presence in him and around him. His new beliefs led him to change the direction of his life.

John Newman gradually recovered from his illness. He attended Oxford University. Even though he then decided to become an Anglican priest, he became more and more interested in the Catholic Church. After his ordination as an Anglican priest, he traveled through Europe and visited many Catholic churches and shrines.

Returning to Oxford, Newman became well-known as a preacher, teacher, and newspaper columnist. The Anglican bishops did not like some of his writings and eventually made him stop writing. He moved to a small town where he spent much time praying and rethinking his beliefs. He expressed his thoughts in a book called *An Essay on the Development of Christian Doctrine*. Newman's book showed how the Church's doctrines had developed over the centuries.

At that time, Newman lived with a few friends in a community of prayer. Through prayer and study, he came to accept the beliefs of the Catholic Church. Newman was received into the Roman Catholic Church in 1845. He worked with his friends to assist the poor immigrant working people who labored in the factories of the city of Birmingham. Not long afterward, he left England to study in Rome. He was ordained a Catholic priest in 1847.

Some Anglicans were angry with Newman for becoming Catholic. He was also strongly criticized by many Catholics because of his writings. His critics were especially angry about one article called "On Consulting the Faithful

in Matters of Doctrine." Nevertheless, Newman continued to live by his beliefs and to write about them.

When Newman was an old man, he was honored by Pope Leo XIII for his great contribution to the Catholic Church. He was named a cardinal. Few individuals have had such a profound effect on the Church's understanding of Catholic doctrine and its development. Almost every non-Catholic university in the United States today has a Newman Center where Catholic students can worship, study, and learn more about their beliefs.

Activity

How did John Newman come to know God's will for him?

_____

_____

_____

_____

_____

EXPRESSIONS OF FAITH

You have prayed the traditional creeds of the Church that were formulated centuries ago. They have been preserved as they were written, and they are spoken in the same words all over the world. Millions of Christians have lived by these beliefs and many have died for them.

Today, Catholics are writing creeds to express their own experiences, questions, and language. The ancient beliefs are preserved and developed in words that are more meaningful to those who write them. The following is an example of a creed that expresses the beliefs of African Catholics of the Masai tribe.

AN AFRICAN CREED

We believe in the one High God,
Who out of love created the beautiful world
    and everything in it.
He created people and wanted them to be
    happy in the world.
God loves the world
And every nation and tribe on the earth.
We have known this High God in the
    darkness.
And now we know him in the light.
God promised in the book of his word,
The Bible,
That he would save the world and
    all nations and tribes.
We believe that God
Made good his promise by sending his son,
Jesus Christ,
A man in the flesh, a Jew by tribe,
Born in a little village.
Who left his home and was always
    on safari doing good,
Curing people by the power of God,
Teaching them about God and humanity,

Showing that the meaning of religion
Is love.
He was rejected by his people,
Tortured and nailed hands and feet to a cross,
And died.
He lay buried in the grave,
But the hyenas did not touch him.
And on the third day he rose from the grave.
He ascended to the skies.
He is the Lord.
We believe that all our sins are forgiven
    through him.
All who have faith in him must be sorry for
    their sins,
Be baptized in the Holy Spirit of God,
Live the rules of love,
And share the bread together in love,
To announce the good news to others until
    Jesus comes again.
We are waiting for him.
He is alive. He lives.
This we believe.
Amen.

Members of the Masai tribe

OUR CATHOLIC BELIEFS

A creed is never a statement of an individual's belief. It is a statement of the beliefs that a group of people share and express together. You have read the Nicene Creed and the Masai Creed. You may be familiar with the Apostles' Creed. All of these creeds express the key ideas that are central to Christian faith. They do not reflect an individual's opinions. Creeds help Christians to recall and learn the important teachings that identify them as followers of Jesus Christ.

Activity

What are some of the central ideas that the Nicene Creed and the Masai Creed have in common?

_____

_____

_____

_____

Activity

Work with others to create a class creed that professes your Christian faith as a group. Begin by listing the most important Christian beliefs that members of your class share. Then work together to write your creed on the chalkboard. If you wish, refer to the Nicene Creed.

Central Christian Beliefs

1. _____
2. _____
3. _____
4. _____
5. _____

6. _____
7. _____
8. _____
9. _____
10. _____

PRAYING TO REAFFIRM OUR FAITH

FAITH AS A GIFT

Leader: Let us come together to meditate on our faith as a gift, as an assent, and as a challenge.

Reader 1:   When you were a child, you were too small to speak. When you were brought to your parish church to be baptized, you were greeted by the priest. Your parents spoke for you. Now you can speak for yourself.

Leader: What do you ask?

Students: Faith.

Leader: What does faith offer you?

Students: Eternal life with God.

FAITH AS AN ASSENT

Reader 2:   When you were a child, your godparents spoke for you. Now you can express your Christian beliefs yourself.

Students: (Read together the class creed or the Nicene Creed.)

FAITH AS A CHALLENGE

Reader 3:   Our faith leads us to face the challenge of living as followers of Christ Jesus. Reflect for a moment on one of the challenges that you find most difficult.

Describe in writing how you will try to meet this challenge in your life.

_____

_____

CHAPTER REVIEW

Circle the correct answer or answers to complete the following sentences.

1. The Church expresses its faith in these ways:
   a. the way its members live.
   b. the way its members worship.
   c. through creeds and doctrines.

2. Faith is
   a. a belief that is contrary to reason.
   b. a firm belief without having proof.
   c. a loving trust in someone or something.
   d. agreeing because adults say so.

3. Beliefs are
   a. what someone holds to be true or real.
   b. what we give up easily.
   c. what we do not pay much attention to.

4. A creed is
   a. a list of opinions about Church matters.
   b. a summary of the bishops' decisions.
   c. a formal summary of basic beliefs.

5. A doctrine is
   a. an official papal decree.
   b. an official Church statement of belief.
   c. a matter of opinion.

Respond to the following questions based on what you have learned in this chapter.

1. What is meant by the *development of doctrine*?

   _____

   _____

   _____

2. Why does the Church develop creedal statements?

   _____

   _____

   _____

Hold fast to the traditions that you were taught.
2 Thessalonians 2:15

3. Discuss how the world would be different if every Christian lived out his or her beliefs.

A TRINITARIAN PEOPLE

Activity

Complete each web below by writing words that you associate with the topic that is in the center of the web.

Friends

WHAT RELATIONSHIPS SAY THE MOST ABOUT YOU?

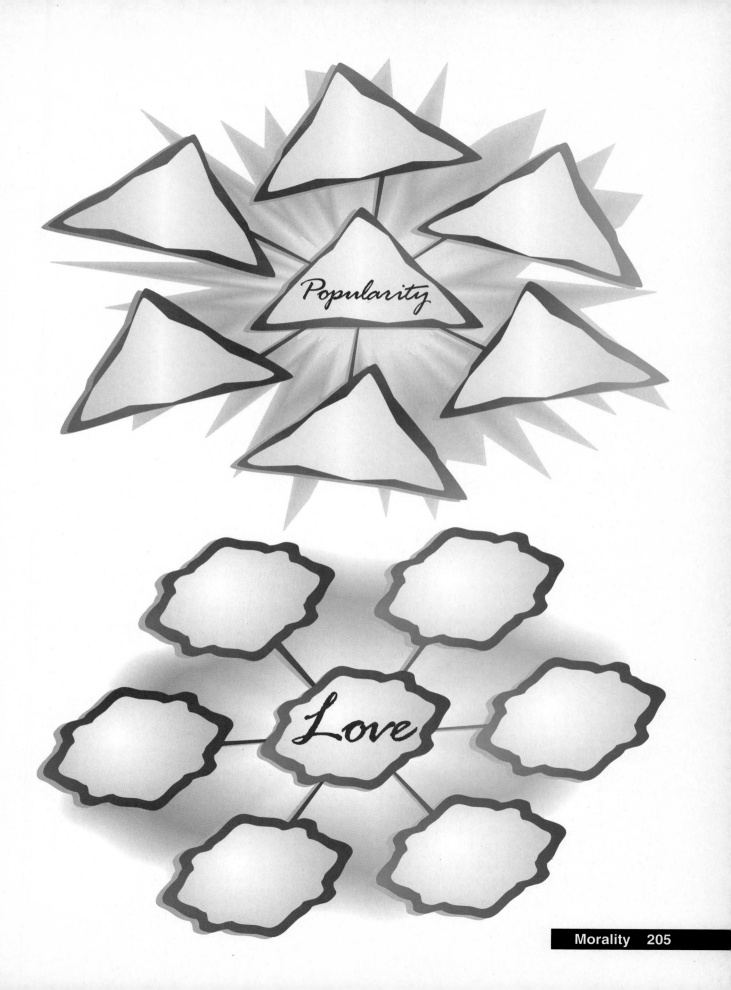

Popularity

Love

LEARNING WHO GOD IS

The original followers of Jesus were devout Jews who believed in the one and only God of the Old Testament. Their God was mighty enough to hold the entire universe, yet caring enough to look personally after each creature.

Those who followed Jesus before his death and resurrection regarded him as more like God than anyone they had ever met. He was strong but gentle, compassionate and forgiving, wise in the ways of happiness, on the side of the poor and victims of injustice, and intimately united with God. After Jesus' resurrection, the disciples came to believe that Jesus was not only like God but actually was God.

At Pentecost they experienced the Holy Spirit, whom Jesus had promised to send. That experience was like the many experiences of God that were recorded in their Scriptures. The Holy Spirit was coming into their lives just as the Bible said that God had come into the lives

of their ancestors. The Holy Spirit gave the new disciples strength and courage, a powerful sense of unity and enthusiasm, a deep love for one another, and a need to go out and tell others about God's love.

The New Testament records the first Christians' faith in God. They experienced God as a Father, as Son (become man in Jesus), and as Holy Spirit.

Just as the early Christians believed that God is Father, Son, and Holy Spirit, so too do we today. We profess that God is the Father who created all things, the Son (Jesus) who is truly human and truly divine, and the Spirit, who guides and enlightens us.

As Christians we respond to this revelation of who God is through praise and affirmation. Christian prayer and song often end in praise of God, who is Father, Son, and Holy Spirit. Our shared prayer during the liturgy is addressed to the Father, through the Son, and in the Holy Spirit.

Activity

For some years now you have experienced God in different ways at different times. Think about who God is for you. Then write as many words as possible that you associate with God. Add as many writing spaces as you need.

DOCTRINE OF THE TRINITY

For about four centuries following Jesus' resurrection, Christians grappled with the question, "How can there be only one God if we believe Jesus Christ is God, and the Holy Spirit is God?"

Attempting to resolve this question, some Christians insisted that there must be three gods, but their views were never accepted by the Church. Others argued that there is only one God, so neither Jesus nor the Holy Spirit was really God.

Most Christians continued to believe that there is and can be only one God. Yet they could not deny that they experienced God also as Jesus Christ and as Holy Spirit.

Finally, the Church arrived at the doctrine of the **Trinity**, which was formalized by the Councils of the early Church. This doctrine stated what Christians believed about the Trinity. The First Council of Constantinople defined that there is one God who is Father, Son, and Holy Spirit. The Father is God. The Son is God. The Holy Spirit is God. There is but one God.

How God can be one-yet-three remained for the Christians then and for us today beyond the power of human understanding.

As Christians we profess our belief in this unending and profound mystery of the Trinity.

We say in the Nicene Creed that God the Son is "one in being with the Father." We profess that the Holy Spirit "proceeds from the Father and the Son." This ancient language suggests that the Father, Son, and Spirit are one God and differ only in their relationships.

For us the doctrine of the Trinity means that the reality of the life of God and of God with us reaches beyond thought, imagination, and expression. And so we bow in adoration, and we continue to grow in our understanding and experience of God.

As we grow in experience of God, we come to know God as Father—the all-powerful, all-knowing, all-loving Creator of all that exists.

We experience and come to know God as Son who became man in Jesus Christ, our Savior and Redeemer.

We experience and come to know God as Holy Spirit, our unifier, reconciler, helper, and guide.

God is revealed to us in these three distinct but related ways. These three ways reflect the inner life of the **triune** God.

The Catholic doctrine of the Trinity puts into words the way we Catholics experience God. Words necessarily fall short of expressing the loving relationship of Father, Son, and Holy Spirit. Nonetheless, the words of the creeds explain to us that God is three-in-one.

THE MYSTERY OF THE TRINITY

Christians have expressed the mystery of the Trinity in symbols and images as well as in creeds and doctrines. The following Irish folk prayer uses simple images to help us express the mystery of the Trinity.

Three folds in the cloth,
yet there is but the one cloth.

Three joints in a finger,
yet there is but the one finger.

Three leaves in the shamrock,
yet there is but the one shamrock.

Frost, snow, and ice . . .
yet the three are only water.

Three persons in God likewise,
but there is the one God.

Activity

These symbols are traditional representations of the triune God. Select the one that you feel says the most to you about the Trinity. Circle it and describe here what it says to you about the triune God.

Activity

Create your own symbol of the Holy Trinity—one that conveys the meaning of the doctrine of the Trinity in your life.

Vocabulary

Trinity: the one God revealed as Father, Son, and Holy Spirit

triune: three-in-one

WE BELIEVE

The one God is revealed as Father, Son, and Holy Spirit. From knowing the one God in three distinct ways, Catholics and many other Christians know God as triune, or three-in-one. The doctrine of the Trinity shows God as so full of life and love as to overflow any single way of being and acting.

In the life of Jesus, we see his commitment to bringing about the reign of God. Jesus was so committed to this, as we know, that he was willing to sacrifice himself on the cross for us. Closely connected with Jesus' sacrifice on the cross is the outpouring of the Holy Spirit, especially on Pentecost.

The early Church reflected on what the life of Jesus revealed about God. The early Christians also reflected on the Spirit that they experienced. However, it was not until about the fourth century that these revelations about the nature of God were formally expressed in the doctrine of the Trinity.

GOD THE FATHER

God is the supreme being, who always was and always will be. God is all-good, all-holy, all-knowing, always just, merciful, and forgiving.

God created all things. Human beings are made in the image and likeness of God. God continually invites us to share the gift of his life and loving presence. God is revealed to us in many ways but especially in the sacred Scriptures, in the life of Jesus Christ, and in the life of the Church.

GOD THE SON

Jesus Christ is the second Person of the Trinity. Jesus is God's own Son and Jesus is one with the Father and the Holy Spirit. He is the Christ, the Messiah, the Anointed One sent by God.

Jesus Christ is both human and divine. Jesus is our Savior. In loving obedience to God's will, Jesus Christ suffered and died to redeem all people from sin and death. Through the power of God, Jesus rose to new life and invites us to share this new life with him. Through Jesus, we share in the fullness of God's grace. The truth of Jesus' resurrection shows us that death is not an ending but leads us to new and everlasting life.

Through the paschal mystery—Jesus' passion, death, resurrection, and ascension—God's salvation of the world is fulfilled.

THE PERSONS OF THE TRINITY

God is revealed in the life of Jesus as Father, Son, and Holy Spirit. This doctrine of the Trinity expresses the mystery of God. Over the centuries, the ways in which theologians discussed and wrote about the Trinity became very technical and hard to understand. Yet this doctrine is at the heart of our Christian faith. It tells us much about the nature of God, the story of salvation, and the way we as Christians should worship with God.

GOD THE FATHER AND JESUS THE SON

Jesus called God *Abba,* which means "Father" and from this we understand God as Father. And if God is Father, then Jesus is Son.

GOD THE HOLY SPIRIT

The Holy Spirit is the third Person of the Trinity, one with the Father and the Son yet distinct. The Spirit leads and guides us in living as followers of Jesus. The Holy Spirit sanctifies, or makes holy, our minds and hearts.

The Holy Spirit has been at work in the world since creation. Under the guidance of the Holy Spirit, for example, the authors of the Bible were inspired to write the word of God.

The Holy Spirit is at work in the Church today, enabling us to carry on the mission of Jesus. We receive the Holy Spirit at Baptism and become temples of the Holy Spirit. The Spirit remains with us, guiding our conscience and helping us avoid sin.

THE MYSTERY OF GOD

The Trinity is not meant to be easily understood. The terms of human language can never adequately express the reality of all that God is. But the doctrine of the Trinity of God as three-in-one reveals to us that God is loving and sustains and cares for his people.

Activity

Read the hymn and then describe what it tells about each Person of the Trinity.

God the Father _____

_____

_____

God the Son _____

_____

_____

God the Holy Spirit _____

_____

_____

Come Now Almighty King

Come, now almighty king,
Help us your name to sing.
Help us to praise.
Father all glorious,
Ever victorious,
Come and reign over us,
Ancient of days.

Come, now Incarnate Word,
Gird on your mighty sword,
Our prayer attend.
Come and your people bless
And give your Word success;
Establish your righteousness,
Savior and Friend!

Come, holy Comforter,
Your sacred witness bear
in this glad hour.
You, who almighty art,
Now rule in every heart
Never from us depart,
Spirit of Power!

To the great One in Three
Eternal praises be
For evermore!
Your sovereign majesty
May we in glory see
And to eternity
Love and adore!

Activity

Think about one person whom you know very well. What would you say are the most important things to know about this person if someone was to really understand him or her? Give one reason why each characteristic or fact is so important.

Key characteristic or fact:
_____

Reason why it is important:
_____

_____

_____

Key characteristic or fact:
_____

Reason why it is important:
_____

_____

Key characteristic or fact:
_____

Reason why it is important:
_____

_____

Key characteristic or fact:
_____

Reason why it is important:
_____

_____

Key characteristic or fact:
_____

Reason why it is important:
_____

_____

Key characteristic or fact:
_____

Reason why it is important:
_____

A PRAYERFUL WOMAN

Julian of Norwich was one of the most famous women of the Middle Ages, yet we know very little about her life. We do know that she lived most of her days alone in a small cottage that was attached to St. Julian's church in Norwich, England. No one is certain whether her name was really Julian or whether she simply used the name of the church where she lived. She was probably born in the year 1342 and died between 1416 and 1423.

Julian lived as an anchoress—that is, a woman who withdraws from family and community life in order to live a solitary life devoted to prayer. Unlike hermits, who usually withdrew to remote places, anchorites and anchoresses usually lived alone in rooms built onto the sides of churches. Townspeople gave her food and other necessities and she became known as an excellent counselor to those who came to her with their problems.

What made Julian of Norwich famous and important to Christians through the ages were her writings about her experiences of God in prayer. In her writings she described her understanding of the presence of the Holy Trinity in people's lives. She wrote in an informal and personal style rather than as a theological scholar.

Julian also wrote extensively about how much God loves us and all creation. Like St. Anselm, she used the image of a mother and child to describe the close personal relationship we can have with God.

She wrote, "The kind, loving mother who knows and sees the need of her child guards it very tenderly." Julian described that in this same way Jesus loved us very much and cares for us: "And he wants us to know it for he wants to have all our love attached to him."

Activity

When Julian spoke of the loving tenderness of our Lord, she repeated an image that is found in the Bible. Read Isaiah 49:15. What does God say about how we are cared for?

_____

_____

_____

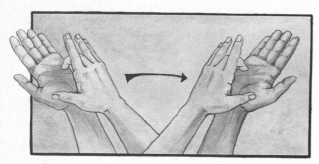

Jesus

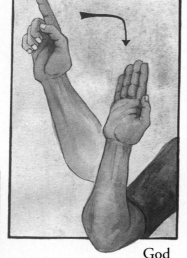

God

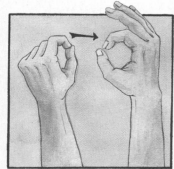

Spirit

Praying in the Trinity

Many of our Christian prayers call to mind the doctrine of the Trinity. For example, when we pray we make the sign of the cross. We address the Trinity when we bless a person or object. At Mass we pray prayers of praise to the Trinity. Many of our hymns also praise the Trinity.

The sign of the cross is an ancient gesture of faith that dates from as early as the second century. This sign is used in the sacraments, such as Baptism and the Eucharist. It is used to begin and end prayers, such as the Rosary and Grace at Meals. The sign of the cross reminds us of our Baptism and calls God's blessing upon us.

An important prayer to the Trinity is called the "Glory Be to the Father." This prayer is actually a hymn of praise to the Trinity. It is also called the Lesser Doxology. A doxology is a hymn of praise to God. (*Doxa* means "glory.") The Greater Doxology is the Gloria recited at Mass. It begins, "Glory to God in the highest." These doxologies were probably adapted from Jewish blessings. The Lesser and Greater Doxologies have been used by Christians since about the fourth century.

Activity

Think about all you have learned about the Trinity.
Then write a prayer, hymn, poem, or rap praising the Trinity.

_____

_____

_____

_____

_____

_____

CHAPTER REVIEW

We can approach the mystery of the Holy Trinity by describing the qualities and the actions of each Person of the Trinity. Write brief answers to describe each of the following.

1. These words describe the Father.

   _____

   _____

2. These words describe the Son.

   _____

   _____

3. These words describe the Holy Spirit.

   _____

   _____

Julian of Norwich's prayer led her to a profound understanding of God. Write a paragraph to describe some of what she understood about God and God's relationship with us.

_____

_____

_____

_____

Respond to the following questions based on what you have learned in this chapter.

1. What is the *Trinity*?

   _____

   _____

2. Name three images that Christians have used to symbolize the Triune God.

   _____

   _____

3. Discuss three ways in which we experience God.

In the name of the Father, and of the Son, and of the Holy Spirit. Amen.

15 A MARKED PEOPLE

Activity

Write a brief description of a well-known person by writing about his or her qualities and character. Do not tell anything about what this person does or what he or she looks like.

WHAT DO YOU ADMIRE MOST IN OTHERS?

_____

_____

_____

_____

_____

_____

Now think of some qualities and attitudes that are characteristic of you. Name and briefly describe these four personality traits.

1. _____

   _____

2. _____

   _____

3. _____

   _____

4. _____

   _____

THE MARK OF DISCIPLESHIP

Our Lord wanted the lives of his followers to be marked in a way that would influence the lives of others. In the Gospel of John, Jesus described this mark of discipleship on the night before he died.

> I give you a new commandment:
> love one another.
> As I have loved you,
> so you also should love one another.
> This is how all will know that you are
> my disciples,
> if you have love for one another.
>
> *John 13:34–35*

Active, self-giving love was to be the distinguishing characteristic of Jesus' disciples. Jesus Christ, the Son of God, demonstrated the depth and intensity of Christian love by sacrificing his life for all people. After Jesus' resurrection and ascension, the early Christians, enlivened by the Holy Spirit, strove to practice the same unconditional love as Jesus.

Activity

The Apostle Paul, in Galatians 5:22–23, lists nine signs of the presence of Christ's Spirit in a person or community. Find these signs in Paul's letter and write them below.

1. _____
2. _____
3. _____
4. _____
5. _____
6. _____
7. _____
8. _____
9. _____

Activity

Read Acts 2:42–47 and Acts 4:32–35 to discover the dynamic ways the early Christians showed their love for others. Write four of these ways below.

1. _____
   _____

2. _____
   _____

3. _____
   _____

4. _____
   _____

The Marks of the Church

The earliest Christian communities continued to follow most of the traditional Jewish ways of living and worshiping. They also tried to live as good citizens under Roman law. But there was something different about the early Christians. Gradually the Christians themselves, and their Jewish and Roman neighbors, came to recognize that they were really a new religious movement, rooted in but branching out from Jewish life, and coming into open conflict with official Roman rule.

The early Christian communities in Jerusalem, according to the New Testament, were marked by (1) a strong sense of community, (2) respect for the teachings of the apostles, (3) lives of prayer, and (4) mutual service and help (Acts 2:42–47; 4:32–35).

These Christian communities remembered the command of Jesus: "As I have loved you, so you also should love one another" (John 13:34–35). For Jesus, unconditional love for one another was the clearest sign that someone was his disciple. This love for others characterized his own life.

For these early Christian communities, it was not just a matter of imitating Jesus as they remembered him. They also continued to experience his presence and actions in their own lives as well as in their communities. They were identified with him. "Where Jesus Christ is, there is the Catholic Church," wrote St. Ignatius of Antioch, on his way to martyrdom. The attitudes and actions of the early Christians reflected the presence of the risen Christ with them.

The early Christians stood out because of their strikingly unselfish care for others. In the second century, a famous Christian writer named Tertullian described how Christian communities cared for the poor, for orphans, for the elderly, for slaves, for shipwrecked sailors, and for prisoners. He concluded: "Such works of love. . . put a mark upon us in the eyes of some. 'Look,' they say, 'how they love one another . . . and how they are ready to die for each other.' " As the Church began to formulate its creeds, four **marks of the Church** were singled out. These were identifying signs by which Christ's Church is still recognized. Like the first communities of Christians, the Church was to be "one, holy, catholic, and apostolic."

ONE

Over the centuries, Catholics experienced these traits in their communities in different ways. They were united in their beliefs, in their sacramental worship centering on the Eucharist, and in the bonds between the many local churches and the bishop of Rome, the pope. There were conflicts and divisions, but these difficulties made Catholics more aware of the oneness to which Christ called his Church.

HOLY

The early Christians experienced holiness in their individual and community lives, even though they also recognized their own sinfulness. The Catholic Church is holy. God's plan to unite all things in Jesus Christ is revealed and fulfilled in the Church's holiness. The Church is **transcendent**—established by Christ and having a supernatural character.

CATHOLIC

The growing Church experienced itself as catholic—that is, universal and adaptable. Not only were the local communities open to people of all kinds but missionaries started new Christian communities all over the world. Christ is the head of the Church, who continues his mission to bring the entire human race to salvation.

APOSTOLIC

Through time, the Church has remained faithful to the teachings of the apostles. Catholics believe that Christ governs the Church through the pope and the bishops, who are the successors of Peter and the apostles. Through apostolic activities, the Church has responded to the call to share Christian ideals and beliefs with the world.

The four marks of the Church were, and continue to be, the manifestations of the love Christ demanded of his followers. The four marks of the Church identify Christ's Church in the world.

Activity

Identify how your parish exhibits the four marks of the Church.

one

_____

holy

_____

catholic

_____

apostolic

_____

Vocabulary

marks of the Church: identifying signs by which Christ's Church may be recognized: one, holy, catholic, and apostolic

transcendent: supernatural character of the Church, established by Christ

✦ ✦ ✦ ✦ ✦ ✦ ✦ ✦ ✦ ✦ ✦ ✦ ✦ ✦ ✦

WE BELIEVE

Jesus gathered a community of disciples who became the Church after the resurrection. The traditional identifying marks of Christ's Church are unity, holiness, catholicity, and apostolicity. In different times and places these marks are expressed in different ways. Christ's Church today expresses these marks by its respect, compassion, justice, freedom, and solidarity with the poor.

WE ARE ONE

The first mark of the Church is that the People of God are one, or united. This does not mean that Catholics throughout the world are identical in every way. We are one in our faith, in the sacraments, and in Church leadership, but we enjoy much diversity in the way in which we worship God.

In the Catholic Church today there are more than twenty different Rites, or distinct liturgical and spiritual traditions. The Latin, or Roman, Rite is just one of these, although it is the largest. The Catholic Church began in Palestine and as it spread, the early centers of Christianity became Jerusalem, Alexandria, Antioch, Rome, and Constantinople. The way the churches in these early centers expressed the same faith differed in theology, liturgy, hierarchy, government, tradition, and culture. These differences still exist and find their expression in the individual Rites of the one Catholic Church.

Most of the Rites of the Church are called Eastern Catholic Churches or Eastern Rites because historically these Rites originated from Eastern Christianity. They are now in union with Rome. Persons who follow these Rites are referred to as Eastern Rite Catholics. Eastern Rite Catholics are not members of the Orthodox Churches. They are Catholics in union with Rome, just as Catholics of the Latin Rite are.

Activity

What does it mean that the Church is one even though every Catholic Mass is not identical in its outward expression?

_____

_____

_____

Rites of the Catholic Church

Alexandria
Coptic Rite
Ethiopic Rite

Antioch
Malankar Rite
Maronite Rite
Syrian Rite
Chaldean Rite
Syro-Malabar Rite

Armenia
Armenian Rite

Rome
Latin Rite

Constantinople
(Byzantium)
Albanian Rite
Belorussian Rite
Bulgarian Rite
Greek Rite
Hungarian Rite
Italo-Albanian Rite
Melkite Rite
Romanian Rite
Russian Rite
Ruthenian Rite
Slovak Rite
Ukrainian Rite

WE ARE HOLY

Holiness means being dedicated to God and the worship of God through our prayers, thoughts, and actions. The Church is holy because the Church is dedicated to God and to doing his will in our world.

One of the ways in which the Church acknowledges lives led in holiness is through the recognition of saints, or the process of **canonization**. When a person is canonized, the pope declares that he or she has led a life of Christian virtue to a heroic degree. This means that the person is now with God in heaven and is worthy of our honor. He or she can become a role model for us. To be considered for canonization, a person must be dead and must have led a life of great virtue.

Before someone can be canonized he or she must first be beatified. **Beatification** is the process for naming someone blessed, or worthy of our honor. First, his or her life is investigated. The person's writings (if any) and deeds are examined and, except in the case of martyrs, one miracle must have been worked by God through his or her intercession. If the person is found to have lived a life of extraordinary virtue and one miracle has been certified, the pope declares this person blessed.

Once someone has been beatified, he or she may be considered for canonization. This entails another investigation of his or her life, writings, and deeds as well as the certification of another miracle. The rules and procedures of the process of canonization are the responsibility of the Congregation for the Causes of Saints, a department in the Vatican.

It is important to remember that the Church recognizes that everyone in heaven is a saint, not just persons whom the Church has officially canonized. The Church canonizes saints so that these people may be honored and venerated for their sanctity and goodness. They show us new paths to holiness. We can and should pray to the saints for their intercession with God on our behalf. By learning about the lives of the saints we can imitate those who have shown us the best possible examples of being truly Christian.

Facts About Canonization

- The Congregation for the Causes of Saints, a department in the Vatican, handles the work and research involved in beatifying and canonizing someone.
- The official list of saints and martyrs is called the *Roman Martyrology*.
- The volume containing all the information relating to a person's cause is called a *positio*.
- Elizabeth Bayley Seton was the first American-born person to be canonized (1975).
- The lives of the saints are commemorated at Mass throughout the liturgical year—usually on the day of the saint's death.

Activity

Identify the names of four saints and then describe something about them that you admire.

1. _____

_____

2. _____

_____

3. _____

_____

4. _____

_____

Vocabulary

canonization: the process for naming someone a saint

beatification: the process for naming someone blessed

❖ ❖ ❖ ❖ ❖ ❖ ❖ ❖ ❖ ❖ ❖ ❖ ❖ ❖ ❖

Percentages of Catholics in Countries of the World
(Statistics not available for every country.)

99 Malta	83 Slovenia	28 Zambia	7 Vietnam
98 Italy	82 Chile	27 Australia	6 Korea
95 Ireland	82 Austria	23 Madagascar	5 Senegal
95 Mexico	81 Guatemala	23 Malawi	5 Swaziland
95 Poland	80 Lithuania	22 Kenya	4 Barbados
95 Spain	79 Puerto Rico	22 Suriname	4 Singapore
94 El Salvador	78 Uruguay	22 Tanzania	3 Indonesia
93 Colombia	70 Lebanon	22 United States	3 Iraq
93 Ecuador	68 Croatia	21 Benin	3 Liberia
93 Honduras	68 Czech and Slovak	19 Bosnia	3 Malaysia
93 Paraguay	Federative Republic	19 Botswana	2 Sweden
93 Portugal	62 Belize	17 Bahamas	2 Syria
92 Bolivia	60 Hungary	15 Bermuda	1.7 India
92 Peru	55 Angola	15 Scotland	.9 Libya
92 Venezuela	52 Zaire	14 Namibia	.8 Ethiopia
91 Argentina	47 Switzerland	14 New Zealand	.7 Bulgaria
91 Nicaragua	45 Canada	14 Romania	.7 China
90 Costa Rica	44 Rwanda	13 Ghana	.6 Denmark
90 Dominican Republic	41 Cuba	13 Mozambique	.5 Greece
90 Haiti	41 Uganda	9 England	.4 Egypt
88 Brazil	38 Lesotho	9 Nigeria	.35 Japan
88 Panama	37 Netherlands	9 Zimbabwe	.18 Bangladesh
86 Belgium	36 Congo	8 South Africa	.12 Algeria
84 France	36 Germany	7 Sri Lanka	.1 Finland
83 Philippines	28 Cameroon	7 Sudan	.02 Iran

WE ARE CATHOLIC

The third mark of the Church is that it is catholic, or universal. Through the centuries, the Church has indeed become universal. From Albania to Zimbabwe, Catholics are found throughout the world.

The influence of the Church, especially in the areas of morality and social justice extends throughout the world, too. As head of the state of Vatican City, the smallest sovereign state in the world, the pope and his representatives participate in international political organizations, such as the United Nations. A number of countries maintain diplomatic ties with the Vatican and have ambassadors in Vatican City. A diplomat who represents the Vatican in a country and who has the rank of ambassador is called a nuncio.

The Church is catholic and speaks to the whole world about the message of Christ and how it should be lived today.

Activity

Examine the chart above and then answer the following questions.

1. What percentage of the population of the United States is Catholic? _____

2. What country has the highest percentage of Catholics? _____

3. According to this chart, what is one of the countries with the lowest percentage of Catholics? _____

WE ARE APOSTOLIC

The Church has remained faithful to the teaching of the apostles, and the leadership of the Church has been passed from them, especially Peter, down through the centuries. According to the Gospel of Matthew, Jesus gave the authority to lead his followers to Peter.

> And so I say to you, you are Peter, and upon this rock I will build my church, and the gates of the netherworld shall not prevail against it. I will give you the keys to the kingdom of heaven. Whatever you bind on earth shall be bound in heaven; and whatever you loose on earth shall be loosed in heaven.
>
> *Matthew 16:18–19*

This apostolic authority is passed down from generation to generation in the Church's hierarchy, or structure, of pope, bishops, priests, and deacons. Bishops ordain priests and deacons, and bishops themselves are consecrated by other bishops. The pope is elected by the College of Cardinals, a special group of bishops who have been chosen as special advisors to the papacy.

When a pope dies, a meeting of the College of Cardinals takes place to elect a new pope. This meeting, called a conclave, is closed to the world so that no one can influence the members of the College of Cardinals. A candidate must receive a two-thirds majority vote by secret ballot.

When a pope is elected and the last ballots are burned, a plume of white smoke rises from the Vatican. This is the first indication to the rest of the world that a new pope has been elected. The cardinals pledge their obedience to the new pope, and then his election is proclaimed to the world from the main balcony of St. Peter's Basilica. At this time the new pope gives his blessing to Vatican City and the rest of the world. A pope is elected for life.

The pope is sometimes referred to as the Roman Pontiff, the Vicar of Christ, and the successor of St. Peter. As head of the Church, the pope has full authority over the Church. The pope states official Church teaching in agreement with Scripture, tradition, and the experience of the Church. In addition, the pope, with the assistance of the departments of the Vatican, administers the institutional concerns of the Church—for example, by appointing bishops to dioceses.

Activity

What qualities do you think the College of Cardinals looks for in choosing a new pope?

_____

_____

_____

_____

_____

Why are these qualities important?

_____

_____

_____

_____

_____

A MARKED MAN

During World War II, several million Jews were imprisoned in concentration camps and executed by the Nazis, who ruled Germany and conquered much of western Europe. This terrible tragedy is called the holocaust. Among those arrested were some Christians.

In the concentration camp at Auschwitz, Poland, Maximilian Kolbe wore the number 16670 on his prison clothes. But the guards in the camp and the prisoners who suffered with him noticed a mark much deeper within him. One prison doctor wrote, "Although tuberculosis consumed him, he remained calm . . . ; through his living belief in God and God's providence, with his unshakable hope and, before all else, in his love of God and his neighbor, he distinguished himself from all."

Maximilian Kolbe was a Franciscan priest. Before World War II and his imprisonment in Auschwitz, he had published successful magazines, founded lay organizations, and established Franciscan communities in Poland and Japan. But little of that was known to his captors or his fellow prisoners. Instead, what everyone saw was simply someone they admired and wanted to imitate.

During the night of July 30, 1941, a prisoner escaped from Auschwitz. Even though the guards were Christians, that meant harsh punishment for the rest of the prisoners. The camp commander ordered all the prisoners from Cell Block 14 to line up. He chose ten of them to be locked up until they starved to death.

One of them began to cry out, "My poor wife and children! I will never see them again!" Maximilian heard the man and quickly offered to take his place. Kolbe's offer was accepted.

Years later an inmate described what had happened in the windowless bunker where the ten prisoners were locked up. "Father Kolbe never complained. He prayed aloud, so that his fellow prisoners could hear him in order to join him. He had the special gift of comforting everybody."

During those horrible weeks of starvation, Father Kolbe's eyes were marked by calmness and peace. The guards soon ordered him to look at the ground so that they would not have to look into his eyes.

By the third week, only Father Kolbe and three others were alive. The guards finally injected them with poison. They died on August 14. Thirty years later, Pope Paul VI said of number 16670, Father Maximilian Kolbe, O.F.M., "His name will remain among the great."

Activity

In what ways did Father Kolbe demonstrate the traditional marks of the Church?

_____

_____

_____

_____

_____

In His Place

Father Kolbe was canonized as a martyr on October 10, 1982. The man he saved, Franciszek Gajowniczek, witnessed the ceremony. His story, too, shows how the marks of the Church are lived in everyday life.

Although Kolbe had sacrificed his own life so that Gajowniczek could see his family again, it did not quite work out that way. Gajowniczek saw his wife Helena after nearly five and a half years in Auschwitz, but he never saw his sons again. They were killed during the war.

Gajowniczek avoided execution, but while he was in Auschwitz, the other Catholic prisoners in the camp hated him. Because of him they had lost their priest and confidant. In the brutal concentration camp, just the presence of a priest could inspire them to deeper faith and greater inner strength. But Gajowniczek had robbed the other Catholic prisoners of the comfort and hope that Kolbe could have brought them.

Gajowniczek spent much of his life after World War II giving talks about Kolbe and working for his canonization. The man Kolbe saved had had his life transformed by Kolbe's heroic sacrifice. Kolbe's selflessness taught Gajowniczek to be more selfless, too. Throughout the rest of his life, he had a strong sense of the presence of Kolbe and believed that Kolbe guided him. He waited for Kolbe to take him to heaven with him. Franciszek Gajowniczek died in 1995.

Activity

If Gajowniczek had had the chance to talk to Kolbe about what had happened at Auschwitz, what do you think he would have said?

_____

_____

_____

_____

_____

If you had been one of the prisoners at Auschwitz, what might you have said about Kolbe to Gajowniczek?

_____

_____

_____

_____

_____

What do you think we can learn from Kolbe's sacrifice?

_____

_____

_____

_____

_____

Lord, help me to appreciate
    and develop the gifts you have given me.
Keep me faithful to the call of the gospel
    and lead me in using my gifts
    for the good of your creation.
Give me the strength and patience
    to act with gentleness and concern
    for others.
May I be a witness of your love to the world
    and courageously persevere
    in following your will.
Amen.

PRAYING AS A MARKED PEOPLE

When you were baptized, one of the first things the celebrant did was to mark you as Christ's own. Calling you by name, the celebrant said the following words as he traced the sign of the cross on your forehead.

" . . . . , the Christian community welcomes you with great joy. In its name I claim you for Christ our Savior by the sign of His cross. I now trace the cross on your forehead, and invite your parents [and godparents] to do the same."

Rite of Baptism for Children

The marks of Christ's Church apply not only to the institution of the Church but also to individual Catholics. Each of us is called to care about others as well as to work for unity, to pray and try to do God's will, to be accepting of people of all kinds, and to know better and share with others the teachings of Christ that came to us from the apostles.

Activity

Select one of the marks of the Church and decide on some practical action you plan to take to live it out more fully.

The mark I select for my resolution is

_____

I plan to _____

_____

_____

CHAPTER REVIEW

There is an incorrect fact in each one of these sentences. Write each sentence correctly on the lines below.

1. The early Christians were distinguished by their sense of social justice.

   _____

2. The word *catholic* refers to the idea that the Church is holy.

   _____

3. Jesus gathered a community of disciples who became the Church before the resurrection.

   _____

4. Maximilian Kolbe saved ten men from execution.

   _____

Choose one of the four marks of the Catholic Church and write a paragraph explaining what the mark means and how it identifies the Church today.

   _____

   _____

   _____

   _____

Respond to the following questions based on what you have learned in this chapter.

1. What are the *marks of the Church*?

   _____

   _____

   _____

2. Why is love one of the characteristics of Christians?

   _____

   _____

3. Discuss what you feel is the most convincing sign today that the Church is living out its call to be one, holy, catholic, and apostolic.

This is how all will know that you are my disciples, if you have love for one another.
John 13:35

16

A HOPEFUL PEOPLE

MYSTERIES OF LIFE AND DEATH

WHAT DO YOU THINK AND FEEL ABOUT DEATH?

There is an old Jewish story about a tourist who went to visit a world-famous rabbi. When the tourist found himself standing in the rabbi's home, he was shocked to find that there was no furniture in the house except for two simple chairs and a desk.

"Where is your furniture?" the surprised tourist asked.

"Where is yours?" the rabbi replied.

"What do you mean?" the tourist exclaimed. "I have no need for furniture. I'm just passing through."

The rabbi smiled and said, "So am I."

Activity

1. What do you think the rabbi's reply meant?

_____

_____

_____

2. How did the rabbi view life? Death? Life after death?

_____

_____

_____

_____

THE REALITY OF DEATH

At some point, we will all die. The certainty of death affects people in different ways. As Christians, we accept death as a natural part of life and an important transition to the afterlife with Christ. For Christians, death is both sad and hopeful, a time of grief and a time of quiet joy.

In death, we Christians recall our future resurrection. In the face of the anguish of our grief at the death of a loved one, we trust that Christ has conquered the power of sin and death. We realize that in death there is physical separation, but in Christ we are never truly parted from one another.

Activity

Below are some of the many different views about death and what happens after death. Mark each statement with which you agree.

1. Death is the end, period. There is nothing after death.

2. Any living being that dies is later reincarnated as another living being in a higher form of life if the being lived a good life, in a lower form if not.

3. Death is the end of the body, but the soul lives on forever.

4. After death, the person lives on temporarily without the body until the end of the world, when all will rise again with their bodies.

5. Since God loves everyone, no matter how people live, all will be happy forever with him.

6. After one dies, God judges the person on the basis of how he or she has lived. Those who have lived good lives will live happily forever with God, while those who have lived evil lives will not.

With which of these views are you most comfortable? Why?

_____

_____

_____

_____

_____

_____

_____

Mark your answers to identify some of your experiences connected with death.

	No	Yes
Have you ever been to a funeral?	☐	☐
Have you ever been to a wake?	☐	☐
Have you ever been to a memorial service?	☐	☐
Have you ever experienced the death of a relative?	☐	☐
Have you ever experienced the death of a friend?	☐	☐
Have you ever experienced the death of a pet?	☐	☐

If someone said to you that death is a natural part of life, how might you respond to this person?

_____

_____

_____

DEATH AND HOPE

When a Catholic dies, we gather together to celebrate his or her life and to pray that he or she is united with Christ. As Christians, we believe that when a person of faith dies he or she passes to a new life with Christ. Death is not the end.

By attending a **funeral**, we can comfort and console the living and ask God for forgiveness of the sins of the deceased person. Although death has separated us from those whom we love, we affirm in faith and hope that in Christ we are still united.

There are three services we can celebrate together when someone dies. These are the vigil service, the funeral Mass, and the **rites of committal**.

THE WAKE

During a vigil, or **wake**, we sit with the family of the deceased and offer them our support and consolation at a difficult and sad time. The wake is frequently held at a funeral home, but it may also be held at the home of the deceased.

A Catholic vigil service may be held at some point during the wake. In this prayer service, the family and the community hear the word of God proclaimed as a source of our faith and hope. The reading of Scripture and our prayers remind us of the presence of Christ and the life we have in him. We call upon God to receive the soul of the deceased and to forgive his or her sins.

THE FUNERAL MASS

Usually there is a procession from the funeral home to the church, where the body of the deceased is received. At a funeral Mass, the church becomes a symbol of the community of Christians, both living and dead. During the Mass, we thank God for Christ's victory over sin and death in the resurrection. We also pray that God's mercy will be extended to the deceased and that we will be consoled and find strength and hope.

Much of the symbolism of the funeral Mass reminds us of our Baptism and the Baptism of the deceased. Just as in Baptism we gain a new life in Christ, so too in death we pass to a new life with Christ. For example, the casket is sprinkled with water, recalling the waters of Baptism. The casket may also be covered with a **pall**, or white cloth, which symbolizes the white garment worn in Baptism.

The funeral Mass celebrated by Catholics does not dwell on our grief and loss but strengthens us in our faith and hope. Someday we too will be united with Christ and pass into a new life with him. We also look forward to our future resurrection at the end of time.

THE RITES OF COMMITTAL

After the funeral Mass, there is frequently a procession of cars to the final resting place. The rites of committal may be held at the grave or in another place, such as a chapel at the cemetery.

The farewell prayers of the community are prayed so that the deceased may pass into the welcoming company of those who have gone before. There may be a custom of leave-taking. This might include placing flowers on the casket, sprinkling soil on it, or sprinkling it with holy water.

Vocabulary

funeral: the services held when a person dies

rites of committal: the last prayers said at the place where the body will rest

wake: the vigil of the family and friends of the deceased

pall: a white cloth that covers the casket at a funeral Mass

✦ ✦ ✦ ✦ ✦ ✦ ✦ ✦ ✦ ✦ ✦ ✦ ✦ ✦

Activity

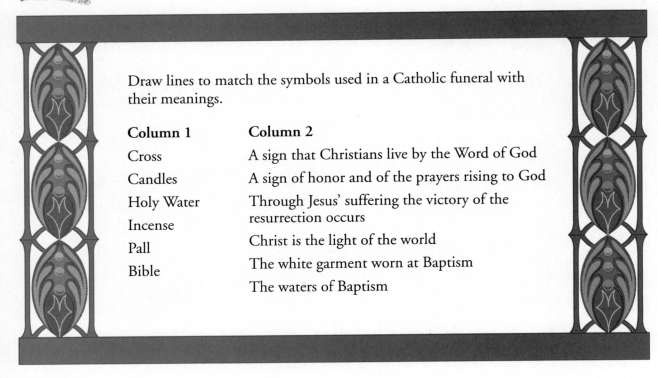

Draw lines to match the symbols used in a Catholic funeral with their meanings.

Column 1

Cross

Candles

Holy Water

Incense

Pall

Bible

Column 2

A sign that Christians live by the Word of God

A sign of honor and of the prayers rising to God

Through Jesus' suffering the victory of the resurrection occurs

Christ is the light of the world

The white garment worn at Baptism

The waters of Baptism

Activity

Write a paragraph explaining the hope that Christians see in the tragedy of death. Use the following phrases in your paragraph.

forgiveness of sins

Christ's resurrection

new life in Christ

God's merciful love

prayers of the community

faith and hope

_____

_____

_____

_____

_____

_____

_____

EXPERIENCING GRIEF

When someone dies it is natural to experience feelings of grief, loss, and sadness. These may be accompanied by feelings of depression, loneliness, and hopelessness. Depending on how close we were to the person who died, these feelings may be very intense and last several months or a year or more. Each person grieves in his or her own way and in his or her own time.

Sometimes even after we have begun to feel more like ourselves again, there may still be times when we miss the person or experience intense pangs of loss. These may be triggered by a familiar object, sound, or place associated with the deceased person. Other times these feelings occur on anniversaries connected with the person or around holidays.

It is important not to deny these emotions to ourselves, and it is important to respect these feelings in others. A period of grieving, or **mourning**, is a necessary part of acknowledging the death of a loved one and respecting his or her memory. In some cultures, people wear black clothing to funerals, do not hold parties or other social events for several months or a year, and follow other customs. Many families still observe customs that help them to acknowledge and express their loss and grief when death occurs.

Whether or not we were close to the person who has died, we must act with respect and compassion toward others who may be experiencing deep grief and intense loss. Our sensitivity, gentleness, and courtesy at these times are also ways of respecting the memory of the person who has died.

Activity

What are some ways that people today acknowledge the death of someone they know?

_____

_____

_____

_____

_____

How can you show support and sympathy for someone who has lost someone close?

_____

_____

_____

_____

_____

Vocabulary

mourning: a period of grieving after a loved one has died

✦ ✦ ✦ ✦ ✦ ✦ ✦ ✦ ✦ ✦ ✦ ✦ ✦ ✦ ✦ ✦

THE FORMULATION OF HOPE

Rooted in faith in Christ's resurrection, the hope of the early Christians in life forever with God was soon put to the test by the persecutions. Many Christians proved their hope by lovingly giving their lives for their faith. The Christians who survived the early persecutions believed that they retained a bond with those who had died, and soon they came to speak of this bond as a **communion of saints**—a union beyond death among those who call themselves Christians.

The early creeds of the Church confirmed this bond with statements of belief in life after death: "We look for the resurrection of the dead and the life of the world to come" (Nicene Creed). "I believe in . . . the communion of saints . . . the resurrection of the body and life everlasting" (Apostles Creed).

Over the centuries, Christians grew in their belief that death marked an encounter with the living God. The Church called this encounter a **particular judgment**, a moment in which the individual's faith, hope, and love come face to face with God in all his completeness. Recognizing that the Church is a community of people, there also developed an understanding of a **general judgment** occurring at the end of time, a moment when the entire community of humanity will stand before God as a people.

Those whose faithfulness has been proved by lives of active love will find their hope fulfilled in the eternal life with God, promised by Christ.

This unending happiness with God and with each other, we call **heaven**. Those who were unwilling to reach out in love to others in this life will not reach out in love to God or neighbor in the life beyond death. They have separated themselves forever from God and from everyone else. This state of complete separation is called **hell**.

For those whose faithfulness wavered, whose hope lagged, or whose love faltered, after death there will be purification—a stripping away of all the things that have made their lives less than fully human. This process of **purgatory** must happen before complete unity with God can take place.

Christians also looked to the final pages of the Bible, the Book of Revelation, to speak to them about the mystery of death and Christian hope. There, we read about God making all things new, with "a new heaven and a new earth" (Revelation 21:1). Therefore, Christians believe that Christ will come again at the end of time to complete the goodness and justice of God's reign. He will do this so that the whole of creation might share in God's promise of life fulfilled. That is why Christians everywhere pray, "thy kingdom come; thy will be done," in the Lord's Prayer.

Like any mystery, the mystery of death cannot be solved and can never be completely understood. And yet, our Christian hope grows ever brighter. Vatican II says, "Through Christ and in Christ, the riddles of sorrow and death grow meaningful. Apart from His gospel, they overwhelm us. Christ has risen, destroying death by His death. He has lavished life upon us. . . . " (Pastoral Constitution on the Church in the Modern World, #22).

Activity

Choose one of the following questions to answer in a sentence.

1. How does the Church's teaching about the afterlife give you hope?

2. What appeals to you about the teaching of the communion of saints?

3. What is the Catholic belief about the end of the world?

_____

_____

_____

_____

Vocabulary

communion of saints: the community of those still living in Christ's Church on earth, of those souls in purgatory, and of those in heaven

particular judgment: God's judgment of each person at the moment of death

general judgment: the judgment of all people at the end of the world

heaven: unending happiness with God and with each other

hell: eternal separation from God and others

purgatory: the process of purification after death from all traces of sin

WE BELIEVE

The Church has continually taught that death is not the end of life. All share in Christ's victory over death. We will rise to unending life. The quality of our eternal life depends on how we live now. God judges each of us at death (particular judgment) and all people at the end of time (general judgment). He judges us as worthy of unending joy with God (heaven) or of painful separation from God (hell).

Activity

Think about the life you are living. What does this say about your beliefs about life and death?

_____

_____

_____

_____

_____

LIFE AND HOPE

Death and life after death are great mysteries. Oddly enough, much of the fear, concern, and misunderstanding of these mysteries has its source in searching to understand the mystery of life. The way in which we view life affects the way we look at—or refuse to look at—death and life after death.

We are called to live a life of hope, and hoping is more than wishing. Hope means trusting that God will never abandon us and that God will be with us now and forever. As Catholics, our ultimate hope is the **Beatific Vision**—our face-to-face encounter with God after our lives on earth.

Christian hope is rooted in Christ's promise of eternal life with God. The Gospel of John includes many references to this promise. Read and discuss the following passages.

> For this is the will of my Father, that everyone who sees the Son and believes in him may have eternal life, and I shall raise him [on] the last day.
>
> *John 6:40*

> I am the resurrection and the life; whoever believes in me, even if he dies, will live; and everyone who lives and believes in me will never die.
>
> *John 11:25–26*

Eternal life with Christ is the goal of our lives here on earth. The faith we have in our lives gives us a taste of what it will be like to be united with God. As St. Basil, the father of Eastern Christian monasticism said, "It is as if we already possessed the wonderful things which our faith assures us we shall one day enjoy."

The proof of our faith and the test of our hope lie in our willingness to love and put our love into action. In speaking about the importance of faith and hope tested by love, Jesus himself said: "Why do you call me 'Lord, Lord,' but not do what I command? I will show you what someone is like who comes to me, listens to my words, and acts on them" (Luke 6:46–47).

In this Scripture passage, Jesus reminds us that it is not enough to say we have faith and love. We must prove that we do by witnessing, or giving evidence by the way we live every day. What we believe and how we act shows how strong our faith is and how deep our love has grown.

Activity

What do you think it means to say that we will see God face to face after our lives on earth?

_____

_____

_____

_____

_____

_____

_____

_____

A WOMAN OF HOPE

Agnes Bojaxhiu (Boh hax - hyoo) was born in Skopje, Yugoslavia in 1910. Today, she is known as one of the greatest Catholic women of our time—Mother Teresa. When Agnes was a girl, she saw in her mother a positive example of Christian service and love of neighbor. Her mother gave money to the poor and visited the sick. She nursed the dying.

One day Agnes heard a priest read a letter from a missionary sister in India. Agnes decided to become a religious sister and do God's work in India.

Agnes Bojaxhiu entered the Sisters of Loretto and took the name Sister Teresa. At age 17 she went to India as a missionary and taught in a private school in Calcutta for twenty years. But each day, Sister Teresa saw the terrible poverty of India. She saw homeless and sick people on the street. She saw tiny babies who had been abandoned. It made her heart ache to see the poor dying alone in the gutters.

Sister Teresa asked permission to live outside the convent and minister to the poor. She began to serve the poor, sick, and dying people of Calcutta, India. At first, she worked alone, spending part of each day in the slums. She taught the children of the poor by using a stick to print words and numbers in the dirt. She comforted the dying. In 1948, she founded her own religious order, the Missionaries of Charity.

Mother Teresa's order expanded around the world. The order has over 200 branches in India and 25 other countries. The Missionaries of Charity operates hospitals, schools, orphanages, youth centers, and shelters for the poor.

In 1979, Mother Teresa was awarded the Nobel Peace Prize for her work. She has taught us that the poor—wherever they are found—are our brothers and sisters. She has taught us that by acting out of love for God, anything is possible. The world can be transformed through the simplest acts of kindness. She and the Missionaries of Charity give us wonderful examples of Christian hope.

Activity

Think about the kind of life you are living and the kind of life you hope to live when you are an adult. Write how you would like to be thought of at the end of your life.

_____

_____

_____

_____

Vocabulary

Beatific Vision: our face-to-face encounter with God after our lives on earth

◆ ◆ ◆ ◆ ◆ ◆ ◆ ◆ ◆ ◆ ◆ ◆ ◆ ◆ ◆ ◆

Leader:	Eternal rest grant unto them, O Lord.
All:	And let perpetual light shine upon them.
Leader:	May they rest in peace.
All:	Amen.
Leader:	May their souls and the souls of all the faithful departed, through the mercy of God, rest in peace.
All:	Amen.

PRAYING FOR THE DEAD

In early Christian art, the Church was sometimes pictured as a ship. Christ himself steered the ship. Those who had died and were with God in heaven were pictured as guiding the ship, sometimes floating above it. Those rowing the ship were the faithful in this world. Others who seemed to be only passengers on the ship were seen as those in the state of purgatory.

This artwork depicted the Church's hopeful vision of itself as the communion of saints—the faithful who supported one another and were bound to one another through the journey of life through death into life forever with God.

It is Catholic tradition to pray for the dead. We not only pray at the time of a person's death, but we remember all our deceased brothers and sisters in daily prayer and in our weekly celebrations of the Eucharist. We do not know for certain the state of those who have died before us, but we have faith that God has fulfilled their hope. We recognize that it is our duty to remain united to them in active, prayerful love.

Activity

List the names of your deceased relatives and friends for whom you will pray.

_____

_____

_____

_____

_____

_____

_____

_____

_____

_____

Describe in your own words why Christians can find hope in the reality of death.

_____

_____

_____

_____

Complete the following sentences.

1. _____ is unending joy with God.

2. The judgment at the end of time is the _____.

3. The community of Christ's Church, both the living and the dead, is sometimes called

    _____.

4. _____ is the unending separation from God and others.

5. The judgment at the moment of death is the

    _____.

Respond to the following questions based on what you have learned in this chapter.

1. What is *purgatory*?

    _____

    _____

2. Why are Christians so hopeful of rising to new life after they die?

    _____

    _____

    _____

Death is swallowed up in victory.
1 Corinthians 15:54

3. Discuss why Catholic beliefs about life after death will help us better appreciate the importance of our own lives.

Complete the Unit Organizer below by explaining how each of these is important to Catholics.

*D*OCTRINE

_____
_____

*C*REED

_____
_____

*T*RINITY

_____
_____

*T*HE CHURCH IS APOSTOLIC

_____
_____

*T*HE CHURCH IS CATHOLIC

_____
_____

*C*OMMUNION OF SAINTS

_____
_____

*P*ARTICULAR JUDGMENT

_____
_____

UNIT **4** REVIEW

Fill in each blank by choosing a word or phrase from the box below.

> particular judgment   Mother Teresa   hell   heaven   life
> communion of saints   hope   purgatory   general judgment   resurrection

1. _____ brings hope to the dying and those who are ill.

2. The Church has continually taught that death is not the end of _____ .

3. The judgment of all peoples at the end of time is called the

   _____ .

4. _____ is the process of purification after death from all traces of sin.

5. God's judgment of each person at the moment of death is called the

   _____ .

6. We refer to the event in which God raised Jesus from the dead as the

   _____ .

7. The _____ are those members of the Church who are living, those who are in purgatory, and those in heaven.

8. Christians are called to a life of _____ .

9. _____ is a term for unending happiness with God and all who love him and one another.

10. The anguish of being separated from God and everyone else forever is known as

    _____ .

Identify the correct word next to its definition.

1. _____ an official Church statement of belief.

2. _____ three-in-one.

3. _____ the vigil with the family of the deceased.

4. _____ the farewell prayers at the final resting place.

5. _____ a loving commitment to and trust in someone or something.

UNIT  REVIEW

Place a **T** before each true sentence. Place an **F** before each false sentence.

1. _____ A creed is a formal summary of basic beliefs.

2. _____ A belief is something that one holds to be true or real.

3. _____ The Church continues to develop its understanding of what it means to be a follower of Jesus.

4. _____ There are three Gods.

5. _____ For Jesus, unconditional love for one another was the clearest sign that someone was his disciple.

6. _____ At the moment of death, there is a general judgment of each person.

7. _____ Christians share in Christ's victory over death.

Write a brief response that describes each of the four marks of the Church below.

one _____

_____

holy _____

_____

catholic _____

_____

_____

apostolic _____

_____

Think about and then write a paragraph explaining how we, as members of the Church, can be recognized as living the four marks of the Church.

_____

_____

_____

_____

Letting Go and Moving On

The transition from one school to another is always exciting, but there is also probably some anxiety over what the experience will be like. Common concerns include making new friends and fitting in, the amount of schoolwork to be done, the expectations of teachers, and participating in activities, such as making an athletic team.

Activity

Three Things I Will Miss About Grade School

_____

_____

_____

_____

_____

Three Things I Am Looking Forward to About High School

_____

_____

_____

Three Things That Concern Me About High School

_____

_____

_____

What are the top three things your class will miss about grade school?

_____

_____

_____

What are the top three things your class is looking forward to about high school?

_____

_____

_____

What are the top three things about high school that concern your class?

_____

_____

_____

MANAGING ANXIETY

What can you and your classmates do about the concerns you have about high school?

▶ Share these with one another. It can help just to find out you are not alone.

▶ Find out more about the high school you will be going to.

▶ Talk to a high school student about the things that concern you.

▶ Visit the high school, if possible, to find out more about it.

Prayer

Jesus, share my anxiety and joy about moving on to high school. Be with me as I move toward this new experience. O Lord, please bless my classmates and keep all of us safe and happy as we begin our high school years.

OPENING DOORS
A Take-Home Magazine™

COMMUNICATE

It is easy to make others feel bad. Tell them that they do not know what they are talking about or that they do not have a right to their own opinions. Use words like *just* (as in "You're just a kid" or "You're just a third grader"), *jerk, stupid, fool,* and *only* ("You're only on the junior team" or "You only got a C"). These words make people feel bad about themselves.

Which words are you guilty of using too easily?

_____

_____

_____

Here are some other common ways we put people down.

Ignore. Worse than being rejected is being totally ignored. It is important to acknowledge *out loud* the contributions of each family member. Ignore little Roxanne and you are telling her that not only do you think that her idea is no good but also that she is not any good.

Insult. Sometimes we belittle the accomplishments of others when we feel insecure about ourselves. Remind others of the things they do of which you are proud, and they might be more enthusiastic about you.

Change the conversation. Has this ever happened to you? You try to tell your folks about school, but every time you bring it up, they ask you whether you have finished your homework. Changing the conversation tells the other person that what he or she has to say is not worth a response.

Say they are wrong. There are two good ways to make others feel bad for voicing opinions. First, just tell them they are wrong. "What are you talking about? There's no way the Rolling Stones are the best." Second, tell others that they do not have a right to their opinions. "Grandma, you don't know anything about the way kids dress today. You're too old." Some people thought the same way in Jesus' day. If you were a sinner or did not have the right occupation, you did not deserve to speak to Jesus, they said.

Do you use any of these ways to tell members of your family that they do not deserve to be heard?

FAMILY ACTIVITY

The opposite of hurtful communication is supportive communication. Tonight, encourage family members to feel good about themselves. Have each person tell one good thing about him or herself. When each person speaks up, you should smile, listen, and do not interrupt (unless they are having difficulty). Start with the oldest member of the family. Remember, what makes accomplishments special is that we have done them, not that other people find them special.

STUFF

Clothes are not the only things we love to buy. Look at the list below and choose (or add to the list) those things you think you will need by the time you are a senior in high school.

VCR	35mm camera	tickets to a sold–out concert
TV	dirt bike	
stereo	car	compact disc player
telephone	motorcycle	
personal computer	jewelry	your own credit card
camcorder	designer clothes	
moped		
_____	_____	_____

Look at your choices. Then, without using the word *need*, explain what these things will give you. What is it that you think having these things will do for you? (Actually, you do not *need* any of these things. They are all luxuries and conveniences.)

Let's say you really want a new jacket, okay? You bug your parents with all the usual arguments: "I really like it," "Everybody's wearing this kind," and "I need a new one anyway." Finally, your parents relent and say you can get it. You're so excited. You can't wait. You know you're going to look terrific. You're going to be great wearing this jacket.

You get it. Maybe the first day everyone compliments you and you look GOOD. The jacket's just as great as you thought. After a while, though—sometimes even the first time you wear it, sometimes not until the third or fourth time—well, it's a nice jacket and you like it, but the excitement is gone. The jacket just does not have the power it once did.

This happens with stuff all the time. You think, "I need this thing. This is THE thing. I've got to get it." And after you've got it, well, it's just there, and you find yourself looking at some new thing that you just have to have. *It's not the thing you want so much as the excitement and the sense of well-being you think you will have.*

The truth is that stuff —the latest stuff, getting the same stuff that everyone else has—will never satisfy you. There's always the big buildup of excitement. You get the thing. And then—nothing. A letdown. The thing just sits there. Maybe it doesn't even work right. In a couple of days, the cycle begins again when you think you need something else. It's a vicious cycle and it doesn't mean anything. Stuff doesn't make you happy. It doesn't make you a better person and it doesn't take your problems away.

Things are not evil in and of themselves. They have their purposes and it's not wrong to enjoy them. It is wrong, however, to get addicted to the excitement of getting new things and to spend a whole lifetime chasing after stuff in order to get that feeling of well-being.

Jesus told us not to worry about things, even things like food and clothing. He pointed out that the birds do not worry about their food, and yet God feeds them. God makes the flowers more splendid than the best clothing can make us. Jesus said that we should seek after the kingdom of God and depend upon God for all that we need. We should be careful that we do not lose sight of what is really important in our lives and keep the purpose and place of stuff in perspective.

A STORY ABOUT SAINT FRANCIS OF ASSISI

One day one of the friars came to Saint Francis and asked his permission to own a book of prayers. This was in the time before printing, and books were expensive and copied by hand. Now, Saint Francis felt that it was very important that the friars not own anything because too many things would distract the friars from God. Saint Francis thought about the friar's request. How bad could a book of prayers be? "Well," Saint Francis said, "if you get this book, you will need a shelf on which to keep it." The friar nodded. "You will need walls to hold up the shelf." The friar nodded again. "You will need a roof to keep the rain off the book." The friar nodded yet again. "You will need a door to keep out the wind and the snow and a lock on the door to keep the book safe from thieves." The friar nodded sadly. "You will need a fence around the house and a gate with a latch to keep the house safe." The friar looked very sad. "You will need..." Saint Francis began again, but the friar had turned and gone away.

Challenge!

What do you understand about our most important act of worship—the Mass? Think you know it all? Take the following challenge. Start at Level 1. You must accumulate the indicated number of points to go on to subsequent levels. Who among your friends and classmates really understands all that they have learned about the Mass?

START

Level 1: ○○○○○○

Provide the correct *question* for each answer.
1. *Answer:* The special meal shared with members of our Catholic Christian family
   Question: _____
2. *Answer:* The word that means "thanksgiving"
   Question: _____
3. *Answer:* The Liturgy of the Word
   Question: _____
4. *Answer:* Under the appearance of bread and wine
   Question: _____
5. Answer: The meal at which Jesus first gave us the gift of himself
   Question: _____

Scoring: 10 points for each correct answer. You must have 40 points to proceed to the next level.

Answers Level 1: 1. What is the Mass? 2. What is the meaning of the word Eucharist? 3. What is the part of the Mass in which we hear the Word of God in Scripture? 4. What is the body and blood of Jesus? 5. What is the Last Supper?

Level 2: ○○○○○○

Complete each sentence with the correct word. (Hint: The first letter of each answer is provided.)
1. The Mass is a c_____ of thanksgiving.
2. At Mass we share the p_____ of Jesus' body and blood.
3. The Mass is a celebration of the r_____ with us in our lives.
4. The Mass is the s_____ of Jesus giving himself to us.
5. At Mass Communion still has the appearance of ordinary bread and wine, but through the power of the H_____, it has become Jesus' body and blood.
6. The Mass is a call to continue Jesus' m_____ to others.
7. In the Mass we are called to love and serve others and to r_____ the presence of Jesus in others.
8. At Mass we are n_____ and renewed.
9. At Mass we are renewed to become better disciples of Jesus, to work to build up the C_____
10. At Mass we also are renewed to work to build up the k_____ _____.

Scoring: 10 points for each correct answer. You must have a total of 120 points from Levels 1 and 2 to go on to the next level.

Answers Level 2: 1. celebration 2. presence 3. risen Christ 4. sacrifice 5. Holy Spirit 6. mission 7. recognize 8. nourished 9. Church 10. kingdom of God

Level 3: ○○○○○○

Answer the following.

1. Name three ways to describe the body and blood of Christ we receive at Mass:

_____, _____

and _____.

2. At Mass, in the Penitential Rite we ask for _____.

3. In the gospels, Jesus taught his followers about the meaning of the Eucharist twice after his resurrection. Name or describe these two incidents: _____

and _____.

4. The two major parts of the Mass are the Liturgy of the Word and the

_____.

5. Name three ways we share in Jesus' presence at Mass: _____,

_____, and _____.

6. At the Last Supper, Jesus gave new meaning to the symbols from the Jewish ritual of _____.

7. Jesus is called the

L_____ _____ _____ and the

B_____ _____ _____

8. In the story of the journey to Emmaus in the gospel of Luke, when did Jesus' disciples recognize him? _____.

9. The Eucharist is a _____

_____ of the Last Supper.

10. The Mass ends with what commission being given to us? _____

_____

Scoring: 7 points for each correct answer (For questions with multiple answers, give 7 points for each correct answer.) You must have a combined total of 190 points to proceed to the Bonus Level.

Bonus Level: ○○○○○

Answer the following.

1. When are Catholics required to attend Mass?

_____

_____

2. What does the fast before Communion require? _____

3. Name the Holy Days of Obligation for the United States.

_____ _____

_____ _____

_____ _____

4. Where does the word *Mass* come from and what does the original word mean?

_____

5. At what Church council was the language of the celebration of the Eucharist changed from Latin to the vernacular?

_____

Scoring: 5 points for each correct answer. (For questions with multiple answers, give 5 points for each correct answer.)

Although the depth of our faith and the quality of our participation in the celebration of the Eucharist cannot be determined by answering questions such as these, it is important to understand the teachings of the Church regarding the celebration of the Eucharist. Often, understanding something can help us to appreciate it and enter into it more completely. How well do you understand the purpose and meaning of the Mass?

Tribulation This term is frequently used to describe a time of troubles immediately before the end and to persuade people how awful the events of today are. Yet the world has long known crisis and calamity.

Actually, the Church is very clear about the end times. Only God knows the time of the end of the world and the Second Coming of Christ.

THE END TIMES

For centuries people have been warning of the end of the world. For example, people were convinced the world would end in the year 1000 because it was approximately one thousand years after Christ had lived. Other groups have prophesied the years 1845, 1913, 1988—and practically every year in between. Many groups have looked to the Book of Revelation in the New Testament for their proof and read into this book's symbolism all kinds of meanings. Here are some common terms that have become associated with the end of the world.
Armageddon This is the final battle between good and evil. The word means "Hill of Megiddo," an actual historical battlefield in the Middle East.
Rapture This term indicates that immediately before the end of time, the chosen will be united with Christ and sinners will be left behind.

State troopers confiscate illegal alcohol.

DID YOU KNOW?

During Prohibition in the United States (1920–1933) the Church had to apply to the Internal Revenue Service for permits to buy wine for sacramental purposes.

Looking Ahead

In Unit 5 you will learn about the way of Christ. Christ lived and calls his followers to live lives of compassion, care, and concern for their fellow human beings, particularly those most in need. The way of Christ, and therefore the way Catholic Christians are called to live, is a way of respect for God's will, for every human being, and for all creation.

WE FOLLOW THE WAY

When is it hard to be a Christian?

17 A RESPECTFUL PEOPLE

HAVE SOME RESPECT

Today, people frequently talk about the importance of respecting others and respecting themselves. It is said that our world would be a better place if everyone just showed some respect. But what is respect? Who deserves it? How should it be expressed?

Activity

Explore your understanding of and expectations about respect by completing the following. Share your responses with your class.

What do you think respect is? Mark one or more of the characteristics below or add your own.

_____ Acknowledging a superior

_____ Having admiration and affection for someone

_____ Being polite

_____ Holding a high opinion of someone

_____ Obeying another person

_____ Having correct behavior

_____ Never showing disapproval or disagreement

_____ Other: _____

Whom do you think you are most likely to respect? Mark your top three choices below and, if you want, add your own description.

_____ Someone who is popular

_____ Someone who has authority

_____ Someone who is outgoing and friendly

_____ Someone who is successful

_____ Someone who is attractive

_____ Someone who is talented

_____ Someone who is in control

_____ Someone who is right most of the time

_____ Someone who likes to hear other points of view

_____ Someone who is wealthy

_____ Other _____

_____

What are the characteristics of someone whom you are not likely to respect?

_____

_____

_____

_____

JESUS CHRIST: RESPECTFUL SERVANT

The first Christians described Jesus in the Gospels as a man with a strong respect and reverence for all people and things. The actions of Jesus reveal a profound respect for God, for the commandments, and for the Temple. Jesus acted respectfully toward Mary and Joseph. He acted with extraordinary respect toward women, poor people, sick people, foreigners, prostitutes, tax collectors, public sinners, and Samaritans—a group despised among the Jewish people. Jesus' respect for all living things and for nature came through in many of his parables.

In the Gospel of Matthew, the life of Jesus is summarized in poetic words taken from the Hebrew prophet Isaiah and used to describe a servant of God. These words tell us about Jesus' respect and care for others.

A bruised reed he will not break,
a smoldering wick he will not
quench.

Matthew 12:20, from Isaiah 42:3

Activity

The following passages relate events in Jesus' life that seem to explain his deep reverence for all life. Look up and read one of the passages. Circle it. Then describe how Jesus demonstrated his respect for life.

Mark 10:13–16

Luke 15:1–7

Matthew 15:21–28

John 8:3–11

_____

_____

_____

_____

_____

_____

_____

_____

THE GOD OF LIFE

From its very beginning, the Bible tells us that all life comes from God, and all life is good. At the same time, the Bible quickly reminds us that human beings are to be life's caretakers.

In the two Creation stories found in the Book of Genesis, God creates all the world for human beings, who are made in his image and who live by his lifegiving breath. The man and the woman are made for each other; all else is made for them to care for, use, enjoy, and share (Genesis 1, 2).

The prophets continually called the people back to ideals of respect. They contrasted God's people with nations that showed no respect and that exploited everyone and everything.

It is in the covenant of Sinai, however, that humanity's responsibility to respect all of creation is emphasized. The Ten Commandments give concrete expression to the absolute basics of respect due to God, people, self, and all creation. Special respect was owed to the weakest and neediest—widows, orphans, children, and the aged.

Activity

If someone asked you to give three rules for getting respect from others, what would you say?

1. _____
_____
_____

2. _____
_____
_____

3. _____
_____
_____

COMMANDMENTS OF RESPECT

The Ten Commandments, also known as the decalogue, are found in two places in the Bible: Exodus 20:2–17 and Deuteronomy 5:6–21. According to Scripture, they were given by God to Moses on Mount Sinai.

We are accustomed to thinking about the commandments as laws that must be obeyed, but for the Jewish people, the Hebrew word for "commandment" is *mitzvah*, which also means "a good deed." In this light, a commandment is not a burden but an opportunity to extend oneself for the good of others. Understood this way, the Ten Commandments are not burdensome prohibitions but joyful ways to live with respect for God, neighbor, and self.

When we are uncertain how to live and how to treat others with respect, we can look to the Ten Commandments.

THE TEN COMMANDMENTS
(Exodus 20:2–17)

1. I, the Lord, am your God. You shall not have other gods besides me.
2. You shall not take the name of the Lord, your God, in vain.
3. Remember to keep holy the sabbath day.
4. Honor your father and mother.
5. You shall not kill.
6. You shall not commit adultery.
7. You shall not steal.
8. You shall not bear false witness against your neighbor.
9. You shall not covet your neighbor's wife.
10. You shall not covet anything that belongs to your neighbor.

Activity

Select any five of the commandments. Write the numbers of the five you have chosen and after each number indicate how that commandment directs us to live respectfully for God, our neighbors, and ourselves.

_____ _____

_____

_____ _____

_____

_____ _____

_____

_____ _____

_____

_____ _____

_____

How do you think the Ten Commandments help us to respect life?

_____

_____

THE CHURCH AND HUMAN RIGHTS

Especially during the past one hundred years, the Church, under the leadership of the popes and bishops, has been developing a **social doctrine** that spells out the implications of the gospel for human rights. Beginning with Pope Leo XIII in 1891 and continuing today with Pope John Paul II, the basic principle of the Church's modern social teaching is respect for the dignity of every person. Just as Jesus respected all people, so must we. Each person has basic rights, Pope John XXIII wrote, that all are called to respect.

Human Dignity

RELIGIOUS RIGHTS	Right to religious beliefs	Right to religious freedom	Right to private and public worship
FAMILY RIGHTS	Right to choose a state	Right to found a family	Right to economic, social, cultural, and moral conditions necessary for family life
ECONOMIC RIGHTS	Right to work	Right to adequate working conditions, a just wage, and to organize a union	Right to own property
COMMUNICATION RIGHTS	Right to communicate	Right to be informed truthfully	Right to freedom of expression, education, and culture
POLITICAL RIGHTS	Right to political participation	Right to juridical protection of political participation	Right to freedom from arbitrary arrest

Activity

Respect or reverence for all includes respecting people's basic human rights. The chart above sums up the rights that the Catholic Church upholds for all persons.

Study the chart carefully. Think beyond the borders of your town or city and of our country. Place a check by those rights that you feel are least respected in the world today. Mark an X by any you feel are not respected in your town or city. Explain specifically how these rights are not respected.

_____

_____

_____

_____

Now think of an example of a time when people have worked together to respect the rights of others. Write about this example below.

_____

_____

Vocabulary

social doctrine: Church teachings that state the implications of the gospel for human rights

✖ ✖ ✖ ✖ ✖ ✖ ✖ ✖ ✖ ✖ ✖ ✖ ✖ ✖ ✖ ✖ ✖ ✖

WE BELIEVE

Respect or reverence for human life is the basis of Catholic social doctrine. Respect for all human beings and for all creation is based on our belief in God's act of creation and in the incarnation of God's Son. Jesus Christ not only provides an extraordinary example of respect and reverence for all but he also identifies himself with all human beings, particularly the weakest and the poorest.

LIVING THE CHRISTIAN IDEAL OF RESPECT

Mary Josephine Rogers (1882–1955) grew up in Massachusetts and went to Smith College. After she graduated, she worked in the college's biology department, and then she was a teacher in the Boston public schools.

While she was in college, she had begun a mission study club to help the Church grow in other countries. She had been helped in getting the club started by Father James A. Walsh. When Father Walsh asked for help with his new organization, the Catholic Foreign Mission Society of America (now known as Maryknoll), Mary volunteered to be a secretary.

In a few years, she and other women volunteers decided to start a new religious order dedicated to the missions. In 1920, the order became known as The Maryknoll Sisters of St. Dominic, and Mary became the first mother general.

As head of the new order, Mother Mary Joseph prepared and trained other young women to carry the good news of the gospel to China and other countries, especially those in Latin America. She was also active in training the people of the countries where the sisters of her order worked. She helped the people there to become catechists, nurses, teachers, and religious sisters.

Along with the priests and brothers associated with the Maryknoll Society, Mother Mary Joseph and her sisters shared in the vision of spreading the gospel message while being open to the insights of other cultures. They engaged in pastoral work that sought to meet the needs of peoples throughout the world.

Today, through the Maryknoll Mission Association of the Faithful, lay people can minister to Christians in other countries. More than forty years after Mother Mary Joseph's death, Maryknoll continues to be committed to fostering local, self-sustaining Christian communities throughout the world.

Activity

How did Mother Mary Joseph show respect for other peoples?

_____

_____

_____

How do members of Maryknoll today continue to show respect for other cultures?

_____

_____

_____

_____

ACTING FOR OTHERS

As Christians, we believe that all human beings are made in God's image and likeness. We believe that to be a human being is to be a person for God and others. Our Lord stressed this in all he said and did. At the same time, Jesus identified himself with all people. He also taught that only those who act for him and others will inherit the kingdom of God.

Through its social doctrines, the Church teaches us how to be for Christ and for others. Perhaps the Church's greatest teaching is that we must be for others together—that is, as a Church and as a people, not just as individuals.

In his great social encyclical *Mater et Magistra (On Christianity and Social Progress),* Pope John XXIII described the way we are to act together for others in a given situation:

"First the actual situation is examined . . . then evaluated . . . then only is it decided what can and should be done . . . These three steps are at times expressed by the three words: *observe, judge, act . . .* it seems particularly fitting that youth not only reflect upon this order of procedure, but also . . . follow it to the extent feasible, lest what they have learned be regarded merely as something to be thought about but not acted upon" (236–237).

Activity

Think of an example of a human right being ignored and then follow the steps given by Pope John XXIII to decide on something that can be done for others in this particular situation.

Situation: _____

_____

Observations: _____

_____

Judgment: _____

_____

Actions: _____

_____

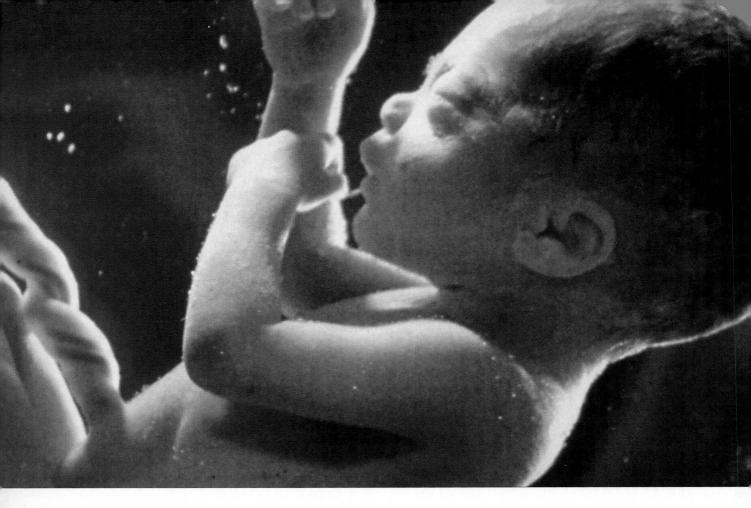

REVERENCE FOR LIFE

All life is a gift from God and must be treated with reverence, recognizing that it is precious and sacred because it comes from God. Christ's call to love one another means putting the needs of others ahead of our own. And certainly we can never be so selfish as to put our own interests ahead of the very lives of others.

Of all the human rights, the very first is that of the right to life. If we claim as Christians to be concerned about human rights, we cannot mean only our own lives; we must be concerned about all members of society. We must be concerned about the weak, the elderly, the ill, and the unborn. The Father calls each of us to recognize that every human being is made in the image and likeness of God.

We as Christians are to defend and promote life, to show reverence for life, and to show loving concern for life in all its forms. We are also to recognize that because life is a gift from God, we do not have the last word about when life begins and ends. Only God has complete control over human life. This is why the Church teaches that abortion, infanticide, and euthanasia are forms of great evil. Human beings do not have the power over and against others to decide when someone will live or die. Only God has that power.

Life is a treasure entrusted to human beings. This treasure must not be wasted but must be cherished well. In the end, we are accountable to God for how we have treated this great and precious gift. We are responsible for the lives of others and must do all we can to preserve life wherever it is found.

SELF-RESPECT

Some people say that respect of any kind is not possible if we do not respect ourselves. Self-respect is not the same as selfishness or arrogance. It is a recognition that we are made in the image and likeness of God. To honor God for giving us this great gift, we must show honor and care for ourselves.

Self-respect means many things and includes an awareness of how to take care of ourselves physically, mentally, emotionally, and spiritually. Just as we would never wish to see others hurt or doing harmful things, so too a person with self-respect makes good choices and good decisions about how he or she lives every day. Good diet, plenty of exercise, a serious attitude toward school, good relationships, and prayer and worship are the beginnings of self-respect.

The next step toward self-respect is to respect others. When we consider the effects of our actions on others, when we avoid hurting others and treat others with courtesy, we are actually deepening our self-respect. Respecting others also means that we recognize that we are not better than anyone else and that to get respect, we must first give respect.

There are other things about self-respect to know as well. It is important to know ourselves, to face up to our faults, to take responsibility for our actions, and to appreciate our own talents. As we are able to do this, we develop the capacity for self-control. We can overcome bad habits, exercise self-discipline, and recognize that while we do not have control over everything in our lives, we do have control over how we choose to react to what happens to us. The ability to step back and choose the action that is best for us opens us up to life. We see more possibilities both for ourselves and others. We live less in fear and more in joy.

Our power to achieve our goals increases greatly when we have self-respect. We are able to better our lives and to make a positive difference in our world. We not only become more skilled at taking care of ourselves and others but we also show our appreciation for the gift of life that God has given us.

Activity

Identify three ways in which some people fail to respect life.

1. _____

_____

2. _____

_____

3. _____

_____

Suggest ways that Christians can encourage other people to show respect for life in all its forms.

_____

_____

_____

_____

Praying About Human Rights

What issues in our world matter to you? What can you do about them? One thing we can all do is pray. We are accustomed to praying about problems in our own lives, for the people we love, and for the things that we want. But the power of prayer should never be underestimated. Prayer is part of the way we can find solutions to the crises and tragedies that our world faces. It is especially important to pray about issues that affect large numbers of people.

One of these issues is human rights. God calls us to bring to the attention of others times when basic human rights are violated. Violence, political oppression, and failing to address the causes of poverty are all violations of human rights. Prejudice based on religion, race, ethnicity, gender, language, or way of life is also a violation of human rights. Be imaginative and get others involved in bringing these sufferings before God.

Ideas

_____ Ask everyone in your school to stop at a certain time of day and pray about a social problem in the world.

_____ Plan and hold a candlelight vigil. Prepare prayers, hymns, and Scripture readings beforehand. Hold your vigil in the evening and arrange for candles to be burning in a safe place while everyone prays together.

_____ Invite all the classes in school to attend a prayer service about a world problem. Include news clippings and, if possible, video footage about the problem as part of the prayer service.

_____ Write a prayer about a social problem, have copies of it made, distribute them, and ask people to pray the prayer each night with their families.

_____ Hold a prayer breakfast about a social problem. Plan Scripture readings, grace, simple food, and perhaps even a speaker.

_____ Other: _____

_____

_____

Mini-calendar

October	Respect Life Month
November 1	Worldwide Peace Day
December 10	Human Rights Day
February 8–14	National Crime Prevention Week
March 8	International Women's Day
April 7	World Health Day

Explain each of the three steps by which a respectful Christian should act for others.

Observe _____

_____

Judge _____

_____

Act _____

_____

Why did Pope John XXIII insist that young people follow these principles?

_____

_____

_____

_____

What does reverence for life entail?

_____

_____

Respond to the following questions based on what you have learned in this chapter.

1. What is *social doctrine*?

_____

_____

_____

2. What is the basic principle of Catholic social doctrine?

_____

_____

Be gentle with everyone, able to teach, tolerant, correcting opponents with kindness.

2 Timothy 2:24

3. Discuss what chance for success the respectful, nonviolent approaches to social change have in our world today.

18

A COMPASSIONATE PEOPLE

A CALL FOR COMPASSION

Ryan White was born in Kokomo, Indiana, on December 12, 1971. He was born with hemophilia, an incurable disease that causes excessive bleeding from even minor injuries. Like all hemophiliacs, Ryan had to be careful about everything he did. A fall or a cut could cause him to bleed to death. However, Ryan was luckier than hemophiliacs who had lived in earlier times.

Medical research led to the development of a blood-clotting product called factor VIII. It was made from donated blood and contained a concentrated dose of the clotting factor. Factor VIII was given intravenously to hemophiliacs to help slow massive bleeding. Before factor VIII was invented, most hemophiliacs only lived

about fourteen years. With factor VIII, Ryan was able to live a more normal life.

In the early 1980s, AIDS, or Acquired Immune Deficiency Syndrome, was discovered. AIDS is caused by a virus that makes the body unable to fight off infections. As scientists studied the disease, they learned that three groups of people were at risk for AIDS: people who have unprotected sexual intercourse with an infected person, people who come in contact with contaminated hypodermic needles, and hemophiliacs and others who are dependent on blood products.

At some point, Ryan was unknowingly treated with AIDS-contaminated blood. Shortly after his thirteenth birthday, Ryan was diagnosed with AIDS when he became ill with pneumonia. While Ryan was still in the hospital, burglars broke into his home and stole the family's Christmas presents. Word of the burglary and Ryan's illness spread throughout the small town of Kokomo. While some people were outraged that a family struggling with a terminal disease should be victimized in such a tragic way, others responded with fear and hatred.

The school board barred Ryan from school. When the Whites sued and won, some parents signed petitions to keep Ryan away from their children. The Whites' mailbox was filled with hate letters and threats. People called Ryan names on radio talk shows and when they saw him. When he was finally re-admitted to school, students backed away from him and wrote obscenities on his locker. The Whites were even shunned by the members of their own church, who insisted that Ryan and his family sit in a special area when they came to church, so that they could be watched. The front window of Ryan's house was shot out. Finally, the Whites moved to Cicero, Indiana, where they were welcomed with acceptance and friendship.

Journalists reported about Ryan's plight and the unfair treatment he received. Ryan became a national symbol for helping people confront their prejudices about AIDS. He taught us that it is the disease, not its victims, that is frightening. Ryan testified before the President's Commission on AIDS. He told the commissioners that he did not hate those who had treated him unjustly. He said that they were victims, too—victims of ignorance.

Ryan helped us recognize that ignorance and prejudice can be conquered by compassion and understanding. Ryan White died on Passion Sunday, April 8, 1990.

Activity

Imagine that a classmate has been diagnosed with AIDS. On the lines below, write about how you would respond to and behave toward this individual. What would you say to other students who behaved unfairly toward your sick classmate?

_____

_____

_____

_____

JESUS, THE COMPASSION OF GOD

Compassion is probably the characteristic we most associate with Jesus. Compassion is also at the core of his teachings.

The first Christians remembered how compassionate Jesus was, and they told others. Many Gospel stories show Jesus touched by someone's pain and doing something to take it away. Jesus felt the crowd's hunger in the desert, and he fed them (Matthew 15:32). He was moved by the pain of two blind men, and he touched their eyes so that they might see (Matthew 9:27). A widow's sorrow at the loss of her son moved him to restore the boy to life (Luke 7:13). Feeling the isolation of a leper, Jesus reached out his hand and cured him (Mark 1:41). The confusion of the people moved Jesus to teach them about God and about life's meaning (Mark 8:2).

Activity

Read Matthew 25:31–40. Then list the acts of compassion we are called to practice.

_____

_____

_____

Activity

Here is how the dictionary defines compassion.

> **com•pas•sion** \kəm-'pash-ən\ *n* [ME, fr. MF or LL; MF, fr. LL *compassion-, compassio,* fr. *compassus,* pp. of *compati* to sympathize, fr. L *com-* + *pati* to bear, suffer — more at PATIENT] (14c): sympathetic consciousness of others' distress together with a desire to alleviate it— **com•pas•sion•less** \-ləs\ *adj*

Study the definition. Then describe the two dimensions of compassion.

1. _____

2. _____

List four other words that have almost the same meaning as compassion.

1. _____

2. _____

3. _____

4. _____

Use one or two of these words in a complete sentence.

_____

_____

_____

A COMPASSIONATE CHURCH

Throughout the centuries, the Catholic Church has tried to live up to and live out the ideal of compassion given to it by Christ. The earliest Christian communities cared for the sick, poor, and elderly. The Apostle Paul collected **alms**—money or other goods given by Christians for the poor. Almsgiving was an accepted part of life in the early Church.

The Church's monasteries and religious communities of men and women continued and expanded these forms of compassionate service.

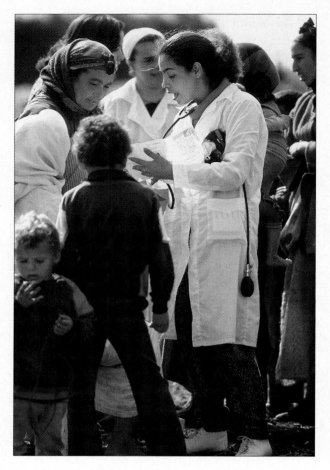

The history of the Church is filled with the deeds of women and men who followed the challenging model of compassion to which Jesus Christ calls all his followers. Many modern social service organizations can trace their beginnings back to the compassionate acts performed by Christians centuries ago. These include such services as hospitals, hospices, orphanages, soup kitchens, low-cost housing, emergency shelters, prison reforms, and food distribution programs.

Although cruelty, neglect, and silence perpetuated the sufferings of people throughout the centuries, compassionate acts by some Christians have been a bright spot in the history of our Church. The Catholic Church today continues the commitment to the Christian ideal of compassion. Many parishes have social action committees. Dioceses have offices of Catholic Charities. The American Catholic Church has the Campaign for Human Development and Catholic Relief Services.

The National Conference of Catholic Bishops continues to speak out compassionately on the many difficult issues that face our society. For example, *Economic Justice for All: Pastoral and Letter on Catholic Social Teaching and the Economy* issued in late 1986, speaks eloquently and compassionately to the inequalities that exist in and sometimes are fostered by our United States economy. In this document, the bishops boldly state that they write in order to discover "what it means to serve 'the least among us' " (#4).

Catholic men and women actively support charitable organizations and social services. They work for and with the poor, feeding them, and tending their physical and emotional wounds. Two modern Catholics admired by Catholics and the world at large are Mother Teresa of Calcutta and Dorothy Day of New York—both have given examples of extraordinary compassion for the poor and the outcast. In emerging nations today, the poor themselves find ways to reach out to one another and to their struggling neighbors.

If Jesus is considered the "compassion of God," the Church and each Christian are called to be the "compassion of Christ" in today's suffering world. This rediscovery of ancient charitable practice is growing in the Catholic Church today.

Activity

Review the stories of great Catholic men and women told in the previous chapters. Choose two who appeal most to you and describe what each did that exemplifies Christian compassion.

1. _____

_____

_____

_____

_____

2. _____

_____

_____

_____

_____

Vocabulary

alms: money or goods given for the poor

✖ ✖ ✖ ✖ ✖ ✖ ✖ ✖ ✖ ✖ ✖ ✖ ✖ ✖ ✖ ✖ ✖

WE BELIEVE

Jesus' life and teachings gave human form to God's compassion. Jesus was deeply moved by people's sufferings and reached out to ease or remove those sufferings. He called his followers to regard compassion as their chief characteristic. The Church continues to live out, even if imperfectly, Christ's ideal of compassion for all who suffer.

Activity

Think about the people you know—people in your family, your neighborhood, your town or city. List below the names of individuals and organizations you know about that reach out in compassion to those who are in need or who are suffering.

_____

_____

_____

_____

_____

WORKS OF MERCY

The Church has long summarized its ideals of compassion in two practical lists. These lists are based on the Gospel of Matthew's parable of the final judgment as well as on centuries of Christian experience. These are called the Corporal and Spiritual Works of Mercy.

THE CORPORAL WORKS OF MERCY

1. Feed the hungry.
2. Give drink to the thirsty.
3. Clothe the naked.
4. Visit those in prison.
5. Shelter the homeless.
6. Visit the sick.
7. Bury the dead.

THE SPIRITUAL WORKS OF MERCY

1. Help sinners.
2. Teach the ignorant.
3. Give advice to the doubtful.
4. Comfort those who suffer.
5. Be patient with others.
6. Forgive injuries.
7. Pray for the living and the dead.

Activity

Select one Corporal Work of Mercy and one Spiritual Work of Mercy. Then write an example of how each might be lived.

1. _____

_____

_____

_____

2. _____

_____

_____

_____

_____

A COMPASSIONATE WOMAN

Rose Hawthorne grew up in a loving family in Massachusetts. Her father was one of America's most famous authors, Nathaniel Hawthorne.

When Rose was seventeen, she fell in love with a young writer named George Lathrop. The two were married three years later and moved to New York. They had a son who died at the age of five. About the same time, Lathrop began to drink heavily.

Rose met Emma Lazarus, the woman who wrote the inscription for the Statue of Liberty. They became friends. Not long afterward, Rose learned that Emma had cancer. This information was to give Rose's life a whole new direction.

When Rose discovered that hospitals at that time refused to care for poor people with incurable cancer, she felt called to do something to help them. She began to dedicate herself to the needs of these people. She made the words of St. Vincent de Paul her motto: "I am for God and the poor."

After Rose became a widow, she took a basic nursing course and rented a small apartment on the Lower East Side of New York City. She was convinced that to help the poor she must be one of them. She went each day to care for the dying cancer victims in the slums. She took some into her own apartment.

She advertised in the newspapers for bandages, medicines, and helpers. A few volunteers joined her but found the life too depressing and left. In 1897, Alice Huber, an art student, joined Rose and stayed.

The two women bought a large house so that they could serve more patients. Housing and treatment were free.

In 1900, Rose began the Dominican Congregation of St. Rose of Lima, calling her order Servants of Relief for Incurable Cancer. Rose died in 1926 at age seventy-five.

Activity

Think of one person or group of persons who are suffering in our world today. Explain why you feel this compassion. Then suggest what you think should be done to help this person or group.

Person or Group: _____

Why you feel compassion: _____

What you think should be done: _____

Activity

Write a brief description of what you think a good Christian is like.

_____

_____

_____

_____

_____

Give a brief description of what you think the kingdom of God is like.

_____

_____

_____

_____

_____

THE BEATITUDES

A beatitude is a prayer form found in both the Old Testament and the New Testament. It declares someone blessed in the eyes of God, explains why this person is blessed, and what reward he or she will receive from God. In the Old Testament, beatitudes are found in books such as Psalms. They usually praise the person who enjoys the friendship of God. In the New Testament, beatitudes are found primarily in the Gospels of Luke and Matthew. In the New Testament beatitudes also express the characteristics of the true follower of Christ: anyone who lives out Jesus' command to love and reminds us of the promises God has made us through Jesus Christ.

When Christians refer to the beatitudes, they usually mean the list of eight blessings in Matthew 5:1–10. These are given at the beginning of the Gospel chapter in which Jesus' Sermon on the Mount is presented. In the Gospel of Matthew, the eight beatitudes focus on describing the characteristics of the person who participates in and hopes for the final coming of the kingdom of God.

The Gospel of Matthew describes this person as being one of the poor. This has been interpreted to mean those who lack a fair share of the world's goods as well as those who recognize their need for and complete dependence on God. The beatitudes proclaim the blessings that Christ has gained for us.

The beatitudes call us to happiness with God. By giving us examples of the kind of person who will enjoy union with God in the kingdom, the beatitudes are also providing us with a blueprint to help us make the right choices in our lives. The beatitudes teach us the true meaning of love and compassion.

The first part of each beatitude identifies the reasons God has blessed a person, and the second part of the beatitude specifies the blessing. According to the Gospel of Matthew, the blessing is participation in the kingdom of God begun in Christ and fulfilled at the end of time. Established by Christ, the kingdom is present with us now and will be completed by God in the future. God's kingdom is present wherever there are examples of Christ's love and compassion.

BLESSED ARE THE POOR IN SPIRIT, FOR THEIRS IS THE KINGDOM OF HEAVEN.

This beatitude has been interpreted to mean both those people who have no material possessions as well as those who recognize their complete dependence on God. This beatitude teaches us to recognize our need for God. The poor in spirit know that God is more important than anything else in life.

BLESSED ARE THEY WHO MOURN, FOR THEY WILL BE COMFORTED.

To mourn means to grieve over a loss or a painful event. This beatitude helps us to acknowledge the pain that others experience as well as the need to grieve over the sin and suffering caused by evil in our world. We trust that God comforts anyone who suffers from loss and injustice. We are reminded to reach out to those who need to be comforted.

BLESSED ARE THE MEEK, FOR THEY WILL INHERIT THE LAND.

In the Old Testament, the phrase *the land* refers to the promised land, or Palestine. In this beatitude, however, *the land* refers to the kingdom of God. This beatitude reminds us to humbly recognize that all our gifts and talents come from God. With kindness and patience, we should share these gifts to serve God and others.

BLESSED ARE THEY WHO HUNGER AND THIRST FOR RIGHTEOUSNESS, FOR THEY WILL BE SATISFIED.

In this beatitude, the word *righteousness* means "behavior that is in accord with God's will." This beatitude also reminds us that God's rule of peace, love, and justice has been established by Christ and will be fully realized at the end of time. As followers of Christ, we should imitate his life and act with equality, truth, and fairness. It is also important to speak out for the rights of those who are suffering from any kind of oppression or injustice. We are called to share our possessions with those in need.

BLESSED ARE THE MERCIFUL, FOR THEY WILL BE SHOWN MERCY.

Mercy is a readiness to forgive those who have harmed or hurt us. This beatitude calls us to forgive anyone who has hurt us, reminding us that our reward for forgiving others is that we ourselves will be forgiven the hurt and harm that we have caused. In this beatitude, we are also reminded of the importance of accepting others and showing compassion for them.

BLESSED ARE THE CLEAN OF HEART, FOR THEY WILL SEE GOD.

The phrase *clean of heart* is found in the Old Testament, and there it sometimes refers to worshiping at the Temple. In this beatitude, it refers to those people who place God first in their lives and who are not distracted by other interests. To be clean of heart means that we want only to do God's will and to follow his commands. This beatitude reminds us to keep our minds and hearts focused on God, always seeking good, avoiding evil, and having hope in the coming kingdom.

BLESSED ARE THE PEACEMAKERS, FOR THEY WILL BE CALLED CHILDREN OF GOD.

A peacemaker is not just someone who works to settle arguments but also someone who actively works for the wholeness and harmony that reflects God's love for us. This beatitude reminds us to be a sign for others of God's forgiveness and compassion. It calls us to try to settle disputes as well as to pray for peace and unity in our families, in our communities, and in the world.

BLESSED ARE THEY WHO ARE PERSECUTED FOR THE SAKE OF RIGHTEOUSNESS, FOR THEIRS IS THE KINGDOM OF HEAVEN.

This beatitude acknowledges that it can be difficult to follow God's will and that we may sometimes face others' hostility and persecution. We must stand up for our beliefs even if we are made fun of or criticized. In this beatitude, we are reminded that since our reward will be the kingdom of heaven, we are part of Jesus' mission in the world. We still must speak out against situations that prevent God's rule.

The eight beatitudes teach us how wonderful the kingdom of heaven will be in comparison to the suffering of this world. The beatitudes also show us how to love God above all things and how to serve others in compassion and a spirit of mercy. When we are uncertain about how to live our daily lives, we can look to the beatitudes, which show us that happiness is to be found in living in Christian hope.

Activity

Explore the meaning of the beatitudes by creating your own beatitudes that describe characteristics and virtues for which Christians may be blessed by God. After each, give your reason for suggesting this beatitude.

Blessed are ————— for they ——————————————————————————

Reason: ——

Blessed are ————— for they ——————————————————————————

Reason: ——

Blessed are ————— for they ——————————————————————————

Reason: ——

Blessed are ————— for they ——————————————————————————

Reason: ——

The psalms have been very popular in both Jewish and Christian prayer and worship. One reason for their popularity is that the psalms deal with the real problems of human existence. By praying the psalms, we can ask God for safety from enemies, for freedom from all kinds of oppression, and for mercy and forgiveness for wrongdoing.

Some psalms speak of God's compassion and mercy. Others speak of the need for human beings to have compassion, since our lives are so brief. These psalms remind us that while we do not live very long, our deeds and good works continue to last after we are gone.

PRAYING THE PSALMS

The Book of Psalms is a collection of songs found in the Old Testament. Some of the psalms are ancient and may date back to the time of King David, 1,000 years before the birth of Jesus. Today, they are an important part of Christian prayer. They express the joy, thanksgiving, and longing for God that human beings experience.

The psalms are a significant part of Jewish daily prayer, and Christians have included the psalms in their daily prayer since the early Church. Psalms are adapted as songs, they become parts of prayers and prayer responses, and they are favorite readings for certain times of the year and on special occasions.

As a father has compassion on
     his children,
so the LORD has compassion on
     those who fear him.
For he knows how we are formed;
     he remembers that we are dust.
Man's days are like those of grass;
     like a flower of the field he blooms;
The wind sweeps over him and he
     is gone,
     and his place knows him no more.
But the kindness of the LORD is from
     eternity
     to eternity toward those who fear
     him,
And his justice toward children's
     children
     among those who keep his covenant
     and remember to fulfill his precepts.
Psalm 103:13–18

Activity

What are some images in this psalm describing the shortness of human life?

_____

How is God's compassion described in this psalm?

_____

What insight about compassion have you learned from this psalm?

_____

CHAPTER REVIEW

Complete the following by naming the Works of Mercy.

The Corporal Works of Mercy	The Spiritual Works of Mercy
1. _____	1. _____
2. _____	2. _____
3. _____	3. _____
4. _____	4. _____
5. _____	5. _____
6. _____	6. _____
7. _____	7. _____

Write a paragraph explaining what a beatitude is and how a beatitude can help us to become better followers of Christ.

_____

_____

_____

_____

_____

Respond to the following questions based on what you have learned in this chapter.

1. What are *alms?*

_____

_____

_____

2. In what ways has the Church lived out Jesus' ideal of compassion?

_____

Be merciful, just as [also] your Father is merciful.
Luke 6:36

_____

_____

3. Discuss what obstacles get in the way of our being more compassionate.

19   A JUST PEOPLE

YOU BE THE JUDGE!

Everyone expects to be treated fairly in life, and when justice does not occur, we feel outraged. Yet it is not always easy to be fair. Some situations are complicated, and fairness may seem to change, depending on one's point of view.

WHAT DOES IT MEAN TO BE FAIR?

Activity

Explore your idea of justice. Read each of the situations below. Then explain whether or not you think what happened was fair. Explain your response.

1. Tracy failed her science test because she was sick and missed several days of school. She asked her teacher if she could take the test over again, but her teacher said no. Is this fair? Why or why not?

_____

_____

_____

Would your opinion change if you found out that Tracy had not been doing her work all marking period? Why or why not?

_____

_____

_____

Would your opinion change if you found out that the teacher allowed another student who had been ill to take the test again? Why or why not?

_____

_____

_____

2. Mark needed a pen for class and took Carl's without asking. After class he forgot to return it, and a day or two later he lost it. Carl had to borrow a pen from someone else. Was this fair? Why or why not?

_____

_____

_____

Would your opinion change if you found out that Carl had originally taken the pen from Tanya without asking? Why or why not?

_____

_____

_____

Would your opinion change if you found out that Mark was never prepared for class and always took pens from other students? Why or why not?

_____

_____

_____

What do you look for in determining whether or not someone is being treated fairly?

_____

_____

_____

_____

UNDERSTANDING FAIRNESS

Our understanding of fairness, or justice, is part of our understanding of morality. As human beings, we grow and mature in our awareness of morality, or what is right or wrong, and in our awareness of justice. We grow in our ability to recognize and work for the good.

When children are very young, they may think of goodness as a matter of obeying the laws and other demands of those in authority. When disobedience occurs, very young children would expect that justice demands punishment.

As children grow older, they may see doing good as part of gaining a reward. In this stage of moral growth, young children may understand justice as being anything that satisfies their own needs. This may include doing something for others, or it may include acting mainly for oneself.

In the next stage of moral growth, children want to please God, Jesus, their parents or guardians, and other persons in authority, such as a teacher. After this, children begin to recognize that right and wrong are important concepts in themselves. The rules of games must be followed. A code of conduct—the things we like and the things we do not like—may be enforced.

As a person continues to grow, he or she will probably begin to question the reasoning behind the laws of a particular group or society. He or she may be critical of laws and what they accomplish or fail to accomplish.

In the final stage of moral development, a person acts out of a concern for truth, justice, and love. He or she recognizes that trying to achieve these important principles are the reason people make laws in the first place, however imperfect these laws may be. Justice means giving to God and neighbor. The person of justice is distinguished by his or her ability to think rightly and act properly toward others.

All of us continually face the challenge of maturing morally. By trying to live our Christian ideals, we deepen our awareness of and capacity for justice.

COMPASSIONATE AND JUST

As the Son of God, Jesus Christ acted from the highest stage of morality. As both God and man, he never sinned. Jesus brought truth, justice, and love to us. He stood out against powerful institutions in his single-minded care for all who came to him. Jesus' heart went out to those whose lives were burdened, and his anger flashed when he realized that the powerful and self-contented placed heavy burdens on those who were without power or influence.

One such story of Jesus' care and of his anger at the source of injustice happened when Jesus went to a local synagogue.

A man with a shriveled hand happened to be there, and they put this question to Jesus, hoping to bring an accusation against him: "Is it lawful to work a cure on the sabbath?"

Jesus said in response, "Suppose one of you has a sheep and it falls into a pit on the sabbath. Will he not take hold of it and pull it out? Well, think how much more precious a human being is than a sheep. Clearly, good deeds may be performed on the sabbath."

To the man he said, "Stretch out your hand." He did so, and it was perfectly restored; it became as sound as the other.

Based on Matthew 12:10–13

Jesus responded to the immediate physical and spiritual needs of those who came to him. He also pointed out the source or cause of people's difficulties and confusion. He often faced the misuse of power by some of the religious leaders of his time. He acted in anger against the misuse of the Temple, which he saw as a house of God and prayer rather than as a place of business.

All who seek to follow Jesus must imitate his example, as did his first followers. As we grow in our understanding of what goodness is, we are continually called as Christians to tend to the immediate needs of our brothers and sisters. We must work to eliminate the sources of injustice and must participate in making a better world.

Activity

Complete the following sentences to help create a just and peaceful classroom.

What are some of the injustices that might occur in a class of eighth graders?

_____

_____

_____

_____

Work to resolve issues of injustice in your class by completing the following
open-ended statements.

In our classroom, in order to study and learn in peace, we can _____

_____

_____

In our classroom, in order to make sure that everyone is treated fairly, we can _____

_____

_____

_____

In our classroom, in order to make sure that all

classmates are included, we can _____

_____

_____

_____

_____

Activity

Specify the qualities you think a person of justice should have.

_____

_____

_____

_____

_____

_____

_____

BEING AWARE

In order to develop a sense of justice, it is important to understand the role evil plays in our sinful world. We know that evil does not come from God, because God is totally good. We know too that evil can occur in the actions people choose, in what people fail to do, and in the harm that people experience as a result of natural forces, such as earthquakes and hurricanes, or from accidents, such as plane crashes.

God enters into a relationship of love with all people. God gives us the gift of **free will,** the freedom to choose to do what is right or wrong. God creates all human beings with this freedom to choose between right and wrong.

When we choose to do wrong or to fail to do what we know we should, we **sin.** Sin prevents us from living as followers of Jesus. Sin is a free decision, and when we sin, we make a conscious decision to turn away from the Trinity and the teachings of the Church.

Human beings have a tendency to be selfish. Catholic Christians call this sinful condition within our lives and into which we are all born **original sin.**

The direction of the Holy Spirit is our greatest help in overcoming sin and living as a follower of Jesus. The Spirit guides our **conscience,** the ability to judge whether something is right or wrong. The Spirit helps us to resist **temptation,** the attraction or pressure that may lead us to sin.

Very serious sins that completely break off our relationship with God are called **mortal sins.** There are three conditions that make a sin mortal.

- The act must be seriously wrong.
- We must know that the act is seriously wrong.
- We must make a free choice to commit the sin.

Mortal sins must be confessed in the sacrament of Reconciliation. Through Jesus, we receive God's mercy and forgiveness and once again begin to live a life of grace.

Less serious sins are called **venial sins**. Venial sins weaken but do not destroy our relationship with God and the Church community. Venial sins not only hurt ourselves and other people but also turn us away from God.

Mortal and venial sins committed by the individual are called personal sins. Personal sins have social consequences. These sins often hurt others or tempt them to turn away from God and the Church.

Social sins are ingrained in the unjust and oppressive systems and structures of the community, the country, and the world. Racism, failure to pay just wages, ignoring the homeless, fighting unjust wars, sexism, and prejudice in any form are all social sins.

The Church teaches that there are seven **capital sins**. These sins represent the most basic temptations for all people and are the source of many other personal and social sins.

> Pride is an exaggerated love for self; it makes us think and act as if we were better than others.
>
> Covetousness is a greedy desire for wealth or material possessions.
>
> Lust is an uncontrolled desire for sexual pleasure.
>
> Anger is an uncontrolled emotion that causes us to lose temper and strike out at others, verbally and physically.
>
> Gluttony is excessive eating and drinking.
>
> Envy is resenting the achievements and success of others.
>
> Sloth is avoiding work and responsibility through laziness.

We cannot work for justice if we do not understand the harmful effects of sin and evil in our world. We also must recognize that because we are sinful beings we do not always act justly and are not always able to understand where justice may best be found. We must rely on prayer, Scripture, and Church teachings to guide us.

Activity

Look at the list of actions below. Mark those with which you are familiar.
I know people who . . .

_____ write in books they do not own.

_____ fail to return library books.

_____ scratch their initials into everything.

_____ throw food in the cafeteria.

_____ make fun of classmates.

_____ avoid classmates who cannot afford expensive clothes.

_____ always choose to be with the most popular students.

_____ pick popular classmates for group work rather than those who will really help.

_____ act as if the unpopular classmates do not exist.

How do the actions you have selected sometimes develop into attitudes of indifference and sources of injustice?

Vocabulary

free will: the freedom to choose to do what is right or wrong

sin: a free decision to do wrong or fail to do the good that we should

original sin: the sinful condition within our lives and into which we are all born

conscience: the ability to judge whether something is right or wrong

temptation: the attraction or pressure that may lead us to sin

mortal sins: very serious sins that completely break off our relationship with God

venial sins: less serious sins that weaken but do not destroy our relationship with God and the Church community

capital sins: the seven basic temptations

✗ ✗ ✗ ✗ ✗ ✗ ✗ ✗ ✗ ✗ ✗ ✗ ✗ ✗ ✗

WHO WILL ANSWER?

When Christianity became the official religion of the Roman Empire and Christians became wealthy and powerful leaders of society, Christians had the opportunity to exercise the ideals of justice in new ways. Although Christians sometimes failed to do this, Church fathers—such as Clement of Alexandria, Augustine, Basil, Cyprian, John Chrysostom, and Ambrose—reminded people to act on Christ's ideals of justice. The Church fathers and other Christians stood up and spoke out for the poor and powerless as strongly as Jesus and the Hebrew prophets before him had done.

In the last hundred years, the Catholic Church has developed its social teaching and its commitment to **social justice**, a term that describes the systematic respect for human rights within society and its institutions. Social justice is the expression of respect and compassion through the structures of society—laws, values, business practices, government, taxes, art forms, and culture.

In contrast to compassionate action, which responds to heal people's pain, social justice attempts to discover and remove the causes of the social and economic pain. It seeks to change for the better the habits, policies, and purposes of social structures and institutions. Social justice works against social sin, for social sins thwart God's plan to bring peace, love, and justice to our world.

The world's Catholic bishops have declared that the gospel of Christ calls every believer to work for social justice throughout the world. The goal of this important statement is to help bring about a world in which nations and other important institutions respect the dignity and rights of all human beings. As Catholics, we are responsible for working to change the unjust situations and institutions that allow social sins to exist.

Today, the Church judges the quality of social justice in any country or institution in the same way the prophets, Jesus, and the early Church leaders judged it—that is, by the way the poorest and weakest members of the society are treated.

The Church today is aware of how Jesus chose to identify himself with the poor and the weak. As Christians and members of the Catholic Church, we are called to stand with and for the poor and against every form of social and political injustice and oppression. As we think about how we might change the unjust systems that create poverty and oppression, we ask "Why?" and try to identify the causes of the pain and oppression people suffer.

IDENTIFYING THE SOURCE

An ancient Chinese proverb says that a journey of a thousand miles begins with a single step. Christians are called to undertake long journeys toward solving injustice even when the sources of the injustice seem far away and very complex.

Throughout the world, thousands of men and women, young as well as old, devote their lives to helping people who are poor, hungry, and homeless. They give them food, shelter, and medical care. Yet the number of people in need continues to grow.

Consider the statistics below and ask "Why?" The facts themselves provide clues to some possible causes.

1. More and more people around the world are becoming poor as the nations of the world spend about $22 for military purposes for every $1 spent to aid the poor.

2. Although more and more women in the United States are working, they continue to earn just $.69 for every $1 that men earn.

3. In the United States, 8.7% of white families, 30% of African American families, 34% of Native American families, and 21% of Hispanic families are living at what is officially considered to be poverty level.

4. In the United States, 79% of the people who are officially considered to be poor are women and children—and the percentage is growing.

5. The fastest-growing group of poor in our country is made up of children.

Activity

Choose one of the real-life statistics given above. Identify an immediate remedy and then describe a possible long-term solution.

_____

_____

_____

_____

Vocabulary

social justice: the systematic respect for human rights within society and its institutions

✖ ✖ ✖ ✖ ✖ ✖ ✖ ✖ ✖ ✖ ✖ ✖ ✖ ✖ ✖ ✖ ✖

WE BELIEVE

The Church teaches that action for social justice is a vital part of the gospel message. Social justice expands individual compassion into efforts to change society so that everyone's rights are respected. The Church and all its members are called by Christ to work for a more just society worldwide. The Church today chooses, as Jesus did, to stand with, for, and on the side of the poor and against the powerful forces of injustice.

A FRIEND OF THE POOR

During Frédéric Ozanam's studies at the University of Paris in the 1830s, he made many friends and began a discussion group that became very popular with both faculty and students. Religion was a frequent topic because most of the professors were anti-Catholic.

One evening as Frédéric was defending the Church during a discussion, a member of the group challenged him. "What do you do besides talk to show what good your faith is?" the challenger asked.

The remark hit home. Frédéric had no reply. A few weeks later he came to a decision that changed his life. One spring evening, he told a friend, "We must do what our Lord Jesus Christ did when preaching the gospel—we must go to the poor."

That night they gave to a poor family their own small supply of wood for heating their room. In the next weeks, five more students joined them in visiting the unemployed poor in the slums of Paris.

Frédéric's group continued to grow. He called it the Society of St. Vincent de Paul and its members helped the needy.

In 1848, France was torn apart by a revolution between the poor and the wealthy. Frédéric decided to try to change the situation. He ran for election to the National Assembly. Though he was defeated, he helped to negotiate a truce. After the fighting stopped, however, the social conditions for the poor did not improve as he had hoped.

When Frédéric became a professor, he published learned studies on literature. Yet he also began publishing a newspaper aimed at changing society so that there would be social justice for the poor. He continued his efforts for social justice until his health gave out in 1850.

At the time of his death the St. Vincent de Paul Society numbered 15,000. His society today exists everywhere in the world with over 700,000 members helping the poor.

FREDERIC OZANAM

Activity

1. Do you think that Ozanam was effective at saying how good his faith was? Why?

   _____

   _____

   _____

2. What made him do more than talk?

   _____

   _____

   _____

3. What did Ozanam immediately begin doing?

   _____

   _____

4. What was the result of Ozanam's work?

   _____

   _____

Activity

Christ calls each of us to do what we can to ease the suffering of individuals and to change the unjust conditions that cause the suffering. Complete the following story to express your ideas about how people of justice might work for a better world.

It is the year 2020 and people of justice rule the world. This means that the

top priority of all governments is _____ because

_____

_____ .

Taxes are _____ .

There are very few extremely rich people, but there are many people who

_____

because _____ .

The most important subject taught in school is _____

because _____

_____ .

When asked in a survey what the goals of their lives are, most people

responded _____ .

The most popular television show is _____

because _____ .

The biggest hit on the music charts last year was _____

because _____ .

The best thing about the influence of persons of justice is _____

_____ .

PRAYING THROUGH A STORY

Once upon a time there was a small village on the banks of a quiet river. The village people were good, caring people who lived simple lives farming and fishing. Their work and recreation centered on the river.

One day a boy shouted from the riverbank, "Quick, come here! Look!"

The villagers rushed down to the river. The boy was pointing upstream to where the river was narrowest. A few trees were jammed between the two shores, making a small dam. The flow of the river was slowed to a trickle. Behind the logjam the waters were rising over the riverbanks.

"Our village will be flooded!" a young man exclaimed.

"We must do something quickly!" cried an older woman.

About a dozen young men and women ran along the riverbank to the dam. Some jumped into the river and began to free the logjam. Others helped them from the riverbank. Everyone tried to help.

Soon the jam was broken and the river was flowing naturally.

Everyone cheered and shouted. "We have stopped the flood! We have saved our village!"

But the next day a young girl who was fishing called out, "Look! The river is flooding again!"

The young men and women rushed upriver and again broke up the new logjam.

The same thing kept happening. Each day, small tree trunks and branches floated down the river and made a logjam that caused flooding. Each day, the men and women had to break down the jam. They were no longer able to do their regular jobs.

After a time, a wise old woman asked the villagers to call a meeting to deal with the emergency. The wise woman stood up before the assembled village. She praised the men and women for working so hard each day to keep the river from flooding the village. "But why are there so many trees floating down the river all of a sudden?" the old woman asked.

Everyone was silent. The question was so obvious. But they had been so busy removing the daily logjam that they had not stopped to wonder why there were now so many trees floating down the river. So they organized a team to go upstream and discover the cause.

Activity

Reflect quietly about this story. Then answer the questions below.

1. What might the villagers find upstream? What would be a solution to the problem?

   _____

   _____

   _____

2. What "logjams" do you experience in your life? What might be causing them? How can you find out?

   _____

   _____

   _____

Match the terms in Column 1 with their correct definitions in Column 2.

Column 1

_____ capital sins

_____ sin

_____ conscience

_____ mortal sins

_____ temptation

_____ original sin

_____ free will

_____ venial sins

Column 2

a. the freedom to choose to do what is right or wrong

b. the seven basic temptations

c. a free decision to do wrong or to fail to do the good that we should

d. less serious sins that weaken our relationship with God

e. the sinful condition within our lives and into which we are all born

f. very serious sins that completely break off our relationship with God

g. the attraction or pressure that may lead us to sin

h. the ability to judge whether something is right or wrong

Write a paragraph explaining how Jesus is an example of justice for us.

_____

_____

_____

_____

Respond to the following questions based on what you have learned in this chapter.

1. What is *social justice*?

_____

_____

2. Why must actions for social justice go hand in hand with individual, immediate acts of kindness or charity?

_____

_____

_____

_____

Only if you thoroughly reform your ways and your deeds . . . will I remain with you.
Jeremiah 7:5, 7

3. Discuss why it is so important for the Church and individual Catholics to be with and for the poor.

20 A LIBERATING PEOPLE

Freedom is _____

IF YOU COULD DO ANYTHING WHAT WOULD YOU DO?

Activity

Here are photographs that might be found in commercials and advertisements. These attempt to express something about the concept of freedom. After each photograph, complete the statement about how this image expresses something about freedom.

Freedom is _____

Freedom is _____

Freedom is _____

Freedom is _____

Freedom is _____

According to the Gospel of Luke, Jesus began his ministry with these words of Scripture. This was his promise that he was the liberator of people, particularly the poor, from all manner of slavery.

Part of Jesus' mission was to teach us to struggle against a basic form of slavery—one that was at the root of political, social, and economic injustice. As God's suffering servant, Jesus lived and taught his followers a message of freedom from selfishness for the sake of truth, love of others, and justice.

He did this by speaking the truth, acting with love, working nonviolently for justice, protesting, living free of prejudices, and freely breaking religious laws and social customs that were violating people's basic rights. When Jesus was killed and was raised, he broke the bonds of death, freeing humanity from even this last enslavement of death.

Jesus' followers proclaimed their partnership with Jesus in his death and resurrection. They followed his teachings and acted toward victims of injustice as he had. They proclaimed life in the risen Lord.

JESUS, OUR LIBERATOR

Jesus Christ is the one who brings God's freedom to all humankind. Jesus lived in a Jewish society that longed for liberation from Roman rule. Some people looked upon Jesus as a messiah who would lead a violent uprising against the Romans. But Jesus proclaimed another kind of freedom—a freedom from sin and from the lifeless burden of sin.

> The spirit of the Lord is upon me,
>   because he has anointed me
>   to bring glad tidings to the poor.
> He has sent me to proclaim liberty
>   to captives
> and recovery of sight to the blind,
>   to let the oppressed go free,
> and to proclaim a year acceptable
>   to the Lord.

Luke 4:18–19

Activity

Complete the following open-ended statements.

1. Jesus proclaimed freedom from

   _____

   _____

2. One way Jesus taught us about this freedom was

   _____

   _____

3. Jesus' resurrection freed us from

   _____

   _____

Activity

Think about what freedom means to you and who Jesus is for you. Then imagine how the world might be different if we all lived in Christ, as he calls us to. Use the writing lines below to give four examples of what Jesus' freedom means to you.

FREEDOM IN JESUS IS

1. _____
_____
_____
_____

2. _____
_____

3. _____
_____
_____
_____
_____

4. _____
_____
_____

Activity

What does it mean to be truly free? As Christians, we have learned from Jesus that to be truly free means to live for the sake of others. It means serving others and leading a life of goodness. Brainstorm some of the characteristics of a life of goodness.

_____

_____

_____

_____

_____

_____

CHOOSING FREEDOM

Some people say that being free is being able to do anything we want whenever we want. But our actions always have consequences. The things we choose to do always affect ourselves and others—sometimes in ways we cannot accurately predict. True freedom is acting for the good of ourselves and others. Our lives actually become happier and more enriched when we make decisions for the best, going beyond self-interest and acting on our ideals.

This is because we are made in the image and likeness of God and he has given us the capacity to seek wisdom about what is right and true. We call this wisdom natural law, which states the moral principles upon which our lives should be based. For example, some acts are always wrong to choose, even if we mean well or think that good may be the result. Natural law remains the same throughout all times and places and can be grasped through human reason. True freedom means following God's natural law and not living selfishly.

There are times, however, when living our Christian ideals is a challenge. We may be able to get away with less than our best in a given situation. Or we may be tempted to do the wrong thing. Under such circumstances, we need to take the time to think through the situation, considering the consequences of our actions, and to pray for the grace to do the right thing, even if it is difficult.

MAKING MORAL DECISIONS

1. Identify the decision that needs to be made. Tell all that you know about it. What do you need to decide?

2. Consider possible options. What choices can you make?

3. Evaluate the consequences of the options. How will your choice affect you and others?

4. Reflect and pray. How do the Bible and the moral teachings of the Church guide you in making this choice? How will this decision show that you are a follower of Jesus?

5. Decide what you will do. Using your intellect and your free will, what choice will you make?

Activity

How do you make a good decision? From the choices below, mark what you are most likely to do when trying to make a difficult decision.

> 1 - I would never do this.
> 2 - I might do this.
> 3 - I would definitely do this.

_____ Ask advice from others who are responsible.

_____ Distinguish between what you want and what you should do.

_____ Face the consequences of your action.

_____ Admit you made a mistake.

_____ Pray about the issue.

_____ Refer to Church teachings.

_____ Read a Scripture passage.

_____ Think about similar situations you have heard of and how these turned out.

_____ Other: _____

Activity

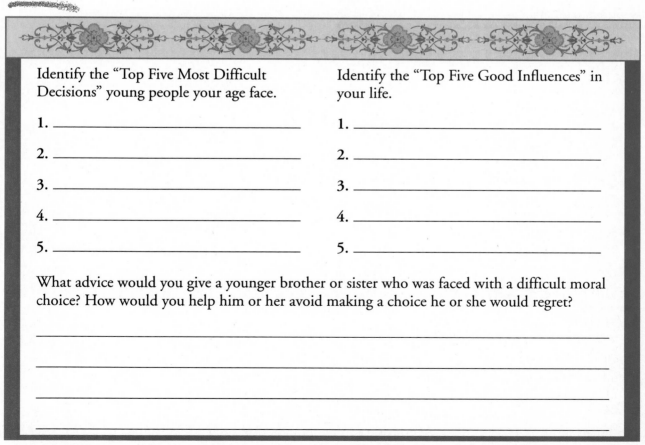

Identify the "Top Five Most Difficult Decisions" young people your age face.

1. _____

2. _____

3. _____

4. _____

5. _____

Identify the "Top Five Good Influences" in your life.

1. _____

2. _____

3. _____

4. _____

5. _____

What advice would you give a younger brother or sister who was faced with a difficult moral choice? How would you help him or her avoid making a choice he or she would regret?

_____

_____

_____

_____

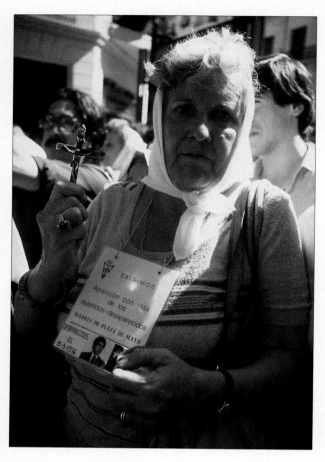

Freedom For the Children of God

The early Church struggled against the continued oppression of Roman rule. Finally, after more than three centuries of struggle and persecution, Christians were granted religious freedom. With this newfound freedom from martyrdom or imprisonment came new responsibilities—namely, the obligation to stand up for the freedom of other oppressed groups.

Throughout the 2,000 years of the Church's life, great men and women have always taken their stand on the side of freedom for all peoples. However, these Christian men and women were not always successful. At times in the Church's long history, members cared more about their own acceptance and safety in society than they did about the freedom of others.

However, while some Christians were tolerating abuses and wrongs, others struggled to keep alive the reality of the freedom from sin in Jesus Christ. In the early centuries of Christianity, men and women established hermitages and prayed and labored alone to keep the Christian faith alive. Later, monasteries were established to strengthen and preserve the faith. These hermitages and monasteries enriched the lives of all who came into contact with these men and women whose purpose was to live holy lives.

About four centuries ago, religious orders and lay societies began to turn their energies to the needs of working men and women. The efforts of these Christians made a difference and influenced life in the new and fast-growing cities of Europe and the Americas. These Christians worked hard to improve the living conditions of laborers and factory workers.

Gradually, practicing Catholics came to realize that injustice and sin could live within the very foundations of national institutions and attitudes. They began to see that tolerance of their own personal sin and evil could result in social evils that burden and exclude some of God's children. Catholics are not only called to struggle for freedom from personal sin, but by their baptism, they are also called to enter into the struggle to free their nation and their national institutions from fostering evil.

Some Christian thinkers and activists use **liberation** theology to express this commitment to transforming the world. Liberation theology reminds us that the kingdom of God was established by Christ and not only exists for the end of time but also is present to some degree in our world today. Our Christian faith calls us to spread Christ's freedom throughout the world.

Today, many Catholics and Catholic groups continue to work to free people from all kinds of oppression. We, too, are called to work for justice. Whether our efforts are great or small, as Christians we participate in preparing the world for the final fulfillment of the kingdom of God. Each of us has the responsibility to make our world a better place in whatever way we can, no matter how seemingly insignificant. Many individual voices joined with others can make a mighty sound that will be heard.

Activity

The voices of many were heard in a letter by the bishops of the United States and titled "Economic Justice for All." Read the following excerpts from that letter. In your own words, give the meaning of each statement and then write an example that illustrates the same point.

"Our faith calls us to measure [the] economy, not only by what it produces, but also by how it touches human life and whether it protects or undermines the dignity of the human person" (#1).

Meaning: _____

_____

Example: _____

_____

"Economic decisions. . . help or hurt people, strengthen or weaken family life, advance or diminish the quality of justice in our land" (#1).

Meaning: _____

_____

Example: _____

_____

"As a community of believers, we know that our faith is tested by the quality of justice among us, that we can best measure our life together by how the poor and the vulnerable are treated" (#8).

Meaning: _____

_____

Example: _____

_____

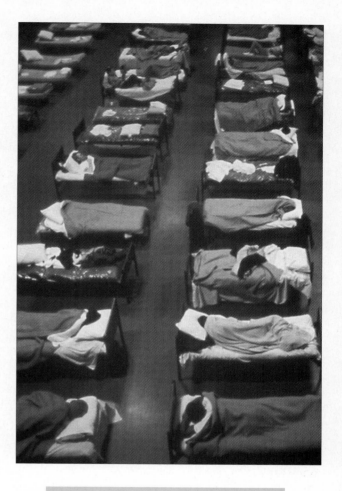

Vocabulary

liberation: being released or freed

✖ ✖ ✖ ✖ ✖ ✖ ✖ ✖ ✖ ✖ ✖ ✖ ✖ ✖ ✖ ✖ ✖ ✖ ✖

WE BELIEVE

Jesus Christ is the world's Savior or liberator. He devoted his life to freeing people from every form of slavery, beginning with slavery to sin. The life and message of Jesus are calls to cooperate with his Spirit in liberating all people everywhere from sin and from social, political, and economic structures that are marked by sins of injustice.

Activity

Name someone in the history of the Catholic Church who interests you.

_____

Name one quality you admire in this person and explain why.

_____

_____

_____

Explain how you think this person's life embodies true freedom in some way.

_____

_____

_____

_____

A LIBERATING PEOPLE

For centuries, men and women have recognized that Jesus Christ, the source of our true freedom, can be found in the Church. In accepting the challenge to live as Jesus did, these men and women have been liberated from sin. As Christians, we too are offered the same wonderful liberation. By virtue of our Baptism in Christ, we are freed from the fear, the ignorance, the hate, and the prejudice that sin engenders.

Christ freed us by his death and resurrection. And through the grace of the Holy Spirit we are continually led to grow in this freedom. We are guided to lives of joy, kindness, charity, and peace.

It can be helpful to us to appreciate the lives of those exemplary Catholics who have lived before us. We can recognize in their struggles and triumphs the same problems and anxieties we ourselves face. We can also recognize the same gentle guidance of the Spirit and learn to better respond to this loving tenderness in our lives.

A WOMAN OF FREEDOM

The Church looks to Mary, the mother of Jesus, as the model of a true disciple of Jesus Christ. She lived out perfectly the life of faith that all Jesus' followers are called to live. Mary is the image of a perfect Christian.

We know little about Mary's daily life. The Gospels describe her in the light of what Jesus' followers believed after his resurrection. To learn about Mary, it is necessary to understand the time in which she lived.

In Jesus' time, most people married young. It is likely that Mary was a teenager when Jesus was born. She must have been very special for God to have chosen her to be the mother of Jesus, but she was probably much like the other teenage girls of Nazareth in many ways. She probably had little education, was skilled at cooking and caring for the home, and enjoyed the simple pleasures of life in a rural village. She observed the Jewish rituals, prayed at the usual times, and attended the synagogue with the other women in the village.

It is not clear whether Mary traveled with Jesus and his disciples once he began his public ministry. The Gospels mention her only a few times. The Gospel of John mentions that she was with Jesus at Cana as the first believer in his mission and that she was at his side at the end on Calvary. The Acts of the Apostles portrays her as being with the disciples after Christ's resurrection.

Although the New Testament tells us little of the details about Mary's life, it does tell us what she was like and what was most important about her. The Gospels show Mary to be a woman of faith. She was open to God's word and ready to respond with her whole being. "I am the servant of the Lord. Let it be done to me as you say," sums up her life. She was the perfect disciple of her son, and her life's goal was to be God's servant.

Mary lived as her son lived, in the service of God and people. The song that we call "Mary's Canticle" and which is found in the Gospel of

Luke, suggests that her faith was committed to the poor and the hungry. She shared in God's efforts to liberate people from sin and pride.

Mary was free because she was dedicated to the freedom of all. As Pope John Paul II wrote, "She is the most perfect image of freedom and of the liberation of humanity and of the universe."

Activity

Read Luke 1:46–55, "Mary's Canticle." Choose a verse of the prayer to write in your own words, expressing God's ways of justice and freedom of all.

_____

_____

_____

_____

_____

_____

PRAYING WITH THE PROPHETS

We are called to be a just and liberating people. We learn what this means by reading the Scriptures, especially the prophets, who spoke out many times about the suffering of the oppressed. One of these prophets is Isaiah, who tells us God's answer to those who asked how to follow God's will.

Read this adaptation of Isaiah's message prayerfully with your class.

People: What laws shall we follow? What fasts shall we perform? How can we get you to draw near, O God? No matter what we do, you never seem to notice!

God: Now look here! On your fast days, you treat your workers badly. You strike the poor with your fists. If you fast like this, I will never attend to you. Never.

People: How shall we fast?

God: I tell you, hanging down your head and wearing sackcloth will not do. This is what I ask. Pay attention!

Speaker 1: Break unjust bonds. Undo the leather straps that bind the heavy yoke of people's shoulders. Let the burdened go free and break every yoke that binds them.

Speaker 2: Share your food with the hungry. Give shelter to the homeless poor ones. Clothe those who have no clothing. Do not turn your back on your own family.

Speaker 3: Then the light will come. Then your own wounds will heal quickly. People will know of your wholeness. The Lord will stand by you. Then you will call, and the Lord will answer you.

God: I am here. I will guide you, and I will strengthen you. You will be as refreshed as a watered garden. Dancing waters will bubble on and on. For I am here with you.

Based on Isaiah 58:3–11

CHAPTER REVIEW

Complete the sentences below by filling in the missing words.

1. Jesus freed us by his _____ and _____ .

2. The _____ guides us in living Christ's freedom.

3. We are also called to make the _____ a better place.

4. We must work to _____ people from all sources of _____ .

5. We live in Christ's freedom when we make moral _____ in our lives.

What was the slavery from which Jesus liberated people?

_____

_____

_____

_____

_____

_____

_____

Respond to the following questions based on what you have learned in this chapter.

1. What is *liberation*?

_____

_____

2. Why is Mary considered the model of a true disciple of Christ?

_____

_____

_____

_____

_____

For freedom Christ set us free.
Galatians 5:1

3. Discuss why people who work for the liberation of the poor and weak are often criticized and even attacked.

UNIT 5 ORGANIZER

Review this unit by writing key words and phrases in the boxes below.

A Respectful People

_____

_____

A Compassionate People

_____

_____

A Just People

_____

_____

A Liberating People

_____

_____

UNIT 5 REVIEW

Complete each sentence by supplying the correct word(s).

1. Church teaching that states the implications of the gospel for human rights is called

   _____ .

2. _____ are goods or money given to the poor.

3. Systematic respect for human rights within society and its institutions is termed

   _____ .

4. A _____ is one who releases or frees another from slavery or prison.

5. Respect for the dignity of each person forms the basis of _____ .

6. True freedom is freedom in _____ .

Circle the letter of the correct ending for each sentence.

1. The basis of Catholic social doctrine is   (a) reverence for human dignity.
   (b) obedience to God.   (c) the Corporal Works of Mercy.
2. A Catholic may no longer struggle for spiritual freedom without in some way joining
   with   (a) governments.   (b) oppressed people.   (c) lay people.
3. The Church teaches that action for social justice is a vital part of the
   (a) general judgment.   (b) social service.   (c) gospel message.
4. To liberate all people from sin and unjust structures, Jesus calls us to cooperate with
   (a) base communities.   (b) his Spirit.   (c) charities.
5. The Catholic Church stresses the link between social, economic, and political evils and
   (a) compassion.   (b) freedom.   (c) personal sin.

Write the name of the person described in each statement.

1. _____ She is the most perfect image of freedom and liberation.

2. _____ She founded The Maryknoll Sisters of
   St. Dominic.

3. _____ She dedicated herself to the needs of poor cancer patients.

4. _____ He was the founder of the Society of St. Vincent
   de Paul.

UNIT **5** REVIEW

Explain the meaning of promise of each beatitude.

1. Blessed are the poor in spirit, for theirs is the kingdom of heaven.

   _____

2. Blessed are they who mourn, for they will be comforted.

   _____

3. Blessed are the meek, for they will inherit the land.

   _____

4. Blessed are they who hunger and thirst for righteousness, for they will be satisfied.

   _____

5. Blessed are the merciful, for they will be shown mercy.

   _____

6. Blessed are the clean of heart, for they will see God.

   _____

7. Blessed are the peacemakers, for they will be called children of God.

   _____

8. Blessed are they who are persecuted for the sake of righteousness, for theirs is the kingdom of heaven.

   _____

Identify the number of the Commandment described in each sentence below.

1. _____ We respect all human life.

2. _____ We pray and rest on Sunday.

3. _____ We are truthful.

4. _____ We share our resources.

5. _____ We obey and respect our parents.

6. _____ God is first in our lives.

7. _____ We use God's name with love.

8. _____ We fight against greed.

9. _____ We respect the husbands and wives of others.

10. _____ We are faithful in marriage.

Fitting In

Making new friends and fitting in is important to most young people—particularly as they begin high school. Unfortunately, there are also new temptations to act in ways that might be dangerous or lead away from solid Christian values. Some young people succumb to social pressures because they think that saying "yes" is the only way to gain social acceptance. Being honest with oneself and clear about one's beliefs are two of the biggest challenges young people face.

Activity

Read each of the following situations about fitting in. Then discuss the questions below.

1. Rachel's parents will not permit her to go to the mall with her friends. Her parents worry that the mall is not safe and that Rachel is too young to be on her own in such a busy place. Rachel feels embarrassed when all of her friends make plans to go to the mall and she has to tell them she cannot go. She thinks her parents are old-fashioned and will never understand her. Rachel's best friend, Julia, invites her to spend the night at her house. Once at Julia's, the girls decide to go to the mall to see a movie. Rachel figures that what her parents do not know will not hurt them.

    How is Rachel trying to fit in?

    Do you think Rachel is acting responsibly? Why or why not?

    How would Rachel's parents feel if they found out that she went to the mall?

    Is Rachel being dishonest with her parents in doing something she knows they would not approve of?

    If you were Rachel's parents, how might you respond if you found out what Rachel had done?

    If going to the mall with friends is really important to Rachel, how might she discuss this issue with her parents and demonstrate that she is capable of handling greater freedom?

    Has going to the mall without her parents' approval helped or hurt Rachel's quest for greater autonomy?

2. Tim knows that there will be drinking at the party he is going to tonight. Tim's parents said he could go because the parents of the person giving the party will be there to chaperone. By the time Tim and his friends arrive at the party, most kids are drinking and several are already drunk. Tim hears someone saying that the parents are home, but are upstairs. Tim's best friend calls him aside, beer in hand, and asks Tim to drink with him. Tim refuses, but his friend keeps insisting. "Come on," he says, "I don't want to do this alone. Just try it this once with me. What could be so bad about a few sips of beer?"

How is Tim's friend trying to fit in?

What do you think Tim will decide to do? Why?

Do you think Tim's choice will be a responsible one? Why or why not?

Why might Tim choose not to drink at the party? What other ways can he fit in without risking the things he values and believes in?

What are some of the short-term and long-term consequences of Tim's friend deciding to have a beer? Are these risks worth it?

What makes someone want to drink? What can help prevent someone from giving in to the temptation?

3. On Friday, John and his friends usually meet to go to the movies. John always looks forward to this time with his friends. Tonight when the group gets together, they decide to go to another friend's house instead of going to a movie. John calls home to let his father know of the change in plans.

How is John trying to fit in?

Was John acting responsibly?

What does John's decision to phone home say about what he values?

Does your family expect you to call when plans change?

Why would this be a good thing to do?

Why might someone your age resent having to make such a call?

Prayer

Write a prayer asking for Jesus' guidance as you face social pressures.

Dear Jesus,

Help me _____

_____

I'm tempted to _____

_____

I believe _____

_____

I feel _____

_____

OPENING DOORS
A Take-Home Magazine™

Does your family meet your needs?

NEEDS NEEDS NEEDS NEEDS

Your first reaction might be a resounding "NO!" Think about it more carefully and you will probably find that individual family members often do help you to feel better about yourself in different ways.

Mark the needs members of your family help you to meet.
_____ physical (food, shelter, clothing)
_____ affection
_____ being included
_____ feeling good about yourself
_____ personal privacy
_____ feeling closer to God
_____ independence and responsibility
_____ communication
_____ fun
_____ other

UNMET NEEDS
When needs go unmet, we feel anxious, lost, or empty. If your need for affection goes unmet, you will feel unloved. If you are not included, you will feel lonely. Never have the opportunity to lead others and you will have little self-confidence. Remember that other people have needs, too, and experience the same bad feelings when these needs go unmet.

Sometimes we think needs are being met but we still feel rotten. What's going wrong? Suppose you let your little sister be with you, but the whole time you keep telling her what a pest she is. Do you think you are really meeting her need to be included? Sure, she gets the privilege of being with you, but she is still going to feel rotten because you are treating her meanly. Sincerity and honesty are important in meeting needs.

FAMILY ACTIVITY
Tonight, sit down with your family and brainstorm all the ways just one need can be met. For example, you might decide to determine how each member of the family can feel that they have more independence and responsibility for their own lives. Maybe you would like to help make more family decisions. Maybe your dad wants you to talk to him about the things happening in your life to make him feel more on top of things and more included.

UNDERSTANDING OTHERS
Meeting one another's needs is not as difficult as you might think. Most of the time it is a matter of being sensitive and caring for another person. Treat others this way and they often will respond by being more sincere and considerate.

Lifestyles

What do you want to be?

More importantly, what kind of lifestyle do you want to have?

When someone asks you the first question, he or she is usually asking about the kind of job you will have. The second question, however, has to do with the values and ideals by which you will live. Your lifestyle influences the kind of person you will be.

Describing your dreams and goals can help you to identify the values and ideals that you think are the most important. Complete the following statements.

I want to be _____.

Success is _____.

I wish _____.

I do not want _____.

If I were God, I would _____.

Ten years from now I will be living _____.

I wish I did not have to _____.

Rate the following qualities and values according to their importance to you. Use the following scale: Unimportant **(U)**, Okay **(O)**, Important **(I)**, and Very important **(V)**. Refer to your responses above to help you to identify the importance of the qualities and values.

	U	O	I	V
honesty				
loyalty				
caring				
ambition				
courage				
sympathy				
generosity				
organization				
thrift				
caution				
patience				
commitment				
self-discipline				
humor				
opportunity				
determination				
education				
wealth				
health				

Circle the five qualities or values that you rated as most important.

What kind of person do these five qualities reveal? Do they reflect a person of integrity, someone upon whom others can depend? Do these five qualities reflect Jesus' teachings more than your own selfish wants?

TAKE CHARGE!

People today frequently see themselves as victims of circumstances. We tend to think that things happen to us that make us inevitably who we are. Rather than rising above circumstance and taking control of our own fate, we make excuses: "I didn't get good grades because the tests were bad," "I didn't do my homework because I'm under a lot of stress," or "I can't do any better because I'm a C student."

Jesus did not make excuses. He did not sit at home and complain to his mother that the Jewish religious authorities were not being fair to him. He went out and did what needed to be done. He did not sit around playing the victim and feeling sorry for himself. He took risks. He acted on the things that were important to him. Jesus' lifestyle was one of integrity and trust in God. What kind of person will you be? You have the power to decide.

Imitate Jesus in your lifestyle!

Follow the Ten Commandments.
Live the Beatitudes.
Follow the Great Commandment to love God and your neighbor.
Pray and worship with your parish community.
Receive the sacraments.
Pray and read Scripture.
Consult the Church's teachings for guidance in making moral decisions.
Work for peace and justice.

PRIVATE TIME

Private time should be a part of every lifestyle. Everyone needs time to be by themselves and to renew themselves. Use this time for prayer and meditation on a regular basis.

Prayer is more than talking to God. It is the *yearning* for something more complete, more satisfying—God. We do not need dramatic spiritual experiences. Just as closeness grows up in the everyday things two friends share, we grow closer to God in the ordinary circumstances of our lives.

Meditation is listening to God. God has much to tell us and a lot to which we must be open. We cannot always do the talking. Meditating is sitting quietly and focusing on one idea or concept. Meditate, think about, the meaning of a Scripture passage or story, the life of a saint, or a quote. Meditate five or ten minutes at a time. If your mind wanders, refocus, but do not feel guilty or frustrated. Just sit and be quiet for a while.

TOWARD THE FUTURE

What will our celebration of the Eucharist be like in the twenty-first century? From what you have learned, the meaning and purpose of the Mass remain the same as when Jesus gave us the gift of himself at the Last Supper. Yet there have been changes in some of the ways people have celebrated the Eucharist. The language of the Mass has changed, for example, as have the music, the placement of the altar, and the styles of churches. Other changes also might occur in the future. What do you think these will be?

It is impossible to predict the future accurately, of course, but the present can give valuable clues to the future. Here are some of the characteristics that may affect the Church in the twenty-first century. Which ones might influence or change the way we celebrate the Eucharist together?

- Catholics of Third World areas such as Africa and South America are likely to have more influence in the Church.

- Technology and science continue to change the way we live and think about our world and the universe.

- Poverty continues to increase, not only in Third World countries, but also in developed nations, such as the United States.

- The Church continues to emphasize the importance of the celebration of the Eucharist and Christ's priesthood and ministry.

- Base Christian communities unite poor Catholics in small organized groups of Christian families in order to help them improve their lives.

- The Church seeks to identify itself with the vast majority of its members who live in poverty.

- Lay people today participate more actively in the life of the Church than in the past. Both men and women serve as lectors and eucharistic ministers.

- The Catholic Church in the United States is experiencing a crisis in religious vocations. Some parishes have trained lay people to lead prayer and communion services; some have priests from other countries; and other parishes have been closed.

- Conservative and liberal Catholics sometimes have different expectations and concepts of the Mass.

- Permission has been given by Pope John Paul II for priests to celebrate the Tridentine Mass (the Mass used before Vatican II) under certain conditions.

    Choose one of the above and explain how you think it might affect the way Catholics celebrate the Eucharist in the twenty-first century.

_____

_____

    What do you think will change in the Mass? Brainstorm your ideas about the Mass of the future by focusing on one of the following areas.

1. What uses can you predict for any of the following: computers, holograms, lazers, synthesizers, and other technological advances? What will the place where the community gathers look like? What kinds of songs will be sung at Mass? What kinds of instruments will be played? What kinds of vestments will priests or others wear?

2. How might space exploration affect the way Catholic Christians worship and celebrate together? What will Mass be like for those living in outer space? What other religious and spiritual issues might occur through space exploration?

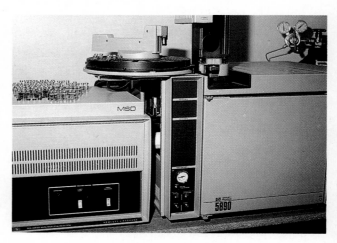

DID YOU KNOW?
Many cities in the United States are named after saints. St. Louis, Missouri, for example, was named by French explorers after Saint Louis IX, king of France. Whenever Spanish explorers founded a settlement, discovered a new river, or built a mission, they named it after the saint whose feast day it was. Saint Augustine, Florida; San Antonio, Texas; and San Diego and San Francisco, California were all named this way. Can you think of other cities and places in the United States that are named after saints?

LEGEND AND LORE

The unicorn is a horse with a single horn on its forehead. This popular creature of myth was said to be very strong and quick and to have a gentle nature. Over the centuries, the unicorn became a symbol for Jesus. According to the tale, a unicorn could not be caught by hunters but would only trust a pure young girl (just as Jesus was born of the Virgin Mary). The unicorn could then be killed by the hunters, a sacrifice to its trust, just as Jesus trusted in the will of God. There are many other variations of the legend of the unicorn. One story has it that a unicorn could detect poison by dipping its horn into the suspect liquid.

CATHOLIC!

R.C.I.A. . . . Mother Teresa . . . sacraments . . . papacy . . . monasteries . . . saints . . . Eucharistic liturgies . . . Dorothy Day . . . Sign of the Cross . . . Rosary . . . Thomas Merton . . . Church councils . . . Curia . . . Opus Dei . . . charismatics . . . canonization . . . deacons . . . Eucharistic ministers . . . encyclicals . . . Peter's Pence . . . absolution . . . ordination . . . dispensation . . . Easter duty . . . Paschal candle . . . Pax Christi . . . Vatican . . . retreat . . . How many can you identify?

Celebrating the Journey

Gathering

Leader: This year we have journeyed together and have learned about our Church, past and present. We have also begun to prepare ourselves for the future when Jesus comes again. Remember our journey together this year. Reflect upon what has most impressed you about what we have learned about the Church.

Sharing

Leader: Call to mind what you have learned best and share these things with one another. They may help us as we live our faith as members of the Catholic community.

[Sharing]

Leader: Our journey of faith is not yet over. The words of Scripture guide us and protect us no matter how difficult our journey might be.

The Word of God

Reader: [Read Matthew 28:16-20]

All: Thanks be to God.

Blessing

Leader: May Jesus Christ be with us as we seek and discover his love and peace. May we share his way of love with all whom we meet.

All: Amen.

Amen

Our Church Celebrates Advent

THE SECOND COMING

The Gospel readings for the First Sunday of **Advent**, the first season of the liturgical year, refer to the Second Coming of Jesus. Each reading consists of a warning to be prepared for Jesus' Second Coming.

According to the Gospel of Matthew, Jesus said, "Two men will be out in the field; one will be taken, and one will be left. Two women will be grinding at the mill; one will be taken, and one will be left. Therefore, stay awake! For you do not know on which day your Lord will come" (Matthew 24:40–42).

According to the Gospel of Mark, Jesus warned his disciples to "be watchful" (Mark 13:23). The Gospel of Luke shows Jesus predicting what will happen at the Second Coming. "There will be signs in the sun, the moon, and the stars, and on earth nations will be in dismay, perplexed by the roaring of the sea and the waves. People will die of fright in anticipation of what is coming upon the world, for the powers of the heavens will be shaken. And then they will see the Son of Man coming in a cloud with power and great glory. But when these things begin to happen, stand erect and raise your heads because your redemption is at hand" (Luke 21:25–28).

It is important that we understand that all of these Gospel accounts were written before the end of the first century. They reflect the idea that the return of Jesus would come within that generation. Other readings from the New

Testament, however, show the early Church after the death and resurrection of Jesus, and after the Holy Spirit descended upon the apostles on Pentecost. These early followers of Christ compiled sayings and teachings of Jesus and interpreted them for their own lives. The advice to stay awake and be watchful reminded them that in the past, the Jewish people had not always heeded the warnings of the prophets. It was important to follow God's way of love.

If the exact time of Jesus' Second Coming had been the important part of the message, surely the news would have been given of that time to his disciples. However, Jesus cautions his listeners then and now that the time is known only to the Father. The key to the message is that Jesus will come again in glory. Christians live with this view of the future and it should make a difference in our daily lives. The Christian community gathers for that purpose: to celebrate the Lord's coming into our midst and to await his return.

During Advent, we prepare for the celebration of Jesus' birth in Bethlehem, knowing that after that event, human history and humankind were never the same. His coming into our midst ushered in the "final age." This is not measured in years but in the way we live our lives. Just as the early Church began to increase its missionary activity and draw up guidelines for living, we, too, must concern ourselves with the situations in which we find ourselves. If we listen to the Lord's call in our present situations, we can be assured that we will hear him when he comes again.

As we prepare for the celebration of Christmas, let us do so in the true spirit of believers who have not lost sight of the real meaning of the Incarnation. Jesus came many years ago and lived his life to show us the way and teach us the truth. He died, rose, and returned to the Father, promising to come again. His victory and promise give us hope. This belief in the Second Coming of Jesus is the beacon on the horizon for us and our pledge of a future destiny with him in glory.

Activity

Unscramble the four Memorial Acclamations of the liturgy below and write each correctly in the spaces provided.

Christ will come again
rising you restored our life
until you come in glory
you have set us free
Dying you destroyed our death
Christ has died
Lord, by your cross and resurrection
When we eat this bread and drink this cup
You are the Savior of the world
Christ is risen
we proclaim your death, Lord Jesus
Lord Jesus, come in glory

1. _____

_____

_____

_____

2. _____

_____

_____

_____

3. _____

_____

_____

_____

4. _____

_____

_____

_____

THE PROMISE OF ADVENT

During the Advent season, the Church prepares us to welcome Christ in our daily lives. The readings of Advent are often taken from the Book of Isaiah. Scholars think that this book of the Bible was written by three or more people over a period of about two hundred years.

The Book of Isaiah is divided into three periods of time. First Isaiah (chapters 1 through 39) was probably written around the time of the fall of the northern kingdom of Israel in 722 B.C. Second Isaiah (chapters 40 through 55) was compiled when the Jewish people were struggling through their humiliating **exile** in Babylon between 585 B.C. and 539 B.C. when, having been forcibly removed from their homes, they were forbidden to return. Third Isaiah (chapters 56 through 66) was probably written shortly after the Jewish people returned from Babylon in 539 B.C. to face the immense task of rebuilding their land, which lay in ruins.

The Book of Isaiah, then, was written to help and comfort the Jewish people as they faced the threat of war, the pain of exile, and the task of renewing Jerusalem. The Book of Isaiah overflows with hope for the Jewish people.

Each year, Christians gather during the wintertime, when we face the shortest days and the longest nights. We remember that sometimes we are frail and stubborn. We prefer to stay in the darkness of our own sinfulness and wrongdoing. The Church reads the words of the Book of Isaiah to call us to come into the light and to depend on the kindness of God.

Every Advent we are reminded that the words of the Book of Isaiah again come true for us and for those we care about. As Christians we recognize God's kindness and mercy in the birth of Jesus.

Activity

Read the references to the Book of Isaiah, and complete the exercises that accompany each reading.

1. In First Isaiah, the prophet warned the people that their lazy and careless ways would lead to their downfall. He warned that a stronger nation, Assyria, would invade and conquer them. The prophet also longed for someone who would be a perfect king and protect the Hebrew people. He called this person a messiah, an anointed one.

   Read Isaiah 9:5–6. Describe in your own words the anointed one Isaiah hoped for.

   _____

   _____

   _____

   _____

Now look again at verses 15–16. How would these words give comfort and peace?

_____

_____

_____

2. In Second Isaiah, we learn that when the southern kingdom also fell, the people were taken into exile. They lost their homeland, their Temple, and their way of life. Isaiah was faced with the work of comforting the people. He had to provide them with the spirit to overcome their anguish and their humiliation.

   Read Isaiah 49:8–16. Look specifically at verse 10. Write your ideas about how these words would give hope to the people.

   _____

   _____

   _____

   _____

3. The author of Third Isaiah used word pictures to tell about the great joy of the exiles. Those who had seen their family members die and who had spent years away from home without adequate food and clothing were now able to return to Jerusalem. God talks to the people through the words of Isaiah 55:1–2 and 12–13.

   Read these words. Think about your hopes for yourself, your family, and the world. Write your images or ideas of freedom and fullness that the words of Isaiah inspire.

   _____

   _____

   _____

   _____

THE REASON FOR THE SEASON

Just after Halloween, stores and shopping malls begin to decorate for Christmas. By Thanksgiving weekend, advertisers are urging us to take advantage of the low prices to be found in pre-Christmas sales. It is no wonder that critics say that Christmas has become too commercial and that people have lost the true meaning of Christmas in the rush of the holiday season.

As Catholics, we are called to look at life with eyes of faith and to keep our "eyes fixed on Jesus" (Hebrews 12:2). In the Gospels we read that Jesus told his followers that they must be on guard against anything that might turn them away from his teachings: "False messiahs and false prophets will arise and will perform signs and wonders in order to mislead, if that were possible, the elect. Be watchful!" (Mark 13:22–23).

Advent is a time to think about the meaning of the things we do to prepare for Christmas. Our Advent traditions can help us to welcome Jesus into our hearts at Christmas or they can be "false prophets" that tempt us to be selfish and interested only in what we will get for Christmas. They can help us to enter into the joy and anticipation of Jesus' Coming or they can keep us so busy with distractions that we never bother to take the time to reflect on what Jesus' birth means to us.

During Advent, we can reexamine the significance of some of our traditions and discover anew how they help us to celebrate the mystery of Jesus' presence among us.

ADVENT WREATH

The custom of the Advent wreath began in Germany in the sixteenth century. The wreath, an ancient symbol of victory worn by heroes, was combined with the practice of lighting candles and bonfires during winter festivals. The Advent wreath represents the Coming of Jesus, our Savior. The round shape of the wreath symbolizes that God's love for us is never ending and that Jesus is the completion of God's plan for the world. The candles are a sign that Jesus casts out darkness and sin by his life and light. The candles represent the four Sundays of Advent and the three purple candles remind us that Advent is a season of preparation. The rose or pink candle represents our hope in the promises God made to us through Jesus.

JESSE TREE

The Jesse Tree helps us to remember the Jewish people from whom Jesus was descended, and it is named for King David's father, Jesse. The tree is decorated with symbols that represent the people and events described in the Old Testament. There might be an apple to represent Adam and Eve; a rainbow for Noah; a tent to represent Abraham and Sarah; a colorful cloth for Joseph; tablets for Moses and the Ten Commandments; and a star for David. Throughout Advent it is customary to place a new symbol on the Jesse Tree each day. This activity helps little children to count the days until Christmas. The Jesse Tree is a visual reminder of our faith story, from creation to the present moment. Through Baptism we became a part of Jesus' family. We too have a place on the Jesse Tree.

SENDING CHRISTMAS CARDS, BAKING, AND DECORATING

Sending Christmas greetings, preparing special foods, and decorating our homes are all important ways of preparing for Christmas. Each year during Advent we take the time to do these things. If we are caught in the trap of selfishness, we will see these activities only as chores that have to be done. If we look at them with eyes of faith, we can see that they are a way of offering hospitality to relatives, friends, and neighbors. They are also a way of reaching out to someone who may need a word of cheer and encouragement at this time of year.

Jesus welcomed strangers. He fed the hungry, comforted the sorrowful, and reached out to anyone who needed him. Our Advent preparations give us the opportunity to be Jesus for others. The foods we make, the decorations we create, and the cards we write can be prepared with others in mind. In these ways, our actions can echo the Advent prayer: "God of power and mercy, open our hearts in welcome. Remove the things that hinder us from receiving Christ with joy, so that we may share his wisdom and become one with him when he comes in glory." (Opening Prayer, Second Sunday of Advent)

Activity

In the space below, write three Advent resolutions that describe how you will prepare to welcome Jesus on Christmas.

_____

_____

_____

_____

_____

LET YOUR LIGHT SHINE

This Advent, prepare yourself to be a light for others. Let your good works shine and let your face shine with welcome. Create a path of light for others by making luminarias, a wonderful custom that is very popular in Mexico and in the southwestern United States. People light paths to their homes or church to guide the footsteps of the faithful and of all who come in the name of the Lord.

Materials:

- a medium-sized, brown paper bag
- a jar of vegetable oil
- scissors or hobby knife
- a supply of paper towels and newspapers
- a votive-type candle
- a sack of sand

Procedure

1. Select designs or symbols of Christ's coming.
2. Cut small designs near the top of the bag. If you use a hobby knife, you can cut out double designs by laying the bag flat on a cushion of newspapers and carving through both sides of the bag.
3. When your design has been cut out, rub oil on the top of the bag.
4. Put sand in the bottom of the bag.
5. Place the candle in the center of the sand.
6. Line up the luminarias along the path to your church or home.
7. To light your luminaria, use a long wick or taper to reach the candle inside.

IN THE MORNING YOU WILL SEE GOD'S GLORY

OPENING PRAYER

Leader: The Vigil Mass of Christmas helps us remember Jesus' ancestors.

Group 1: A circle of stars remembers Abraham whose faith was great.

Group 2: A bundle of firewood remembers Isaac, Abraham's only son.

Group 1: A ladder remembers Jacob's great dream.

Group 2: A sheaf of wheat recalls Ruth, who is remembered as David's grandmother.

Group 1: A crown reminds us of David, the great king.

Group 2: The tablets of the Ten Commandments bring to mind Moses.

Group 1: A simple home recalls another Jacob, the father of Joseph.

Group 2: And carpenter's tools are for Joseph himself.

Based on Matthew 1:1–16

All: God of endless ages, Father of all goodness, we keep vigil for the dawn of salvation and the birth of your Son. With gratitude we recall his humanity, the life he shared with the sons of men. May the power of his divinity help us answer his call to forgiveness and life. We ask this through Christ our Lord.

Alternative Opening Prayer, the Vigil Mass of Christmas

THE WORD OF GOD

Reader: Now, let us all stand for the Gospel of Matthew, the Gospel of the day before Christmas. (Read Matthew 1:18–25.)

CLOSING PRAYER

Leader: God, our Father, every year we rejoice as we look forward to this feast of salvation. May we welcome Christ as our Redeemer and meet him with confidence when he comes to be our judge, who lives and reigns with you and the Holy Spirit, one God, for ever and ever.

Opening Prayer, the Vigil Mass for Christmas

Our Church Celebrates Christmas

A FAMILIAR STORY

The journey to Bethlehem had been long and difficult. Mary's time to deliver her baby was very near. Joseph was worried and anxious to get his young wife settled. He knocked on the door of an inn and when the door was opened, Joseph could hear sounds of laughter and talking. Joseph patiently explained his plight to the innkeeper, who informed him that there was no room for the young couple at the crowded inn. The census ordered by Caesar had brought many people to the little town.

The innkeeper told them that there was a stable nearby. At least it would be shelter. The couple went to the stable and prepared as best they could for the birth of the child. Before the night was over, the birth of this baby would be announced by angels and celebrated by shepherds. Another account of this story would tell of wise men, astrologers from another land, visiting the baby and bringing gifts.

The Christmas story is so familiar. Yet it is powerful in its simplicity. Once again we prepare ourselves for the coming of Jesus into our world. He enters our world whenever and wherever there is room. He does and will come to each of us if we let him.

CHRISTMAS PRESENCE

The giving of ourselves to others can be one means of keeping the real meaning of Christmas alive. In addition to (or in place of) giving a material gift to each member of your family, consider a nonmaterial way to be present to them. You might try one of these or think of one of your own.

Christmas card insert: Use plain note paper to write the members of your immediate family a note thanking them for the gift of themselves. Mention some quality about them that you like. If you need forgiveness for something, ask for it in your note. If you need to forgive, do it now.

Group Gift: Get together with family members and plan an appreciation night for your parents or guardians during the holidays. Perhaps you can give them a night off for themselves during the week after Christmas. You could take care of preparing the dinner and cleaning up after the meal.

Activity

Consider the characters in the story and the role that each played. There is a suggested activity for imitating the role of each character. In the space provided, write another activity that you can do.

Person	Role	Suggested Activity	Other Activity
Joseph	Guardian, protector, husband, and foster father	Be a big brother or sister to a younger boy or girl; do free babysitting for a neighbor.	
Mary	Said "yes" to God; changed her life to do God's will	Put up with an inconvenience today.	
Angels	Announced the good news to the shepherds	Cheer someone up; send a card to a shut-in.	
Shepherds	Humbly accepted the message and responded immediately	Show gratitude for a gift received.	
Wise Men	Followed the star; took risks	Do a good deed for someone you do not know very well.	

Activity

What is the best gift you have ever received?

_____

_____

What is the best gift you have ever given?

_____

_____

What made these gifts important to you?

_____

_____

THE GREATEST GIFT

Christmas is a time of gift giving. We spend time finding the perfect gift for family members and special friends. We make lists of gifts that we would like to give as well as lists of gifts we would like to receive. We give gifts to people who have helped us, supported us, or served us throughout the year. We wrap our gifts with care and wait anxiously to see how people react when they open them. When we see our names on a present under the Christmas tree, we are eager to open it, anticipating that we will be happy.

On the first Christmas, God gave us the most precious gift we will ever receive: Jesus Christ. Through the miracle of the Incarnation, God became man in Jesus and lived among us. Jesus is **Emmanuel**, God with us.

In giving us Jesus, God offers us a model for how we should live. It has been said that "God became human so that humans might become God." Through the gift of Jesus, God made it possible to share in Jesus' life. In the First Letter of John we read, "See what love the Father has bestowed on us that we may be called the children of God. Yet so we are. The reason the world does not know us is that it did not know him. . . . And his commandment is this: we should believe in the name of his Son, Jesus Christ, and love one another just as he commanded us" (1 John 3:1, 23).

Although we are all familiar with the story of the Magi bringing gifts of gold, frankincense, and myrrh, the custom of gift giving did not begin with the first Christmas. The date for the celebration of Jesus' birth was not established until the fourth century. December 25 was probably chosen in part to offset a pagan festival held on the same date in honor of the sun. It was customary to exchange gifts around the time of this pagan festival.

As Christmas grew in popularity, the pagan customs of the day were forgotten and it became a holy day. The tradition of giving gifts remained, however, and took on new meaning as people came to recognize that Jesus is God's ultimate gift to the world. We accept God's gift of love with gratitude and we offer gifts to others as a sign of our love for them. Our joy in Christ's birth must be shared with others and giving gifts is a tangible sign of that joy.

Exchanging Christmas presents is a meaningless custom if we give someone a gift only because it is expected of us or because we know that they are going to buy something for us. It is equally meaningless if we measure our feelings for others by the amount of money they spend on us at Christmas or if we buy expensive gifts to impress others.

God wants our gifts to come from our hearts. A gift from the heart is a gift of self, a sharing of our time and our talent with others. At Christmas, we remember that Jesus calls us to serve others out of love.

Activity

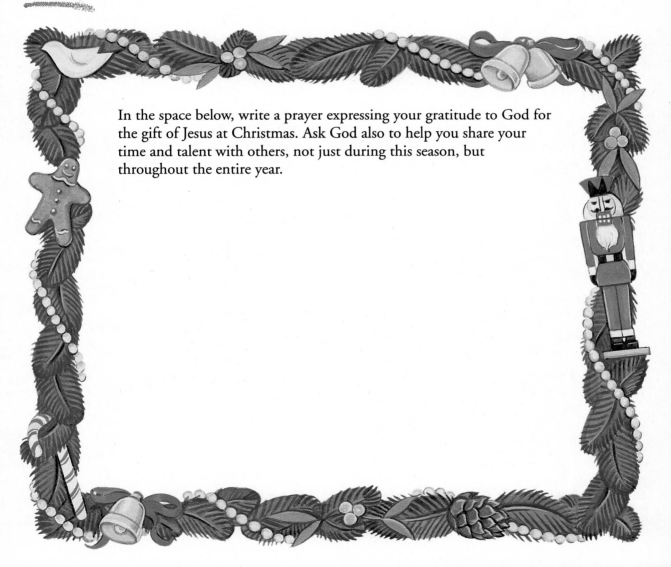

In the space below, write a prayer expressing your gratitude to God for the gift of Jesus at Christmas. Ask God also to help you share your time and talent with others, not just during this season, but throughout the entire year.

A Time of Tradition

Every family has its own, unique way of celebrating Christmas. The decorations we display, the foods we eat, our gift-giving customs, and even the songs we listen to and sing are all an important part of our family's story. Yet, we often forget that many of our family traditions have evolved from centuries-old customs that helped people express their joy and belief in the birth of our Savior, Jesus Christ.

The Christmas Crèche

It is said that St. Francis of Assisi began the tradition of the Christmas nativity scene, or crèche, in 1224 in Greccio, Italy. St. Francis' manger scene was a tableau with live characters and a wax figure of the baby Jesus. Each day during the twelve days of Christmas (from December 25 to the original feast of the Epiphany on January 6) St. Francis preached about the birth of Jesus and its meaning, using the crèche to help people understand the story. It is possible that the idea for Christmas pageants developed from the tradition of a living nativity scene.

The tradition of the crèche soon spread throughout the world. People began to recreate the Christmas scene in their own homes, using small statues and handmade stables. In France, small figures called *santons,* or little saints, have been added to manger displays. The santons represent different townspeople: mayor, shopkeepers, and even neighbors. It is a sign that we are all witnesses to the great event of Christ's birth.

In Latin America the manger scene is called a *nacimiento.* In Italy it is called a *presepio.* They may be small enough to fit under a Christmas tree or they may be so large that they occupy the entire front yard or a room in the house. Some nativity scenes are family treasures, handed down through the generations. In many places on Christmas Eve, neighbors go from home to home, sharing food and admiring one another's Christmas cribs.

Christmas Carols

A most beloved Christmas carol, "Silent Night" was first sung at St. Nicholas Church in Obendorf, Austria, on Christmas Eve in 1818. After discovering that the church organ was broken, Father Joseph Mohr quickly wrote a

Christmas poem. He brought it to the parish organist, Franz Grüber, who wrote a melody that could be sung by a chorus accompanied only by a guitar.

"O Little Town of Bethlehem" was written by an American Episcopal priest, Father Phillips Brooks. It was inspired by a trip he took to Palestine. During his visit, he rode on horseback from Jerusalem to Bethlehem. As he traveled, he could not help thinking about the journey of Joseph and Mary so many centuries before. The song was first sung in 1868 by the children's choir at Holy Trinity Church in Philadelphia.

CHRISTMAS GREENERY

The tradition of Christmas trees began in Germany. Legend has it that Martin Luther, the German monk who led the Protestant Reformation, brought a fir tree into his church and had candles placed on its branches. During Christmas services, the candles were lit to symbolize the star that led the Magi to Jesus.

Holly is another decoration frequently used at Christmas. Holly is a green plant with sharp, prickly leaves and red berries. It is said to be nature's way of reminding us of God's appearance to Moses in the burning bush. Another legend says that the sharp leaves and red berries are a bittersweet reminder of the crown of thorns Jesus would wear and the blood he would shed to save us from sin and death.

A legend is also told about poinsettia plants, so often used to decorate for Christmas. On Christmas Eve long ago, a poor Mexican boy had no gift to bring the infant Jesus. As he walked along, he noticed a small bush. Since he did not want to arrive at church empty-handed, he decided to offer Jesus a few branches from the bush. As he gathered them, they burst into bloom with beautiful, red, star-shaped flowers. Later that night, a star appeared in the sky over the church. It was said that the star was a sign that God was pleased with the boy's simple gift.

Christmas traditions help us to enter into the great celebration of Christmas in a very personal way. They prepare a place for Jesus in our hearts and give us the opportunity to thank God, with people of every time and place, for the greatest gift of all: God's Son.

Activity

Think about a favorite Christmas memory that you associate with each of the customs below. Write about your memories and traditions in the space provided.

Christmas crèches, nativity scenes, and pageants

_____

_____

Christmas carols _____

_____

_____

Christmas decorations _____

_____

_____

SPICED POTPOURRI ORNAMENT

Since the Middle Ages, some people have decorated their Christmas trees with apples. The apples were a symbol of the sin committed by the first man and woman who ate of the fruit from the Tree of Knowledge in the Garden of Eden. Because Jesus was born to save us from our sins and make it possible for us to live forever in heaven, some people called the apple-covered Christmas tree a "Paradise Tree."

In order to prepare the apples, they were first soaked in fragrant spices and herbs, as a reminder of the gifts give to Jesus by the Magi. Then the apples were tied with ribbons. Guests who visited during the Christmas season were given an apple to take home. The apple ornaments were called pomander balls at that time. Today we know them as potpourri ornaments.

Materials Needed:
- 1 small, firm apple or orange
- 1 small box of cloves
- 2 tablespoons of cinnamon
- 1 tablespoon of all-spice
- 1 tablespoon of sage
- 1 cup lemon juice
- 1 small bowl
- a square of transparent plastic wrap
- a plastic bag
- 1 ribbon
- several small straight pins

Instructions

1. Insert cloves into the fruit, covering the entire surface.

2. Add the rest of the spices to the lemon juice and mix in the small bowl. Place the fruit in the mixture, turning it over several times to coat it. Cover the bowl with plastic wrap and place it away from the sun. Turn the fruit once or twice daily for three days.

3. Remove the fruit and put it in a sealed plastic bag for several days to dry.

4. Tie ribbon around the dried fruit, securing it at the top with small straight pins.

5. Make a loop at the top of the ribbon so the ornament can hang on a tree branch.

6. Give your spiced ornament to someone important in your life. Be sure to tell him or her the story of the Paradise Tree!

BELOVED ONE

INTRODUCTION

Leader 1: On the last day of the Christmas season we remember the Baptism of Jesus. When Jesus began his public life, he was baptized by John in the River Jordan. The voice of God was heard over the Jordan Valley, saying of Jesus, "You are my beloved Son; with you I am well pleased" (Mark 1:11). Through our own baptism we are united with Jesus' dying and rising. The words of God spoken at Jesus' Baptism can be spoken to us as we present ourselves in service to God. We can count on God's blessings for us.

Leader 2: Now I invite you to bring your dreams before God.

Students: (Each student who is willing to read his or her dream should do so now.)

All: (After each reading say) You are my beloved one. On you my favor rests.

RITE OF ANOINTING

Leader 1: Lord, you hear our voices as we say our dreams. You hear the wishes of our hearts as we ponder our dreams.
(Invite the students to come forward. Anoint the palms of their hands with oil, symbolic of commissioning and blessing, while saying the following.)
You are my beloved one. On you my favor rests.

A LITANY FOR JOURNEYING

Leader 2: Now we ask God's saints to journey with us:
St. Ignatius of Antioch and St. Anthony of Egypt,

All: Journey with us.

Leader 2: St. Brigid and St. Patrick of Ireland,

All: Journey with us.

Leader 2: St. Francis and St. Clare of Assisi,

All: Journey with us.

Leader 2: St. Dominic and St. Catherine of Siena,

All: Journey with us.

CLOSING PRAYER

All: Dear God, we are mindful that we are your works of art, created in Christ Jesus to live good lives as you intended from the beginning of all time. Be with us as we journey to bring all good works to their fullness and to your glory, for endless ages. Amen.

Our Church Celebrates Lent

LEARNING TO PRAY

The season of **Lent** provides us with a forty-day preparation for the great feast of the death and resurrection of Jesus. Lent is a special season in which Catholics take time to listen, reflect, and respond to the word of God. It is a time to separate ourselves from the world to pray. Just as Jesus was led by the Spirit into the desert for forty days, we too are led by the Spirit to deeper prayer and reflection.

Jesus prayed often. He teaches us to pray by his example and teaching. Jesus rose early in the morning to have time for prayer. He also prayed at night. Jesus prayed before he faced an important decision or event in his life, before he called the Twelve, and in the garden before he experienced his passion and death. Jesus prayed on a mountaintop, at sea, in a desert, and in an olive grove.

Lent is a time for each Christian to follow the example of Jesus and be led into a desert place, a place of solitude and quiet. Lent is an invitation to each faithful Christian to take time to be alone with oneself and with the Lord, and to discover who God is and who we are as his people. In our quiet desert place of prayer, we discover our weaknesses and faults. We see the need for a savior, and we are asked to accept Jesus and receive his redemption, forgiveness, and love. We discover that we are loved by a loving Father, and we understand that he is the truth that sets us free.

PRAYING WITH SCRIPTURE

Learning to be a friend of Jesus requires spending time with him in prayer. Praying with Scripture is a good method for growing in holiness. To learn to pray well with Scripture, follow these simple steps.

1. Find a quiet place where you are comfortable and relaxed. Think of Jesus and ask him to help you pray.

2. Open your Bible to the New Testament and select a passage, then read it slowly.

3. Imagine the scene in your mind. Imagine that you are there and Jesus is speaking to you. Ask yourself these questions:
   • Who is present there?
   • What is happening?
   • What does it mean to me?

4. Talk to Jesus. Tell him what is on your mind. Ask him what he is saying to you. Listen to the answer. Remember to thank him for his love and support. Ask for the grace to live out his message in your life.

Activity

Sometimes it helps to write your thoughts and feelings when you are beginning to pray. Keep a journal of your spiritual journey with the Lord by recording your thoughts and feelings. Use the example and format below to practice your journal writing.

Read Luke 8:4–15. Summarize briefly the key idea of the parable.

_____

_____

_____

_____

Who was present when Jesus told this parable?

_____

_____

_____

_____

What does it mean to me?

_____

_____

_____

_____

Talk to Jesus and ask him what he is saying to you. Write what you think his message is.

_____

_____

_____

_____

_____

Listen quietly to his word in you. Thank him.

_____

_____

_____

_____

Ask him to help you live out his message in your life.

_____

_____

_____

NOW IS THE ACCEPTABLE TIME

Lent is the Church's sacred time of growth, a time when we are called to turn toward God just as surely as spring plants turn toward the sun. It is a season that offers us an opportunity to turn our thoughts and efforts toward working for peace and justice. This season also reminds us that we are called to join in the following traditional Lenten practices.

Almsgiving: We are called to attend to those who are poor and in need of material and spiritual goods.

Prayer: We are called to look carefully at our prayer life and to take responsibility for praying in solitude as well as for praying with the Church at the Sunday Eucharist and at other traditional Lenten **devotions**, or special ways of praying, such as the Stations of the Cross.

Fasting: We are called to eat less food and put aside those habits and actions that cause us to

grasp and hoard for ourselves rather than to be open and generous to all.

Read the following two passages from Scripture to discover Jesus' instructions for almsgiving, prayer, and fasting.

> When you give alms, do not blow a trumpet before you, as the hypocrites do in the synagogues and in the streets to win the praise of others. Amen, I say to you, they have received their reward. But when you give alms, do not let your left hand know what your right is doing, so that your almsgiving may be secret. And your Father who sees in secret will repay you.
>
> *Matthew 6:2–4*

> But when you fast, anoint your head and wash your face, so that you may not appear to be fasting, except to your Father who is hidden. And your Father who sees what is hidden will repay you.
>
> *Matthew 6:17–18*

Activity

Today the Church responds to Jesus' call to serve, to give alms, and to fast. Read the statements in each speech balloon. Then inside the cross, write what you can do to respond to Jesus during Lent.

The Stations of the Cross

The holy city of Jerusalem has long been known as a place of **pilgrimage**, or a journey to a sacred shrine or place. In Luke 2:22–38, we read that shortly after Jesus' birth, Mary and Joseph traveled from Bethlehem to the Temple in Jerusalem to present him to God. They made this pilgrimage because they were devout Jews who followed the tradition of consecrating their firstborn son to the Lord. According to Luke 2:41, every year Jesus and his family traveled approximately seventy miles from their village in Nazareth to Jerusalem to celebrate the feast of Passover.

All four Gospels found in the New Testament record the fact that in the days before his death, Jesus again journeyed to Jerusalem, where he would die on the cross and rise from the dead. In the Gospel of Matthew the reason for this journey is given: "Behold, we are going up to Jerusalem, and the Son of Man will be handed over to the chief priests and the scribes, and they will condemn him to death, and hand him over to the Gentiles to be mocked and scourged and crucified, and he will be raised on the third day" (Matthew 20:18–19).

Over the centuries, Christian pilgrims began to visit Jerusalem and other sites in Palestine connected with Jesus' life. They went to retrace Jesus' final hours and to pray at these sacred places. There is also a devotion that enables Christians to recall the events of Jesus' passion, death, and resurrection without traveling far. Some believe the legend that Mary began this tradition of the Stations of the Cross after Jesus' ascension. According to the story, Mary made frequent visits to pray at the places where Jesus suffered, died, and was buried.

Although the earliest known Stations of the Cross outside of Palestine were erected in Bologna, Italy, in the fifth century, they did not replace the desire of Christians to visit the sites where Jesus suffered and died. During the Crusades, between the eleventh and thirteenth centuries, many pilgrims visited Palestine, where walking "the way of the cross" became a popular devotion. Once the Muslims ruled this territory, it became too dangerous for Christians to risk making such pilgrimages. The popularity of the Stations of the Cross grew.

It became customary to create statues or pictures in local parishes to represent the stops, or stations, along Jesus' journey to Calvary.

Originally, these stations were erected outdoors, but they are now found inside Catholic churches around the world.

Through the centuries, the number of stations in the Way of the Cross has varied greatly. There were as few as five or as many as twenty. In 1731, Pope Clement XII established fourteen as the official number of stations. In recent years, a fifteenth station, representing Jesus' resurrection, has been suggested.

When we pray the Stations of the Cross, we recall the event that occurred at each station, meditate on its meaning in our lives, say a prayer, and ask Jesus to be with us on our journey through life. The Stations of the Cross can be prayed at any time of the year, but they have special meaning for us during Lent, as we try to imitate Jesus' example of sacrifice and service to others. Many Catholic churches have the Stations of the Cross on their interior walls.

THE STATIONS OF THE CROSS

1. Jesus is condemned to death.
2. Jesus accepts the cross.
3. Jesus falls the first time.
4. Jesus meets his mother.
5. Simon helps Jesus carry the cross.
6. Veronica wipes the face of Jesus.
7. Jesus falls the second time.
8. Jesus meets the women of Jerusalem.
9. Jesus falls the third time.
10. Jesus is stripped of his garments.
11. Jesus is nailed to the cross.
12. Jesus dies on the cross.
13. Jesus is taken down from the cross.
14. Jesus is buried in the tomb.
15. Jesus rises from the dead.

Activity

Prepare a prayer celebration of the Stations of the Cross to share with younger students in your school. In the panels below, write out the name of each station for which your group is responsible. Identify who will play the parts of the people for each station. Then work together to create a description of the event that occurred at each station. Finally, write a brief prayer to be prayed aloud at each station.

Station: _____

Characters: _____

Description: _____

Prayer: _____

Station: _____

Characters: _____

Description: _____

Prayer: _____

TAKE UP YOUR CROSS

According to the Gospel of Luke, once when Jesus was praying, his disciples came to him. Jesus asked them, " 'Who do the crowds say that I am?' They said in reply, 'John the Baptist; others, Elijah; still others, "One of the ancient prophets has arisen." ' Then he said to them, 'But who do you say that I am?' Peter said in reply, 'The Messiah of God.' He rebuked them and directed them not to tell this to anyone.

"He said, 'The Son of Man must suffer greatly and be rejected by the elders, the chief priests, and the scribes, and be killed and on the third day be raised.'

"Then he said to all, 'If anyone wishes to come after me, he must deny himself and take up his cross daily and follow me. For whoever wishes to save his life will lose it, but whoever loses his life for my sake will save it' " (Luke 9:18–24).

The question that Jesus asked his disciples, "Who do you say that I am?" is a question that each of us must answer for ourselves. Our response is a sign of how much we believe in Jesus. If we can say, as Peter did, with complete faith and love, "You are the messiah sent by God," then our words and actions will reflect our trust in Jesus as our Savior. This passage from the Gospel of Luke occurs just before the Gospel writer shows Jesus and his disciples on their way to Jerusalem and ultimately, his death at Calvary. There, he would demonstrate his perfect love and faithfulness to God by sacrificing himself on the cross. In this Gospel passage, Jesus is shown telling his followers that being his disciples meant that they would have to change the way they were thinking and acting. This decision to change, Jesus warned them, was not something that they could decide once and for all. Each day they would have to decide to give up their former way of living and make a conscious choice to follow him.

Jesus knew that his disciples would face many temptations. They would be tempted to deny their faith in him because they feared for their own lives. They would grow tired of the demands people would make of them. They would become angry at those who mocked them for their faith in Jesus. They would be tempted to feel that they were better than other people because they had been chosen by Jesus to share his good news with others. They would grow discouraged if people did not believe in the message they shared. They might even be tempted to doubt Jesus. Every day they would have to work to overcome the temptations they faced.

We, too, face many temptations as we try to live as Jesus' disciples. During Lent, we are challenged to turn away from the things that prevent us from being faithful to our commitment to follow Christ. It is not easy to avoid the things that attract us or the pressure from peers to do things that we know are wrong. This is what Jesus means by telling us to take up our cross. Because we are his disciples, we will follow his example of faithfulness to God's ways and selfless service to others.

During Lent, Jesus calls us to keep our minds and hearts focused on our belief in him. He asks us to trust that he alone knows what is best for us. If we follow Jesus' example during Lent, then we will be able to share in his new life at Easter and in the kingdom that is to come.

Activity

Journey through the maze to the risen Jesus. Then choose two of the temptations that junior high students face. Write how someone your age can fight against and overcome these temptations because of his or her faith in Jesus.

_____

_____

_____

A LENTEN DEBATE

A debate is a formal discussion in support of or against a particular viewpoint or question. Before debating, participants should research the issue. They should have facts and figures to support their positions. With your classmates, debate the following statement.

Statement

If you want to know what charity is, you should look around you and take care of the problems nearest to you. For example, you can become aware of world hunger by doing something about the attitude toward hunger and the waste of food in your school cafeteria. That is enough charity.

Process

Divide the class into two teams. Team 1 will agree with the statement. Team 2 will disagree with the statement. Each group should choose one person to speak for the team. All team members should work together to help plan the speeches. When both teams are ready, begin the debate.

Constructive Speeches

Team 1: Give a speech that explains why you agree with the statement.

Team 2: Give a speech that explains why you disagree with the statement.

Rebuttal Speeches

Team 2: Argue against the speech given by Team 1.

Team 1: Argue against the speech given by Team 2.

Team 2: Again argue against the speech and rebuttal given by Team 1.

Team 1: Again argue against the speech and rebuttal given by Team 2.

A Lenten Prayer Service

Gathering

Leader: Let us gather under the sign of the cross, in the name of the Father, and of the Son, and of the Holy Spirit.

All: Amen.

Leader: Let us pray.

All: Merciful Lord, open our eyes to the selfishness that lies locked in our hearts. Give us new hearts. Where sin has brought death, may your Spirit raise us to new life. This we ask in the name of Christ Jesus.

The Healing Word

Reader: (Read Ezekiel 11:17–20.)

Leader: Lord God, sin and selfishness harden our hearts, crush our spirits, and leave us feeling hopeless. We try to rid ourselves of all that keeps us from you and from one another. Sometimes, O Lord, we succeed, and sometimes we fail. Then our hearts grow cold, our hands clench, and we close up inside.

All: Hear us, O God, as we call upon you. Help us to open our closed hearts and clenched hands. Help us to welcome you and all your children.

Leader: (Invite the students to clench their fists as each petition is prayed and then open and lift their hands as they respond to each of the following.) O God, we say we love you most of all, but we choose things first.

All: Lord, banish the selfishness of sin in us.

Leader: We complain and do nothing.

All: Lord, banish the selfishness of sin in us.

Leader: We see injustice, and we decide we are powerless.

All: Lord, banish the selfishness of sin in us.

Leader: We talk about being concerned, but mostly we are concerned about ourselves and our little needs.

All: Lord, banish the selfishness of sin in us.

Leader: We make the sign of the cross, but we dread taking on even the tiniest burden of the cross.

All: Lord, banish the selfishness of sin in us.

Leader: Lord, take away the selfishness of these sins. Open our cramped hearts, open our clenched hands. May our hearts welcome and heal. May our hands greet and serve. We ask this through Christ our Lord.

All: Amen.

Leader: Let us offer each other a sign of peace.

Closing Prayer

All: (Pray the Lord's Prayer. Either join hands or hold hands in a gesture of prayer.)

Our Church Celebrates Holy Week

DAYS OF PALMS, PROCESSIONS, AND PASSOVER

Holy Week begins with Passion Sunday and ends with the celebration of the Easter Vigil on Holy Saturday evening. These seven days, the holiest of the year, are filled with centuries-old religious traditions and cultural practices that help us to celebrate the mysteries of our faith.

PASSION SUNDAY

Passion Sunday is popularly known as Palm Sunday. On this day, we remember Jesus' triumphant entrance into Jerusalem, when he was greeted as a king by people waving palm branches. On Passion Sunday, the vestments worn by the priest are red, a color sometimes associated with royalty. Yet the color of the vestments has a deeper, bittersweet meaning for Christians. Red is also the color of blood. On Passion Sunday we recall that days after Jesus' royal welcome, he was executed like a common criminal and died on a cross, shedding his blood for the redemption of all people.

On Passion Sunday, palm branches are blessed with holy water and distributed. The priest then leads the community in a procession into church to celebrate the Eucharist.

After Mass, people take their palms home. Palms are **sacramentals**—objects, blessings, or actions that remind us of Christ's presence with us. Some people place their blessed palms behind a wall crucifix or a picture of Jesus. Others place them in the family Bible. Some people braid the palms into the shape of a cross. In rural areas, palms may be scattered in the fields to ask God to bless the soil.

PASSION PLAYS

In medieval times, religious dramas were performed that reenacted the passion, death, and resurrection of Christ. These dramas, which came to be known as passion plays, were especially popular in Germany and France. They were originally performed during Holy Week and were often quite lengthy. One German passion play was performed over a period of three days.

Modern versions of the passion play still exist today. Every ten years, the town of Oberammergau, Germany, stages an elaborate play, keeping a vow made by village leaders in the seventeenth century. At that time, a deadly plague swept through Germany, killing thousands of people. The people of Oberammergau solemnly promised to dedicate one year out of every decade to the presentation of a passion play if they were saved from the plague. Legend has it that there were no further deaths from the plague in the village and ever since the play as been performed every ten years. It is now considered the highest of honors to be asked to participate.

On Good Friday each year, Mexican Americans in Chicago process through the streets. The pageant is called *Via Crucis*, or "Way of the Cross." People line the streets, praying and singing as a man chosen to portray Jesus carries a 150-pound cross. The procession ends in a public park where thousands of people gather to witness the reenactment of Jesus' crucifixion. The Via Crucis is a way for Chicago's Mexican Americans to share their faith with others.

SEDER MEALS

Our celebration of the Eucharist has its roots in the Jewish tradition of the Passover, or Seder meal. On Holy Thursday, we remember that at the Last Supper Jesus gathered with his disciples, possibly during the time of Passover. This seven-day festival commemorates when God saved the Israelites from slavery in Egypt. During the Passover celebration, Jewish people eat a ritual meal of lamb, matzoh bread, bitter herbs, boiled eggs, and parsley dipped in salt water. Wine is blessed and shared. During the meal, the story of the Exodus is retold.

Many Catholic parishes and families share Seder meals during Holy Week. Catholics should not add Christian elements to Seder celebrations, but should participate in them in their Jewish form. These celebrations will help us to understand our Jewish roots better and appreciate our Jewish friends more.

SIGNS OF NEW LIFE

Easter decorations are filled with images of Spring: rabbits, decorated eggs, baby chicks, and flowers. All of these signs of new life seem to be the Earth's confirmation of Jesus's rising.

On Holy Saturday, it is traditional to have a blessing of foods. People bring to church the foods they will prepare and eat on Easter. The food is brought in baskets which may be carefully decorated and arranged. Other parishes collect food for the poor during Holy Week. As we prepare to celebrate Jesus' passage from death to new life, we are called to share our joy by reaching out to those who are most in need of Jesus' help and care.

Activity

Working in small groups with several classmates, plan a service project for Holy Week. You might volunteer to run a babysitting service during Triduum services or make Easter baskets for needy families. Write what you will do in the space below.

The Triduum

The Church celebrates the culmination of the entire liturgical year during the Easter **Triduum**, or last three days of Holy Week. These three most sacred days, which begin at sundown on Holy Thursday and end at sundown on Easter Sunday, recall the passion, death, and resurrection of Jesus Christ. The manner of counting these days from sundown to sundown follows the Jewish tradition of determining days.

In the early Church, Jesus' passion and resurrection were celebrated in one liturgy. This celebration began at sundown on Holy Saturday and ended at dawn on Easter Sunday. This liturgy had two distinct parts. The first part focused on mourning the death and burial of Jesus. After midnight, the emphasis shifted from sorrow to joy as the community recalled Christ's resurrection, celebrated the Eucharist, and baptized new members into the Church.

Over time, Jesus' passion and resurrection came to be celebrated over three days. Our modern celebration of the Eastern Triduum is drawn from liturgies that were established in the fifth century. These help us to celebrate our own dying and rising in Baptism as we experience again the power of God's love for us in the death and resurrection of Jesus.

The Evening Mass of the Lord's Supper

On Holy Thursday evening, we remember the Last Supper when Jesus gave us the gift of himself in the Eucharist. At the Last Supper Jesus also commanded his followers to serve others as he did. As a sign of the importance of service, he washed his disciples' feet. On Holy Thursday we remember his command by including the washing of feet in our worship.

Also on Holy Thursday, the holy oils, consecrated by the bishop at the Chrism Mass in the cathedral church of the diocese and used in celebrations of the sacraments in every parish, are sometimes received in parishes during the Introductory Rites of the Mass. The oils include chrism, the oil of the sick, and the oil of the catechumens. These oils will be used during the next year.

During Mass on Holy Thursday, the priest consecrates bread for Good Friday services because there is no Mass on Good Friday. The hosts for Good Friday are taken to the tabernacle in a solemn procession. After adoration of Jesus' presence in the tabernacle, the altar is stripped and crosses in the church are covered. This is a reminder that Jesus' body was stripped before his crucifixion. It is also a sign that we are preparing to mourn Christ's death.

THE CELEBRATION OF THE LORD'S PASSION

Good Friday services begin in silence as the priest and other liturgical ministers prostrate themselves before the altar, imitating the way Jesus prayed in the Garden of Gethsemane. As the ministers lie face down before the altar, we kneel in prayer.

The Scripture reading is the story of Jesus' passion, taken from the Gospel of John 18:1–19:42. During the General Intercessions, the community stands and kneels at each petition. This is a way of more fully involving ourselves in prayer. We pray with our bodies as well as our words.

The veneration of the cross also occurs during this liturgy. The cross is unveiled as the priest proclaims three times, "This is the wood of the cross, on which hung the Savior of the world." We show reverence for the cross by kissing it, kneeling before it, or touching it with love and respect.

Later in the liturgy is the reception of Communion. We pray the Lord's Prayer and receive the Body of Christ that was consecrated on Holy Thursday. We leave the church in silence, to wait and watch with Jesus.

THE EASTER VIGIL

No Masses are celebrated during the day on Holy Saturday. After sundown, the Easter celebration begins with the service of light. The Easter fire is blessed and the Easter candle is lit from the fire. The candles held by everyone are lit from the Easter candle and the light of the risen Christ fills the church.

During the Liturgy of the Word, seven readings from the Old Testament are proclaimed, along with an epistle and a Gospel reading from the New Testament. The readings tell the story of God's saving actions in the world, from creation to the resurrection of Jesus. The Liturgy of Baptism follows the readings. We pray the litany of the saints, witness the Baptism and Confirmation of those being initiated into the Church, and renew our baptismal promises. During the Liturgy of the

Eucharist, the newly baptized receive Communion for the first time and the rest of the community receives the body and blood of Christ as well. We rejoice in Jesus' resurrection, expressing our faith and hope that we will share in his victory over death.

Activity

Study the celebrations of the Easter Triduum and mark each statement true or false by circling the appropriate word. Then explain the reason for your choice.

1. The Easter Triduum celebrates only Jesus' sacrifice on the cross.

   True   **False**

   _____

   _____

2. The Mass is celebrated on Holy Thursday, Good Friday, and Holy Saturday.

   True   **False**

   _____

   _____

   _____

3. We venerate the cross on Good Friday by blessing it with holy water.

   True   **False**

   _____

   _____

   _____

4. Baptism is an important part of the Easter Vigil.

   True   **False**

   _____

   _____

Our Church Celebrates Easter

THE RESURRECTION

"Why do you look for the living among the dead?" asked one of the messengers.

The question startled the women who were visiting the tomb of Jesus. What could he possibly mean? They were not looking for the "living." They fully expected to find the body of Jesus just as they had seen it placed in the tomb. After all, some of them had witnessed his brutal death only two days before and had followed closely as friends brought him to the tomb. This day they even brought spices and herbs with which to anoint him.

The insistent messengers went on: "He is not here, he is risen." The women were stunned and confused. They hurried to the disciples and told them of the experience. But most of the disciples did not believe them. Peter and John, however, went to the tomb and found the situation to be as the women described. The linen burial cloth and the headband had been folded and carefully left in place. Jesus was nowhere to be found. Later that same day he appeared to several people. Slowly, it dawned on his followers what had taken place. As unbelievable as it seemed, Jesus had risen from the dead.

Based on Luke 24: 1–12

Over the weeks and months that followed the **resurrection**—Jesus' rising from death to new life—the small group of disciples who had experienced the risen Lord shared their story with anyone who would listen.

There was certainly no logical explanation for the resurrection. If it were a hoax of some kind, it would die out soon enough; people would see through it eventually and lose their enthusiasm. Yet this story has become the cornerstone of the Christian faith.

The Church, energized by the Spirit, grew around the followers of Jesus and their converts, who told the story of the resurrection over and over again. Each group added and explained parts of it with which they were familiar. Gradually, collections of stories, sayings, and teachings of Jesus were added to the phenomenal story of the passion, death, and resurrection. Eventually, these stories were written down by the evangelists and became the four Gospels.

When we look at the Gospels, we see that they appear to be written in chronological order. It is important, however, to remember that the story was originally told backward.

In the days after Jesus' resurrection, the events of Holy Week were related first.

Jesus' resurrection is a promise of our own resurrection. When we feel most defeated, alone, or abandoned, we can recall the meaning of the resurrection.

If we have a "resurrection faith," we will believe that the God who raised his Son, Jesus, from the dead will transform our lives and restore us to the fullness of his love in this life and in the next. All we hope to do is trust in God as Jesus did.

Activity

Use a Bible to find the accounts of Jesus' resurrection in the four Gospels. Complete the chart below by writing the names of the women who visited the empty tomb and the people to whom Jesus appeared.

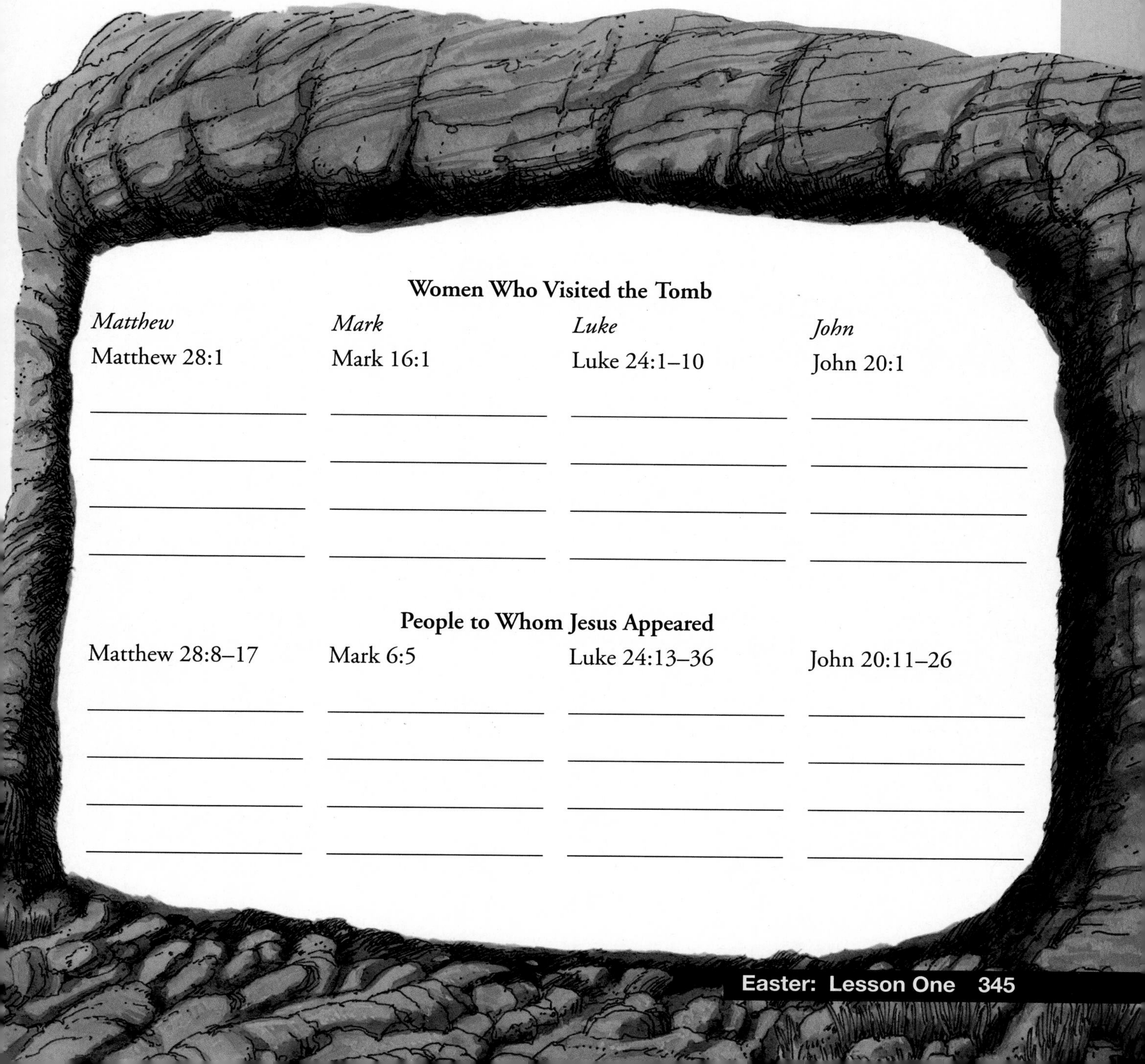

Women Who Visited the Tomb

Matthew	*Mark*	*Luke*	*John*
Matthew 28:1	Mark 16:1	Luke 24:1–10	John 20:1
_____	_____	_____	_____
_____	_____	_____	_____
_____	_____	_____	_____
_____	_____	_____	_____

People to Whom Jesus Appeared

Matthew 28:8–17	Mark 6:5	Luke 24:13–36	John 20:11–26
_____	_____	_____	_____
_____	_____	_____	_____
_____	_____	_____	_____
_____	_____	_____	_____

PETER'S COMMISSION

Jesus—as teacher, leader, and friend—loved and cared for his followers as a shepherd cares for his sheep. "When he has driven out all his own, he walks ahead of them, and the sheep follow him, because they recognize his voice" (John 10:4). Jesus expects us to hear his voice and to follow him. "My sheep hear my voice; I know them, and they follow me" (John 10:27).

Without Jesus we wander through life without purpose; we are lost like stray sheep. Yet if we follow Jesus, he guides us. "For you had gone astray like sheep, but you have now returned to the shepherd and guardian of your souls" (1 Peter 2:25).

Jesus loves and cares for his Church as a shepherd cares for his sheep. After his death and resurrection, Jesus returned to the Father in heaven. However, he entrusted the care of his flock on earth to one of his faithful followers—Peter. We call this Peter's **commission**, which means that Jesus gave him the authority to be the head of Jesus' Church. Jesus even uses the example of a shepherd when he asks Peter to be the leader of the Church. Jesus asks Peter to feed his lambs and his sheep, as a shepherd would care for his flock.

Peter has an interesting relationship with the Lord. He learns to be faithful and loyal to Jesus and eventually to die for Jesus. However, Peter, like each of us, had to grow in love and commitment to Jesus Christ.

In his youth and enthusiasm, Peter chose to follow Christ. However, he discovered that following Christ is not always easy. Peter denied Jesus three times because he was afraid that he would be arrested and sentenced to death.

Activity

Read John 18:15–18 and 25–27. How do you think Peter felt after this experience?

_____

_____

Later, after Jesus died and rose from the dead, Peter answered three more questions. But this time his response was not a denial of Jesus but a declaration of love for him. Read John 21:15–19. How do you think Peter felt after this experience?

_____

Peter had grown through his weakness. He had turned his life toward Jesus and had found meaning and purpose. When Jesus appeared to the apostles after his resurrection, he asked Peter three questions and Peter answered humbly. Two times Peter answered, "Yes, Lord, you know that I love you." In his third response, Peter gave his total self to Jesus. "Lord, you know everything; you know that I love you" (John 21:17).

Once Peter committed himself to Jesus, he was commissioned by Jesus to become the shepherd of the Church. Jesus said to Peter, "Feed my sheep" (John 21:17). In loving faithfulness to Jesus, Peter became the leader of the Christian community, the solid rock of foundation for the Church. All the popes through the centuries can trace their authority to Peter to lead the Church under the guidance of the Holy Spirit.

Activity

Pretend that Jesus is standing before you. He asks you three questions. Write your response to the first question and then write two other questions that Jesus might ask you and your responses to each. Then follow the directions to complete the prayers below.

Jesus: Do you love me?

Response: _____

_____

Jesus: _____

Response: _____

_____

Jesus: _____

_____

Response: _____

_____

Write a prayer asking the Lord to help you live a life committed to him and his Church.

_____

_____

_____

_____

Write a prayer asking the Lord to help the pope in his leadership of the Church.

_____

_____

_____

_____

THE GOOD NEWS

Jesus' followers were called to spread the good news of the resurrection. As you have seen, the Gospel accounts announce Jesus' resurrection from four different perspectives and experiences. As Jesus' followers broke bread together in memory of him, they continued to tell of his great works. Scholars feel that the first of the Gospel accounts were written about forty or fifty years after the resurrection.

About A.D. 65 or 70, the earliest of the four Gospels was written. It seems to have come from a Christian community that had been through a terrible ordeal, such as persecution. This Gospel was named after Jesus' disciple, Mark.

About A.D. 85, another Gospel was written from and for the Christian communities in the Greco-Roman world. This Gospel, named after someone who traveled with the Apostle Paul, is called Luke. The Gospel of Luke portrays Jesus as the one who brings healing, peace, and reconciliation.

Still later, in about A.D. 95, a third account of the good news was set down in writing. The Gospel of Matthew may have been written in Galilee or Antioch. Jesus as teacher is an important theme of this Gospel.

The fourth Gospel to be written is called the Gospel of John. It was written about A.D. 90 to 100. In this Gospel Jesus is the Word of God made flesh.

All four Gospels tell of Jesus' teachings, the events of his life, and his mission. They proclaim the good news that Jesus suffered, died, and rose again to save us from the power of sin and darkness. The resurrection is the climax and pivotal event of all four Gospels.

Activity

Those who wrote the Gospels were aware of the importance of the ministry of the word. Compare the opening words of each of the four Gospels.

1. Read Mathew 1:1 and write the verse here.

    _____

    _____

2. Read Mark 1:1 and write the verse here.

    _____

3. Read Luke 1:1–2 and write the verses here.

    _____

    _____

    _____

4. Read John 1:1 and write the verse here.

    _____

    _____

    _____

Activity

In the space provided, plan a publicity campaign that will spread the good news of Easter.

Radio: _____

_____

_____

Television: _____

_____

_____

_____

_____

The Good News

Newspaper: _____

_____

_____

_____

_____

_____

REJOICE AND BE GLAD

The following banner project will help you, your classmates, and your parish community celebrate the Sundays of Easter. You may want to ask if the banner may be carried in the entrance procession of each Sunday Mass celebrated during the Easter season.

Materials

- light, silk-like fabrics in bright colors
- assorted small bells or other materials that make chime-like sounds
- metallic strips that reflect the sun
- a ball of string
- scissors
- inexpensive pine lathes or wood strips
- carpenter's staple gun
- needles and spools of colorful thread, glue, or rubber cement
- sturdy string or cord

Procedure

1. Plan the shape, color, and decoration of your banner. Remember that you want your banner to be a celebration for both the eye and the ear.

2. Cut out letters and designs from smaller pieces of fabric.

3. Sew or glue the letters and designs to the large base piece of fabric.

4. Staple the top of the banner to a wood strip.

5. Tie and staple (to hold in place) sturdy string or cord to the ends of the wooden strip.

6. Use string or ribbon to attach small bells to each end of the wood strip.

7. Suspend the banner so that it moves freely in the wind.

THIS IS THE DAY THE LORD HAS MADE

During Lent, Church custom invites us to take our stand with Jesus as we pray the Stations of the Cross. During the fifty-day celebration of Easter, we take our stand as we process in gladness through the "Stations of the Resurrection." Establish seven places in your classroom. Have a banner at each station. Appoint one student to carry a resurrection cross. As he or she stops at each station, say the following prayers.

Opening Prayer

Crossbearer: Let us proceed in peace.

All: In the name of the Lord. Amen.

The Stations

Crossbearer: At the first station we pray,

All: God, our Father, you raised Christ your Son and conquered death.
   You opened the way to life. Renew our lives through the Spirit who is with us. Amen.

Crossbearer: At the second station we pray,

All: God of endless mercies, as we celebrate the resurrection of Christ,
   help us grow in the awareness of your blessings, renew the gift of your life in us. Amen.

Crossbearer: At the third station we pray,

All: God our Father, grant that we may rise and come into the new light of
   your day and stand before you until eternity dawns. Amen.

Crossbearer: At the fourth station we pray,

All: Almighty and eternal God, renew our strength as we look to Christ,
   the good shepherd, and lead us to the saints in heaven. Amen.

Crossbearer: At the fifth station we pray,

All: God our Father, look lovingly upon us today. You have saved us
   and made us your children in Christ. Grant us true freedom, and bring us
   into the inheritance you promise. Amen.

Crossbearer: At the sixth station we pray,

All: Ever-living God, come to our aid as we celebrate the resurrection of
   the Lord. Help us to show forth in our lives the love we celebrate today. Amen.

Crossbearer: At the seventh station we pray,

All: Father, help us to remember that Christ, who lives with you,
   promises to stay with us now and through all eternity. Amen.

Our Church Honors Saints

THE NORTH AMERICAN MARTYRS

Throughout the history of the Church, thousands of people have given their lives for their faith. We call these people **martyrs** because they chose to die rather than renounce their beliefs.

The people of North America honor a group of individuals who gave their lives for their faith. Called the North American Martyrs, these eight Jesuit missionaries were martyred between the years 1642 and 1649 in what is now New York State and Canada.

After the French began arriving in America in the early 1600s, Father Isaac Jogues and his fellow Jesuit missionaries wanted to come and minister to their French countrymen who were living in Quebec. At the same time, they wished to spread the Christian faith to the Huron Indians who lived in the vast country in which

Quebec was located. In the 1630s these missionaries taught the Hurons about God and baptized many of them with "waters of importance," as the blessed water used in Baptism was called. The priests moved from Huron village to Huron village, spreading the good news of God's saving love for all. For six years Father Isaac and his companions worked among the Hurons in what is now Toronto, Ontario, and Albany, New York.

Then on one of their journeys farther from French outposts, Father Isaac, Father Charles Garnier, and René Goupil, a Jesuit laybrother, were attacked and captured by the Mohawks, the enemies of the Hurons and the French. They were taken as slaves to nearby Mohawk villages and tortured.

During this period of slavery, Father Isaac was permitted to visit a Dutch settlement and to call upon a Dutch minister. The minister devised an escape plan for Father Isaac. The priest escaped and returned to France, but he still desired to continue his work in America.

Within a year Father Isaac got his wish and was permitted to return to North America. A peace treaty had been made with the Mohawks and Father Isaac wanted to teach them about God. He and Jean de Lalande began the journey into Mohawk territory in the fall of 1646. They never made it to their destinations. About six o'clock in the evening of October 18, 1646, Father Isaac was killed by the Mohawks. His death occurred at the same time that an Indian council was meeting to decide if the missionaries would be allowed to work among the Mohawks. Father Jean was killed the next day.

St. René Goupil, the Jesuit laybrother captured with St. Isaac in the earlier Mohawk ambush, had been killed by two Iroquois in the fall of 1642. The Jesuit missionaries who gave their lives in 1648 and 1649 were Sts. Jean de Brébeuf, Antoine Daniel, Charles Garnier, Noel Chabanel, and Gabriel Lalemant.

These eight Jesuit missionaries certainly are a treasure to the Church. From their blood, spilled on the soil of New York and Canada, grew the faith of succeeding generations.

Activity

How can we stand up for what we believe? Imagine that a group of your friends asks you the following questions. How would you respond?

1. Do you really believe in that "God stuff"? I think Jesus Christ is as much a fairy tale as the Easter bunny. What do you think?

   _____

   _____

2. Why do you go to church on Sunday?

   _____

   _____

3. Religion class is for little kids. Do you get anything out of it?

   _____

   _____

4. You Catholics are a bunch of goody-goodies. Do you ever have any fun?

   _____

   _____

MARTYRS IN JAPAN

St. Francis Xavier, the legendary apostle to the Far East, brought the gospel to Japan in 1549. Missionaries and traders from Spain and Portugal soon followed him to this isolated island world. They found themselves enchanted by ancient and beautiful customs, but also plagued by constant persecution.

At that time Japan was a collection of small states, each ruled by a shogun. Each shogun commanded his own samurai, or warrior knights. The swords of these samurai were kept busy as the shoguns maintained their territories and sometimes sought more power.

In this complex political situation, the European traders and missionaries found themselves at great risk. The European traders knew they had to try to work with the shoguns if their businesses were to succeed. This placed them and the missionaries in the dangerous position of being used by the shoguns.

For the missionaries, the gospel was their first priority and they tried to avoid political rivalries. They preached the gospel and showed kindness to the Japanese people. In time, churches and monasteries were built. Young Japanese men became priests and taught their own people.

In 1587, the powerful shogun Hideyoshi made a bid to rule all of Japan. To succeed, he needed to control the property and influence of European foreigners in Japan. Though he seized Church holdings and officially expelled the missionaries, some missionaries worked underground to keep the Church alive. After a decade-long struggle, Hideyoshi decided to strike the final blow to the Christian presence in Japan. He seized a stranded Spanish ship off the coast of Nagasaki and ordered twenty-six of the missionaries on board to be condemned to death. Hideyoshi ordered a dramatic form of execution—the missionaries were to be crucified on a hill overlooking Nagasaki harbor.

The twenty-six missionaries (Europeans and Japanese, priests and lay men) saw their coming martyrdom in the pattern of Jesus' death. On the morning of February 5, 1597, Paul Miki, who was the leader, and twenty-five others dressed in their finest clothing. They sang psalms of joy as they walked to their death. From among the crowds of onlookers, three more Christians stepped forward and joined their brothers on their painful journey to eternal life.

The persecution of Christians continued for fifty long years. For 200 years the Church was banned from Japan. However, the deaths of the martyrs of Nagasaki were deeply engraved in the memory of the struggling Church in Japan. In 1855, when missionaries were again permitted to work in Japan, they found there several thousand Christians who had quietly and steadily practiced and passed on the faith that was so dearly bought by the martyrs of Nagasaki. The Church remembers Paul Miki and the other martyrs of Nagasaki on February 6.

DO NOT BE AFRAID

In the Bible there are many passages that give comfort and courage to those who are being persecuted. Read the following example of Jesus' words as restated in haiku, a Japanese form of poetry.

> Do not be afraid.
> (five syllables)
> You are worth many sparrows.
> {seven syllables}
> I will be with you.
> (five syllables)
>
> *Based on Matthew 6:26–27*

Activity

Look up Psalm 23 in your Bible. This familiar psalm of the Lord as shepherd sings the praises of God's loving care and generosity. Choose one or two of the verses from this psalm and write them below. Then restate your selection in haiku form. You may want to use a separate piece of paper to work out the final version of your haiku.

Psalm 23
Verses:

_____

_____

_____

_____

_____

_____

_____

_____

_____

Haiku:

_____

_____

_____

BLESSED KATHARINE DREXEL

Katharine Drexel was born into a wealthy Philadelphia family in 1858. Katharine's mother died when Katharine was an infant and she was raised by her father's new wife. Katharine's new mother loved her as a daughter. Because Katharine's father was a successful banker, she enjoyed many privileges and opportunities about which other children could only dream. She was educated by a tutor at home and spent a great deal of time traveling with her family throughout the United States and Europe.

Even though her family was wealthy, Katharine was not spoiled. She was raised to show care and concern for others, especially those who lived in poverty or who were the victims of prejudice. The Drexels were devout Catholics and lived their faith by contributing great sums of money to charity work in Philadelphia and elsewhere in the United States. From the time Katharine was a little girl, she was taught that her family's money was meant to be shared with people in need.

One experience affected Katharine profoundly. Her father hired a private train to take the family to visit the western part of the United States. As they rode through the state of Washington, Katharine saw Indian reservations for the first time. She was shocked by the conditions in the villages and the poverty of the Native Americans who lived there. Through her family's charity work, Katharine was already aware that African Americans throughout the United States were treated unjustly. Seeing the plight of the Native Americans convinced Katharine that something had to be done to put an end to the discrimination against these two groups of people.

Some time later, the Drexel family visited Rome. They were granted an audience with Pope Leo XIII. During the audience, Katharine begged the pope to send missionaries to the United States to help the Native Americans. Pope Leo reportedly challenged Katharine by saying, "Why don't you become a missionary yourself?"

When Katharine's father died, she inherited a fortune. Although she could have continued to live comfortably in Philadelphia while donating money for others to do charitable work, Katharine was unable to forget what the pope had said to her. She felt that God was calling her to dedicate her life to the education of those who suffered from the effects of prejudice.

Katharine decided to become a religious sister and work among African Americans and Native Americans. When she joined the convent, the newspapers reported her decision. They called her "the richest nun in America." People were astonished to learn that Katharine intended to spend her 12-million-dollar inheritance caring for others. In 1891, after two

years of training in religious life with the Sisters of Mercy, Katharine founded the Sisters of the Blessed Sacrament. Katharine's order was devoted to educating Native Americans and African Americans and to sharing with them the message of Jesus' love and concern.

Word of Katharine's work spread quickly and other women, attracted by the idea of making a difference in the lives of those who were discriminated against, soon joined the Sisters of the Blessed Sacrament. These women gave Katharine the title "Mother" because her love for them and the people they served was like a parent's affection and devotion.

With Mother Katharine's money and direction, the Sisters of the Blessed Sacrament built their first school for Pueblo Indians in Sante Fe, New Mexico. Eventually, Katharine's order opened more than sixty-three schools in twenty-one states. In 1925, Katharine established Xavier University for African Americans in New Orleans, Louisiana. At that time, African Americans were not allowed to enroll at most colleges in the South because of the unjust segregation laws.

Initially, most of the sisters' work was done in the South and Southwest regions of the United States. After World War I, when African Americans began to move to the big cities in the North and Northeast to find employment, Katharine and her sisters followed them to continue their mission of service and education.

Mother Katharine lived to be ninety-six years old. Her order continues her work for equality and justice among the Native American, African American, and Haitian peoples.

Pope John Paul II beatified Mother Katharine Drexel in 1988, calling her a woman who saw the "evil of racial prejudice and set out with determination to combat it and overcome it." We honor Blessed Katharine Drexel on March 3, asking God to allow her prayers and example to inspire us to work for justice among the poor and oppressed.

Activity

Katharine lived by the words of Jesus, "If you wish to be perfect, go, sell what you have and give to the poor, and you will have treasure in heaven" (Matthew 19:21). Blessed Katharine Drexel inherited more money than most of us can even imagine. Instead of spending it on herself, she spent her entire fortune helping others. How would you use money to serve others? Imagine you have inherited millions of dollars. Write below how you would spend your inheritance.

_____

_____

_____

_____

_____

_____

_____

Saint Thomas Aquinas

Thomas was born into a rich family in Aquino, Italy, the youngest of many children. His father was the Count Landulf, and the whole family lived in a castle in a mountainous area. Young Thomas went to school at Monte Cassino, a great and influential Benedictine monastery near his home. He was very intelligent, and in little time he found himself at the University of Naples.

While there, he joined the company of a new **order**, or religious group, of preachers and teachers, called the Dominicans. However, his father, the grand and rich count, refused to allow his son to join this poor and common order. He sent Thomas's older brothers to bring him home. Thomas was kept at home for two years, but his kind sisters saw how miserable he was and helped him escape from his prison-like room. The young man went off to Paris and then to Cologne to take up life again with the Dominicans.

During his student days with the Dominicans, Thomas was quiet and attentive. His classmates called him "the dumb ox." Little did they realize how powerful his mind was. His teacher, St. Albert the Great, assured the class,

that one day, quiet Thomas's voice would be heard throughout the world.

And so it was. Thomas was quiet—mostly because he was always thinking. He would solve problems while he was eating—even when dining with the king.

Thomas from Aquino became the famous St. Thomas Aquinas, a saint whose greatness of heart matched the brilliance of his mind. Thomas began as all Christians begin. He was baptized and claimed forever as God's own. His interest in and love of God grew deeply. He began seeking a depth of understanding that would match the depth of his love.

Thomas began to talk and write about God. He became a theologian, one who studies God. Theology is faith seeking understanding, the head explaining things to the faithful heart. By the time Thomas reached middle age, he had written a whole series of books of theology. Taken together these books are called the *Summa Theologiae*. This Summa is part of every Catholic theologian's study today.

Thomas Aquinas fell sick and died while he was journeying to the Council of Lyons. He died in 1274. Finally, Thomas would meet face to face the God whom he had known and loved all his life.

PROCLAIM GOD'S GREAT DEEDS

Introduction

Leader: We invite you to raise your voices in praise and joy to God.

Opening Prayer

Group 1: Sing a new song to the Lord.
Sing out, all nations.

All: Proclaim God's great deeds to the whole world.

Group 2: Sing out freshly and bless God's name.
Announce God's saving power each and every day.

All: Proclaim God's great deeds to the whole world.

Group 1: Tell God's glory all around the world.
Announce to all people God's great deeds.

All: Proclaim God's great deeds to the whole world.

Group 2: Let the heavens sing out in gladness and let the earth rejoice.

All: Give glory and praise to the Lord.

Group 1: Let the sea and all within it echo the sound.

All: Give glory and praise to the Lord.

Group 2: Let the winds whisper through the fields of grain.

All: Give glory and praise to the Lord.

Based on Psalm 96:1–3, 11–12

Reading

Students: (Read haiku poems of verses from Psalm 23.)

Closing Prayer

Leader: God our Father,
source of strength for all your saints,
you led Paul Miki and his companions
through the suffering of the cross
to the joy of eternal life.
May their prayers give us the courage
to be loyal until death in professing our faith.
We ask this through our Lord Jesus Christ, your Son,
who lives and reigns with you and the Holy Spirit,
one God, for ever and ever.

Opening Prayer, Memorial Mass for
Paul Miki and Companion Martyrs

Our Church Honors Mary

MARY, MOTHER OF THE CHURCH

After the Second Vatican Council in the early 1960s, Pope Paul VI conferred the title "Mother of the Church" on Mary. He honored the Blessed Virgin with this special title because he saw her as a loving mother of the Church from its early days with the apostles to the present time. She is the mother of the members of the body of Christ.

With the message of the angel at the **Annunciation**, the Virgin Mary received the Word of God in her heart and in her body. We acknowledge and honor Mary as being truly the Mother of God and the Mother of the Redeemer. From ancient times, the Blessed Virgin has been praised and honored with the title "God-bearer."

Mary leads us to Jesus and draws us closer to God. The Church has endorsed many forms of piety and devotion toward the Mother of God. At times devotion to Mary has been stimulated by word of her appearances to devout people at Lourdes, Fatima, and Guadalupe.

Mary is considered to be the Mother of the Church because she is a God-bearer to the members of the Church. Mary is our example of faith and charity. In honoring Mary and imitating her virtues, we too will be God-bearers to the world.

Activity

Complete the following open-ended statements about Mary.

Mary is the Mother of the Church because

_____

_____

At the Annunciation, Mary _____

_____

Mary is called "God-bearer" because _____

_____

Activity

Next to each virtue of Mary, write one thing you can do to imitate that virtue.

- Patience: I can _____

_____

- Peace: I can _____

_____

_____

- Holiness: I can _____

_____

_____

- Purity: I can _____

_____

_____

- Love: I can _____

_____

_____

Activity

Name three ways that a mother shows love for her children.

1. _____

2. _____

3. _____

Look at the three ways you listed above. Do any of them apply to the ways Mary cares for the Church? How?

_____

_____

_____

_____

_____

GOD-BEARER

HONOR OF OUR PEOPLE

The good news has been proclaimed to the ends of the earth. Christians of all nations share the same faith in the risen Lord. They celebrate the Eucharist in their own land. They speak in their own language. With paintbrush and chisel and clay, they create their own images of their faith, among them images of Mary. To Catholics in Japan, Mary looks Japanese; to Catholics in Africa and the Caribbean islands, Mary looks African. To Catholics in Europe, Mary looks European. And so it is with people everywhere. These images help us to worship Jesus and to give honor to his mother, Mary.

Catholics in many nations, such as the United States, Poland, and Mexico, have taken Mary as their patron and protector. Just as Mary cared for her home in Nazareth, so too would she care for our homes and our countries.

All people are drawn to Mary. They see her as one who knows the great joy of being the Mother of God. The words of the Magnificat, "My soul proclaims the greatness of the Lord; my spirit rejoices in God my savior" (Luke 1:46–47), express the happiness of all people who have found God.

People everywhere honor Mary, whose life in all its joy and sorrow was given to God. Throughout her life, Mary remained one with God. People of all races honor Mary and pray that they may be like her—one with God in both sorrow and joy.

Activity

Look at the many different images of Mary on these two pages. They represent the work of artists throughout the world. Discuss each image and how you feel about it.

Now think about an image you would draw that would represent Mary. In the space provided on this page, either describe your image of Mary, or find a picture that represents how you see Mary and paste it here.

Mary Chase Stratton, Salve Regina, mosaic, 20th century American

D.G. Rossetti, The Annunciation, painting, 19th century English

Artist Unknown, Our Lady of Yevsemanisk, icon, 16th century Russian

Artist Unknown,
The Annunciation,
manuscript, 15th
century Ethiopian

Koseki, Nativity, oil, 20th century Korean

Sister Corita Kent, Virgin and Child
Enthroned, serigraph, 20th century American

Leonardo da Vinci, Virgin of the Rocks,
painting, 15th century Italian

Studio of Dieric
Bouts, Mater
Dolorosa,
painting, 15th
century Dutch

Artist Unknown, The Annunciation,
Coptic illumination, 10th century Egyptian

Artist Unknown, Nativity, detail, stained glass window,
late 12th or early 13th century English

Artist Unknown, The Virgin
and Child, wood sculpture,
15th century Slovenian

THE LITANY OF OUR LADY

The Church has an ancient tradition of praying **litanies**. The word *litany* comes from a Greek word that means "to pray in earnest." When we pray a litany, we invoke, or call on, God, Jesus, the Holy Spirit, Mary, or the saints. The invocations we pray can be statements of belief, titles we use to praise God or the saints, or petitions. During the Mass, we pray three short litanies. The first is found in the Penitential Rite when we pray the Kyrie: "Lord have mercy; Christ have mercy; Lord have mercy." We pray another litany during the General Intercessions, or Prayers of the Faithful. The third litany occurs during the Breaking of the Bread, when we pray the Lamb of God.

One of the most ancient and beloved litanies of the Church is the litany honoring Mary, the Mother of Jesus. This litany has been called by different names throughout the centuries. It was initially known as the Litany of Loreto because it was first prayed at a shrine dedicated to Mary in the small town of Loreto, Italy. Later, it became known as the Litany of the Blessed Virgin Mary. Today we call it the Litany of Our Lady.

Mary is our greatest saint and we pray to her to praise God and to ask her to help us learn to follow Jesus. We do not pray to Mary in order to worship her; instead, we pray that she will lead us to Jesus. When we pray the Litany of Our Lady, we honor Mary's grace-filled life, which gave glory, praise, and honor to God.

The Litany of Our Lady was first prayed during the Middle Ages, and over time, new invocations have been added to the prayer. The litany is divided into three parts. The first part addresses Mary as Virgin and Mother and describes her relationship to God and humanity. In the second part we praise Mary using the different titles that have been associated with her throughout history. Many of these titles are taken from the prophecies in the Old Testament; others simply try to express Mary's perfect love for God. The third section describes Mary as Queen of heaven and earth.

When we pray the Litany of Our Lady, we repeat the phrase, "Pray for us" after each invocation.

Activity

Look at the picture on this page. What does it tell you about Mary?

_____

_____

What are some words, phrases, and titles you would use to describe Mary?

_____

_____

LITANY OF OUR LADY

Holy Mary
Holy Mother of God
Most honored of virgins
Mother of Christ
Mother of the Church
Mother of divine grace
Mother most pure
Mother of chaste love
Mother and virgin
Sinless Mother
Dearest of mothers
Model of motherhood
Mother of good counsel
Mother of our Creator
Mother of our Savior
Virgin most wise
Virgin rightly praised
Virgin rightly renowned
Virgin most powerful
Virgin gentle in mercy
Faithful Virgin
Mirror of justice
Throne of wisdom
Cause of our joy

Shrine of the Spirit
Glory of Israel
Vessel of selfless devotion
Mystical Rose
Tower of David
Tower of ivory
House of gold
Ark of the covenant

Gate of heaven
Morning Star
Health of the sick
Refuge of sinners
Comfort of the troubled
Help of Christians

Queen of angels
Queen of patriarchs and prophets
Queen of apostles and martyrs
Queen of confessors and virgins
Queen of all saints
Queen conceived without original sin
Queen assumed into heaven
Queen of the rosary
Queen of peace
Queen of the family
Lamb of God, you take away the sins of the
world, have mercy on us.
Lamb of God, you take away the sins of the
world, have mercy on us.
Lamb of God, you take away the sins of the
world, have mercy on us.
Pray for us, holy Mother of God, that we may
become worthy of the promises of Christ.
Let us pray.
Eternal God,
let your people enjoy constant health in mind
and body.
Through the intercession of the Virgin Mary,
free us from the sorrows of life
and lead us to happiness in the life to come.
Grant this through Christ our Lord. Amen.

Activity

Working with a small group of classmates, choose one of the invocations to Mary from the Litany of Our Lady. In the space below, explain what this invocation means to you, an eighth grader living in today's world.

_____

Create a modern invocation to Mary below:

_____

Our Church Celebrates Holy Days and Feasts

IMMACULATE CONCEPTION

On December 8, we celebrate the Solemnity of the **Immaculate Conception**. It is the most important feast during the Advent season. The Solemnity of the Immaculate Conception celebrates that Mary was free from all sin, including original sin, from the first moment of her life when she was conceived in the womb of her mother. This special grace was a gift from God that prepared Mary to be the Mother of God's Son, Jesus. The Immaculate Conception was the beginning of God's divine plan for Mary. Nine months after her Immaculate Conception, Mary was born.

We do not know the circumstances of Mary's birth nor do we know anything about her childhood. Catholic tradition says that Mary was raised by her parents, Ann and Joachim, whom we honor as saints. Like other young Jewish women of her time, Mary was taught to believe in God. She practiced the traditions of her faith and probably worshipped with her neighbors at the local synagogue on the Sabbath. She may have journeyed to the Temple in Jerusalem for important celebrations like Passover.

Some people misunderstand the meaning of the Immaculate Conception, thinking that it celebrates Mary's conception of Jesus through the power of the Holy Spirit. The Church celebrates Jesus' conception at the Feast of the Annunciation on March 25. In the liturgy for that day, we remember that the angel Gabriel appeared to Mary when she was a young woman and announced that she was to be the Mother of Jesus.

The Immaculate Conception, however, focuses on the very beginning of Mary's life and God's plan for her to become Jesus' mother. In the Immaculate Conception of Mary, we celebrate the belief that God kept Mary free from original sin. We have learned that original sin is the sinful condition within ourselves into which we are all born. This sinful condition is the human tendency to be selfish.

By freeing Mary from sin, God gave Mary the gift of selflessness. Unlike every other human being, she would not have to struggle against selfish desires. Her life was one of complete cooperation and openness to God's plan. Mary's response to God can be summed up in one sentence; "May it be done to me according to your word" (Luke 1:38).

Mary, freed from the tendency to sin, was able to put her life in God's hands. She trusted that God alone knew what was best for her. In allowing herself to be open to God's plan, Mary became a channel, or way, for God's love to come into the world.

The Immaculate Conception is a dogma of the Catholic Church. A dogma is a doctrine of the Church that is publicly taught by the pope and the bishops and must be believed by all Catholics. The tradition of honoring the conception of Mary was celebrated as early as the eighth century. In 1477, Pope Sixtus IV listed the feast on the official Church calendar for the diocese of Rome for the first time. In 1708 Pope Clement XI extended observance of the feast to the entire Church. However, the Immaculate Conception did not become an official dogma of the Church until it was proclaimed and taught by Pope Pius IX in 1854. Interestingly, an important development in the United States led up to this official statement of the Church's belief.

In 1846, the bishops of the United States petitioned Pope Pius IX in Rome, asking permission to name Mary as the patroness of our country, using the title of the Immaculate Conception. The bishops believed that there could be no greater model for the Catholics of the United States than the faithful, sinless life of Jesus' Mother, the Immaculate Conception.

By celebrating the Solemnity of the Immaculate Conception, we remember that Mary was the first to hear the good news that Jesus would fulfill God's mission for the world.

Activity

In the Opening Prayer at Mass on the Solemnity of the Immaculate Conception, the priest prays the words that are found in the puzzle below. Follow the directions to discover how we ask God to help us to imitate Mary.

1. Circle the names of the mysteries of the Rosary.
2. Circle the titles by which we know Mary.
3. Circle the names of Mary's relatives.
4. Circle the names of places associated with Mary.
5. Circle the names of prayers that honor Mary.
6. Write the remaining uncircled words on the lines below.

Bethlehem Mother Lord Annunciation Ann help Patroness Guadalupe us Assumption Elizabeth through Angelus Nazareth handmaiden Mary's virgin prayers Jerusalem to Magnificat live Visitation in United States your John the Baptist presence Queen without Joachim sin Rosary

_____

_____

THE FEAST OF PENTECOST

As the end of Jesus' life drew near, the disciples became anxious and afraid. They did not understand how Jesus' death could fulfill his mission. Jesus understood their fear and tried to encourage them: "Do not let your hearts be troubled. You have faith in God; have faith also in me" (John 14:1). He promised his disciples that he would not abandon them and that he would send them a helper, the Holy Spirit, whom Jesus called "the Advocate" and the "Spirit of Truth."

On the evening after the resurrection, Jesus appeared to his disciples. He breathed on them and said, "Receive the holy Spirit" (John 20:22). Then Jesus sent them forth to carry on his work.

Fifty days later, the disciples were gathered together on the Jewish feast of **Pentecost**, a celebration of the giving of the Torah to Moses. They were worried and afraid to preach about Jesus, thinking that they, too, would be killed. Suddenly there was a great wind and the Holy Spirit came upon them in the shape of tongues of fire. According to the account found in the Acts of the Apostles, they went out and began teaching about Jesus, speaking in all the languages of the world, and three thousand people were baptized that day. The Church began on Pentecost, just as the people of Israel became a people at Mt. Sinai.

The disciples now understood that Jesus' promises had been fulfilled. They could see from the many people who were baptized that Jesus was really with them. The Holy Spirit helped them to find the right words to teach about Jesus. As the Church grew, it carried on Jesus' mission by caring for the poor and by announcing his message to all.

Jesus rose from the dead and gave his disciples the gift of the Holy Spirit. We celebrate the first event on Easter and the second event on Pentecost. Between Easter Sunday and Pentecost, we celebrate the fifty days of the Easter season. It is a time when the Church rejoices in Jesus' passage from death to new life, celebrates his ascension into heaven, and awaits the final fulfillment of the kingdom of God.

When the Holy Spirit descended upon the disciples, the Church was born. After the disciples preached to the people in the streets, new members joined their community. All of this happened because of the power of the Holy Spirit.

The feast of Pentecost is the last day of the Easter season. It has been called the crowning glory of Eastertime because on Pentecost the mystery of Christ's life, death, resurrection, ascension, and continued presence among us is brought to completion. With the coming of the Spirit in our own lives, we can share in these mysteries. Today the Holy Spirit first comes to us, not in wind and fire, but through the waters of Baptism.

At the Vigil Mass on Pentecost Eve, one of the Scripture readings tells us what a confusing struggle life can be if we do not have the presence of God in our lives to help and guide us. The Holy Spirit is still present in the Church today. Whenever we preach, teach, or do any good work, it is because the Spirit enables us to do so. The Spirit is present in every believer. The Spirit helps us grow in faith, trust in Jesus, forgive those who hurt us, and be generous and patient with others.

Activity

Use the clues below to fill in the word puzzle.

Across

2. The Spirit helps us _____ in faith.
3. A symbol of the Holy Spirit
6. Another symbol of the Holy Spirit
7. Jesus promised to _____ the Spirit.
8. Number of days in the Easter season
9. The last day of the Easter season

Down

1. What the Spirit gave the disciples
2. The _____ of the Holy Spirit
4. _____ thousand were baptized on Pentecost.
5. Another symbol of the Holy Spirit
6. We _____ in the Holy Spirit.

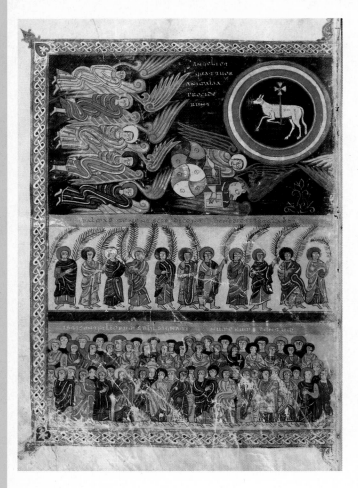

The Solemnity of All Saints

Each year on November 1, we celebrate All Saints Day. During the Opening Prayer at Mass on November 1, we say that we have gathered together to celebrate the lives of all the holy men and women of the past and present. We ask that the saints' prayers on our behalf will bring us God's forgiveness and love. We honor all the **saints** in heaven on this day—the saints we know of and especially, those whose names and lives are unknown to us.

The word *saint* comes from a Latin word that means "consecrated to God." The saints were people who dedicated themselves to lives of service to God. We believe that they were holy because they chose to follow God's call in their lives. The saints all lived very different lives. Some were born in poverty, like Pius X, who said, "I was born poor. I live poor. I will die poor." Other holy people, like Katharine Drexel, were born to wealth and gave it away.

Some saints were popular and famous, like Francis of Assisi, Joan of Arc, and John Vianney. Teresa of Avila and John Neumann were well-educated; others had little education. Margaret of Scotland and Elizabeth of Hungary were royalty. Augustine and Mary Magdalene were public sinners before they responded to the teachings of Jesus.

The saints come from every country, race and ethnic background: Kateri Tekakwitha, a Native American; Martin de Porres, from Peru; Paul Miki, from Japan; Charles Lwanga, from Uganda, Africa; Patrick from Ireland; and Elizabeth Seton, from New York City. They were fishermen and housewives, doctors and teachers, priests and parents, royalty and peasants. They were also missionaries, barbers, nuns, lawyers, accountants, knights, and nurses. Yet all the saints, no matter what they did or where they lived, share two special qualities. They loved God with all their hearts and their love for God was visible in the way they lived their lives.

Activity

Think about a saint whom you admire. On the lines below, identify the saint and explain why you think this saint is holy.

_____

_____

_____

_____

_____

The Tradition of Honoring Saints

The saints have been important examples for the Christian community since the earliest days of the Church. Paintings and writings about the saints' deeds are found on the walls of the catacombs in Rome, where many of the first saints were buried. By the fourth century, it had become a custom for local churches to set aside one day to honor the martyrs from the community who had died for their faith.

In 609, Pope Boniface IV took over the Pantheon, a pagan temple that had been empty for some years. He dedicated it to Mary and all the Christian martyrs. For many years, the feast honoring the martyrs was observed on May 13 in Rome. In 732, Pope Gregory III had a chapel built in St. Peter's Basilica in the Vatican. It was consecrated to all the saints, not just the martyrs. However, it was not until about a century later, in 844, that the current date of November 1 was established as All Saints Day. Pope Gregory IV petitioned the emperor to make it a day of celebration for the entire Roman Empire.

It is appropriate that we celebrate All Saints Day in the Fall, after the crops of the summer have been harvested. The saints are our harvest, the products of God's work among us. Their desire to know, love, and serve God made it possible for the Holy Spirit to work through them. We see in them the attitudes and qualities we call the fruits of the Holy Spirit: charity, joy, peace, patience, kindness, goodness, endurance, humility, fidelity, and self-control.

The Church teaches that everyone in heaven is a saint. Some of these saints have been canonized and are included in the prayers we pray at Mass. They have feast days honoring them throughout the Church year. However, the majority of the saints are unknown to us. They are simply good people who made a decision to follow Christ. They have been rewarded for their lives on earth and live with God, now and forever, in a state of complete happiness that we cannot fully understand.

All Saints Day is a time for us to remember those who have gone before us in faith. Yet the celebration honoring the saints is about each one of us, too. All Saints Day is a source of hope to all who believe in Jesus. Each of us is part of the communion of saints, the entire community of God's people, both living and dead. We are the Body of Christ. Some of our members are saints in heaven, looking forward to the day when we will all be one. Others who have died are in purgatory, awaiting the time when they will see God face to face. Those of us still on earth are trying to live as God's people.

We have hope that one day we, too, will share in God's kingdom. The saints have shown us how to follow Christ. We honor them as examples. We pray to them so that they will pray for us, encourage us, and inspire us to be the saints that we are all called to be.

Activity

Many dioceses and parishes have patron saints. Research your diocesan and parish saints. Find out who they are, when we celebrate their feast days, and why they have special meaning for the people of your diocese and parish.

_____

_____

_____

_____

_____

Recall the characteristics that make up the fruits of the Holy Spirit. Identify the gift you most need to grow in to be a sign of God's kingdom on earth. On the lines below, explain what you will try to do to grow in this quality.

_____

_____

_____

_____

_____

_____

In the Spirit of Jesus

SISTER ELAINE ROULET

" ' For I was hungry and you gave me food, I was thirsty and you gave me drink, a stranger and you welcomed me, naked and you clothed me, ill and you cared for me, in prison and you visited me.' Then the righteous will answer him and say, 'Lord, when did we see you hungry and feed you, or thirsty and give you drink? When did we see you a stranger and welcome you, or naked and clothe you? When did we see you ill or in prison, and visit you?' And the king will say to them in reply, 'Amen, I say to you, whatever you did for one of these least brothers of mine, you did for me.' "

Matthew 25:35–40

This powerful passage from Matthew clearly and sharply reminds us that Jesus is present in each person, especially in those who are suffering in any way. Whatever is done to the least of our brothers and sisters is done to Jesus.

Living in the spirit of Jesus is to live like Jesus, to act like Jesus, and to see people as he saw them. It means putting the needs of others before our own and treating others with **compassion**—sympathetically desiring to help them. Thinking and acting in this way often requires heroic effort on our part. Finding examples of people who do this can help us see how we can serve Jesus.

Sister Elaine Roulet, a Sister of Saint Joseph from Brentwood, New York, is such a person. She is the founder and director of the Children's Center at Bedford Hills Correctional Facility, a maximum security prison for women. This center allows women in prison to spend quality time with their children. Through Sister Elaine's leadership and guidance, the center is staffed mainly by prison inmates themselves. It is the only center of its kind connected with a state prison in the country. The staff organizes workshops and projects for the visiting children and helps with their transportation arrangements. In the summer, the children can come daily to the center. Through the nursery program, the staff conducts parenting classes and distributes baby clothing and equipment as needed. They also supplement the services of the counseling staff.

In addition to this center, Sister Elaine is the founder and executive director of Providence House, a temporary shelter for homeless women and their children. Women who have been battered, evicted, or recently released from prison are welcomed at any of the three Providence House facilities. Sister Elaine has been the subject of articles and television interviews and the recipient of several awards, including the 1984 "Wonder Woman Award,"

given by the president and publisher of DC comics. The award was given to "women who take risks" and was presented to Sister Elaine on the fortieth anniversary of the publication of Wonder Woman Comics.

While these accomplishments may seem beyond our capabilities, we must remember that Sister Elaine's actions and activities flow from the attitudes and values that she holds. She worked for many years as a teacher and a school principal before taking a position with Catholic Charities. By simply being open to the spirit of Jesus and attuned to the needs of others, she has been able to bring the sensitivity of Jesus to difficult situations. She has made a difference in the lives of countless number of mothers and children.

Activity

Read Luke 15. What do you think is Jesus' attitude toward sinners or those who have done wrong?

_____

_____

What attitude does the older brother have in the story of the Prodigal Son?

_____

_____

Do you agree with the elder brother? Why or why not?

_____

_____

_____

Mother Teresa once said that many people hunger for something more than food. What do you think she meant?

_____

_____

_____

A CLASS OF DREAMERS

In the spring of 1980, Eugene Lang was invited to give a graduation address to the sixth grade class at Public School 121 in New York City—the same elementary school he had attended many years earlier. Mr. Lang had prepared a speech, but as he sat on the stage waiting his turn, he looked at the 61 sixth graders sitting there on the folding chairs. He remembered when he worked as a dishwasher at age 14, earning ten cents an hour. He remembered Mr. Jackson, who offered to help pay his way through college if Eugene promised to work hard. Eugene did work hard and founded a successful company, of which he was president.

Mr. Lang sat there looking at this small group of children who had no more money than he did when he was their age. He thought about what the children dreamed they would be when they grew up, and he decided he would help them realize their dreams. So when the time came for Mr. Lang to give his speech, he set aside his prepared talk. He promised the children that if they graduated from high school, he would pay their tuition to any city or state college in New York.

Mr. Lang did more than just make an offer. He kept track of the students of the class of 1980. He met with them, talked to them, and sometimes had to be firm with them when they failed to work hard.

By 1986, 90 percent of those Public School 121 sixth graders did graduate and were able to take advantage of Mr. Lang's offer. One of those graduates was Rafael Rodriquez. Rafael's father died when Rafael was seven years old. He had no hope of going to college until Mr. Lang offered his help. Rafael said, "It's like a tree. He put out branches for all of us." In the fall Rafael went to college, the first person in his family to do so.

This is just the beginning of the story. Mr. Lang's idea caught on. Today his idea is called the I Have a Dream project. Other individuals and businesses are spending their time and money on America's greatest resource—its young people.

Activity

God does not make clones. God makes each of us one of a kind. We are each given skills and talents. And we each have been specially called by God to use our talents and skills to follow our dream. When we do what we love and love what we do, we are happy. And when we are happy, we work and live well.

Complete the following activity, which will help you discover and follow your dreams. Put a check before any appropriate phrases.

1. I'm afraid to

_____ lose.

_____ fail.

_____ speak up.

_____ make a mistake.

_____ join groups.

_____ try to make friends.

_____ try new things.

2. I like

_____ building.

_____ drawing.

_____ painting.

_____ cooking.

_____ performing.

_____ collecting.

_____ teaching.

_____ babysitting.

_____ playing sports.

_____ watching sports.

_____ listening to music.

3. If I have free time, I spend it

_____ listening to music.

_____ reading.

_____ building something.

_____ talking with my friends.

_____ solving something.

_____ using a computer.

_____ playing sports.

_____ playing video games.

_____ making something.

_____ spending time outdoors.

4. I think that God is calling me to realize my dreams by using my best talents and skills and becoming a person who

_____

_____

_____

_____

OUR CATHOLIC HERITAGE

What Catholics Believe

Catholics are on a lifelong journey of faith. The Holy Spirit is with us as we journey, offering direction and help along the way. In this section of THIS IS OUR FAITH, the important truths of our faith are presented. These shared beliefs are like a beacon—guiding us as we journey together.

ABOUT The Bible

1. What is the Bible?

The Bible is a collection of books that tells the story of God and his people.

2. Who wrote the Bible?

The Bible was written over a span of 1,000 years. It was written by many different people at many different times. Each of the writers was inspired by the Holy Spirit to write, but each one wrote in his own way and for his own time. Authors of the Bible did not sit down to write a book that would be revered for generations. They simply wrote their experiences of God and of his love.

3. Why do we call the Bible the word of God when other people actually wrote it?

God was the reason the Bible was written. The Holy Spirit used human instruments to communicate revelation to people. These authors were not taking dictation from the Holy Spirit. Their writings, however, were prompted by God and led by the Spirit.

4. Why was the Bible written?

The Bible was written by people who wanted to give the message of God to others. We read it today to hear that same message. Times change, the world changes, but the message of God remains the same. When we read the Bible, we listen to God speaking to us, right here, right now.

5. How do you look something up in the Bible?

The Bible is divided into two parts: The Old Testament and the New Testament. Each part of the Bible is divided into different books. Each book is divided into chapters and each chapter into sentences. These sentences are called verses. All of the chapters and verses are numbered. To look up Matthew 5:14, you would turn to the New Testament, the book of Matthew; then the fifth chapter, and finally the fourteenth verse. If there is more than one book of the same title, then these books would also be numbered. This number would appear before the name of the book. An example is 1 John 3:11.

6. What is a Gospel?

The word *gospel* means "good news." There are four Gospels written by Matthew, Mark, Luke, and John. Each of the Gospels tells in its own way the good news of Jesus.

7. What is a parable?

A parable is a story, told usually by Jesus, to teach a lesson. An example of a parable is found in Luke 10:30–37.

PAUL THE MISSIONARY

Besides the four Gospels in the New Testament, we also find twenty-one Epistles, or letters. A number of these letters were written by the Apostle Paul, who was one of the greatest missionaries of the Church. Once he realized what Jesus was all about, Paul began to preach about him. In his zeal to spread the good news of Jesus, he not only wrote letters urging the Christians to follow the way of Christ but he also traveled extensively to bring the good news of Jesus in person.

The map traces the three missionary journeys of St. Paul as well as his journey to Rome. His journeys were long, difficult, exhausting, and dangerous. During the course of the journeys he was kicked out of synagogues, shipwrecked, and imprisoned twice. After his release from prison each time, he stood firm in his great love for Jesus Christ and continued to preach and teach about him.

Paul was probably executed in Rome during the persecutions of Christians under Emperor Nero. His feast is celebrated on January 25.

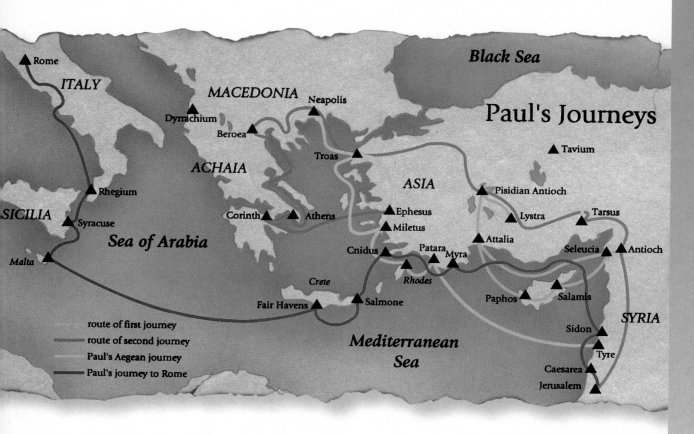

Paul's Journeys

- route of first journey
- route of second journey
- Paul's Aegean journey
- Paul's journey to Rome

ABOUT
The Trinity

WE BELIEVE IN GOD

There is only one true God, who is revealed to us as three distinct persons—God the Father, God the Son, and God the Holy Spirit—in the union of the Blessed Trinity.

God is the supreme being, who always was and always will be. God is all-good, all-holy, all-knowing, always just, merciful, and forgiving.

We believe that God speaks to us in many ways. God's self-communication is revealed especially in the sacred Scriptures, in the life of Jesus Christ, and in the life of the Church. The Church preserves, cares for, and keeps alive God's word.

WE BELIEVE IN JESUS

Jesus is the second person of the Blessed Trinity, God's own Son. Jesus is one with the Father and the presence of God among us. Jesus is the Christ, the **Messiah**, the anointed one sent by God.

Jesus Christ is both human and divine. When we say that Jesus is divine, we mean that he is God. Our belief that the second person of the Trinity, the Eternal Word of the Father, took flesh and became like us in all things but sin is called the **Incarnation**.

Jesus had a four-fold mission: to proclaim the good news of God's reign to all people, to claim us as God's own people and form with us a new and everlasting covenant, to free us from sin and reconcile us with God and one another, and to save us from death and unite us with

God by bringing us eternal life. Jesus carried out his mission by teaching, healing, forgiving, and working miracles as signs of God's love.

Jesus is our Savior. In loving obedience to God's will, Jesus Christ suffered and died and so redeemed all people from sin and death. Jesus' suffering and death is the ultimate sign of his love for us.

Through the power of God, Jesus rose to new life and invites us to share this new life with him. Through Jesus, we share in the fullness of God's grace. Christ came to offer us full and everlasting life. Catholics see the **resurrection** as God's victory over sin and death and the source of our hope. The truth of the resurrection is that death is not an ending but leads us to new and everlasting life.

After the resurrection, Jesus appeared to his disciples. He entrusted his mission to the apostles and promised to send the Holy Spirit to be with them. Then Jesus returned in glory to his Father. Catholics call Jesus' glorification and return to God the **ascension**.

The heart of our faith is found in the **Paschal Mystery**. The Paschal Mystery is Jesus' passion, death, resurrection, and glorification. Through these events, God's salvation of the world is fulfilled.

We Believe in the Holy Spirit

The Holy Spirit is the third person of the Blessed Trinity, one with the Father and the Son yet distinct. The Holy Spirit is the bond of love and unity between the Father and the Son. The Spirit leads and guides us in living as followers of Jesus. The Holy Spirit sanctifies, or makes holy, our minds and hearts.

The Holy Spirit has been at work in the world since creation. Under the guidance of the Holy Spirit, the authors of the Bible wrote God's inspired word. At **Pentecost**, the Holy Spirit descended upon the disciples, giving them the courage, energy, and all the gifts necessary to be Jesus' witnesses and to bring Jesus' truth to all people.

The Holy Spirit is at work in the Church today, enabling us to carry on the mission of Jesus. At Baptism we receive God's grace and become temples of the Holy Spirit. The Spirit remains with us, guiding our conscience and helping us avoid sin.

ABOUT
The Catholic Church

Catholics are followers of Jesus and, under the leadership of the pope and bishops, spread God's word, worship the Lord through the sacraments, and serve those in need.

The Church has four marks, or qualities, that show its truth and its origin in God. The Church is **one**, in our faith, sacraments, and authority. The Church is **holy**, because we draw our life from God and offer people the way to him. The Church is **catholic**, or universal, and brings together all people without exception. The Church is **apostolic**, founded on and faithful to the apostles' teachings.

The chief teacher of the Church is the pope. The pope is the successor to St. Peter, the first bishop of Rome. We also call the pope the Vicar, or representative, of Christ on earth. Catholics believe that when the pope speaks officially and deliberately, alone or with the bishops, to define a matter of faith or morals, he teaches infallibly. The doctrine of **papal infallibility** assures us that the pope teaches with the guidance of the Holy Spirit and that his teaching is free from error.

The official teaching office of the Church is called the **Magisterium**. The responsibility for teaching the authentic message of Jesus is carried out by the pope and bishops.

The Church is a mystery that reveals God's love in Jesus through the power of the Spirit. We are able to more fully grasp the mission and mystery of the Church through images that describe the Church as People of God, Body of Christ, and Pilgrim People.

ABOUT Mary

Mary, the Mother of Jesus, is a model of holiness for all Catholics. We believe that Mary was conceived without original sin. This special privilege from God is called the **Immaculate Conception**. Through our belief in the Immaculate Conception, we recognize that from the moment of her conception, Mary was filled with grace and lived a sinless life.

We revere Mary as the Mother of God and Mother of the Church. By recognizing Mary as the mother of God, we affirm that Jesus is God. As mother of the Church, Mary shows us how to live with faith and love. She is our mother, too, and cares for us.

Through the Holy Spirit's power, Jesus was conceived without a human father. We honor Mary's virginity as a sign of God's power in saving us and of Mary's loving response to his plan.

Catholics believe that Mary was taken up to heaven, body and soul, and fully shares in Jesus' resurrection. This belief is called Mary's **assumption**.

ABOUT Life Everlasting

We believe that God's kingdom, or reign, will one day be fulfilled, or completed. At the end of time, Jesus will come again in glory to reveal God's peace, love, and justice. We call this longed-for return of Jesus the **Second Coming**. We await the Second Coming of Jesus with faith and hope in God's promises. Catholics prepare for Jesus' triumphant return by making a way ready for the coming of God's reign in the world.

Our personal destiny depends on God's mercy and how well we have responded to the call to love God, ourselves, and others. If we have tried to live as faithful followers of Jesus, we will be forever united with God in **heaven**. Heaven is unending happiness with God and all who love him. Catholics believe that heaven is the experience of God's unimaginable and infinite love.

After death, any remaining faults of imperfect love and selfishness will be cleansed through the process the Church calls **purgatory**. We believe that this process of purification will enable us to fully respond to the complete love and happiness prepared for us by God.

Those who deliberately have refused, in serious ways, to love God and their neighbor separate themselves for all eternity from God and those who love him. Catholics call this everlasting separation **hell**.

ABOUT The Communion of Saints

The **communion of saints** is the entire community of God's people, whether living or dead. The communion of saints includes all those who are in heaven, all those who are living as God's faithful people on earth, and all those in purgatory waiting to be fully united with God for all eternity.

How Catholics Worship

Catholics have a unique tradition of **worship.** Worship is giving honor and praise to God. Through the sacraments and the **liturgy,** the official, public worship of the Church, as well as through our public and private prayers, we deepen our relationship with God.

ABOUT The Sacraments

The **sacraments** are sacred signs that celebrate God's love for us and Jesus' presence in our lives and in the Church. There are seven sacraments. Through the sacraments, we are united with Jesus and share in God's life—grace.

THE SACRAMENTS OF INITIATION

We become full members of the Church through the three sacraments of initiation. The sacraments of initiation are Baptism, Confirmation, and Eucharist.

Baptism welcomes us into the Christian community, frees us from original sin and personal sin, and unites us with Jesus.

During the celebration the priest or deacon pours water over the head of the person being baptized as he prays, "I baptize you in the name of the Father, and of the Son, an of the Holy Spirit."

from the Rite of Baptism

Each of us is born into a sinful condition that separates us from God. This condition is called **original sin.** Baptism frees us from original sin and restores our dignity as children of God.

Through the waters of Baptism, which represent life and death, we share in Christ's death and resurrection. We die to sin and rise to new life in the mystical body of Christ.

Confirmation strengthens the new life we received at Baptism and makes us living witnesses of Jesus in the world.

During the celebration the bishop or priest lays his hand on the head of the one to be confirmed and anoints the forehead with chrism as he prays, "Be sealed with the Gift of the Holy Spirit."

from the Rite of Confirmation

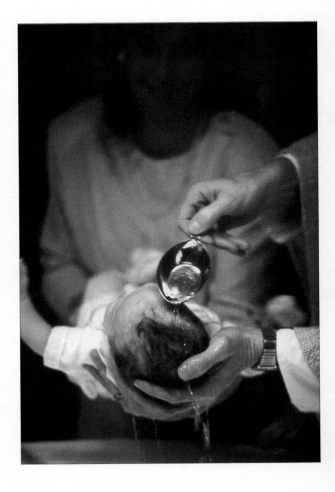

The Eucharist makes present Jesus' sacrificial death on the cross and his resurrection from the dead. The word *Eucharist* means "thanksgiving." During the Mass we praise and thank God for all our gifts, especially the gift of God's Son, Jesus.

Jesus is truly present in the Holy Communion we receive at Mass. Although the Eucharist still has the appearance of ordinary bread and wine, through the power of the Holy Spirit it has become Jesus' body and blood. This sacred mystery, in which bread and wine are changed into the real presence of Christ, is called **transubstantiation**.

The Eucharist unites us with Jesus and the Church community. Jesus is also present in the people gathered to celebrate the Eucharist, in the word that is proclaimed, and in the priest who presides.

A bishop is the ordinary minister of Confirmation. At Confirmation we receive gifts from the Holy Spirit that assist us in building up the Body of Christ and carrying on the mission of the Church.

Eucharist celebrates the real presence of Jesus' body and blood under the appearance of bread and wine.

During the celebration the priest calls on the power of the Holy Spirit and prays the words of consecration over the bread and wine, which become the body and blood of Christ.

The **Eucharist** is the central celebration of the Church and our greatest act of worship. Jesus taught that he was the bread of life. He promised to give his followers his body and blood so that they could live forever. Jesus fulfilled this promise at the Last Supper, on the night before he died.

THE SACRAMENTS OF HEALING

The sacraments of healing—Reconciliation and the Anointing of the Sick—celebrate Jesus' forgiveness and healing.

Reconciliation celebrates God's healing and forgiveness of our sins.

During the celebration the priest prays the prayer of absolution, ending with the words, "I absolve you from your sins in the name of the Father, and of the Son, and of the Holy Spirit."

from the Rite of Penance

When we sin, we make a conscious choice to turn away from God, Jesus, and one another. Through Reconciliation, we experience a conversion, a turning back, to God and the Church. **Conversion** is a lifelong process in which the Holy Spirit works through us, transforming our lives to the image of Jesus.

The sacrament of Reconciliation is always celebrated with a priest, sometimes individually and sometimes as part of a communal or group celebration. We may celebrate Reconciliation any time we feel the need of God's mercy and forgiveness or when we have committed a mortal sin.

The Anointing of the Sick brings Jesus' healing, comfort, and strength to those who are seriously ill, elderly, or in danger of death.

During the celebration the priest anoints the person with the oil of the sick as he prays, "Through this holy anointing may the Lord in his love and mercy help you with the grace of the Holy Spirit. May the Lord who frees you from sin save you and raise you up."

from the Rite of Anointing

Before the anointing, the sick may celebrate Reconciliation. The Eucharist may be received after the anointing. When we receive Eucharist as we approach death, we call the Blessed Sacrament **viaticum**. Viaticum means "food for the journey," our journey to everlasting life with God.

Like Reconciliation, the Anointing of the Sick may be celebrated privately or communally.

THE SACRAMENTS OF COMMITMENT

In the sacraments of commitment, the Church celebrates two special ways that people serve others by sharing their gifts. The sacraments of commitment are **Matrimony** and **Holy Orders.**

Matrimony celebrates the permanent and lifelong love of a man and woman for each other.

During the celebration the bride and groom exchange marriage vows, promising always to be faithful to each other.

In Matrimony, the couple's love for one another is a sign of God's love and faithfulness for all people and Christ's love for the Church.

God gives married couples a special grace to help their love grow. Through their sexual love, which is a complete giving of themselves to each other and a sharing in God's life-giving creative power, they become one. This is why sexual intercourse is reserved for married couples who have made a lifelong commitment to faithfulness.

Catholic parents accept the responsibilities and joys of raising their children as members of the Body of Christ. Through their unselfish love and care for their children, parents are a living sign of God's love and forgiveness.

In **Holy Orders**, bishops, priests, and deacons are ordained to serve the Church in a special way.

During the celebration the bishop lays his hands on the head of the person to be ordained. Afterward he prays a prayer of consecration, or blessing.

The word *ordain* means "to set aside." Bishops are "set aside" or empowered to carry on the work of the apostles and serve the Church by leading a diocese. Bishops have the special responsibility of teaching, leading, and sanctifying the Catholic Church.

Priests are ordained by a bishop to help him in ministering to the community. Priests, like bishops, do this by celebrating the sacraments, proclaiming God's word, and guiding the Church community.

The word *deacon* means "helper" or "server." Deacons care for the needy in the community. They also baptize, proclaim the Gospel at Mass, witness marriages, and preside at funerals.

ABOUT The Mass

INTRODUCTORY RITES

Gathering Song

In the Mass we come together to pray and worship as the family of Jesus. We stand and sing a gathering song.

Greeting

With the priest we make the Sign of the Cross. The priest welcomes us in Jesus' name and then says, "The Lord be with you." We answer, "And also with you."

Penitential Rite

As a community we acknowledge our sins and failures and ask for God's forgiveness.

Gloria

We sing or say this hymn of praise to God.

Opening Prayer

The priest says the Opening Prayer of the Mass.

Liturgy of the Word

There are usually two Scripture readings before the Gospel is proclaimed. They include readings from both the Old Testament and the New Testament.

First Reading

From the Old Testament, the lector reads about the beginnings of God's covenant with us.

Responsorial Psalm

The song leader sings a psalm and we respond with an acclamation after each verse.

Second Reading

The lector reads from the New Testament, usually from the letters.

Gospel Acclamation

This psalm verse with its response serves as an introduction to the gospel.

Gospel

In honor of Jesus, who speaks to us in the gospel, we stand when it is proclaimed by the deacon or priest.

Homily

The priest speaks about the scriptural readings, especially the gospel.

Profession of Faith

We profess our faith by saying either the Nicene Creed or, at times, the Apostles' Creed.

General Intercessions

As a community, we pray for the whole Church, for those in authority, for people in special need, for our parish community, and for our own intentions. To each petition we respond with "Lord, hear us," or a similar prayer.

LITURGY OF THE EUCHARIST

Preparation of the Altar and Gifts

We bring our gifts of bread and wine to the altar.

Prayer Over the Gifts

The priest says the Prayer Over the Gifts. We answer, "Amen."

Eucharistic Prayer

In this prayer of praise and thanksgiving, the priest addresses God the Father in our name. Together with the priest, we sing a hymn of praise to God for God's many blessings and especially for Jesus. We sing or say,

"Holy, holy, holy Lord, God of power and might, heaven and earth are full of your glory.

Hosanna in the highest.
Blessed is he who comes in the name of the Lord.
Hosanna in the highest."

The Eucharistic Prayer continues. With the priest we call upon the Holy Spirit to change bread and wine into the body and blood of Christ. Using the words and actions of Jesus at the Last Supper, the priest consecrates the bread and the wine.

Memorial Acclamation

We proclaim the mystery of faith by singing or saying these or other words of joy and praise:
"Christ has died,
Christ is risen,
Christ will come again."

With the priest, we continue praying for unity, peace, and the salvation of all the world.

The Great AMEN

The priest concludes the Eucharistic Prayer by lifting up the host and the cup as he sings or says,
"Through him,
with him,
in him,
in the unity of the Holy Spirit,
all glory and honor is yours,
almighty Father,
for ever and ever."

We show our assent and approval by singing or saying, "Amen."

COMMUNION RITE

The Lord's Prayer

We pray the Lord's Prayer, asking for our daily bread, the coming of the kingdom, and the forgiveness of our sins.

Sign of Peace

We share a sign of peace with each other.

Breaking of Bread

In the early Church this gesture of Jesus at the Last Supper—the breaking of bread—gave the Mass its first name. In this rite, the priest places a small particle of the host in the cup. This is a sign that we are all one in Christ.

Communion

Raising the host and the cup, the priest says, "This is the Lamb of God . . . "
We respond, "Lord, I am not worthy to receive you, but only say the word and I shall be healed."

When we receive Communion the priest or deacon or eucharistic minister says, "The body of Christ." We answer, "Amen." If we are to receive from the cup, the minister says, "The blood of Christ." We answer, "Amen."

Prayer After Communion

The priest prays the Prayer After Communion. We answer "Amen."

CONCLUDING RITE

Blessing

The priest blesses us in the name of God. We answer, "Amen."

Dismissal

The priest sends us out to bear witness to the gospel. "Go in peace to love and serve the Lord." We answer, "Thanks be to God."

Closing Song

We sing a song of praise and thanksgiving.

ABOUT Reconciliation

The sacrament of Reconciliation, or Penance, celebrates God's love and forgiveness which reach out to us through the ministry of the Church.

Preparation

I prepare for the sacrament of Reconciliation by looking back over my words and actions since my last confession. How do I fulfill God's command to love my neighbor as myself? Do I try to "get even" when others hurt me? Do I hold grudges? Do I show reverence and respect for my own body? Am I sorry for my sins and do I ask God for help with these problems?

RITE FOR RECONCILIATION OF INDIVIDUALS

Priest's Welcome

The priest, the minister of Reconciliation, greets me in the name of Jesus and of the Church.

Reading from Scripture

The priest may read with me a Bible passage about God's mercy.

Confession

I confess my sins to the priest. I tell him how I have offended God and what I would like to improve in my life. The priest then advises me. He suggests ways in which I might serve God better. The priest then asks me to say a prayer or to do an act of kindness to show that I am sorry and wish to change the direction of my life. This is called my penance.

Prayer of Sorrow

The priest then asks me to tell God I am truly sorry for my sins. I say aloud a prayer of sorrow, also called an act of contrition.

Absolution

Acting in the name of the Christian community, the priest extends his hands and asks God to give me pardon and peace. The priest forgives me in the name of the Father, and of the Son, and of the Holy Spirit. This is called absolution. I answer, "Amen."

Prayer of Praise and Dismissal

I praise God with the priest. Then the priest says, "The Lord has freed you from your sins. Go in peace." I answer, "Amen."

CELEBRATING RECONCILIATION IN COMMUNITY

Sometimes we gather together as a community to celebrate the sacrament of Reconciliation.

Introductory Rites We sing an opening hymn. Then the priest greets us and invites us to pray for God's forgiveness.

Celebration of the Word of God We listen to readings from the Bible. The priest reads the Gospel and preaches a homily.

Examination of Conscience We examine our conscience and tell God we are sorry for our sins.

Rite of Reconciliation We make a general confession and sing or say the Lord's Prayer. Then we make our individual confessions to a priest and receive absolution.

Proclamation of Praise for God's Mercy When individual confessions are finished, the priest invites us to praise and thank God.

Concluding Rite The priest blesses us and tells us to "Go in peace." We sing a song of praise and thanksgiving.

ABOUT The Liturgical Year

The prayer life of the Church revolves around the events of Jesus' life, death, resurrection, and glorification through the seasons of the liturgical year. Throughout the liturgical year, we are reminded of our call to follow Jesus.

Advent The liturgical year begins with the First Sunday of Advent. Advent is a season of joyful waiting in which we prepare to celebrate the coming of Christ at Christmas and at the end of time.

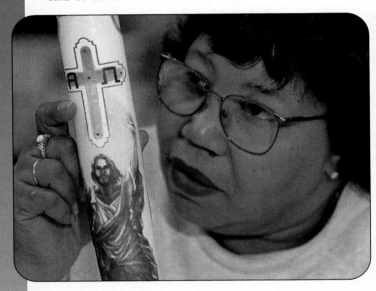

Christmas Season During the Christmas season we celebrate Christ's birthday; the feast of Mary, Mother of God; the Epiphany; and the Baptism of the Lord.

Lent During Lent we prepare to celebrate Easter. Lent is a forty-day period of prayer and sacrifice. It begins with Ash Wednesday, a day on which the priest traces a cross on our forehead with ashes. The Sixth Sunday of Lent, known as Palm Sunday, or Passion Sunday, signals the beginning of Holy Week.

Easter Triduum The Easter Triduum begins with the Mass of the Lord's Supper on Holy Thursday. It continues with the celebration of the Lord's passion on Good Friday and the Easter Vigil service on Holy Saturday. It ends with the evening prayer on Easter Sunday. Easter is the greatest feast of the liturgical year.

Easter Season In the Easter season the Church continues to celebrate Christ's resurrection. Toward the end of this season, we celebrate the Lord's ascension and prepare for the great feast of Pentecost that marks the coming of the Holy Spirit upon the apostles.

Ordinary Time During the Church year there are two seasons called Ordinary Time. The first runs from the feast of the Lord's Baptism to the day before Ash Wednesday. The second begins the Monday after the feast of Pentecost, and ends on the Saturday before the first Sunday of Advent. Ordinary Time consists of thirty-three or thirty-four weeks. During this time we celebrate all that Jesus has taught us and listen to stories about his life.

Sundays and Holy Days Sunday, the first day of the week, commemorates the resurrection of Jesus and is observed as the Lord's day. **Holy days of obligation** are special occasions on which Catholics are seriously obliged to assist at Mass. In the United States there are six holy days of obligation: Christmas, Dec. 25; Solemnity of Mary the Mother of God, Jan. 1; Ascension of our Lord, forty days after Easter; Assumption of the Blessed Virgin Mary, Aug. 15; All Saints' Day, Nov. 1; and Immaculate Conception of the Blessed Virgin Mary, Dec. 8.

Commemorations of the Saints During the liturgical year the Church also honors Mary and the saints with special feasts. Some are observed on Sundays; others are celebrated on weekdays. The seasons and feasts of the liturgical year help us to worship God every day and remind us of God's continued presence with the Church.

Each calendar year the Church celebrates Jesus' life, death, and resurrection in a cycle called the liturgical year.

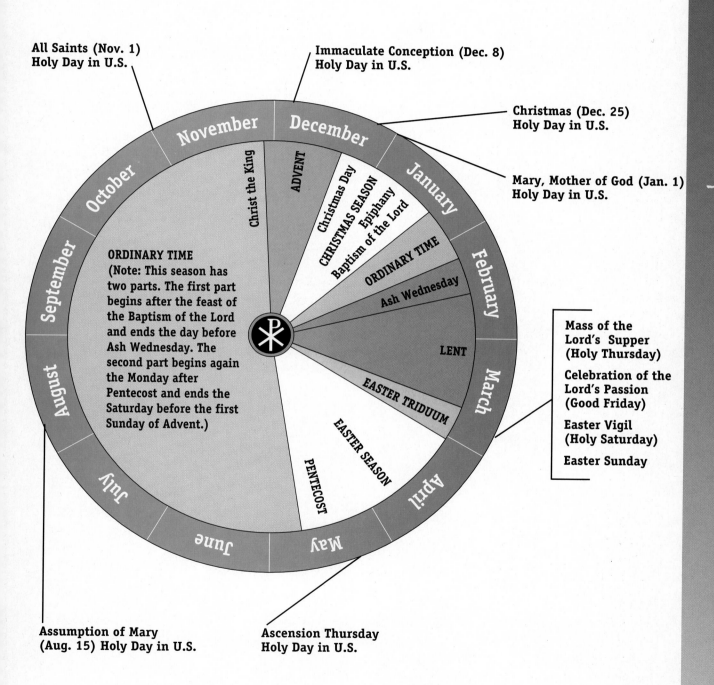

All Saints (Nov. 1)
Holy Day in U.S.

Immaculate Conception (Dec. 8)
Holy Day in U.S.

Christmas (Dec. 25)
Holy Day in U.S.

Mary, Mother of God (Jan. 1)
Holy Day in U.S.

November

December

January

October

Christ the King

ADVENT

Christmas Day

CHRISTMAS SEASON

Epiphany

Baptism of the Lord

September

ORDINARY TIME

Ash Wednesday

February

ORDINARY TIME
(Note: This season has two parts. The first part begins after the feast of the Baptism of the Lord and ends the day before Ash Wednesday. The second part begins again the Monday after Pentecost and ends the Saturday before the first Sunday of Advent.)

LENT

March

August

EASTER TRIDUUM

Mass of the Lord's Supper (Holy Thursday)

Celebration of the Lord's Passion (Good Friday)

Easter Vigil (Holy Saturday)

Easter Sunday

July

EASTER SEASON

PENTECOST

April

June

May

Assumption of Mary (Aug. 15) Holy Day in U.S.

Ascension Thursday
Holy Day in U.S.

How Catholics Live

Jesus calls us to live a moral life. We can live a moral life by following the teachings of Jesus and the Church. The Holy Spirit is always with us to help us make good moral decisions.

ABOUT The Beatitudes

In the Beatitudes, Jesus sums up the basic principles of what life will be like in the kingdom of God at the end of time. The Beatitudes also tell us how to respond to the problems of poverty, injustice, and oppression.

The Beatitudes (Matthew 5:1–10)	Living the Beatitudes
Blessed are the poor in spirit, for theirs is the kingdom of heaven.	We recognize our need for God. We depend on God. The poor in spirit know that God is more important than anything else in life.
Blessed are they who mourn, for they will be comforted.	We mourn the sin and suffering that we see in the world. We trust that God comforts anyone who suffers from loss or injustice. We reach out to anyone who needs to be comforted.
Blessed are the meek, for they will inherit the land.	We humbly recognize that all our gifts and talents come from God. We share these gifts with kindness and patience to serve God and others.
Blessed are they who hunger and thirst for righteousness, for they will be satisified.	We long for God's peace, love, and justice to rule in the kingdom. We work for equality and truth. We share our possessions with those in need.
Blessed are the merciful, for they will be shown mercy.	We forgive anyone who has hurt us. We accept others and have compassion for them.
Blessed are the clean of heart, for they will see God.	We want only to do God's will and to follow his commands. We keep our minds and hearts focused on God, seeking good and avoiding evil.
Blessed are the peacemakers, for they will be called children of God.	We work to be a sign for others of God's forgiveness. We pray for peace and unity in our family, in the community, and in the world. We try to settle arguments and disputes.
Blessed are they who are persecuted for the sake of righteousness, for theirs is the kingdom of heaven.	We continue Jesus' mission in the world. We speak out against situations that prevent the rule of God's peace, love, and justice. We stand up for our beliefs even if we are made fun of or criticized.

The Commandments

Jesus reinforced the importance of obeying the Ten Commandments. The commandments guide us in living as responsible and respectful children of God.

The Ten Commandments (Exodus 20:2–17)	Living the Ten Commandments
1. I, the Lord, am your God. You shall not have other gods besides me.	We believe in God and place him first in our lives. We love God more than anyone or anything else in life.
2. You shall not take the name of the Lord, your God, in vain.	We use the names of God and Jesus with respect and love. We never say God's or Jesus' name in anger or carelessly.
3. Remember to keep holy the sabbath day.	We worship God by celebrating the Eucharist together on Sunday. We never miss Mass without a serious reason. We put aside all unnecessary work on Sunday to praise and honor God for all our gifts.
4. Honor your father and mother.	We love, respect, and obey our parents and all in authority. We promise to care for our aging parents.
5. You shall not kill.	We respect God's gift of life by caring for our bodies. We do not drink alcohol or use drugs. We care about other people's right to life, especially the unborn, the elderly, the poor, and the prisoner.
6. You shall not commit adultery.	We use the gift of sexuality with respect. We are modest in how we dress, act, and speak. We avoid any persons or situations that might tempt us to commit a sexual sin.
7. You shall not steal.	We respect the property of others. We never take things that do not belong to us. We ask permission before borrowing things and we use others' things with care. We never cheat.
8. You shall not bear false witness against your neighbor.	We are truthful and honest. We keep our promises and never tell lies or spread rumors about others.
9. You shall not covet your neighbor's wife.	We respect the promises that married couples have made to each other. We work to overcome those sexual thoughts and desires that might lead us to sin.
10. You shall not covet anything that belongs to your neighbor.	We are satisfied with what we have. We are not jealous of others' good fortune or success. We are not greedy.

THE GREAT COMMANDMENT

"You shall love the Lord, your God, with all your heart, with all your being, with all your strength, and with all your mind, and your neighbor as yourself" (Luke 10:27).

Jesus affirmed the importance of the Ten Commandments in the Great Commandment. The Great Commandment summarizes the Ten Commandments and emphasizes that God's laws are based on love of God and love of neighbor.

THE NEW COMMANDMENT

"This is my commandment: love one another as I love you" (John 15:12).

Jesus' love for us is the standard by which we are called to respond to others. We must love as Jesus loved. We live the New Commandment by acting with compassion, mercy, peace, kindness, justice, and forgiveness.

The Works of Mercy

Jesus treated everyone with love and respect. He always acted with compassion and mercy. Jesus teaches that when we serve others, we serve him. The loving acts described in Matthew 25:31–46 are called the **Works of Mercy**. The corporal and spiritual works of mercy tell us how to respond to the basic needs of all people.

The Spiritual Works of Mercy

1. Help others do what is right.
2. Teach the ignorant.
3. Give advice to the doubtful.
4. Comfort those who suffer.
5. Be patient with others.
6. Forgive injuries.
7. Pray for the living and the dead.

Corporal Works of Mercy

1. Feed the hungry.
2. Give drink to the thirsty.
3. Clothe the naked.
4. Visit those in prison.
5. Shelter the homeless.
6. Visit the sick.
7. Bury the dead.

The Precepts of the Church

The Precepts, or laws, of the Church list specific duties and responsibilities expected of Catholics.

As Catholics, we also have the obligation to contribute to the support of the Church, observe the laws of the Church concerning marriage, and join in the missionary spirit of the Church.

The Precepts of the Church

1. Assist at Mass on Sundays and Holy Days of Obligation. Do no unnecessary work on these days.
2. Confess serious sins at least once a year.
3. Receive Communion during the Easter season.
4. Observe the Holy Days of Obligation.
5. Fast and abstain on the days appointed.

The Gifts of the Holy Spirit

Throughout history, the Church has identified special gifts or blessings that Jesus' followers experience through the Holy Spirit. There are seven traditional gifts of the **Holy Spirit**.

Wisdom helps us know how God wants us to live.
Understanding helps us to be aware of all that God has revealed through Jesus, the Bible, and the Church.
Knowledge helps us to recognize that God is more important than anything else in life.
Right Judgment is the Spirit's guidance in making good decisions.
Courage helps us to be strong when faced with problems.
Reverence is respecting, loving, thanking, and praying to God.
Wonder and Awe fill us with wonder and praise for all that God has made.

The Theological and Moral Virtue

Through the Holy Spirit, we receive **virtues**, or spiritual powers, that help us to do good and avoid sin. God calls us to develop these spiritual powers so that they will become habits or patterns of living the moral life.

The most important virtues are the **theological virtues**: faith, hope, and love. The word theological means "pertaining to God." These three virtues help us to believe in God, trust in God's promises, and show our love for God by living as Jesus taught.

The **moral virtues**, sometimes called the cardinal virtues, guide us in living according to God's plan to bring about the kingdom. There are at least four moral virtues.

Prudence is the habit of making good decisions.
Justice is the practice of treating others with equality and fairness.

Fortitude is a habit that gives us the courage to do what we know is right.
Temperance helps us to live with moderation and control our desires.

ABOUT
Sin and Grace

Sin prevents us from living as followers of Jesus. Sin is a free decision to do what we know is wrong and to omit doing what we know is right. When we sin, we make a conscious choice to turn away from God, Jesus, and the teachings of the Church.

Very serious sins that destroy our ability to love and turn us away from God are called **mortal sins**. There are three conditions that make a sin mortal.

- The act must be seriously wrong.
- We must know that the act is seriously wrong.
- We must make a free choice to commit the sin.

Mortal sins must be confessed in the sacrament of Reconciliation to seek God's mercy and restore our relationship with God and the Church community. Through Jesus, we receive God's mercy and forgiveness and once again begin to live a life of grace.

Less serious sins are called **venial sins**. Venial sins weaken but do not completely destroy our relationship with God and the Church community.

Mortal and venial sins committed by the individual are called **personal sins**. Personal sins have social consequences. These sins often hurt others or tempt them to turn away from God and the Church.

Social sins are ingrained in the unjust and oppressive systems and structures of the community, the country, and the world. Social sins thwart God's plan to bring peace, love, and justice to our world. Racism, failure to pay just wages, ignoring the homeless, abortion, fighting unjust wars, sexism, and prejudice in any form are all social sins. As Catholics, we are responsible for working to change the unjust situations and institutions that allow social sins to exist.

The Church teaches that there are seven **capital sins**. These sins represent the most basic temptations for all people and are the source of many other personal and social sins.

Pride is an exaggerated love for self, which makes us think and act as if we were better than others.

Covetousness is a greedy desire for wealth or material possessions.

Lust is an uncontrolled desire for sexual pleasure.

Anger is an uncontrolled emotion that causes us to lose temper and strike out at others, verbally or physically.

Gluttony is excessive eating and drinking.

Envy is resenting the achievements and success of others.

Sloth is avoiding work and responsibility through laziness.

GRACE

God created all things. Human beings are made in the image and likeness of God. We are invited to share the gift of God's life and loving presence. Catholics call this sharing in God's own life **grace**. With the gift of grace, we become God's stewards, responsible for cooperation with him in caring for all creation and furthering God's plan for the world.

MAKING MORAL DECISIONS

The Holy Spirit helps us to make intelligent, conscious decisions based on the teachings of Jesus and the Church. The Spirit does not force us to make the right decision. One of our greatest blessings is the gift of **free will**. Free will is our freedom to choose to do what is right or wrong.

We can make good moral decisions by using a five-step process.

HELPS IN LIVING A MORAL LIFE

The direction of the Holy Spirit is our greatest help in overcoming the obstacle of sin and living as a follower of Jesus. The Spirit guides our **conscience**, the ability to judge whether something is right or wrong. The Spirit helps us to resist **temptation**, the attraction or pressures that may lead us to sin.

1. Identify the decision that needs to be made. Tell all that you know about it. What do you need to decide?

2. Consider possible options. What choices can you make?

3. Evaluate the consequences of the options. How will your choice affect you and others?

4. Reflect and pray. How do the Bible and the moral teachings of the Church guide you in making this choice? How will this decision show that you are a follower of Jesus?

5. Decide what you will do. Using your intellect and free will, what choice will you make?

ABOUT Social Justice

In the Gospel of Matthew we read: "Jesus went around to all the towns and villages, teaching in their synagogues, proclaiming the gospel of the kingdom, and curing every disease and every illness. At the sight of the crowds, his heart was moved with pity for them because they were troubled and abandoned, like sheep without a shepherd. Then he said to his disciples, 'The harvest is abundant but the laborers are few; so ask the master of the harvest to send out laborers for his harvest'" (Matthew 9:35–38).

With these words, Jesus invited his disciples to share his mission of bringing about God's kingdom. Like Jesus, his followers are to be shepherds, seeking out those who are lost, neglected, and abandoned. Jesus invites us to be laborers, working to harvest God's peace, love, and justice in the world.

Jesus' disciples accepted the mission he shared with them. After Jesus returned to his Father, he sent the Holy Spirit to form his disciples into his Church and to give them the strength and courage they would need to continue his work. The members of the first Christian community lived a communal life devoted to prayer and unselfish sharing: "All who believed were together and had all things in common; they would sell their property and possessions and divide them among all according to each one's need" (Acts 2:44–45). From these basic acts of compassion and caring for those who were poor, weak, sick, and needy, the Church's deep commitment to **social justice** was born.

Social justice is the systematic respect for human rights within society and its institutions. This rich tradition has its roots in the Old Testament, which describes God's covenant relationship with the People Israel. The Hebrew people recognized that God called them to live justly. They understood that living justly meant being right with God and with people and that justice included care for the poor. At Mt. Sinai, God gave them the Ten Commandments, the basic rules for living with peace, justice, and love. The Ten Commandments outline the minimum requirements for loving God, our neighbor, and ourselves.

The Hebrew prophets spoke out against the injustices they observed. They called the Jewish people to return to the covenant with God, live justly, keep the Ten Commandments, and treat others well, especially those who were weak and needy. The prophets said that how a society treated its weakest members showed whether or not that society was just. The prophet Amos told Israel: "Seek good and not evil, that you may live" (Amos 5:14). The prophet Micah challenged the people of Israel: "You have been told, O man, what is good, and what the LORD requires of you: Only to do right and to love goodness, and to walk humbly with your God" (Micah 6:8).

THE EXAMPLE OF CHRIST

Jesus became man to teach us how to live with love, peace, and justice and to save us from sin and death. At the Last Supper, on the night before he died, Jesus washed his disciples' feet to give them an example of how they were to treat others. Like Jesus, they were to serve others. Then he gave them a new commandment: "Love one another. As I have loved you, so you also should love one another" (John 13:34). Love, or the virtue of charity, is at the heart of the Church's social justice teachings.

This radical understanding of love requires us to have a **preferential option for the poor**. This means that we are called to stand with, for, and on the side of the weakest and poorest members of society—the people Jesus called "blessed" in the Beatitudes. Having a preferential option for the poor obliges us to fight against the **social sins** that are ingrained in the unjust and oppressive systems and structures of the community, the country, and the world. Social sins include prejudice and oppression in any form, such as the failure to pay just wages, and failing to meet the bodily and spiritual needs of those who are homeless, elderly, sick, or in some other way neglected by society.

As Catholics we seek to continue Christ's mission in the world by treating others with respect, compassion, and justice. This is not always an easy task. It is sometimes difficult to decide the most just and compassionate way to act. It is not easy to be the prophets of today by speaking out against the injustices we see or to work to change the systems that prevent people from living as God intended. Yet this is our mission as baptized followers of Jesus. Catholic teachings on social justice help us to know and follow the example of Jesus who came to serve rather than to be served.

THE PRINCIPLES OF SOCIAL JUSTICE

Five basic themes are the foundation for all Catholic social teaching.

Respect for Human Dignity

All people are made in the image and likeness of God and we are called to share in his own life. Through his life, death, and resurrection, Jesus, God's Word among us, revealed to us our vocation as children of God. Respect for the dignity of the human person requires that we think about and treat our neighbor just as we think about and treat ourselves. We are all equal before God and are called to respect, or reverence, all human life.

Human Beings Are Social

We are part of a human family, created "male and female" by God (Genesis 1:27). We are part of many inner-related communities: family, Church, neighborhood, nation, and world. Jesus calls us to be a community of disciples who witness to and share his message of peace, justice, and love with all members of the human family to which we all belong.

Called to Solidarity

God calls us to recognize that we are all brothers and sisters. We must share our possessions, resources, gifts, and talents with one another. Solidarity, or unity, must exist between rich and poor, between employers and employees, and among nations and peoples. We express our solidarity in compassion, which means feeling another's pain and wanting to respond to it. Like Jesus, we are to be sensitive and deeply moved by the sufferings of others. We are to be willing to make sacrifices to lessen one another's pain and to put an end to the unjust situations that cause others to suffer.

Our Vocation to Beatitude Love

Beatitude love requires us to move beyond love based simply on a desire for justice. The word *beatitude* means happiness and the Beatitudes point to the only source of our happiness: God. The Beatitudes describe some of the actions and characteristics of Christian life. They also remind us of the blessings we will have in Christ. Most importantly, the Beatitude understanding of love challenges us to recognize that we cannot truly love God if we do not love our neighbor. Love of God and love of neighbor cannot be separated.

Basic Human Rights and Responsibilities

Catholic social teaching acknowledges that because of the basic dignity of all human beings, all people have the right to participate in society. We are each endowed with undeniable economic, political, religious, social, and cultural rights. In addition, we each have the responsibility to respect, promote, and fulfill the rights to which others are entitled. We also have duties which correspond to each of our rights. For example, the right to education requires us to seek knowledge and to be open and attentive to what we are taught. The right to free speech requires us to speak with truth and respect. The right to a just wage carries the duty of giving our employer an honest day's work.

THE MODERN ERA OF CATHOLIC SOCIAL TEACHING

During the past century or so, the Catholic Church has formally addressed issues of social justice, human rights, and peace in encyclicals, or papal letters, and pastoral letters issued by synods, or conferences of bishops. These documents guide us in living gospel values of peace, love, and justice in our modern world. Some of the most important Catholic social teachings are found in the following documents.

Rerum Novarum (On the Condition of the Working Person, 1891) Pope Leo XIII described the rights and obligations of workers.

Mater et Magistra (Christianity and Social Progress, 1961) In this document, Pope John XXIII addressed the rights and duties involved in the growth and development of a country. The pope also described three steps for how to act toward others: observe, judge, act.

Pacem in Terris (Peace on Earth, 1963) In this encyclical, Pope John XXIII outlined the responsibilities of wealthy nations toward poor nations and discussed the urgent problems of nuclear disarmament and racial discrimination. The pope stated that true peace can only come about when human beings relate to one another in truth, justice, love, and freedom.

Gaudium et Spes (The Pastoral Constitution on the Church in the Modern World, 1965) This document was the final document from the Second Vatican Council. It describes the Church's mission in the contemporary world.

The Challenge of Peace (1983) This letter, issued by the National Catholic Conference of Bishops in the United States, addresses issues of war and peace.

Economic Justice for All: Pastoral Letter on Catholic Social Teaching and the Economy (1986) This letter, issued by the United States bishops, states that an economy is judged not by what it produces as much as how it touches human life and how society serves the poorest and weakest among us.

Sollicitudo Rei Socialis (On Social Concerns, 1987) In this encyclical, Pope John Paul II analyzed why the rivalry between nations diverted society from meeting the basic human needs of the world's peoples. The pope criticized the thirst for power and wealth that creates "structures of sin" which prevent all people from sharing in the goodness of creation. The pope also explained that sin is not just personal but a part of all society.

Vocations

For most of us, our Baptism took place when we were infants. Our parents and godparents wanted to give us the opportunity to grow within a Catholic community. They knew that we would need strong values and guidelines in order to live a full and happy life.

Now we are beginning to think about what choices we will make in the future. Because of our life in the church, we know that those choices will include devoting time to service in the Catholic community. We call the choices we make about our place in the Church our **vocation**, or what we feel we are called to do by the gospel message of Jesus.

All Christians have a vocation. We know that God is calling or inviting us to live in a way that allows us to serve others in the community and in the world. Although people live different lifestyles—single, married, raising a family, living in community—all of us are called to hear and respond to the same gospel message.

MANY WAYS OF SERVING

For most people, their vocation is to devote some of their time to service within the Christian community. They choose particular ministries in their parish or diocese, such as caring for the poor, teaching, planning and leading the liturgy, helping with parish management, or inviting others to join the Church. In these and other ways, they help the parish community fulfill its mission to reach out to all in the spirit of Jesus.

Some women and men choose to devote their lives completely to the ministry of the Catholic community. Many decide to join religious communities of sisters or brothers, who take **vows**, or promises of poverty, chastity, and obedience so that they can be completely devoted to their ministry and to growing spiritually. Each religious community chooses to concentrate their efforts on particular ministries, such as teaching, working with the sick and the poor, preaching, prayer and contemplation, or parish work.

In the Catholic Church, there are also ordained ministers—bishops, priests, and deacons. Men who feel that they are called to the priesthood have the special vocation of leading the community in worship as well as serving in a wide variety of ministries in the Church. There are diocesan priests who serve as pastors of parishes, educators, counselors, and in many other capacities. There are priests who, like sisters and brothers, belong to religious communities. They may also be assigned as pastors, teachers, or to the particular ministry of their community.

There are also men who are ordained as permanent deacons. Usually, they assist the pastor of a parish by leading the celebrations of Baptism and marriage, preaching at Sunday Mass, and helping with parish management. Unlike priests, deacons can be married and they live with their families.

DISCERNMENT

In what ways are we being called to serve? Answering this question is called **discernment**, or deciding who God is calling us to become. We should pray that God will help us understand what the gospel is calling us to do. We should also try to know more about the possibilities for us in the Christian community. Ask a priest, brother, teacher, parish minister, or religious brother or sister to find out more about how God's invitation can be answered.

ABOUT
Religious Life

Religious life includes sisters (also known as women religious), brothers (also known as men religious), and religious priests, who differ from diocesan priests. The religious priest, similar to a religious brother and sister "professes" or makes, three vows, or promises: poverty, chastity, and obedience. The diocesan priest promises to be celibate, or unmarried. Both the religious priest and the diocesan priest have the same sacramental ministry. Sisters and brothers, on the other hand, do not preside at the sacraments, although part of their ministry is to encourage people to share in the sacraments of the Church.

Religious priests, sisters, and brothers live a communal life which helps to give their three vows meaning. Much is shared in the communal lives which they live. They pray with their communities as well as alone. Living in community also provides support and challenges them to grow in every way. In an atmosphere of mutual concern, a religious priest, sister, or brother is able to move forward in reaching out to God's people.

RELIGIOUS VOWS

Poverty A religious sister, brother, or priest is committed to sharing all things with the members of his or her community. This refers to material things such as money as well as spiritual things such as prayer. One goal of the vow of poverty is simplicity of life, or having few possessions. Another goal is to be poor in spirit. This means that the religious brother, sister, or priest relies on God in all things and not only on his or her plans and desires.

Chastity A religious sister, brother, or priest promises to love everyone with a celibate love. This means that he or she will love people

without possessing them romantically, leaving them free to be who they are. Religious women and men have strong friendships with many people, but their calling from God invites them not to focus on having one exclusive relationship and their own family. The vow of chastity invites the religious to be available to all people in a loving, caring manner without engaging in sexual activity.

Obedience Religious priests, brothers, and sisters understand this vow to mean always being at God's service at any time. The needs of their particular community as well as their own prayers to God about their abilities and talents determine how they will serve. Women and men religious try to be always in tune with God so as to understand where he is leading.

COMMUNITY LIFE

Men and women religious belong to communities called Orders or Congregations. The members of an Order or Congregation share similar goals and are bound together by their three vows. The Congregation's vision is lived out through the efforts of each member in loving service to those in need. Many Congregations are worldwide, while others are local and serve only one geographical area. Members of Congregations may be asked to serve in any place in which the Congregation has a ministry.

A diocesan priest, on the other hand, usually only serves in his local diocese. A young man chooses to be a diocesan priest rather than a religious priest because he wishes to serve the local Church. He works in a particular diocese under a particular bishop who is the pastor of the entire diocese.

Becoming a religious brother, sister, or priest requires a training period. During this time— usually two years—the woman or man, called a novice, is not engaged in fulltime ministry. Instead he or she is involved in theological and spiritual study as well as personal growth under

the guidance of a novice director. At the end of the novitiate the novice professes first vows for one year. After he or she has renewed these vows for a few years, the religious man or woman is invited to profess his or her vows perpetually— that is, permanently.

After a man who is going to become a religious priest makes his profession of vows, he enters another training period to become a priest. He attends a seminary for further theological and philosophical studies, leading up to ordination—consecration as a priest. A diocesan priest does not go through a novitiate because he does not join an Order or Congregation. He simply attends a seminary and is then ordained.

Whatever a Catholic's vocation in life, he or she feels the call and desire to be a person of prayer. Reflection on the Scriptures, Catholic heritage, and the signs of the times is necessary in discerning one's vocation. As you get ready to leave elementary school and move on to high school, how does your life as a Catholic measure up? Could you make any improvements? Do you think your vocation might include joining a Religious Order?

How Catholics Pray

Catholics seek to draw closer to God through prayer and devotion. As a community and as individuals we can praise, thank, adore, and petition God in prayer. While all Christians pray the Lord's Prayer, for example, some forms of prayer, such as the Rosary, are unique to Catholics. We develop and deepen our relationship with God through prayer.

About Prayer

Prayer is often described as talking and listening to God. It is also described as conversation with God. Some people say that prayer is longing for and listening for God. Others say that prayer is a cry of praise and wonder from our hearts in response to the goodness of God. Prayer is the way we relate to the loving God who made us. In Scripture we read that Jesus taught his followers that a change of heart is necessary to truly pray. For example, to pray we must not hold anger and hate in our hearts. We must be willing to forgive those who wrong us.

Sometimes it is not easy to pray. We may doubt that prayer matters if God did not answer our prayer the way we wanted. We may feel discouraged and doubt that God even hears us or loves us. We may not feel like praying. Sometimes we are distracted by things we find more interesting or by the problems and anxieties we face.

At these times we need to ask ourselves what really matters to us. Do we turn to God only when we need something? Or do we turn to God regularly, placing him in the center of our lives as most important in our lives? Even the greatest saints found it hard to pray sometimes. It happens to all of us. Yet if we truly believe that God comes first in our lives, we will set aside our doubts and our expectations of what we want and turn to him in prayer simply because he is our Father.

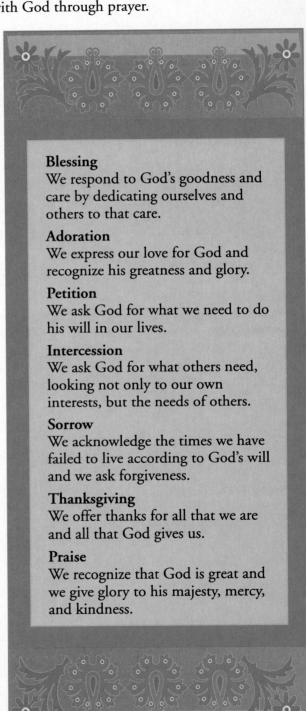

Blessing
We respond to God's goodness and care by dedicating ourselves and others to that care.

Adoration
We express our love for God and recognize his greatness and glory.

Petition
We ask God for what we need to do his will in our lives.

Intercession
We ask God for what others need, looking not only to our own interests, but the needs of others.

Sorrow
We acknowledge the times we have failed to live according to God's will and we ask forgiveness.

Thanksgiving
We offer thanks for all that we are and all that God gives us.

Praise
We recognize that God is great and we give glory to his majesty, mercy, and kindness.

About Meditation

Meditation is a way of praying in which we seek to listen to God. In our minds and hearts we quietly reflect upon and listen to the inner voice of the Holy Spirit. We can prepare ourselves for meditation by reading a Scripture passage, thinking about a person of holiness, or focusing on a sacred object or the beauty of creation. As we quietly reflect, we can think about our relationship with God and respond to his call to us. Meditation involves our thoughts, imagination, and emotions.

There are many different meditation methods. Christian meditation always focuses us on trying to understand the will of God for us as followers of Jesus. It helps us to understand more deeply the mission of Jesus and what Jesus means for our lives.

About Contemplation

Contemplation has been described as a quiet resting in God's presence. It is not as much a method of prayer as an inner orientation—a gaze of faith fixed on God. Contemplation cannot be practiced by the mind because it is not a method of thinking. Neither is it a method of imagining or visualizing God. It is more a way of being. Saints who were great contemplatives, such as St. Teresa of Avila, have taught us that contemplation is a way to be with God as one would be in the presence of a very close friend.

Some saints have said that true contemplation is a gift from God and cannot be achieved by effort alone. Also, contemplation is not a form of prayer that always requires us to set aside time for it. Contemplation is a state of constant inner prayer, of constant inner gaze upon God. It can take place during every moment of daily life: eating, working, playing, and reading. The silent, continual love of God that is the goal of contemplation is reached by very few, but can be attempted by all Christians.

About The Liturgy of the Hours

The Liturgy of the Hours is the official morning, daytime, and evening prayer of the Church. It is made up of prayers, psalms, readings, and hymns taken from the Scriptures, the Mass, and the writings of the saints. Through the Liturgy of the Hours, we unite ourselves with the worldwide Church as together we praise, thank, adore, and petition God.

The purpose of praying the Liturgy of the Hours is to remind us to strive for holiness in every hour of the day from morning to night. By praying in the morning, at midday, in the early evening, and at night, we join the rest of the Church in following Jesus' teaching to "pray without ceasing." The Liturgy of the Hours is sometimes called the Divine Office. These daily prayers have been prayed by Christians for centuries.

ABOUT Devotions

Sometimes we pray directly to God. Other times we express our love for God through our devotion to Jesus, Mary, or the saints. We call these special prayers **devotions**.

THE WAY OF THE CROSS

The Way of the Cross, or Stations of the Cross, is a traditional Catholic devotion most often prayed during the season of Lent. As we pray the stations, we reflect on the passion, death, and resurrection of Jesus.

The Stations of the Cross

1. Jesus is condemned to death.
2. Jesus accepts the cross.
3. Jesus falls the first time.
4. Jesus meets his mother.
5. Simon helps Jesus carry the cross.
6. Veronica wipes the face of Jesus.
7. Jesus falls the second time.
8. Jesus meets the women of Jerusalem.
9. Jesus falls the third time.
10. Jesus is stripped of his garments.
11. Jesus is nailed to the cross.
12. Jesus dies on the cross.
13. Jesus is taken down from the cross.
14. Jesus is buried in the tomb.
15. Jesus rises from the dead.

THE ROSARY

The Rosary is a devotion honoring Mary. In praying the Rosary we repeat the Hail Mary over and over to show our love and respect for Mary, the mother of God and our mother. As we pray, we reflect upon the joyful, sorrowful, and glorious events in the lives of Mary and Jesus. We call these events the Mysteries of the Rosary.

The Joyful Mysteries

The Annunciation
The Visit of Mary to Elizabeth
The Birth of Jesus
The Presentation of Jesus in the Temple
The Finding of Jesus in the Temple

The Sorrowful Mysteries

The Agony of Jesus in the Garden
The Scourging at the Pillar
The Crowning with Thorns
The Carrying of the Cross
The Crucifixion and Death of Jesus

The Glorious Mysteries

The Resurrection of Jesus
The Ascension of Jesus into Heaven
The Descent of the Holy Spirit upon the
    Apostles (Pentecost)
The Assumption of Mary into Heaven
The Crowning of Mary as Queen of Heaven

ABOUT The Lord's Prayer

Jesus himself taught his followers to pray the Lord's Prayer. This prayer is actually in the form of seven petitions. The first three of these are to the glory of God. In the next four we present our needs to God who is truly our Father.

The Lord's Prayer	Living the Lord's Prayer
Our Father, who art in heaven, hallowed be thy name.	God, who made us and who continues to love and care for us, is like a loving parent, our Father. We give glory to God by acknowledging his majesty and holiness.
thy kingdom come,	We recognize that, through Jesus Christ, the kingdom of God has been established in our midst. We look forward to Christ's return and the final coming of the kingdom of God.
thy will be done on earth as it is in heaven.	Again we acknowledge God's majesty and we ask that his plan of salvation be fulfilled.
Give us this day our daily bread;	Daily bread refers both to the nourishment of our bodies as well as to the nourishment given to us in the Eucharist: Jesus, our Bread of Life.
and forgive us our trepasses as we forgive those who trespass against us;	We ask God for mercy for the wrongs we have done. We recognize that we can only truly receive God's mercy into our hearts and change our lives when we have learned to forgive our enemies.
and lead us not into temptation,	We ask God to help us to avoid sin. We ask God to give us the grace and strength to make good choices and avoid sin.
but deliver us from evil.	We pray that through God's plan of salvation in Christ, we will be saved from the evil which opposes God's will.
Amen.	This word at the end of a prayer expresses our agreement. It can mean "so be it."

Glossary

Advent
the first season of the liturgical year *(page 314)*

alms
money or goods given for the poor *(page 267)*

Annunciation
when the Virgin Mary received the message of the Lord that she was to be the Mother of God *(page 360)*

Assumption
Mary taken up to heaven, body and soul *(page 383)*

beatification
the process for naming someone blessed *(page 221)*

Beatific Vision
our face-to-face encounter with God after our lives on earth *(page 237)*

Beatitudes
the basic principles of life in God's kingdom *(page 396)*

belief
something that one holds to be true or real *(page 193)*

canon
a list of the books of the Bible *(page 25)*

canon law
the collection of laws of the Catholic Church *(page 25)*

canonization
the process for naming someone a saint *(page 221)*

capital sins
the seven basic temptations *(pages 281, 401)*

cardinals
advisors selected by the pope *(page 39)*

catacombs
underground Christian cemeteries *(page 15)*

catechumens
persons wishing to join the Catholic Church who enter into a period of study, prayer, and preparation *(page 113)*

catholic
welcoming or open to the whole world *(page 13)*

Christendom
the one society that Church and State form together *(page 31)*

Christian
follower of Jesus Christ *(page 13)*

Church Fathers
great Christian teachers of the first eight centuries *(page 19)*

collegiality
shared responsibility and cooperation *(page 109)*

commission
Jesus' choosing of Peter to head his Church *(page 346)*

communion of saints
the community of those still living in Christ's Church on earth, of those souls in purgatory, and of those in heaven *(pages 235, 383)*

compassion
sympathetically desiring to help those who are suffering *(page 372)*

conciliarism
the idea that the council of bishops had supreme authority in the Church *(page 43)*

concordat
a treaty or agreement permitting the Church to exist and work within a country *(page 97)*

conscience
the ability to judge whether something is right or wrong *(pages 281, 402)*

contemplation
a prayerful "seeing" of God in nature or people; a quiet resting in God's presence *(pages 141, 411)*

conversion
a lifelong process in which the Holy Spirit works through us, transforming our lives to the image of Jesus *(page 386)*

council
meeting of Church leaders *(page 13)*

crèche
the Christmas nativity scene *(page 326)*

creed
a formal summary of basic beliefs *(page 197)*

Crusades
nine military attempts to liberate Palestine from Muslim control *(page 31)*

curia
officials who assist the pope or a bishop *(page 39)*

development of doctrine
the growth of the Church's understanding of what it means to be a follower of Jesus Christ *(page 197)*

devotions
special ways of praying to God, Jesus, Mary, and the saints *(pages 332, 412)*

discernment
the process of deciding who God is calling us to become *(page 407)*

doctrines
official Church statements of belief *(page 195)*

ecumenical
worldwide; efforts toward Christian unity *(pages 19, 58, 103)*

Emmanuel
God with us *(page 324)*

evangelize
to preach the good news of God's kingdom *(page 73)*

exile
the period of time when the Jewish people were forcibly taken from their homes to Babylon and forbidden to return to their land *(page 316)*

faith
a firm belief without having proof; a loving commitment to and trust in someone or something; being in relationship with God *(page 193)*

feudalism
a social system based on loyalties and protections *(page 41)*

free will
the freedom to choose to do what is right or wrong *(pages 281, 402)*

funeral
the services held when a person dies *(page 231)*

general judgment
the judgment of all people at the end of the world *(page 235)*

Gentiles
people who are not Jewish *(page 13)*

gifts of the Holy Spirit
special gifts or blessings that Jesus' followers experience through the Holy Spirit: wisdom, understanding, knowledge, right judgment, courage, reverence, and wonder and awe *(page 400)*

Glossary

grace
God's gift of God's own life and presence to people *(pages 159, 402)*

Great Schism
the period of time during which there was more than one pope *(page 43)*

heaven
unending happiness with God and with each other *(pages 235, 383)*

hell
eternal separation from God and others *(pages 235, 383)*

heresy
the denial of a Church doctrine *(page 19)*

hermits
people who remove themselves from others and live alone *(page 27)*

icons
sacred images of Jesus Christ, his mother Mary, and the saints *(page 147)*

Immaculate Conception
the feast that celebrates that Mary was free from all sin, including original sin, from the first moment of her life *(pages 366, 383)*

Incarnation
the Son of God becoming truly man while remaining truly God *(page 380)*

indulgence
the removal of all or some of the punishments for sins that have already been forgiven *(page 49)*

Lent
the period of forty days before the great feast of Easter *(page 330)*

liberation
being released or freed *(page 291)*

litanies
brief prayers invoking, or calling on, God, Jesus, the Holy Spirit, Mary, or the saints *(page 364)*

Liturgy of the Hours
the Church's official prayer at certain hours of the day and night; also called the Divine Office. It consists of psalms, readings, hymns, and prayers. *(pages 139, 411)*

magisterium
the official teaching office of the Church. The responsibility for teaching the authentic message of Jesus is carried out by the pope and bishops. *(pages 113, 382)*

marks of the Church
identifying signs by which Christ's Church may be recognized: one, holy, catholic, and apostolic *(page 219)*

martyrs
people killed for being witnesses for Christ *(pages 15, 352)*

Mass
another name for the Eucharist, taken from the Latin word *missa,* which was used at the end of the celebration *(page 171)*

meditation
prayerful reflection on an event, object, truth, or text *(pages 141, 411)*

mendicants
religious persons who supported themselves by begging *(page 39)*

Messiah
a person anointed by God for a mission; Jesus Christ *(page 380)*

monastery
a religious community of monks or nuns; also, the building in which they live *(page 27)*

moral virtues
prudence, justice, fortitude, and temperance; also called the cardinal virtues *(page 400)*

mortal sins
very serious sins that completely break off our relationship with God *(pages 281, 401)*

mourning
a period of grieving after a loved one has died *(page 233)*

order
a religious group of men or women *(page 358)*

original sin
the sinful condition within our lives and into which we are all born *(pages 281, 384)*

pall
a white cloth that covers the casket at a funeral Mass *(page 231)*

papal infallibility
the doctrine that when the pope speaks officially on faith and morals, what he says is free from error *(pages 99, 382)*

particular judgment
God's judgment of each person at the moment of death *(page 235)*

Paschal Mystery
Jesus' passion, death, resurrection, and glorification *(page 380)*

Pentecost
the Jewish feast that celebrates the giving of the Torah to Moses; the Christian feast that celebrates the coming of the Holy Spirit *(pages 368, 381)*

personal sins
mortal and venial sins committed by the individual. Personal sins have social consequences. *(page 401)*

pilgrimage
a journey to a sacred shrine or place *(page 334)*

prayer
talking and listening to God; a cry of praise and longing for God from our hearts *(page 410)*

preferential option for the poor
We are called to stand with, for, and on the side of the weakest and poorest members of society *(page 404)*

purgatory
the process of purification after death from all traces of sin *(pages 235, 383)*

religious pluralism
the free existence of religion in a country or a society *(page 87)*

resurrection
Jesus' rising from death to new life *(pages 344, 381)*

Rites of Committal
the last prayers said at the place where the body will rest *(page 231)*

ritual
a formal religious ceremony that proceeds according to set rules *(page 157)*

sacrament
a special sign within the life of the Church through which Christ truly becomes present with us and acts in our lives *(pages 159, 384)*

sacramental
a blessing, an action, or an object that reminds us of Christ's presence with us *(pages 165, 340)*

saints
the holy men and women of the Church *(page 370)*

Second Coming
the longed-for return of Jesus *(page 383)*

Glossary

serfs
poor farmers who could not leave the farms where they were born *(page 41)*

signs of the times
major experiences, issues, and values of our age through which God speaks to us *(page 109)*

simony
the buying and selling of spiritual things *(page 49)*

sin
a free decision to do wrong or fail to do the good that we should *(pages 281, 401)*

social doctrine
Church teachings that state the implications of the gospel for human rights *(page 257)*

social justice
the systematic respect for human rights within society and its institutions *(pages 283, 403)*

social sins
sins that are ingrained in the unjust systems of the community *(pages 401, 403)*

temptation
the attraction or pressure that may lead us to sin *(pages 281, 402)*

theological virtues
faith, hope, and love *(page 400)*

third orders
lay communities closely united with religious orders of men or women *(page 39)*

tithing
a form of taxation; a portion of the harvest given to the Church *(page 41)*

transcendent
the supernatural character of the Church, established by Christ *(page 219)*

transubstantiation
the mystery in which bread and wine are changed into the body and blood of Christ *(pages 173, 385)*

Triduum
the last three days of Holy Week, beginning on sundown on Holy Thursday and ending at sundown on Easter Sunday *(page 342)*

Trinity
the one God revealed as Father, Son, and Holy Spirit *(page 209)*

triune
three-in-one *(page 209)*

venial sins
less serious sins that weaken our relationship with God and the Church *(pages 281, 401)*

viaticum
the Eucharist given when a person is in danger of death *(page 386)*

virtues
spiritual powers that help us to do good and avoid sin *(page 400)*

vocation
God's call to use our gifts for our own good and the good of others *(page 407)*

vows
promises of poverty, chastity, and obedience taken by those who decide to join religious communities of brothers or sisters *(page 407)*

wake
the vigil of the family and friends of the deceased *(page 231)*

Works of Mercy
acts that respond to basic needs *(page 399)*

Index

Index

Index

Index

Index